COMPREHENSION & COLLABORATION

STEPHANIE HARVEY
HARVEY DANIELS

C*MPREHENSION & COLLABORATION

Inquiry Circles *in Action*

Heinemann
Portsmouth, NH

Heinemann
361 Hanover Street
Portsmouth, NH 03801–3912
www.heinemann.com

Offices and agents throughout the world

The authors and publisher wish to thank those who have generously given permission to reprint borrowed material:

Excerpt from *Nonfiction Matters: Reading, Writing, and Research in Grades 3–8* by Stephanie Harvey. Copyright © 1998 by Stephanie Harvey. Published by Stenhouse Publishers. Reprinted by permission of the publisher.

Lyrics from "Rachel Delevoryas" by Randy Stonehill. Copyright © 1992 by Stonehillian Music (Admin. by Word Music, LLC) and Word Music, LLC. All rights reserved. Reprinted with permission.

Excerpt from *Strategies That Work: Teaching Comprehension for Understanding and Engagement, Second Edition* by Stephanie Harvey and Anne Goudvis. Copyright © 2007 by Stephanie Harvey and Anne Goudvis. Published by Stenhouse Publishers. Reprinted by permission of the publisher.

Excerpt from *Teaching The Best Practice Way: Methods That Matter, K–12* by Harvey Daniels and Marilyn Bizar. Copyright © 2005 by Harvey Daniels and Marilyn Bizar. Published by Stenhouse Publishers. Reprinted by permission of the publisher.

"Women of the Negro Leagues" by Mike Weinstein from *AppleSeeds* February 2000 issue: Jackie Robinson © 2000, Carus Publishing Company. Published by Cobblestone Publishing, 30 Grove Street, Suite C, Peterborough, NH 03458. All Rights Reserved. Used by permission of the publisher.

"Dedicated to Teachers" is a trademark of Greenwood Publishing Group, Inc.

Library of Congress Cataloging-in-Publication Data
Harvey, Stephanie.
    Comprehension and collaboration : inquiry circles in action /
Stephanie Harvey, Harvey Daniels.
        p. cm.
    Includes bibliographical references and index.
    ISBN-13: 978-0-325-01230-8
    ISBN-10: 0-325-01230-X
    1. Inquiry-based learning.   2. Active learning.   3. Group work in education.   4. Motivation in education.   I. Daniels, Harvey   II. Title.
    LB1027.23.H37 2009
    371.3'6—dc22   2009008395

Editor: Kate Montgomery
Production editor: Patricia Adams
Typesetter: Gina Poirier Design
Cover and interior designs: Lisa Fowler
Manufacturing: Louise Richardson

Printed in the United States of America on acid-free paper
13 12 11 10 ML 2 3 4 5

124775

Key Lessons in Comprehension, Collaboration, and Inquiry (SEE CHAPTER 7)

COMPREHENSION LESSONS

COLLABORATION LESSONS

INQUIRY LESSONS

Small-Group Inquiry Projects

Preface

Greetings, colleagues and friends. Thanks for sitting down with us.

Like most books (and most good classroom lessons), this one started with talk. Lots of talk. First and foremost, it began in our conversations with teachers like you all across the country.

We make our living mostly by traveling from school to school and conference to conference, helping teachers with reading and writing, hanging around with great kids, and trying to figure out what will make learning and thinking even more powerful and fun. Between us, we worked in twenty-six states last year. And although the travel can sometimes be trying—lost luggage, canceled flights, bizarre hotels—the great conversations we have with teachers make it worth every minute.

Lately, you have been telling us that you see connections between Smokey's and Steph's work. You say that you have been using the reading comprehension strategies with your kids and doing book clubs with them too, and that they fit together seamlessly. As Betsy Brand, a pal in Texas explains it: "Well, I've just been putting Harvey and Harvey together." And when you tell us about your amazing variations, adaptations, and improvisations on our basic ideas, we are knocked out.

So you got *us* talking, to each other. What becomes possible when kids can both comprehend and collaborate—when they can combine the thinking skills of strategic reading with the social skills of small, peer-led groups? Over the past two years, we have had dozens of short and long conversations about the possibilities by e-mail, phone, and face to face; in restaurants, at convention book booths, in our homes, on airplanes, in cars driving around Denver or Santa Fe; and most of all, in classrooms where we were working side by side with kids. We two have become the living embodiment of a classroom strategy that Steph always promotes: *turn and talk!*

In that spirit, it would seem unnatural for us to write any other way than conversationally, so in this book we are going to continue talking to each other, as well as to you, dear reader.

▲

SMOKEY: Hey, Steph, have you ever noticed how much we have in common?

STEPH: Yeah, I have. It's a little weird, actually.

SMOKEY: Weird? It's just cool. Let me see . . . We both grew up in the Midwest (in the virtually interchangeable states of Minnesota and Wisconsin). We had great family times on northern lakes.

STEPH: Water skiing, oh yeah.

SMOKEY: We went to sister colleges, Northwestern and the University of Denver (both founded by John Evans).

STEPH: Come on, you are really reaching on that one. John Evans?

SMOKEY: OK. But I have lots more:

We both have two kids, an older boy and a younger girl.

All four of our children are talented and lovable.

We married exceedingly well—Elaine and Edward, respectively.

We both love the American West.

We have both had great previous coauthors to whom we are deeply indebted, including Anne Goudvis, Steve Zemelman, Marilyn Bizar, Arthur Hyde, and Nancy Steineke.

STEPH: And how about these? For the last several years we have been presenting together at state and national conferences around the country. We were on the same page professionally before we even knew each other.

SMOKEY: Absolutely.

STEPH: So, should we talk about how our work fits together and how this book came about?

SMOKEY: You bet. I'll start. Steph, I think it's fair to say that you are best known for your work with reading comprehension strategies, teaching kids the same kinds of thinking that skillful readers use to make sense of text. Your book with Anne Goudvis, Strategies That Work, was really a blockbuster—it changed the way that millions of teachers teach reading.

STEPH: Well, "blockbuster" is a little over the top. But if the book has had some impact, that's mainly because Anne and I were translating and classroom-izing the amazing work of David Pearson and others who pioneered the comprehension strategies research.

SMOKEY: But I also know that all along, you've had an abiding commitment to kids' working together in pairs, teams, and literature circles, and that is embedded in all your books and videos.

STEPH: That's right, for sure. And that's one place that our work connects so strongly. Now it's your turn. You are known as "the Literature Circle Guy," having led the development of literature circles, or small, student-led reading discussion groups—in Denver we call them book clubs. And you have been widely recognized for labeling and teaching the social skills used by proficient discussion group members. I think that your inventory of social skills is quite parallel to the repertoire of comprehension strategies that I have been working on all these years.

SMOKEY: Exactly. But sometimes people think I _invented_ literature circles, which I most certainly did not. Since this structure basically involves bringing adult book clubs or reading groups into the school setting, no one can really claim credit for inventing them, just for adapting and popularizing the school-friendly version.

STEPH: In a way, that has been my role with the reading strategies too. So should we talk about how we actually met?

SMOKEY: OK, but let's tell this one together.

▼

The two of us have been casually acquainted for years and always admired each others' work. But it was not until 2001 that we became lifelong friends and close colleagues. Each of us had been separately invited to lead teacher workshops in New York City in mid-September. Then the attacks of 9/11 occurred. We were both stunned when our respective host schools called a few days later to reconfirm our workshops.

"The teachers want to hear you," the principals said. "We need some business as usual in our schools. Please come; we need you."

Feeling jangled and uncertain, we connected by phone and agreed to travel together to New York. As our near-empty plane descended toward LaGuardia, we were horrified by the smoking hole at the foot of a city we loved. It looked like the socket of a rough, brutally yanked tooth, spewing unspeakable pain and gruesome debris.

Later, as we sat in a deserted Thai restaurant in Midtown, there was no time—or need—for professional chitchat. Like people all across the country, we tried to make sense of this unspeakable event whose shadow was all around us— and whose scent drifted the ninety blocks north to where we sat. We connected as people, as citizens, and as educators. How could this kind of thing happen? How could we help the confused and terrified young people in their New York classrooms this week? And what can teachers do to gradually create a world where this kind of disaster never happens again, in the United States or any country? By the time we put down our chopsticks, we'd made a friendship that would last—and a commitment we continue to try to fulfill.

The morning after our New York dinner, we boarded different cabs—Steph off to Chinatown and Smokey to the Bronx. And in both schools, we encountered the most amazing teachers—men and women who were lovingly supporting their students while still in shock themselves. Those days made us especially proud to be educators.

Our work has always been about teaching kids to *think for themselves,* to reason, to understand deeply, to build knowledge, to leverage their thinking with others, and to put knowledge to work in their own lives. Now we hold those goals even more urgently. The only way the world can save itself from future 9/11s is if young people all around the world are educated to be critical, thoughtful, independent-minded readers, writers, speakers, and listeners.

Eleanor Roosevelt said: "Every effort must be made in childhood to teach the young to use their own minds. For one thing is sure: if they do not make up their own minds, someone will do it for them." We can hear you now saying "never more important than today." But if you'd read that quote twenty years ago, you would likely have also said "never more important than today." And if you read it twenty years from now, you'll almost certainly have the same response. Nothing is more important than teaching kids to use their own minds and think. Period.

This book is a small contribution to the worldwide effort to raise children into citizens who think clearly and deeply, who have gained knowledge and acquired judgment, and who take action with humanity in mind.

As you'll soon find out, for us this means:

- Teaching as though kids' own questions really matter

- Favoring topics of authenticity, relevance, and significance

- Focusing all our teaching around thinking, stressing knowledge over information

- Encouraging a curious, questioning, and critical stance

- Constantly offering students more choices—and more responsibility

- Helping young people to work collaboratively in pairs, teams, and inquiry groups

- Fostering the active use of knowledge

- Operating our classrooms as model democracies

This kind of teaching is far from new. Education has a long tradition of progressive practice that traces from educators of antiquity like Marcus Fabius Quintilian forward to great figures like John Dewey, Maria Montessori, and Paolo Friere. Through the millennia, the same key features have defined this enduring view—a student-centered approach; a belief in the inherent goodness of human beings; a faith in experience as the best teacher; a zeal for connecting education to real life; an affinity for inductive, constructivist reasoning and teaching; and a commitment to individual fulfillment, autonomy, and freedom. In short, progressive educators have always seen themselves as preparing *citizens.*

It's time for another, stronger, more intentional era of progressive education. There's damage to repair, yes, but more importantly, there's an ongoing struggle to rejoin and extend. We are part of a movement that has been two thousand years in the making, and may take a little while longer to finish. But even if the final triumph of progressive, student-centered, education will be the work of generations, the way we teach tomorrow morning has supreme importance to each child in our care right now, and to the world we are living in this year.

Our work with young people is not about standards—it is about a life of thinking, questioning, and caring; it is about survival.

Stephanie Harvey
Denver, Colorado

Harvey "Smokey" Daniels
Santa Fe, New Mexico

Acknowledgments

*H*aving authored something like 25 books and videos between us, we have had a lot of people to thank over the years. Looking back over all those acknowledgments pages, we see the same names coming up again and again: our beloved coauthors, Anne Goudvis, Steve Zemelman, Marilyn Bizar, Nancy Steineke, and Arthur Hyde.

We have both been fortunate to come out of strong professional networks—Steph in Denver and Smokey in Chicago—that have nourished us and raised us up over the years. They say you can't make old friends, and that's so true when it comes to lifelong colleagues at the Public Education and Business Coalition and the Center for City Schools at National-Louis University.

Thanks to all the schools that invited us to work with their students and teachers over the past several years. Between the two of us, we have now consulted in dozens of states. In this book, we share extended stories from more than 20 classrooms in all corners of the U.S. Sometimes, we sat in those classrooms, watched master teachers at work, and simply did our best to faithfully document the way they operated with kids. Other times, we "borrowed" the students and taught lessons ourselves, for a day or a semester, getting priceless feedback from the owner-teachers along the way.

Kudos and thanks to the many teachers featured in this book who work tirelessly to promote thinking, curiosity, and collaboration in their classrooms—Joyce Sanchez, Brad Buhrow, Diane Titche, Bodo Heiliger, Holly Occhipinti, Michelle Schirmer, Mary Pfau, Mike Laehr, Sue Fischer, Kristin Elder Rubino, Melissa Oviatt, Sara Ahmed, Lynette Emmons, Nancy Steineke, Jim Vopat, Pamela Battin-Sacks, Julia O'Connell, Shari Storch, George Wood and the whole Federal Hocking High School Faculty. We continue to marvel at kids from all around the country who we are fortunate enough to work with. Their stunning and brilliant work and thinking is sprinkled throughout this book and brings it life. We are most grateful.

A very special thanks to Andrew Hess, technology specialist in the Mamaroneck Public Schools, who contributed the powerful internet chapter to this book. We would love to go back to school and learn more about cyberspace from Andrew!

You'll soon be hearing about Burley School in Chicago, where we are currently filming a companion video for this book. The teachers in every single classroom at Burley, from pre-K through eighth grade, are showing what genuine inquiry-based learning looks like every day. It is a joy to be working with them and their leader Barbara Kent—watch for the video in Fall of 2009.

Thanks to Liz Stedem who created the amazing short nonfiction bibliography that appears at the end of this book as well as the bibliography of series books on our companion website. And thanks to Alex Harvey for sniffing out some extraordinary internet resources for teachers and kids, also found on our website.

This book has been more complicated than most, and that means we worked more closely than ever with the people at Heinemann publishers. They really brought out the A-Team for this one: Kate Montgomery as editor, Maura Sullivan as sage and seer, Charles McQuillen as marketeer extraordinaire, Steph Turner as go-between and Facebook coach, Vicki Boyd building professional development connections, and the redoubtable Lesa Scott at the helm.

Two people need extra wows. Patty Adams, our Production Editor, lived every word of this book with us, even as we misspelled, deleted, restored, italicized, undeleted, and rearranged almost every one. Few people, even veteran authors, ever understand all the things that a production editor does. We finally do, and we are in awe of Patty. And boisterous huzzahs to Lisa Fowler, creator of our gorgeous covers and interior design. Beginning with a casual snapshot of the authors on a mountain hike, Lisa created a "look and feel" that accurately effects our energy—and a level of sophistication we totally don't deserve.

As always, we want to thank our colleagues, teachers, professors, and mentors, many of them giants in the field, who continue to inspire us and stretch our thinking. And above all we want to thank our past readers, who are constantly on our minds as we think about kids, schools, and the future of our country. We really hope you enjoy this one—and that you can put it to work.

The members of Smokey's personal inquiry circle (Elaine, Marny, Nick, and welcome, Tara) have joined him on extended investigations of forensic pathology, saganaki, Sweden, knitting, rabbits, the high desert, baseball cards, wine, Dave Eggers, crust punk, kayaking, Queen, the films of John Waters, and so much more. Thanks, guys, for being the most supportive collaborators and for always giving me "Home Court Advantage." So, what hot topics or burning questions shall we investigate next?

To Steph's nucleus—Edward, Alex, and Jess who are still so intriguing to me that I will never lack for curiosity. We, too, have had our slew of inquiries from Shakespearean authorship, to hot yoga, to the nature of plants. And although we never thought to investigate saganaki, we have happily devoured it. Here's to a curiouser and curiouser journey which I wholeheartedly anticipate.

PART

WHY SMALL-GROUP INQUIRY PROJECTS?

Kids Want to Know

Welcome to *Comprehension and Collaboration: Inquiry Circles in Action.* We invite you to begin by reading stories from four classrooms around the United States. Then we'll look at what these teaching and learning projects have in common.

Where Does the Garbage Go?

It is a bright spring morning in Sheila Booth's first-grade classroom in Chicago. As other kids read at their desks, Billy gazes out the window at the garbage workers on the school's loading dock below. Using a hydraulic lift, the men hoist up the school's big dumpster, and bags, cans, bottles, papers, and boxes tumble into the huge truck. As Sheila walks past, Billy muses, "I wonder where all that garbage goes." And Sheila, smart and vigilant teacher that she is, exclaims: "Whoa, what a great question!"

Within a week, the whole class is engaged in an investigation of garbage— what it contains, where it goes, and why its disposal matters. Searching the Internet, Sheila quickly discovers that there is a kid-driven nationwide trend of schools mindfully monitoring their trash output, and she shows some websites to the kids. They read about how some students have analyzed their schools' garbage by sorting through representative bags and determining exactly what is being thrown away: food, paper, office waste, and other materials.

"Yuk, I'm not going to get my hands into that stuff," says Juan.

"That's OK, I'll do your garbage," rejoins Matt cheerily.

"Don't worry, you guys. If we decide to try this, we will get plastic gloves for whoever wants to try it," Sheila says.

A few days later, the great garbage audit is carried out, and for that day anyway, the greatest culprit is an incalculable load of soggy green beans. As Matt says after scooping out handful after handful, "I guess this is what happens when we don't eat our vegetables at lunch."

The kids continue reading, drawing, and writing about garbage, waste, and recycling. With help from the librarian, Sheila finds some books to feed kids' curiosity: *Recycle: A Handbook for Kids; Garbage and Recycling; The Three Rs: Reuse, Reduce, Recycle; Where Does the Garbage Go?* and *Why Should I Recycle?* As kids delve into these resources, Sheila helps them to jot or draw their responses and further questions, and to save them in a file. And, becoming hooked on trashy reading herself, Sheila discovers the adult nonfiction book *Garbageland* by Elizabeth Royle, a muckracking expose of the garbage industry with all of its smells, secrets, and occasional skullduggery. As the inquiry continues, Sheila reads passages aloud to the class and talks about her own reactions and wonderings.

The investigation culminates in a field trip. The first graders pack up their lists of questions, pile onto a school bus, and follow the garbage truck through its rounds and then off to a huge landfill in the community that none of the kids has ever seen. Trooping off the bus with clipboards in hand (and carefully watched by teachers and parents), the kids observe as the school's garbage cascades into the pit. They jot and draw their impressions of the vastness and ickiness of the landfill.

Next, small groups of kids scatter to interview the different workers who drive the trucks, operate machinery, and run the small office. Each team of kids has brought its own research questions: Why does garbage smell so bad? Do you ever find cool stuff that people throw away by accident? Do you really like working here? The workers are patient and encouraging. The kids interviewing the site manager are surprised to hear that the dump is almost full and that another landfill will have to be started soon.

The kids return to school and commence a buildingwide recycling program aimed at reducing the amount of trash that the school sends to the landfill. Within weeks, the school's trash output is slashed, news of the first graders' initiative is spreading through the community, and many local families redouble their own recycling efforts.

*W*ithin weeks, the school's trash output is slashed, news of the first graders' initiative is spreading through the community, and many local families redouble their own recycling efforts.

*N*ative-Settler Contact in North America

Diane Titche's fifth-grade students in Lowell, Michigan, are just finishing up a round of literature circles. Patterned after adult reading groups, lit circles are simple and sociable. Each kid picks a book that he or she wants to read and three or four friends to work with. Then, over a couple of weeks, the different groups read their chosen book. The kids jot down responses and questions as they read, then bring these notes when they gather after every few chapters to talk about the story and the ideas in the book. In Diane's classroom, lit circles have proved to be one of the students' favorite activities all year long.

For this particular cycle of book clubs, students have chosen from a set of historical novels about encounters between European settlers and native American peoples. To make sure that all students could find a just-right read, Diane made sure to include both easier and harder books among the choices. At the groups' first meetings, before they even started to read their books, each newly formed lit circle took two actions. First, each group made a calendar, dividing the book into chunks to be discussed at two- or three-day intervals. Then the group created some "ground rules," including how to handle a member who shows up unprepared, fails to do the reading, or doesn't join in the group's work. Both of these documents were submitted to Diane for her approval (the spanking of unprepared members is definitely not OK; find another consequence) and filed in the group's folder.

Now, following the usual procedures of lit circles, the six groups in Diane's room have been meeting every few days to discuss sections of the book and are finishing up their novels. Usually, when kids come to the end of a lit circle book, their teachers ask them to create a culminating project—a skit, a poster, a board game, a report about the author. But this time, Diane has another kind of project in mind.

She convenes the students and asks them to think about what new or lingering questions they have after reading these books about natives and settlers. This is not an easy task for kids. Throughout their school lives, they have more often been asked to report what they have learned, not to reflect back, examine their own thinking, and pose *further* questions. It takes time and talk, but over some cycles of writing and discussion, each group gradually develops (or simply recognizes) a question that members want to pursue. Then, groups launch into new inquiries, reading principally nonfiction texts to pursue answers to questions like these:

What causes people to develop prejudice and hate toward each other?

What were the actual cultural traditions of the Seneca Indians?

How did white people get the idea that Indians were savages?

Why did Indian parents allow their kids to attend the boarding schools?

What were the roles of women in Indian life?

How did women get the right to vote?

Some groups' questions are a short step from their books, while others range far away in time, content, and ambition.

For more than a week, the literature circles, now operating as inquiry groups, gather information related to their lingering questions, using a variety of nonfiction materials, books, periodicals, and websites. As a way of sharing their eventual findings, students create a series of tableaux, choreographed frozen scenes, depicting key ideas from their research and accompanied by carefully written oral captions. Each group's tableaux, in their own way, grapple with the eternal human issues of prejudice, misunderstanding, exploitation—and the possibility of peace.

*T*he Many Forms of Prejudice: Investigating *"Isms"*

It is May in Chicago, and the freshman class at Best Practice High School has entered a multiday process to negotiate the curriculum the kids will encounter next year as sophomores. Students work with teachers and other adult facilitators in small groups, repeating cycles of reading, writing, discussion, and reflection to identify concerns they have about themselves and their world. Though the student body at BPHS is a very heterogeneous mix of city kids, their "self" concerns are not much different from those of teenagers anywhere: facing issues of identity, trying to envision the future, getting into college, choosing careers, getting married and having families, dealing with peer pressure, coping with alcohol and drugs, staying healthy, getting along with others. When students look out at the world, they find themselves wondering about racism (will people of different races ever learn to get along?), immigration, violence, pollution and the environment, war, and the effects of technology on the future.

A student team investigating ageism took cameras into the city to document the way older people are sometimes treated, discarded, left alone, and shuffled past—then later hung their best photos in a school gallery for all to see.

As this group of kids works through the negotiating process, one cluster of related issues keeps recurring: Why are there always wars? Why do so many people hate each other? Why do we have to fight? Coming from a variety of city neighborhoods, many of them gang-dominated, the kids are troubled by the disharmony they see every day. As LaShonda puts it: "Why is violence all around?" As the kids continue to frame this big question, they decide that there are different kinds of hate, which they begin to name: racism, sexism, ageism, homophobia, gangsterism.

Fast-forward to the next fall, when two weeks are set aside to pursue this "isms" inquiry. Each faculty member has agreed to step out of his or her usual role (biology, math, physical education, art) and become the facilitator for research into one of the different *isms*. Kids choose the *ism* they are most concerned about and interested in, and head off with a team of like-minded classmates and their teacher-facilitator to dig deep into a single topic. Over the summer, teachers have gathered lots of good books and articles on the topic and bookmarked web pages with valuable information. Kids marinate in this material for a while, begin to pose more pointed questions, and then map out plans for learning more. They ask: what can we read, where can we go, who can we interview to help understand this kind of prejudice better and perhaps to combat it?

For two weeks, the kids and their teachers read, search, interview, and discuss. One group studying ableism toured the city, trying to understand the challenges that disabled people face, and grew angrier at the many obstacles and lack of accommodations they discovered. They wrote letters to inform a variety of businesses and public institutions of their need to provide better service. They also created posters about accessibility problems, entered them in an online design contest, and received two awards. Another student team investigating ageism took cameras into the city to document the way older people are sometimes treated, discarded, left alone, and shuffled past—then later hung their best photos in a school gallery for all to see.

Another group became fascinated with the special individuals who, throughout history, have stood up against prejudice and discrimination. They decided to create a "Wall of Respect" to honor those who courageously opposed the *isms* of their times. After studying each hero's life and achievements, kids wrote short essays and graphic displays for the Wall of Respect. On culminating day, students dressed as the figure they had studied—Rosa Parks, Malcom X, Cesar Chavez, Martin Luther King, Abraham Lincoln, Gloria Steinem—and gave presentations in character, answering questions from other students and visitors about their choices and achievements.

*A*dvocating for a New School

In their crumbling inner-city elementary school, Brian Schultz's fifth-grade students have become increasingly outraged by the deteriorating conditions of the building. Years ago, the community was promised a brand-new school, but that replacement was never built, and Byrd Academy was left to crumble with kids inside. Brian's students began to systematically document the issues that obstructed their learning:

- No heat and broken windows, so kids must study with coats and hats on
- No soap, hot water, paper towels, or toilet paper in the washrooms
- No lunchroom, so lunch is served in hallways
- No gym or auditorium, so all school events must use borrowed space

*S*tudents didn't hesitate to suggest that these city leaders would never let their own kids go to a school in such sorry shape.

As momentum grew around this project, Brian saw that it could become the focus of a whole year's worth of curriculum. "All the subjects in the prescribed curriculum were blended together in a natural way," he recalls. "Kids' research took them to books, magazines, and Internet postings that went well beyond their (supposed) reading level and aptitude. As Hennessy said, 'Before this project, I would never have thought I could read this stuff.'"

Working in small groups, the students created folders documenting each grievance, including photos, written explanations, and data displays, and posted all this content on a website (http://www.projectcitizen405.com). They composed respectful but pointed letters to school district, city, and state officials. They didn't hesitate to suggest that these city leaders would never let their own kids go to a school in such sorry shape. As a result, hundreds of letters, phone calls, and emails of support poured in. A wide range of media (local newspapers, TV stations, and National Public Radio) covered the story, Ralph Nader visited and wrote about the school, and the class was invited to the state capitol to testify before the legislature.

Read More About
These Teachers and
Their Classrooms

Want to hear more about
this chapter's opening
stories? We first learned
about Sheila Booth's
garbage inquiry from our
colleague James Beane,
whose *A Reason to
Teach: Creating Class-
rooms of Dignity and
Hope* (2005) has an inspiring message about the
importance of authentic
inquiry in a democracy.
The work of Brian
Schultz's kids at
Chicago's Byrd School is
the subject of his 2008
book *Spectacular Things
Happen Along the Way:
Lessons from an Urban
Classroom.* The high
school *"isms"* unit
and other negotiated-
curriculum projects are
described in Harvey
Daniels, Marilyn Bizar,
and Steve Zemelman's
*Rethinking High School:
Best Practice in Teach-
ing, Learning, and Lead-
ership* (2001). We dig
deeper into Diane
Titche's literature and
inquiry circles right here
in Chapter 10 of this book.

Still, in the end, students did not succeed in shaming the district into delivering the long-promised new building. Indeed, a few months later, the superintendent proposed the permanent closing of the building, due to low enrollment. But both the students and their teacher felt that powerful lifelong lessons had been learned. In the words of Malik: "Last year was my best year ever in school . . . instead of it being like school it was more like family . . . and I learned a lot too, like learning how to write and interview and ask good questions." In the end, Brian wrote a book about his kids' remarkable action research project, called *Spectacular Things Happen Along the Way* (Schultz 2008).

So what do all these classrooms have in common?

Here's what we see: Students are engaged, activated, and motivated. They dig deep into topics and questions they really care about, gathering and weighing information, building knowledge, and putting that knowledge to work in their lives. They design and conduct investigations much like adult researchers, and bring their findings to the community. They collaborate skillfully, shifting fluidly from individual pursuits into small inquiry groups and then back to whole-class communities.

In short, these kids are *thinking*. They are employing the very same cognitive strategies that proficient grown-up readers, writers, researchers, and collaborators use to get work done in the world every day. And these students are thinking *together*. For key parts of each project, teachers have organized students into small, peer-led investigation teams—a structure we call *inquiry circles*.

But there is even more here than meets the eye. Yes, students are exercising choice in topics, readings, and ways to show their learning, but this is not a temporary treat or a "day off" from the official curriculum. In fact, most of what the kids study in these small-group investigations either comes directly from the required curriculum in their schools or can be "backmapped" to it. For example, Diane Titche's literature circles were formed to address the district-required social studies curriculum at her grade level. The Best Practice High School kids identified their own topics, but look at all the standards-based skills they practiced along the way: reading a variety of challenging nonfiction texts, gathering information, categorizing data, forming hypotheses, graphing findings, making informational displays, giving public speeches and performances, defending their inferences and positions, and writing carefully edited informational, persuasive, and explanatory texts across a wide range of genres. Wherever small-group inquiry questions come from, teachers can match kids' investigations to subject matter guidelines, state mandates, and prevailing high-stakes tests.

And speaking of teachers, what strikes you about their roles in these classrooms? All four have relinquished the sage-on-stage stance to become guides on the side. Instead of telling, they are showing, modeling, coaching, mentoring, and facilitating. They are "leading from behind," working skillfully in the background to channel kids' curiosity, provide materials, structure interaction, and document ideas. They don't dominate, nor do they shy away from adding their own knowledge to advance the inquiry. These teachers have become facilitators of kids' learning.

When we hear about these energized kids and their collaborative investigations, many of us sigh and think, "Wow, that's the way I'd really like to teach." And we have all probably tried a few projects like these over the years. But even as we are charmed by and attracted to the active, cooperative learning portrayed in these accounts, it can also strike us as idealistic, time-consuming, or risky. Can we really trust kids to take and sustain this kind of initiative? Can we cover all the required subjects this way? Will students do OK on the state test? Does this kind of teaching really work?

The short answer is yes.

The long answer is this book.

Collaborative, relevant, deep, and thoughtful learning does work, at all grade levels. Kids *can* operate productively together in small peer-led teams, just like adults do every day in workplaces across the country. This kind of schooling pays off richly for learners. Decades of research confirm that such instruction leads not just to higher student achievement on the customary academic measures, but to better social attitudes, stronger work habits, and more persistence in school (Darling-Hammond et al. 2008; Zemelman, Daniels, and Hyde 2005; Daniels and Bizar 2004; Smith et al. 2001; Newmann et al. 1996).

This engaged, interactive instruction is not a passing fad; it's not the latest faux-new bandwagon rolling through Teachertown. On the contrary, this model of learning and teaching has been steadily developing for decades. And today, fresh discoveries in cognition, inquiry, and collaboration show us even better ways to help learners engage with ideas and drive each others' thinking—not just to remember information, but to build knowledge, to care, and to act. When we combine the new research on thinking with the latest findings about how small groups can best be formed, guided, and managed, we can trust the active learning classroom to challenge kids and help them get smart.

Why We Need a Change

In one of the largest studies of its kind ever undertaken in American schools, Pianta and Belsky (2007) found that American fifth graders were spending 91 percent of their school day either listening to a teacher talk or working alone. The findings were similar for first and third graders. Ninety-one percent! Can you believe that? After decades of research on the benefits of interactive teaching and learning, most of our kids are trapped in solitary, passive activities for almost the whole school day. How could this be happening?

Of course, there's long been a strand of "sit-down-be-quiet-and-listen" pedagogy in American schools—but it has always been balanced by a steadily advancing model of progressive student-centered education. As recently as the 1990s, this progressive tradition was widely in evidence: our schools were filled with cooperative learning, reciprocal teaching, flexible small-group instruction, reading and writing workshops. Classrooms fairly burst with interaction—kids meeting in teams, book clubs, and research groups; students sitting at tables, facing other kids and working collaboratively; teachers offering instruction to small, flexible groups; teachers conferring with individuals and providing mini-lessons in literacy workshops.

But the No Child Left Behind legislation in 2001, along with the testing frenzy that followed its passage, sadly drove kids back to their individual seats for endless drill-and-kill test-prep worksheets. Deep thinking was replaced by shallow "coverage," and enforced by a battery of tests that discouraged schools from venturing beyond the approved minimums. Mandated, scripted instruction pushed discussion, interaction, and debate right out of the school day. In elementary schools, time spent on science and social studies shrank dramatically; art and music all but disappeared. More and more course requirements, with fewer and fewer choices, were piled on secondary programs. In effect, the tests literally became the curriculum.

▲

STEPH: Whoa, Smoke, do you think we are being a little too tough? Is this sounding kinda negative?

SMOKEY: Hmmm, maybe. Probably. But what are we supposed to say? We've both worked in so many schools where all this accountability stuff has boomeranged and hurt the kids.

STEPH: Yeah, all those teachers who have had to let go of some of their best teaching to read off a script instead. And then to lose science and social studies time; I mean, no more sharks, no more rain forest. With teachers so concerned about the high stakes, test scores rule the day. It's sad . . .

SMOKEY: I've been in schools where the grown-ups now view the kids who struggle or those with special needs as problems, because their scores can "get the whole school on the state watch list."

STEPH: Yikes! It should be just the opposite. Schools should be about teaching <u>all</u> of our kids, particularly those who need the most support! It's really unfortunate. But still. There have been some positive outcomes from this whole NCLB thing too.

SMOKEY: You're right. Yes, let's look on the bright side for a while.

STEPH: Deal.

▼

Here are three good things about the NCLB legislation. First, it put education at the top of the national agenda, which is always a good thing. Second, the NCLB era squeezed the slack out of the system. The law exposed any schools that might have been coasting on their laurels. But most important, the NCLB reporting requirements, which mandated disaggregated data, shined a harsh spotlight on the shameful disparity between students of privilege and those from poverty, those with special needs, and speakers of other languages. Schools with small populations of struggling kids used to be able to sweep their low scores under the rug. But under NCLB, even some much-admired suburban schools had to explain why they were just as ineffective with these kids as some underresourced urban schools.

As this book goes to press, new leadership has arrived in Washington, and the unfortunate side effects of the NCLB era are being scrutinized. There's a renewed commitment to progressive ideals and plans for a new federal education policy. President Obama has issued a stirring call for young people to enter a revitalized teaching profession:

> I'm calling on a new generation of Americans to step forward and serve our country in our classrooms. If you want to make a difference in the life of our nation, if you want to make the most of your talents and dedication, if you want to make your mark with a legacy that will endure—then join the teaching profession. America needs you. We need you in our suburbs. We need you in our small towns. We especially need you in our inner cities. We need you in classrooms all across our country.

These bright signs give us hope that we can now return to the mainstream of American education. We can reconnect with the work of the generations before us to make school what it should be for kids. How wonderful it feels to be part of a progressive restoration, to help usher in the next wave of student-centered teaching and learning.

Why Small Groups?

We have a long—wait, let's be honest—*ancient* tradition of students working alone in American schools. We recognize this planned aloneness in the standard classroom seating arrangement that keeps kids from facing each other, in the very idea of "seatwork," in the definition of most kid-to-kid talk as disruption, in winner-loser grading practices, in prizes, punishments, and in ubiquitous warnings like "Do your own work!" And as the recent Pianta and Belsky study pointed out, kids are still doing almost *all* their work in a solitary, individualistic framework.

But the world has changed. In offices and factories across the world, employees who once toiled alone are being reorganized into teams, work groups, or task forces. In the global economy, many forward-looking corporations are flattening their organizations, soliciting more buy-in and input from workers. Many corporations are spinning off smaller "boutique" companies where, freed from the hierarchical structures of business as usual, teams of fired-up workers are empowered to find new ways, new products, new processes.

And guess what? Workers *make more money* if they know how to collaborate. A recent study from the University of Illinois showed that ten years after graduation, people who had honed their teamwork skills while still in high school had significantly higher earnings than classmates who had failed to do so (Science Daily 2008). In fact, the mastery of collaboration skills correlated more closely to annual income than standardized test scores. Even after controlling for students' achievement scores, family socioeconomic status, and educational attainment, the researchers found that "social skills such as conscientiousness, cooperativeness, and motivation were as important as test scores for success in the workplace." Shall we all say it together? Well, *duh!*

If you listen to people in the human resources world, you'll hear them talking about this new cooperative workplace and why it is so important. Human resources expert Susan Heathfield writes: "Fostering teamwork is creating a work culture that values collaboration. In a teamwork environment, people understand and believe that thinking, planning, decisions, and actions are better when done cooperatively. People recognize, and even assimilate, the belief that 'none of us is as good as all of us'" (2006, p. 1). Companies are finding that productivity, quality, and service improve when employees feel ownership, when they are part of a defined, small family within the organization—where they feel they have a voice, and even a home. Now, we understand that these cooperative innovations in the business world are aimed primarily at enhanced profit. But look what the trend says: small groups work. We will talk much more about this in Chapter 3, but for now let us simply list some reasons why small-group work is a must in today's schools.

Benefits of Small-Group Work

- Small groups are lifelike.
- Small groups generate energy for challenging work.
- In small groups, we are smarter.
- In small groups, diversity is an asset.
- Small groups make engaged, interactive learning possible.
- Small groups allow us to differentiate instruction.
- Employers increasingly require small-group skills.
- Well-structured small-group work enhances student achievement.

Back in the School World, the adoption of small-group structures has been sporadic. Although we have gradually infused more group work into schools, it is still too rare—more like an occasional side trip, but not the main thoroughfare. The use of small-group work seems to be inversely related to grade levels. In primary and intermediate grades, teamwork is more common; partner reading and literature circles are not hard to find. Less so in middle school, even though the original middle-level model calls for lots of collaborative work. And then there is high school, where the massive curriculum, tracking systems, and instructional traditions often conspire against widespread small-group work.

But to be honest, it's not just the structures of school that make kid-to-kid collaboration seem like a stretch. As teachers ourselves, we may not feel so confident about adding lots of small-group work to our classroom menus. Hey, we all have our own crash-and-burn stories about cooperative activities that flopped. And maybe we never experienced any well-structured small-group work when we were students in school. Maybe the how-to's of student collaboration were omitted from our teacher training.

Students *can* consistently and effectively work with every other kid in the room. But equipping them to do so requires a repertoire of management tools that most of us were never given. If we can't teach our students the social strategies needed for this kind of learning, disappointment awaits. If the kids don't understand how to think together, to read, write, listen, and view as a team, they will drift off task and off topic. Moreover, if we teachers don't feel clear and comfortable with our own roles in the collaborative classroom, we may struggle, and resort to more conventional teacher-driven projects.

These specific skills, strategies, tools, and roles are exactly what this book aims to provide so teachers don't give up on authentic, kid-driven inquiry projects that engage their hearts and minds.

Comprehension, Collaboration, and Inquiry

As we mentioned in the preface, the two of us go back a number of years. As we spent more time together and became friends as well as colleagues, we discovered a natural convergence in our work: the connection between thinking and conversation.

While Steph's work had focused most prominently on *comprehension* strategy instruction and Smokey's on small-group *collaboration,* both of us had crossed over into the other's territory. Steph has always championed active literacy and getting kids to process information by talking to each other. And Smokey always encourages reading discussion groups to think strategically, to visualize, infer, question, and connect. Steph knew that you don't think in isolation and that in order to really begin to understand and act, you have to engage with other

*H*ey, we all have our own crash-and-burn stories about cooperative activities that flopped.

people. And Smokey understood that you don't get kids into small collaborative groups for the sake of it; rather, the purpose of talking and working together is to ponder big ideas, issues, and concepts.

So it became obvious to us that comprehension and collaboration were a perfect fit. In fact, one without the other was pretty useless. The best way to understand the world we live in is to be alert to it—to read about it, to listen, to view, and then *talk* about it. Teaching kids to think coupled with rich talk about text makes all the difference. Two heads are better than one, three better than four, and so on.

When talking about teaching and learning, we often found ourselves asking, *What's next?* What becomes possible when we merge comprehension and collaboration? Time and again, we noticed that when kids have authentic opportunities to read, think, and talk together, their curiosity explodes and their questions come fast and furiously. The more kids learn, the more they wonder. And it is those questions that propel learners on, that get them excited and engaged in the world around them. This works both when kids pursue their own questions and when they investigate topics from the required curriculum. As long as we keep kids' interests, questions, and curiosity in the forefront, we can build inquiries that engage, enlighten, and educate.

Time and again, we noticed that when kids have authentic opportunities to read, think, and talk together, their curiosity explodes and their questions come fast and furiously.

The Next Step: Inquiry Circles

For us, the answer to "What's next?" is: well-structured small-group inquiry across the curriculum. This book occurs at the intersection of comprehension, collaboration, and inquiry. When we teach kids to think and work together, learning is more seamless. When kids learn and practice strategies to comprehend what they read, hear, and see and when they learn the social skills necessary to work in small groups, their inquiries soar.

In *Comprehension and Collaboration*, we teach the reader, not merely the reading; the communicator, not merely the communication; the researcher, not merely the research. When we focus on teaching strategies for reading, listening, viewing, communicating, collaborating, and researching, learners come away with lots of strategy knowledge for sure, but also a ton of content. Learning, understanding, and remembering subject matter is a direct product of knowing how to think, work together, and wonder.

Keep in mind, however, that we don't teach all of the thinking strategies, collaborative processes, and inquiry steps before kids ever get a chance to answer their questions. They wouldn't last long if we taught countless lessons before setting them free to satisfy their curiosity and search for answers. So we model a few important ideas of how to think and work together and then send them off to investigate. We then continue to teach more about comprehension and collaboration throughout the inquiry process.

What do these small-group inquiries look like? Think of literature circles—but instead of choosing a single book to read, kids select a topic or a question to explore. Picture teachers teaching comprehension strategies and kids making connections, asking questions, and synthesizing the information. Envision teachers modeling social skills and kids planning interviews, asking follow-up questions, and making decisions about what to investigate. Imagine teachers demonstrating research techniques and kids meeting together to pursue answers to their questions and take action. When comprehension, collaboration, and research intersect, inquiry circles take root and grow our kids' learning and understanding. The basic principles of inquiry circles are highlighted here:

PRINCIPLES OF INQUIRY CIRCLES

- Choice of topics based on genuine student curiosity, questions, interests
- Digging deeply into complex, authentic topics that matter to kids
- Flexible grouping, featuring small research teams, groups, task forces
- Heterogeneous, nonleveled groups with careful differentiation
- Student responsibility and peer leadership
- Use of proficient-reader/thinker/researcher strategies
- Drawing upon multiple, multigenre, and multimedia sources
- Going beyond fact-finding to synthesizing ideas and building and acquiring knowledge
- Actively using knowledge in our schools and communities: sharing, publication, products, or taking action
- Matching or "backmapping" kids' learning to state or district standards

*T*his Book Is Different

You don't see many professional books claiming to be for all grade levels, K–12. And even fewer address all subjects across the curriculum. Conventional publishing wisdom says that educational authors must disseminate their ideas to a smaller range of grade levels or a narrower span of the curriculum. Well, sorry; guess we're breaking the rules.

This book is for *everyone who teaches* because the big ideas and processes of education, the really big ones, truly do apply to all learners. From pre-K to college, we are all in the business of teaching thinking. And that's something we are never done with: we don't start children off thinking in primary grades and then assume we're finished. Nor do we hold off on thinking until middle school, give them a couple good years of instruction, and then shut down, figuring they're now ready for anything. We teach thinking all year, every year: we teach students how to listen, view, read, gather, and engage with information; we make sure students acquire cognitive strategies, weigh ideas, develop judgment, and build knowledge; and just as important, we help them to remember, care, choose, and take action.

The social structure within which we nurture kids' thinking matters in all subjects and grade levels, too. How long have we worked inside discredited factory-model schools, but can't ever seem to break out of them? How long have teachers played "the font of wisdom," "sage on the stage," or simply the lecturer—when the testimony of our own sense screams: "The kids are not getting it!" We know we have to change the social relationships in the classroom in order to ramp up the learning power of our time with students. No matter whether we teach kindergarten or Advanced Placement, if we cannot get our students to work in groups productively, actively, and responsibly, we are pedagogically sunk. Back to the paleo-classroom, with its straight rows of unwilling kids and us in the front, spoon-feeding, cajoling, and threatening. Enough!

How the Book Works

Living with the Inevitable Internet (much more on this in Chapter 6), we have all become accustomed to reading in quick, strategic bursts, looking for features, pictures, and sidebars, jumping around the page, and following links. (Come to think of it, how often do we see a thirty-six-word sentence like that last one on a website?) In short, with hypertext, we like to take the wheel and drive ourselves around. Because this book is full of practical materials, suggestions, lists, connections, pictures, and samples of kids' work, we've tried to provide as much of that "webby" feel as we can, within the constraints of a tree-based product.

But there's also merit to sitting down in a comfortable chair, under the glow of a nice bright lamp, for a long, leisurely read. Turning a sequence of pages, stopping to think and react, maybe jotting notes or questions in the margin. Yes, we have tried to pack the book with practical ideas and materials you'll want to grab, but it is also about big ideas: What is school really for? How can we develop kids' thinking? How can we teach for understanding? What is most important to learn? Can we really break free of the old lecture-test method? Where does motivation really come from? Are we sure that kids are ready to take much more responsibility for their education? What roles are most powerful for teachers to enact? Sitting in your comfy chair, with that nice bright light, you can do a whole different kind of reading, and give the ideas in this book a longer, deeper, test.

Need a road map to this book? Here's how *Comprehension and Collaboration* lays out.

*W*e have tried to pack the book with practical ideas and materials you'll want to grab, but it is also about big ideas.

PART 1. Here in **Chapter 1,** we have tried to show the powerful potential of this approach and set it in the context of American education today. Next, in **Chapter 2,** we review research and current insights into *comprehension,* the way learners think as they listen, read, and view. In the complementary **Chapter 3,** we look at *collaboration* and the specific social strategies of small-group learning. There is a robust base of research and information (rarely shared among teachers) that helps us confidently form and manage student-directed inquiries in our classrooms. In **Chapter 4,** we share what we know about *research and inquiry projects* in school. While most of us already do some work along these lines—thematic units, projects, term papers—such projects may lack key elements of true inquiry, and thus contain pitfalls we want to avoid when we launch inquiry circles.

PART 2. **Chapter 5** explains ten fundamental classroom conditions needed for active, small-group learning in all subjects and at all grade levels. This starts with setting up your learning space and extends all the way to the intellectual habit of "living with big ideas in mind." Because our students depend heavily (though not exclusively) on the Internet for research, it is vital that we help them use the web wisely. The remarkable Andrew Hess, technology specialist from the Mamaroneck Public Schools, helps us provide that kind of specific, careful online guidance in **Chapter 6.**

In **Chapter 7,** we help you get started with inquiry learning by sharing the Gradual Release of Responsibility framework for instruction and offering 27 practical, adaptable lessons in comprehension, collaboration, and inquiry.

Versions of these 27 lessons appear in many of the classroom accounts scattered throughout the book. To help you navigate between the baseline versions in Chapter 7 and the fascinating teacher adaptations, we use the Lesson Link icon. When this icon appears in the margin, it will direct you to the page(s) where other versions of the lesson can be found.

Lesson Link icons direct you to the page(s) where other versions of a lesson can be found.

PART 3. Part 3 offers how-to instructions for four types of inquiry circles. **Chapter 8** introduces brief, often spontaneous *mini–inquiries,* in which groups of kids seek answers to a pressing question or quickly gather information about a topic of interest. In these brief investigations, kids may simply scratch a curiosity itch and answer a question, or they may spend several days expanding their knowledge about a topic. Either way, mini–inquiry projects offer an opportunity for teachers to teach some beginning steps of the inquiry process and for kids to practice the strategies of "finding out," the core activity of all deeper learning. In **Chapter 9,** we describe *curricular inquiries,* in which teachers offer students choice within subjects required by the official curriculum and help them to investigate their chosen topics in a group inquiry mode, instead of relying solely on the textbook or seatwork. **Chapter 10** describes literature circle inquiries, small-group research projects that stem from book club discussions. In this variant, students systematically reflect upon books they are reading to notice big or lingering questions, and then reorganize to investigate these important topics. Finally, **Chapter 11** moves on to *open inquiry* or *negotiated project curriculum,* where teams of students identify and pursue their own topics, as teachers support, facilitate, and backmap the process to the official curriculum.

PART 4.   The last section focuses on the distinctive management concerns that arise with small-group inquiries. Whenever kids are working in small groups, teachers wonder how to assess them. In **Chapter 12,** we address issues of assessment, evaluation, record keeping, and grading. Inquiry circles allow us to see kids working at a high and sustained intellectual level, and we want to be sure we capture evidence of all that good thinking. Finally, in **Chapter 13,** we tackle the most commonly asked questions about the setup, management, and predictable problems of inquiry circles.

Threaded through all these pages are 29 extended stories of small-group inquiry projects in action (as well as a variety of shorter ones) from pre-kindergarten through high school and across the curriculum. If you can't remember which story is in which chapter, refer to our Inquiry Project Locator chart on page 17.

To further help you locate classroom accounts from the grade level you teach, we've deployed grade-range icons in the margins of the book.

Primary

Intermediate

Middle School

High School

PRIMARY

INTERMEDIATE

MIDDLE

HIGH SCHOOL

Grade level icons help you locate classroom accounts from your grade level.

While it's always valuable to see innovations at work with the kinds of kids you teach, don't forget that stories from other grade levels often provide structures that can be easily adapted to older or younger learners.

Each of these classroom accounts shows creative teachers putting the principles of inquiry to work with a unique group of students. By studying these distinctive stories, you can see the many different ways that artful teachers adapt the basic inquiry circle model to their own situation, style, and students.

Inquiry Project Locator

GRADE	INQUIRY	TEACHER	PAGE
Primary	Garbage and Recycling	Sheila Booth	1
Intermediate	Native–Settler Contact	Diane Titche	2
Middle/High School	Prejudice and –isms	Best Practice H.S. Faculty	4
Intermediate	Advocating for a New School	Brian Schultz	5
Intermediate	Gun Control	Julia O'Connell	32
Middle	Cell Phones for Soldiers	Brittany Bergquist	94
Primary	Becoming Meteorologists	Chatsworth Avenue Faculty	98
High School	Presidential Debates	Elizabeth Clain & Caren Lee	99
Intermediate	Single Stream Recycling	Steph Harvey	148
Middle/High School	Gakl It's Ipecac	Smokey Daniels	152
Primary	Why Do Mosquito Bites Itch?	Steph Harvey	153
Primary	Kids' Choice Topics	Debbie Miller	web
Primary	Self-Selected Inquiries	Barb Smith	web
Intermediate	From Cheese to Magazines	Bodo Heiliger	155
Primary	Antarctica	Kristen Elder-Rubino & Melissa Oviatt	169
Intermediate	Slavery and Child Labor	Holly Occhipinti & Michele Schirmer	176
Intermediate	Health and Body Systems	Mary Pfau	187
Middle/High School	Sugar and Civil Rights	Sara Ahmed	195
High School	Exponential Functions	Vanessa Breschling	web
Primary	Frog and Toad and Friendship	Steph Harvey	203
Intermediate	Bullying	Mike Laehr & Sue Fisher	206
Intermediate/Middle	Native–Settler Contact	Diane Titche	216
Preschool/Primary	Postal Service, Princesses, and Castles	Pamela Battin-Sacks	233
Primary	Signatures and the Origins of Writing	Brad Buhrow	235
Intermediate/Middle	Kids' Choice Inquiry Projects	Joyce Sanchez & Smokey Daniels	247
High School	Capstone and Senior Projects	Federal-Hocking High School Faculty	263
Middle	Atomic Weapons	Joyce Sanchez & Smokey Daniels	268

Anytime you see this icon in the margin, you'll know that there is additional material available on the web, at www.heinemann.com/ comprehensionandcollaboration.

Companion Website

A vital part of this book is its companion website, www.heinemann.com/ comprehensionandcollaboration. Any time you see this icon in the margin, you'll know that there is additional material available on the web. When you log on, you'll see that many of our chapters have extensions, extra sections, background details, or student work samples posted for your study and enjoyment. Especially valuable are several more full accounts of inquiry circles in action at a variety of grade levels. As we go to press, there are already 200 pages of extra content on the site, with lots more coming from us and, we hope, from you.

On the website you will also find:

- a step-by-step **Study Guide,** specifically designed for faculties or teacher study groups working to support student inquiry. You can start your own "Teacher Inquiry Circle" with this guide.

- three practical **Bibliographies** including a list of websites of interest to teachers and kids, a list of magazines that cover science and history topics as well as current events, and a list of series books on a far-reaching range of topics and issues.

- **Resource Pages** that will offer updates on great new books, materials, processes, classroom stories, podcasts, staff development opportunities, and more.

- Detailed versions of some of the featured **Lessons.**

- A variety of **Graphic Organizers, Forms,** and **Think Sheets** that are used with the lessons and inquiries throughout the book.

What We Know About Comprehension

In our previous books and in our work with teachers around the country, we always talk about the *thinking strategies* that enhance kids' comprehension and about the *social strategies* that help learners collaborate effectively to learn more. Ambitious small-group inquiries depend on both—kids must know how to think and how to work together. So in this chapter, we'll start by exploring the key comprehension strategies that support kids to investigate their questions, get more information, and infer bigger ideas as they read and investigate. Then in Chapter 3, we'll discuss the social strategies of well-structured talk and purposeful collaboration that allow groups of kids to work powerfully together, generating knowledge through inquiry.

Ready to Read?

Will you do us a favor? Just read the following passage. Don't look ahead, just read this text until you feel you understand it well. We'll wait.

MS2 Phage Coat Protein—RNA Interaction

This system is being studied for **three reasons:** (1) it is an example of a sequence-specific RNA-protein interaction, (2) it participates in a **well-behaved** in vitro capsid assembly reaction, and (3) it is a good model system to study how protein finds a target on a large RNA molecule. Available are an X-ray crystal structure of the RNA-protein complex and an NMR structure of the free RNA hairpin target. Current efforts focus on understanding how the **thermodynamic** details of sequence-specific "recognition" is achieved. We have made mutations in all the amino acids believed to make contact with the RNA and are evaluating the affinity of the mutant proteins to the normal RNA target as well as to targets that have single atom changes in either the bases or the phosphodiester backbone. It is already clear that nearly all the contacts predicted by the co-crystal structure contribute to the total free energy of binding. Thus, unlike several protein-protein interfaces that have been analyzed in a similar way, there are **no** "hot spots" that dominate the affinity. However, we have several examples where affinity and specificity are defined by structural elements of the RNA in its **free form.**

—OLKE UHLENBECK, INTERDEPARTMENTAL BIOLOGICAL SCIENCES,
NORTHWESTERN UNIVERSITY

Have fun? We didn't think so.

Isn't it odd how rarely we teachers run across text this tough in our normal lives? And whoa, what if our students' experience with textbooks is just like ours with Dr. Uhlenbeck's passage?

But anyway, now that you've read the passage, it's time for the quiz! Get out your pencil.

Comprehension Test

1. How many reasons are there for studying this system?

2. What is the nature of the *in vito capsid assembly reaction?*

3. Current research focuses on what details of sequence-specific recognition?

4. How many "hot spots" dominate the affinity?

5. In what form are there examples of RNA where affinity and specificity are defined by structural elements?

How'd you do? We're guessing you got all five questions right. Congratulations, class! Everybody got an A!

Very funny. Just like the questions at the end of the chapter in the textbook, right? This shows us how we can "cover the material" and the kids can "pass the test," with no understanding whatsoever. And just as we have done here, many textbooks boldface the correct answers for thought-free plucking.

But let's continue the experiment. Turn the clock back a couple of minutes. Try to remember exactly what was going on inside your head as you tried to make meaning out of these 210 words. What kinds of thinking did you use to make sense of the passage? Think a minute. Do this with a colleague if you like, and talk it over.

We've shared this passage with many adult readers around the country, and here are some things people commonly say as they reconstruct their own cognitive processes.

- I kept getting stuck, and going back and rereading, trying to understand it. I slowed down and read more carefully. But it didn't help much.

- I kept having all these questions, like, What do these words mean? What is a "capsid reaction assembly," for crying out loud?! What kind of document is this anyway?

- I kept trying to connect this to what I have learned before about genetics, DNA, and RNA. I know that RNA is some kind of copy or duplicate of DNA that's formed when cells reproduce, but that's all I remember.

- I was trying to visualize this in my head. I have seen diagrams of the DNA double-helix shape, and I think that they are made of strings of proteins. He was talking about how proteins do or don't attach to the surfaces—I could sort of see that.

- There was so much detail here, I was trying to figure out what were the most important ideas, the main things he was trying to get across.

- Well, I could infer from the information that the author must be some kind of research scientist, and seems to works in some field of genetics.

- I was trying to put it all together, to figure out what was the main idea, the big picture. When I saw at the very end that this was a scientist explaining his research interests, that helped me some—but I still didn't really feel like I understood what his experiments were.

- I tried, I really did—but I just don't understand this at all.

Did you recognize some of your own thinking in these responses? Probably you did. And that's because proficient adult readers like us don't just randomly flail at text when our comprehension breaks down, hoping to shake out some meaning. Instead, we deploy a very specific repertoire of thinking strategies that we have developed over years of experience with reading and texts. As the testimonies above show, we

- monitor our comprehension and make adjustments

- connect new information to background knowledge

- ask questions

- infer and visualize meaning

- determine importance

- summarize and synthesize ideas

It's important to realize that since we are veteran readers, we take these cognitive steps mostly automatically and unaware. We have relegated most of the brainwork of reading to the unconscious level, just like driving a car. But when we encounter some really difficult text like this, just as when the car in front of us comes to a screeching halt, we suddenly become acutely aware of our thinking (or driving!). The cognitive strategies at our disposal are now explicit, right out in the open. We can literally hear our strategic thinking at work as we say, "Hit the brakes!" or "Whoops, I better go back and reread this" or "What's goin' on here?" or "This reminds me of some science I learned in high school . . . how did that DNA stuff go?" See the chart on p. 22 "How Proficient Learners Think as They Read, Listen, or View" for a fuller description of these comprehension strategies.

But even with our grown-up array of meaning-making tools, this was still a truly tough reading assignment. And what made it so hard is that most of us didn't have the background knowledge to understand it. So here's lesson number one about comprehension: the prime determinant of understanding is prior knowledge. Period, point blank, case closed.

Most "reading difficulties" are really prior knowledge problems. A few years ago, Illinois administered a statewide test to kids where the key topic was in-line skating (rollerblading, to the rest of us). Needless to say, kids from inner-city housing projects knew little about this subject and scored poorly, while kids from wealthy suburbs crisscrossed with recreational trails proved to be "smarter." Bah! Some kids just don't have the experience base that makes reading easier for others. With Dr. Uhlenbeck's passage, we had a chance to feel how hard reading can be if you don't bring the right schema to school.

Oh yeah, there is one more thing that some adult readers tell us after being presented with the Uhlenbeck passage: "This made me mad. I felt stupid and I knew I'd never understand it, so I just quit reading it." How many times have we seen this same response from students in our own classrooms when they are confronted with supertough text? Like many adults, kids can get so frustrated by such a high ratio of effort to comprehension that they just check out.

*M*ost "reading difficulties" are really prior knowledge problems.

HOW PROFICIENT LEARNERS THINK
AS THEY READ, LISTEN, OR VIEW

Monitor Comprehension

We monitor our comprehension and keep track of our thinking in a variety of ways. We notice when the text makes sense and when it doesn't. When meaning breaks down, we stop and refocus our thinking to repair meaning. We ask questions, infer, activate background knowledge, and make connections, all in the effort to promote understanding. We teach readers to

- become aware of their thinking as they read

- listen to their inner voice and follow the ongoing inner conversation

- notice when meaning breaks down and/or their mind wanders

- leave tracks of their thinking by jotting thoughts when reading

- stop, think, and react to information

- talk about the reading before, during, and after reading

- respond to reading in writing

- employ "fix-up strategies"—reread for clarification, read ahead to construct meaning, use context to break down an unfamiliar word, skip difficult parts and continue on to see if meaning becomes clear, check and recheck answers and thinking, examine evidence.

Activate and Connect to Background Knowledge

Nothing colors our learning more than what we bring to it. Whether we are questioning, visualizing, or synthesizing, our background knowledge is the foundation of our thinking. We simply can't understand what we hear, read, or view without thinking about what we already know. We teach readers to

- refer to prior personal experience
- make connections between texts and media
- activate prior knowledge of the content, style, structure, features, and genre
- connect the new to the known—use what they know to understand new information
- merge their thinking with new learning to build a knowledge base
- activate their schema to read strategically

Ask Questions

Questioning is the strategy that propels learners on. If we didn't wonder about the text, why would we bother to continue reading? Questions are at the heart of inquiry-based learning. Human beings are driven to make sense of the world, and questions open the doors to understanding. We teach readers to

- wonder about the content, concepts, outcomes, and genre
- question the author
- question the ideas and the information
- read to discover answers and gain information
- read with a question in mind
- wonder about the text to understand big ideas
- do further research and investigation to gain information and acquire knowledge

Infer and Visualize Meaning

Inferential thinking allows learners to grasp the deeper essence of text and information. Readers infer and visualize meaning by taking their background knowledge and merging it with clues in the text or the images to draw a conclusion, gain information, surface a theme, or arrive at a big idea that is not explicitly stated in the text. We teach readers to

- use context clues to figure out the meaning of unfamiliar words
- draw conclusions from text evidence
- gain information from the images and features as well as the text
- predict outcomes, events, and characters' actions
- surface underlying themes
- answer questions that are not explicitly answered in the text
- create interpretations based on text evidence
- create mental images drawn from the reader's background knowledge and the clues in text
- visualize as well as hear, taste, smell, and feel the words and ideas

Determine Importance

What we determine to be important in text depends on our purpose for reading it. When we read nonfiction we are reading to learn, understand, and remember information. When we read fiction, we are often reading to nurture our soul, to connect to embedded themes, or to experience the world from a perspective other than our own. We teach readers to

- sift important ideas from interesting but less important details
- target key information and code the text to hold thinking
- distinguish between what the reader thinks is important and what the author most wants the reader to take away
- make connections between their own life and the text themes
- construct main ideas from supporting details
- choose what to remember

Synthesize and Summarize

Synthesizing information nudges us to see the bigger picture as we read. It is not enough for readers simply to recall and restate facts. Thoughtful readers merge their thinking with the information to come to a more complete understanding of the text and the topic. Sometimes, we add new information to our store of knowledge. Other times, we completely change our thinking based on our reading. But either way, we synthesize to gain a more thorough understanding and acquire knowledge. We teach readers to

- take stock of meaning while reading
- add to their knowledge base
- paraphrase information
- move from facts to ideas
- use the parts to see the whole—read for the gist
- rethink misconceptions and tie opinions to the text
- revise thinking after reading
- merge what is known with new information to form a new idea, perspective, or insight
- generate new knowledge

—Source: Adapted from Harvey and Goudvis 2005
and Pearson, Dole, Duffy, and Roehler 1992

Comprehension Strategies for Active Readers and Thinkers

After our little MS2 Phage Coat Protein comprehension test, you might still be thinking: "Yeah, well, nobody ever taught me those so-called strategies, and I turned out to be a pretty good reader." But not everyone in this society has been as

*E*xtensive research tells us that when kids know and employ comprehension strategies, they better understand what they read and engage in a more fulfilling reading experience.

fortunate with regard to literacy as most of us who teach. Many of us came from homes that valued language and learning, we had someone who modeled a love of books and ideas, became pretty good readers ourselves, and were generally engaged and successful in school. Not all of our students share these advantages. They may not, like us, cobble together a powerful repertoire of reading strategies through a lifetime of literacy opportunities. Instead, many of them will flee from school as soon as they can legally escape, settling into a life of dedicated nonreading.

So, if we know how proficient readers like ourselves think through text, we need to start teaching those specific strategies right now, to every kid we see, from prekindergarten through high school and in every subject across the curriculum.

And teaching works. Extensive research tells us that when kids know and employ comprehension strategies, they better understand what they read and engage in a more fulfilling reading experience. For many years, educators studied struggling readers for clues about the best way to teach reading. Then in the 1980s research took a different tack when researchers identified and systematically investigated the thinking strategies that *proficient* readers used to comprehend what they read (Pearson, Dole, Duffy, and Roehler 1992; Pressley 1976). Today, we build lessons around what skillful readers do. We teach thinking strategies that help learners understand whenever they read, listen, or view.

It's well proven that these strategies enhance kids' comprehension throughout schooling. In the summary below "Research on Reading Comprehension," we review the studies that support comprehension strategy instruction. And with inquiry circles, these thinking strategies pay off, big-time. Kids make better use of the autonomy we offer. They are more likely to learn from their reading, ask questions, contribute to the group, and actively use the knowledge. When they stop and talk about the information, their conversations are more thoughtful. When they realize that active readers think about the text, jot or draw their thinking, and talk to one another to come to a more complete understanding, kids gain insight and build knowledge.

RESEARCH ON READING COMPREHENSION

Studies cited in the National Reading Panel report (Langenberg 2000) as well as a burgeoning body of research reviews (Pearson, Cervetti, and Tilson 2008; Block and Pressley 2002; Block, Gambrell, and Pressley 2002; Ruddell and Unrau 2004) provide substantial evidence that explicit comprehension instruction improves students' understanding of texts they read in school. Some studies of comprehension have examined ways to teach specific strategies, such as questioning (Gavelek and Raphael 1985), drawing inferences (Hansen 1981), or creating text summaries (Brown and Day 1983). When researchers explicitly taught these comprehension-fostering strategies, not only did kids learn to apply the strategies, but the instruction had positive effects on students' general comprehension as well.

More recent studies have described the effectiveness of transactional strategy instruction (Pressley 2002; Guthrie 2003). Rather than focusing on a single strategy, transactional strategy instruction teaches students a repertoire of strategies that they apply flexibly according to the demands of the reading tasks and texts they encounter. Pressley (2002) found that students who were taught a group of strategies performed better than those receiving more traditional instruction when asked to think aloud about and interpret texts. These findings seem to hold true for younger children (Pearson and Duke 2001) and for students learning information in content areas such as science (Reutzel, Smith, and Fawson 2005).

Research studies have also focused on teaching students thinking and learning routines that incorporate comprehension strategies as part of ongoing classroom instruction. Anne Marie Palinscar's original work in reciprocal teaching (Palinscar and Brown 1984) illustrates how comprehension strategy instruction improves students' learning from text. Teaching students to become more metacognitive with respect to thinking about the reading also proved effective. Block et al. (2002) focused on "process-based" comprehension instruction, teaching kids to articulate the processes they used to make meaning. Block found that students' comprehension scores on both standardized and criterion-reference measures improved. In summary, whether comprehension instruction is called transactional strategy instruction or multiple strategy instruction, Trabasso and Bouchard conclude: "There is very strong empirical, scientific evidence that the instruction of more than one strategy in a natural context leads to the acquisition of and use of reading comprehension strategies and transfers to standardized comprehension tests. Multiple strategy instruction facilitates comprehension as evidenced on tasks that involve memory, summarizing and identification of main ideas" (2002).

For those of you just dying for more information on research that supports reading comprehension strategy instruction, we suggest you take a look at *Improving Comprehension Instruction: Rethinking Research, Theory and Classroom Practice* (Block, Gambrell, and Pressley 2002) and *Theoretical Models and Processes of Reading* (Ruddell and Unrau 2004).

For elementary teachers seeking practical teaching ideas on comprehension instruction, check out *Strategies That Work,* second edition (2007), *The Comprehension Toolkit* (2005), and *The Primary Comprehension Toolkit* (2008), all by Harvey and Goudvis; *To Understand* by Keene (2008); Debbie Miller's *Reading with Meaning* (2002), or her newest, *Teaching with Intention* (2008). Secondary teachers will enjoy Cris Tovani's *I Read It But I Don't Get It* (2000) and *Subjects Matter: Every Teacher's Guide to Content-Area Reading,* by Daniels and Zemelman (2004).

—Source: Adapted from Harvey and Goudvis 2007

Now if your inner voice is sighing, "Whew! Do I have to teach all of those strategies *before* I can start kids with inquiry circles?" the answer is a resounding NO. In fact, we generally teach comprehension simultaneously with small-group inquiry. Sure, there are a few things we can teach early on to insure more effective inquiry circles later. For instance, if we have taught our kids to listen to their inner voice and ask questions as they read, as well as a few basic social strategies, they have a more seamless transition to small-group inquiry.

But mainly, we roll out strategy instruction continually over the course of the year as our kids read, write, talk, listen, and investigate in small groups. Chapter 7, "Key Lessons in Comprehension, Collaboration, and Inquiry," shares twenty-seven lessons that will make a big difference as you engage kids in inquiry circles. You will see teachers teaching these very lessons in many of the inquiry circle classroom portraits in Part 3 of this book. So please don't feel overwhelmed. We can foster our kids' curiosity and nurture their need to know from the first day of school, and then teach lessons in comprehension, collaboration and inquiry as needed. These lessons, explicitly taught over time, will ensure that inquiry circles are engaging and illuminating for everyone.

Reading Is Thinking

This may seem obvious, but too often we think of reading as simply word calling. Steph remembers a morning when she was sitting quietly conferring with a student during reading workshop. Suddenly, DeCoven, another fourth grader who'd been reading silently at his seat, shattered the silence by blurting out, "*Reading is thinking!*" The kids in the room were practically shaken out of their skins and it took a while to recover. You know fourth graders! But Steph couldn't have been more delighted, because at the beginning of the year DeCoven was a kid who had described reading as "sounding out the words," "answering questions at the end," and, worst of all, as "something I hate to do." And now here he was reading independently in a book he had chosen and having a very public AHA! His teacher had been modeling thinking strategies for the class that fall, and at the very moment when DeCoven realized that reading was about more than sounding out words, he simply had to blurt it out! DeCoven nailed it; reading is thinking! One of those goose bump moments.

Comprehension is not about answering those literal questions at the end of a story, chapter, or textbook section. Comprehension is not about spitting out facts and filling in blanks. Comprehension is about *understanding*. And reading is not merely about word calling. Reading is about thinking. We haven't always realized this, however. For years, comprehension wasn't even taught; it was merely tested—and tested inappropriately at that, by having kids answer those literal end-of-text comprehension questions. As we experienced with the Uhlenbeck passage, answering literal questions does not guarantee understanding. If students can answer those questions, they might have understood it—*or not*. If they can't answer those questions, they might have understood it—*or not*. Most frequently, students can easily answer a literal question, but they don't understand the concept.

Comprehension is about understanding. And reading is not merely about word calling. Reading is about thinking.

Jessica's Post-it responses that record her new learning while reading.

Jessica, a third grader who had been taught to merge her thinking with the information, jotted down an *L* for learn when she learned something new from a book about animals. She learned quite a bit of information— that snails do not look after their eggs, that pandas like bamboo, and that wool is fiber, among other things. If we had created a quiz with a list of multiple-choice questions for the end of reading, she probably would have chosen the correct answers.

1. What do pandas eat? (bamboo)

2. Do snails look after their eggs? (no)

3. What is wool made of? (fiber)

The problem, as we can see from the fiber Post-it, is that although she wrote down that wool is a fiber, she didn't know what fiber was. She didn't understand the concept, but she could easily answer the question. We see this over and over again with kids in school; they can answer the questions but they don't understand the information.

Fortunately for Jessica, her teacher had taught her to think about information as she read and to ask a question if she didn't understand, which is exactly what she did when she drew a line under the phrase and asked, *What is fiber?* The Post-it reveals a great deal about Jessica as a reader: *She is thinking. She is monitoring her understanding. She knows when she does not understand. She knows that reading should be about understanding. She knows to ask a question to clarify confusion.* An added benefit of having kids interact with text while reading rather than spend their days filling in blanks and bubbles is that we learn so much from their written responses. We can usually tell if they understand or not and we can respond with appropriate instruction.

Understanding emerges from thinking. We lay down a foundation of thinking as we teach because kids learn, understand, and remember so much more when they think actively about the text and then talk to each other to enhance their understanding.

*T*each for Understanding

When we teach comprehension, we are teaching for understanding. Few kids can actually demonstrate their understanding of a concept if they have not been taught to think about the information. We teach kids thinking strategies so that they become aware of their thinking and can gain knowledge and understanding. According to Arthur Costa, "Learning to think begins with recognizing how we are thinking—by listening to ourselves and our own reactions and realizing how our thoughts encapsulate us" (2008, p. 23).

Comprehension is the evolution of thought that occurs while reading, listening, or viewing. It is the inner conversation that we have with text—the voice in our heads that speaks to us. When we are confused, it's the voice that says, *Huh? I don't get this part.* When we learn something new, it's the voice that says, *Wow I never knew that before.* The voice that says, *If anything happens to this character, I will never get out of bed again.* That's comprehension—how our thinking evolves and changes while we read—not being able to answer a list of literal questions afterward. And we can construct meaning and understanding only when we pay attention to our inner voice, to our thinking.

The Comprehension Continuum

The goal of comprehension is to acquire and actively use knowledge. There is really no other reason to think and understand. Arthur Costa goes on to say, "[The] deeper knowledge one has, the more analytical, experimental and creative are one's thought processes" (2008, p. 23). In that vein, we have designed a continuum of comprehension, a spectrum of understanding, from answering literal questions to actively using knowledge, as a representation of what happens when we teach kids to comprehend. See the Continuum on page 30 for the specific language teachers use when questioning students.

ANSWERING LITERAL QUESTIONS. Answering literal questions is the least sophisticated level of comprehension. It shows that the learner has some short-term recall, can skim and scan for answers, and pick out one that matches the question. There are a few things to be gleaned from asking kids to answer literal questions. Probably the most useful is to find out whether they actually read the text. But answering literal questions does not demonstrate understanding.

RETELLING. Retelling the events of a story or the sections of a chapter shows that the learner can organize thoughts sequentially and has some short-term recall of fragments of information. But in primary grades, we have elevated retelling to the crowning achievement in comprehension! Probably the best information we can get from retelling is identifying kids who can't do it. Most kids should be able to retell pieces of a story they have heard or provide some basic information from a reading. Kids who repeatedly have difficulty retelling either orally, in writing, or through drawing may need a closer look. We recognize that retelling is a foundational skill for learners, and it is a more sophisticated thinking skill than merely answering literal questions. But retelling in and of itself does not demonstrate understanding.

Comprehension Continuum

Answers Literal Questions	Retells	Merges Thinking with Content	Acquires Knowledge	Actively Uses Knowledge
Answering literal questions shows that learners can skim and scan for answers, pick one out that matches the question, and have short-term recall. Does not demonstrate understanding.	Retelling shows that learners can organize thoughts sequentially and put them into their own words. Shows short-term recall of events in a narrative and bits of information in nonfiction. Does not, in and of itself, demonstrate understanding.	Real understanding takes root when learners merge their thinking with the content by connecting, inferring, questioning, determining importance, synthesizing, and reacting to information. Understanding begins here.	Once learners have merged their thinking with the content, they can begin to acquire knowledge and insight. They can learn, understand, and remember. Shows deeper understanding.	With new insights and understandings, learners can actively use knowledge and apply what they have learned to the experiences, situations, and circumstances in their daily lives to expand understanding and even take action.
Teacher Language	**Teacher Language**	**Teacher Language**	**Teacher Language**	**Teacher Language**
How many...? What is...? Where did...? Who was...?	Tell me what happened... Tell me what it was about... Retell what you read... What comes first, second, third? When did...?	What do you think? What did you learn? What does this remind you of? What do you wonder? What do you visualize? What do you infer? What makes you say that? How did you come up with that? What makes you think that?	What did you learn that you think is important to remember? Why does it matter? What do you think are some big ideas here? What do you think the author most wants you to get out of this? Say more about that...	What do you want to do about this? Why do you want to take action? Is there a way you can get involved? How do you think you can help? What is your plan?

Comprehension and Collaboration © 2009 by Stephanie Harvey and Harvey Daniels (Heinemann, Portsmouth, NH).

MERGING THINKING WITH CONTENT. True comprehension *begins* here. Real understanding takes root when learners merge their thinking with the content and react to the information. We explicitly teach kids to merge their thinking with the information and to stop, think, and react as they read nonfiction. We even teach the terminology. For example, we might ask, "Did you remember to merge your thinking while you read?" When kids add their own thinking to the text, they pay attention to their inner conversation rather than simply running their eyes across the page, reading without thinking. The familiar comprehension strategies that we have written about reflect the most common ways learners merge their thinking with text—connecting, questioning, inferring, visualizing, determining importance, and synthesizing information.

ACQUIRING KNOWLEDGE. The main reason to read and think is to acquire knowledge. When we were kids in school, we wrote down what the teacher said, crammed on Thursday night, remembered the information long enough for Friday's quiz, and then promptly forgot it over the weekend. Memorizing discrete isolated facts does not help us acquire lasting knowledge; that requires *thinking* about the information. Once readers begin to consciously merge their thinking with the content, they are able to understand and acquire knowledge. That knowledge often leads to fresh insight and may even generate new knowledge.

ACTIVELY USING KNOWLEDGE. With new knowledge come insights and understandings that can potentially change the way human beings function in the world. As David Perkins says, "There is little gain in simply having knowledge and even understanding it for a quiz if that same knowledge does not get put to work on a more worldly occasion: puzzling over a public issue, shopping in a supermarket, deciding for whom to vote . . . and so on" (1992, p. 6). When we think about information and acquire knowledge, we can integrate it and actively apply it to the experiences, situations, and circumstances in our daily lives. We can make informed choices about how to act and behave, persuade others, and even take action.

The End Goal—Applying Knowledge Every Day

As you can see on the comprehension continuum, the main reason we teach kids to think is to foster the active use of knowledge. Sometimes the active use of knowledge means kids learn something new, integrate that information, and apply it in their daily lives. Other times it means kids are inspired to make a difference in the world, form a plan, and take action.

Teachers sometimes come to us and express frustration that their kids are only surface thinkers. They ask us how we get kids to ask more thoughtful questions, to think more rigorously, to "go deeper." For us, "going deeper" means thinking about what we learn and applying that knowledge every day. When learners merge their thinking with the themes they glean from literature, the big ideas they meet in history, the concepts they discover in science, they are more likely to acquire knowledge and act.

Listening to and discussing *Oliver Button Is a Sissy* (by Tomie dePaola) is a great way for second graders to come to understand that bullying is hurtful and to remember this before they pick on someone else. Reflecting on Martin Luther King's "I Have a Dream" speech allows sixth graders to consider the power of words and perhaps get people to pay more attention the next time they want their voices heard. Reading *Fast Food Nation* (by Eric Schlosser) might lead twelfth graders to make healthier choices about food. From our perspective, thinking about what we learn and using that knowledge every day is what it means to "go deeper."

Taking Action

The more kids see that their thinking matters, the more they understand their own power. When we teach kids to think about content, wonder about information, and actively use knowledge, they are far more likely to take action.

Julia O'Connell's third graders in Baltimore, Maryland, engaged in an inquiry into gun laws after one of her students read a newspaper article about a first grader who had tragically been shot and killed at school by a classmate. Saddened and outraged, the kids wanted to do something. Julia discovered that legislators in Maryland were about to debate a new gun lock law. So the class began an inquiry into Maryland's gun laws. They made a list of questions and researched gun incidents, gun locks, gun control, and gun advocacy— all big ideas that emerged from their questions. Their findings led them to help pass gun-lock legislation. After they wrote letters of concern to Lieutenant Governor

March 5 2000

Dear Lt. Gov Townsend,
Thank you for leting us come. You told us that not only grown ups can make a diffence, but children can make a diffence too. Thank You very very much for trying to help put locks on guns. Also thank you for trying to keep us safe. I also learned about the law makers. I learned laws are made and I learned a lot of other things I know you will try to vote for locks.

Your friend,
Derrick Rose

Derrick's letter to the Lieutenant Governor after the third grade gun-lock inquiry.

Kathleen Kennedy Townsend, she invited them to the State House on the day the legislation was to be debated. They arrived at the front steps of the capitol carrying handmade signs and chanting, "Locks on guns. Locks on guns!" When legislators stopped to ask them questions, the kids answered with extensive knowledge gained from studying the issue so thoroughly.

Several weeks later, when the Responsible Gun Safety Act was passed, the class was invited back to attend the formal signing of the new law. These kids learned that when you think about an issue, explore many sides of it, acquire knowledge through research, and make a plan of action, you can truly make a difference. What a great lesson for these thoughtful, committed third graders!

Just think, there are elementary schools and districts whose entire "comprehension" curriculum consists merely of answering literal questions and retelling, before understanding even has a ghost of a chance! And there are middle and high school textbooks in social studies, math, science, and even literature that ask kids for nothing more than to scan for boldfaced correct answers and transport them back to the questions at the end of the chapter! We'll say it one more time. Comprehension begins to take root only when we merge our thinking with the information. And when we do, kids who have discussed Oliver Button just might quit bullying, high schoolers who have read *Fast Food Nation* may eat healthier, and third graders in Baltimore will help pass gun-lock legislation! Teaching for understanding leads kids to take action.

> Comprehension begins to take root only when we merge our thinking with the information.

Growing Great Readers

If we want our kids to ask questions, think about what they are learning, gather information, and actively use knowledge, it sure helps if they are capable readers. No doubt about it: the better we read and think, the more we learn. When engaging in small-group inquiry, we are better able to find answers to our research questions if we are proficient readers. We are more able to acquire knowledge and actively use it if reading is seamless for us. So how do we grow great readers?

Richard Allington reports that when you boil down the research on reading from the past thirty years, you come up with three principles that lead to reading achievement (2003). First is the *reading principle:* The more you read, the better you read. It's that simple. You know this instinctively. Think of an avid reader in your class—you probably picture her with her nose in a book. You may have even noticed that each time you listen to her read or talk to her about her reading, she seems a better reader than the last time you sat down with her. Not surprisingly, she is not only getting better at reading, she is also getting smarter, because we add so much to our store of knowledge when we read extensively.

Now picture a kid in your class whom you have concerns about. Is he reading a book? Not likely. He's probably outside on the field, on the playground, or somewhere as far away from a book as he can get. So here's the Catch-22. Avid readers keep increasing their reading volume as they move up the grades, while reluctant readers actually read less. So the gap between successful and unsuccessful students widens as a direct result of how much they read. We need to build in significant time for kids to read, just plain read. No matter what the grade level, kids need to be reading texts they can and want to read in school every day. According to Shefelbine "Reading volume—the amount students read in and out of school—significantly affects the development of reading rate and fluency, vocabulary, general knowledge of the world, overall verbal ability and last, but not least, academic achievement" (1998, p. 1).

Next is the *response principle:* Learners must have opportunities to respond to their reading every day by talking, writing, and drawing about their thinking. Along with lit circles, inquiry circles provide one of the best possible structures for responding to reading and research. Inquiry circles demand that kids talk to each other, jot down their thinking, and record information as they collaborate in the pursuit of answers to their questions.

Nothing enhances our understanding more than talking about what we are reading and learning. According to Pearson, Cervetti, and Tilson, comprehension and learning can be improved by engaging students in rich talk about text. They note that discussions with peers about texts can sharpen cognitive skills and expand student motivation for reading (in Darling-Hammond 2008).

And writing about reading clarifies thinking and often leads to further inquiry. For our primary kids in particular, drawing and writing are frequently the most direct route to reading and learning (Allington 2005). The more kids talk to each other and interact with text through writing and drawing, the more they learn, the more they wonder, and the more content they absorb.

Let's be clear here. We are talking about authentic response—reading, writing, drawing, and talking about real issues and ideas. For too many years, kids have been asked to do a laundry list of activities when they finish reading books. You know the ones—dioramas, shadow boxes, paper bag puppets, word jumbles, and the ubiquitous book reports. None of this busywork gives us any indication of what the reader learned or understood. Nor do these activities challenge readers to think about what they are learning, synthesize the information, or ask more questions. Real oral and written responses let us know if our students are engaged in their reading and learning. Authentic responses tell us what students are thinking about, what they are learning, and what they are wondering. When kids respond to text by talking, drawing, or writing, their thinking and understanding shine through.

And finally, the *explicit instruction principle:* Readers need explicit instruction in the strategies to decode text if they don't know how. They do not need detailed phonics instruction if they can already read. And readers need explicit instruction in the strategies to comprehend text. Explicit instruction is about *showing* rather than telling. When teachers teach explicitly, they show kids how the reading process happens for them. They think aloud as they read, sharing how they make sense of text, how they tackle difficult parts, and how they clear up misconceptions. They

*T*he more you read, the better you read. It is that simple.

model the thinking strategies proficient readers use to construct meaning, and then they give kids time to practice in small groups and individually. To get a better idea of how we teach strategies, check out the comprehension lessons in Chapter 7.

*W*hen kids see how an experienced adult peels back the layers of her own thinking, they are better equipped to try it on their own.

When kids see how an experienced adult peels back the layers of her own thinking, they are better equipped to try it on their own. This model-and-practice approach falls under an instructional framework known as the Gradual Release of Responsibility, which we subscribe to and discuss at greater length in Chapter 7.

When these three principles are in place—lots of time spent reading, lots of opportunity for response, and explicit strategy instruction from the teacher—kids get better at reading. Inquiry circles click along. School, in general, is more successful. And it is not an exaggeration to say that life is more fulfilling if you are a confident, capable reader. These three principles are really a gift. How great it is that we don't need drill-and-kill worksheets, endless hours of solitary time at our desks, or dull, stand-and-deliver lectures to grow thoughtful readers. If we model our thinking and give kids time to read and respond, they will read to learn and get smarter along the way.

Pearson, Cervetti, and Tilson note that "knowledge is both a cause and a consequence of comprehension. Thus prior knowledge influences how well a reader can comprehend a given text, but that very text, once understood, changes the reader's knowledge base to allow the reader to understand even more ideas the next time...In short, the text has the capacity to actually alter knowledge structures" (2008). The studies of Cunningham and Stanovich remind us that "those who read a lot will enhance their verbal intelligence; that is, reading will make them smarter." (1998, p. 7) So you don't have to be smart to read; you get smart by reading! Kids build knowledge by reading, writing, drawing, talking, listening, and investigating—by thinking! We'd like to hang this banner in every classroom on the planet:

> Smart is not something you are.
>
> Smart is something you get.

What We Know About Collaboration

One of our favorite picture books is *The Conversation Club* by Diane Stanley. Peter is the new mouse in town, and he is delighted to be invited to a meeting of what his neighbors call their "Conversation Club." Eager to make friends, Peter shows up ready to chat, only to find that in this discussion group, all the mice simply holler about their own favorite topic simultaneously, without taking a breath or listening to anyone else. After a few exasperating minutes, Peter heads for the door. As the other mice try to stop him, Peter announces that he has his own organization: "It's a listening club; no one talks, and I am the only member."

To the mice, the idea of another club to join is utterly irresistible, and they plead for an invitation to Peter's next meeting. When they arrive at the appointed hour, Peter makes everyone sit quietly and just listen—to the sound of the wind, of chairs creaking in the room, of their teacups clinking on the table. After a while, Peter adds a new rule: club members may speak one at a time, and everyone else must listen and think about what the speaker is saying. At last, the mice learn how to take turns, listen actively to each other, and actually have a sociable conversation—"the best they had ever heard." To us, the moral of *The Conversation Club* is that too many people lack the social skills of small-group interaction. (And the book is a great read-aloud you can use to begin teaching social skills to your students.)

Our students absolutely *must* be able to work effectively together in small groups. If not, where are we? Thirty kids in straight rows, with the teacher up front with a whip and a chair? Teaching to the middle of the class? When we do this, the subject matter is always too hard for some, too easy for others, and "boring" for many. For learners, the process is profoundly passive; at best kids are hearing about ideas, but not interacting with them. In whole-class discussions, one person at a time speaks, while the other twenty-nine wait for a turn that either never comes or they don't even want. In this classroom structure, it's easy for kids to hide, fake it, or sleep. What pale and wimpy pedagogy!

We cannot provide robust, engaged, and differentiated learning unless kids can break into a variety of groups and work together. Learning is far too weak if we limit students' actions, conversations, and thinking to what the one adult in the room can monitor. If we are truly sponsoring active learning, there must be many people talking and doing at once—not just the teacher. There is no realistic option: we simply must train kids to team, give them plenty of structured practice, and then trust them to work as partners.

Eight Ways That Small Groups Matter

Back in Chapter 1, we offered a list of reasons why small-group work is so important for today's students. Now, let's dig a little deeper. We don't implement small-group inquiries just for the sake of doing something different, or for a refreshing change of pace. We reorganize our students into collaborative groups for several urgent and practical reasons.

1. Small Groups Are Lifelike

Do you recall that Al Gore won the Nobel Prize back in 2007? Do you also remember that the award was *shared* by the United Nations Intergovernmental Panel on Climate Change? It was a group achievement. These days, fewer and fewer people win Nobel prizes or make big breakthroughs or change the world by themselves. As the American Association for the Advancement of Science says: "Scientists and engineers work mostly in groups and less often as isolated investigators . . . the collaborative nature of scientific and technical work should be strongly reinforced by frequent group activity in the classroom . . . [something] very different from the usual individualistic textbook-homework-recitation approach" (1989, web page). In many walks of life today, effective action happens when people work in small groups.

When you think about it, almost everyone in the nonschool world works in some kind of group, crew, office, team, line, shift, or staff.

When you think about it, almost everyone in the nonschool world works in some kind of group, crew, office, team, line, shift, or staff. Even at Jiffy Lube, it's a team. First is the guy with the clean hands who greets you and tries to sell you services that you may or may not need ("Look at that gunked-up air filter! I mean, do you want to be driving around town with *that* thing on your engine?"). Then there are two people who work up top, one focusing on the engine and the other setting tire pressure and cleaning windows. And finally, team member number four is "in the hole," down in the pit under your car, pulling the plug and draining your oil pan. Presumably this person is always working to get promoted up to sea level and hoping that some new hire will take over his sloppy slot below decks.

2. Small Groups Generate Energy for Challenging Work

The British educator Charity James said one of the smartest things we've ever heard: "Every kid wants to work hard and do well." How profound. Kids don't want to be slackers—even those teenage slackers don't really want to be slackers. Every young person has a natural drive to wonder, to do, to ask, to explore. Small groups free kids to work hard and excel.

Humans are social animals. We like to work together. The interaction we enjoy before, around, beside, during, and after the work helps ideas flow, makes the time go quickly, and leaves us eager for the next gathering. As we build personal relationships within a group, we conflate the task and the team. We feel that we are in this together. We do it for our buddies.

But we're not just singing "Kumbaya" and chanting "Go team, go!" Under the surface of this sociability is healthy and positive social pressure. When someone brings an awesome idea or fantastic artifact to the group, it excites other members and makes them want to make big contributions, too. When someone lets the group down, that individual feels responsibility, not because some teacher or boss chastises them, but because their team partners are looking at them saying, silently or out loud: "Man, we need you to get this work done—we can't do it without you."

3. In Small Groups, We Are Smarter

In well-structured groups, we leverage each other's thinking. We learn more not just because we all bring different pieces of the puzzle, but because, through talk, we can actually make new and better meaning together. You may have experienced this, or even sought it out. When a problem arises, we have an instinct to gather a few trusted people and talk things through, hoping to find the best solution or course of action.

Similarly, in school, when kids think together, their understanding can deepen. Let's listen to four high school kids having a "written conversation" (Daniels and Steineke 2004) about Holden Caulfield's attitude toward sex in the early chapters of *Catcher in the Rye*. (Elementary teachers, cover your ears; this is what we sometimes study in high school.) The students are sitting around a table, having a conversation "live," but in writing, not out loud. Each kid starts with a blank piece of paper and writes an initial comment about this section of *Catcher*. After about two minutes, the papers are passed to the right, and everyone then has a friend's thinking about Holden to respond to. After some more reading and writing time, the teacher asks groups to pass the pages once again.

See Lesson 16, "Written Conversation," p. 131.

> **MANDY:** Why did Holden call himself the biggest sex maniac you ever saw? Holden has really good values toward sex. I wonder why Holden doesn't understand that he truly does understand sex.

> **DOUG:** Holden does hold women in high regard, but he still sees them as sexual beings. A classic Madonna–Whore scenario. Not like "boobie cone" Madonna, but as in the psychological sense. He still is an adolescent male and becomes sexually aroused.
>
> **JILL:** I don't think he knows exactly what his thoughts are about sex. He seems really confused by it.
>
> **CECE:** He has values, but he is still confused. He can uphold those values and still wonder why he has them because they might be so different from other guys he knows.

Looking right over these kids' shoulders, you can watch them develop a deeper and more nuanced interpretation of the literature through collaborative conversation.

In this classic small-group activity, every single kid is either reading or writing about a key curriculum topic for *the whole time.* Minds-on, every minute. Compare that to a standard whole-class discussion where only one person can talk at a time, and opportunities for dodging involvement abound. In groups, we get energy not just because working together is more fun than solitary toil, but also because it supports us to think hard and well. For more on written conversations, see pages 131 and 223–227.

There's a reason why we use expressions like "two heads are better than one" and "many hands make light work." Sure, people can occasionally dissolve into "groupthink," and we can all remember groups that managed to be dumber than the sum of their parts. But most of the time, in most combinations, we are smarter together.

4. In Small Groups, Diversity Is an Asset

▲

> **STEPH:** What would be the most boring group in the world?
>
> **SMOKEY:** I don't know. Is this a joke? What?
>
> **STEPH:** A group with four Smokey Daniels in it.
>
> **SMOKEY:** Thanks a lot.
>
> **STEPH:** No, I mean it. Or four Steph Harveys. Groups need people who are different, not alike, don't you think? The more different the better, really.
>
> **SMOKEY:** Absolutely. You know how kids with special learning needs so often enrich a small-group discussion? When you've been labeled and bumped around a bit, you look at the world in a different way. When a literature circle reads a book with themes of trust, or loneliness, or independence, these kids can bring a whole new dimension to the discussion when they speak up.

▼

In small groups we can mesh and jigsaw our different talents as we divide up tasks and set to work.

In small groups we can mesh and jigsaw our different talents as we divide up tasks and set to work. The kid who is great at number-crunching can gather data and create displays. The web-savvy techies can conduct searches and hand off leads to other investigators. The extroverted schmoozers can hit the street and interview people about the topic at hand. The kid who's artistically inclined can illustrate the group's work with drawings, videos, or photographs. In this way, kids can do work they are good at, refine their strengths, and feel accomplishment.

But we don't always let kids take the same role over and over either, getting typecast as good at just one thing. We encourage them to switch around, trying on new roles and attempting new modalities. As kids see groupmates using skills they haven't yet mastered, they can learn from these peers, one to one, as casual apprentices.

▲

SMOKEY: So you do admit that a group with four Steph Harveys would not be so great, right?

STEPH: Exactly. Well, maybe better than four Smokey Daniels, but not that much.

SMOKEY: So funny.

▼

5. Small Groups Make Engaged, Interactive Learning Possible

Over the past few years, every major professional organization and subject matter society in education has issued or revised its own standards document, its statement of "best practice." This includes groups as disparate as the International Reading Association, the American Association for the Advancement of Science, the National Council for the Social Studies, the National Association for the Education of Young Children, and two dozen more. Despite their wide range of curriculum interests, the recommendations of these reports overlap strikingly. (Smokey, Steve Zemelman, and Art Hyde wrote a book about these consensus recommendations called *Best Practice: Today's Standards for Teaching and Learning* [third edition, 2005].) All the reports from these disparate expert groups say that kids' classroom experience should be more:

active	democratic	experiential
developmental	holistic	constructivist
authentic	expressive	sociable
reflective	collaborative	challenging

The match-ups between these elements and small-group learning is so entirely evident that we won't explicate them one by one. The headline is: virtually all the major professional groups in American education have endorsed a paradigm of learning that requires subdividing the classroom and putting kids to work in active, flexible, inquiring, hands-on teams.

6. Small Groups Allow Us to Differentiate Instruction

When we teach in whole-class mode, it's impossible to reach every kid. If we assign the same book to everyone, It will be unreadable for some, a "baby book" for others, and a snoozefest to everyone else.

When we teach in whole-class mode, it's impossible to reach every kid. If we assign the same book to everyone, it will be unreadable for some, a "baby book" for others, and a snoozefest to everyone else. When we present material aloud, kids who speak English as their first language, or already know the information, or just "listen fast" do fine—those who don't, don't. And so on. The only conceivable way to meet every child's needs is to break the classroom down into temporary, flexible, smaller groupings. And we know from decades of research that splitting kids into high, medium, and low groups isn't the answer, and in fact hurts everyone (Wheelock, 1993).

One large school district where Smokey worked was sued by families who blamed their children's low achievement on the school district's failure to offer differentiated instruction in the classroom. The parents argued: if my kid is always placed in books he cannot read, and not given help and strategies at his own level, what kind of education is that? Where's my child's opportunity to learn when the teacher teaches to the middle of the class? The parents won in federal district court. Then the school district brought in teams of consultants who helped teachers decentralize their classrooms, moving from whole-class to small-group instruction. This meant mastering well-structured group activities like buddy and partner reading, literature circles and book clubs, and peer writing groups. As kids' achievement rose, the suit was settled.

7. Employers Increasingly Require Small-Group Skills

Look at the want ads in your local paper, or better yet, jump on Yahoo's Hotjobs. Look at what employers are seeking in new employees. Phrases like these abound:

- Ability to work collaboratively with small core team
- Fit into our team-oriented approach
- Help crystallize thinking of your small creative group
- Be team-oriented with a hands-on, collaborative style
- Work in a collaborative fashion with the other account managers
- Join our exciting biotech collaborative work environment

Of course, your new boss will still also expect you to know your engineering, marketing, or biotech skills. But the message is, if you can't get along with the other folks on the team, it really doesn't matter what you know.

Since the early 1990s, the U.S. Department of Labor, through its SCANS program (still widely disseminated on the web) has been trying to draw attention to the centrality of "people skills" in job success. These findings are continually replicated by states and other agencies. In 2008, the state of Ohio impaneled a special task force to both interview employers and examine the research about what skills are most needed for success in the world of work. The study found ten key workplace skills needed for employment in the future. The number one trait listed: "Good communications skills/Ability to work in teams/Ability to build relationships." Employers don't want to teach these interpersonal skills to their new hires—they want them to arrive with those skills already developed.

8. Well-structured Small-Group Work Enhances Student Achievement

*W*ell-structured small-group work raises kids' academic achievement as well as nurturing effective work habits, attitudes, and skills.

Oh, yeah. We saved the best for last. Several intertwined strands of research, reaching back for decades, show that well-structured small-group work raises kids' academic achievement as well as nurturing effective work habits, attitudes, and skills. Indeed, as this book goes to press, a brand-new study has just been released about the value of teaching social skills in *preschool* classrooms. The researchers found that if you teach children collaboration skills like social problem solving, they not only become more cooperative classmates, but their prereading and other academic skills improve as well (*Science Daily* 2008).

It seems only appropriate to take note of the pioneering research from David and Roger Johnson. The brothers conducted and collected such a vast body of research on collaborative learning that by 1989 they had created a meta-analysis of 947 studies, showing better outcomes for students working together in a variety of settings, subjects, and grade levels. Robert Slavin provided research support for a number of effective variations, the most widely implemented of which involved forming heterogeneous four-member groups and inviting kids to learn in a fun but competitive atmosphere (1994). Shlomo Sharan edited the influential *Handbook of Cooperative Learning* (1999), which included reports from the most prominent researchers and practitioners in the field. A most helpful contemporary review of more recent studies may be found in Linda Darling-Hammond's collection, *Powerful Learning: What We Know About Teaching for Understanding* (2008).

The research on more specific small-group practices has also been encouraging. Hammond's review shows increased student achievement in such diverse cooperative models as project-based learning, expeditionary learning, learning circles, complex instruction, reciprocal teaching, and more. The structure known interchangeably as literature circles or book clubs has also shown good results for kids in elementary and secondary grades, for inner-city children, for English language learners, for children living in poverty, and for resistant learners (http://www.litcircles.org/research.html).

The form of projects we espouse in this book, originally developed under the name "group investigations," has been thoroughly studied by Shlomo Sharan and a variety of colleagues. They showed that when students worked in small groups, taking significant responsibility for planning, undertaking, and reporting on research into subject matter, most scored significantly higher on content-area tests of math, history, literature, science, geography, and reading comprehension. These studies reported gains on both factual recall and higher-order thinking, and also showed a balanced distribution of participation within groups, even when students were socially and culturally highly diverse.

Effective Groups Are Made, Not Born

OK, so small groups are a good idea. But how come they don't always work?

We tend to think that the ability of our students to work together is pretty much a matter of luck. When our classroom book clubs flop, peer editing groups crash, or lab partners bicker, we sometimes write it off to the Great Student Lottery. *Maybe I'll get a better group next year.*

You don't have to wait for a good group to magically materialize next August—you can have one right now.

But you don't have to wait for a good group to magically materialize next August—you can have one right now. There is tons of information about growing groups that work. Research from the field of social psychology, especially group dynamics, explains how people behave in small work groups. There are solutions for typical problems and procedures that ensure predictable, constructive outcomes. Unfortunately, the findings of group dynamics research are rarely shared with teachers in preservice or inservice education. This omission is extremely peculiar, especially since we get paid for getting *predictable outcomes from small groups of humans* (called students).

So, getting kids to collaborate is not mostly a matter of luck. There is a science to small group interaction. We can learn it, apply it, and expect good results.

The Ingredients of Collaboration

Our knowledge about collaboration in the classroom has unfolded somewhat differently from that about strategic reading. With comprehension, a dramatic watershed occurred in 1982, when the research of P. David Pearson and his colleagues blew the lid off our thinking about how readers think and changed the field forever. Our understanding of collaboration among teams of learners— what you might call the *social strategies* of small-group learning—has evolved

Kids join in a structured "mingling" activity to build collaboration skills.

more steadily but perhaps less dramatically. And what exactly are these specific strategies?

Well, since we all enjoyed the MS2 Phage Coat Proteins experience so much back in Chapter 2, let's try another thought experiment. You have found yourself in a million small groups, right? With all different kinds of tasks to get done and a whole range of purposes to pursue? Let's see: faculty committees, grade-level teams, department meetings, special district task forces. Outside of school, maybe a book club, volunteer effort, fund-raising project, political campaign, investment club, knitting circle, a women's or men's group, a neighborhood task force—you name it.

With all this experience, you know plenty about what makes small groups operate effectively—and also how they can become annoying, ineffective or dysfunctional. So, what are some of the things that can wreck a small group, grind its work to a halt, and send everyone off with a bad attitude? What can go wrong with small groups? Take a minute and recollect.

Do any of these problems sound familiar?

- People who talk all the time and dominate everything

- People who never speak up and let everyone else do the work

- People who always show up late and unprepared

- People who must have it their own way

- People who are rude and put others down

- People who never listen and just wait for the next turn to talk

- People who don't follow through on their commitments to the group

- People who always get off the topic and distract everyone from the work

We don't know about you, but we have encountered every single one of these problems, up close and personal, somewhere along the road.

But small groups *do* work when the members share a repertoire of strategies that help them operate effectively. Just as with our comprehension strategies, we proficient adult collaborators have specific social skills that we depend upon, mostly unconsciously and automatically. Only when a group meeting starts to go off track (much like when we feel our comprehension breaking down in a difficult text) do we suddenly become conscious of the skills that group members are failing to display. When the group struggles, we start to consciously tap into our repertoire of social strategies, trying to diagnose the problem (*We gotta get Brenda to pipe down*) or take action (*Maybe I should remind people of everything that's still left on the agenda*) to get the work back on track.

As you look at the charts on the next pages ("How Proficient Collaborators Think and Act" and "What Social Strategy Use Looks and Sounds Like"), you will probably recognize many of the tools in your own social strategies repertoire. These skills are pretty much the reverse versions of the problem behavior we listed above. We've also provided mini-scenarios of how these skills look or sound when in use—and when they are lacking.

Now, just as with the comprehension strategies, you might be thinking, "Well, nobody ever taught me all these small-group skills, but now that you mention it, I guess I do use them." Or you might even want to holler out: "This is just common sense!" Yep, these skills are sensible all right; but based on all the groups we've been in, not all that common. Just as with the comprehension strategies we discussed in Chapter 2, we teachers have probably cobbled together an effective repertoire of social skills through a lifetime of small-group work, trial and error, and exposure to good (and bad) models. As adult schoolteachers, we now possess an inventory of small-group social skills we use all the time, mostly effortlessly and unconsciously.

But if we want a classroom—not to mention a community or a world where all the children and teenagers can team up effectively and reliably, day in and day out, these skills need to be *modeled and taught.* Just as with the comprehension strategies, most of our students will *not* cobble together a complete set of small-group collaboration skills unless we teach them explicitly. And why take a chance?

Bringing Social Skills into the Classroom

Some days, we feel sure that our students have "no social skills at all." We can easily name individual kids who seem unable to stay on the topic, ask good follow-up questions, disagree respectfully, or, come to think of it, show *any* of the other skills of effective small-group interaction. Maybe we have already tried some small-group projects that disappointed us, with kids failing to be productive, supportive, and reliable despite our sincere invitation for them to work together.

But before we start pulling our hair out, we really need to take a field trip into the halls between periods or onto the playground during recess and watch what's happening. Here, you'll find small groups of kids joining eagerly in well-structured, sustained small-group interactions—when the topic is whose skateboard is the coolest or who's hanging out with whom. And these meetings most definitely include the kids with "no social skills."

The point is that many of our students are already growing a promising repertoire of social skills that they put to use every day—just not in our classrooms, where the topics may not seem quite so galvanizing. So our main task is not so much to *introduce* kids to certain social skills, like listening actively or asking

Many of our students are already growing a promising repertoire of social skills that they put to use every day—just not in our classrooms, where the topics may not seem quite as galvanizing.

How Proficient Collaborators Think and Act

Strategy	Examples/Actions
1. Be responsible to the group	• Come prepared: work completed, materials and notes in hand • Bring along interesting questions/ideas/artifacts • Take initiative, help people get organized • Live by the group's calendar, work plan, and ground rules • Settle problems within the group • Fess up if unprepared and take on some other work
2. Listen actively	• Make eye contact • Nod, confirm, look interested • Lean in, sit close together • Summarize or paraphrase • Use names • Take notes when helpful
3. Speak up	• Join in, speak often, be active • Connect your ideas with what others have said • Ask lead and follow-up questions • Use appropriate tone and voice level • Draw upon the notes, materials, or drawings you've brought • Overcome your shyness
4. Share the air and encourage others	• Show friendliness and support • Take turns • Be aware of who's contributing; work to balance the airtime • Monitor yourself for dominating or shirking • Invite others to participate • Build upon and learn from others' ideas
5. Support your views and findings	• Explain and give examples • Refer to specific passages, evidence, or artifacts • Connect or contrast your ideas to others' • Dig deeper into the text or topic; revisit important ideas
6. Show tolerance and respect	• Receive others' ideas respectfully; no put-downs allowed • Try to restate opposing views • Use neutral language in disagreeing • Offer your different viewpoint; don't be steamrolled • Welcome and seek insight in divergent viewpoints
7. Reflect and correct	• Do frequent reflections or "think-backs" on group processes • Identify specific behaviors that helped or hurt the discussion • Talk openly about problems • Make plans to try out new strategies and review their effectiveness • Keep written record of group processing

What Social Strategy Use Looks and Sounds Like

Strategy	Sounds/Looks Like	Doesn't Sound/Look Like
1. Be responsible to the group	"Does everyone have their articles? Good, let's get going." "Let me show you this great website I found…" "I'm sorry, guys, I didn't get the reading done." "Ok, then today I'll take notes on the meeting."	"What? There's a meeting today?" "I left my stuff at home." "Teacher, Bobby keeps messing around." Arriving late, unprepared, without materials.
2. Listen actively	"Joe, pull your chair up closer." "I think I heard you say…" "So you think …" Asking follow up questions	Not looking at others "Huh? I wasn't listening." Playing with pencils, shuffling materials.
3. Speak up	"What you said just reminded me of…" "Can I piggyback on this?" "What made you feel that way?" "Let me show you my drawing."	Silence Whispering or shouting Not using/looking at notes Hiding from participation
4. Share the air and encourage others	"Can you say more about that, Chris?" "We haven't heard from you in a while, Joyce." "I better finish my point and let someone else talk." "That's a cool idea, Tom."	"Blah blah blah blah blah blah blah blah…" "I pass." "You guys are so boring." Declining to join in when invited
5. Support your views and findings	"I think Jim treats Huck as a son because…" "Right here on page 15, it says that…" "The person I interviewed said …" "My thinking was a lot like Jennifer's…"	"This book is dumb." "Well, that's my opinion anyway." "No, I didn't consider any other interpretations."
6. Show tolerance and respect	"Wow, I thought of something totally different." "I can see your point, but what about…" "I'm glad you brought that up; I never would have seen it that way."	"You are so wrong!" "What book are *you* reading?" "Where did you get *that* idea?" Rolling eyes, disconfirming body language.
7. Reflect and correct	"What went well today and where did we run into problems?" "We are not sharing the talk time evenly." "OK, so what will we do differently during our next meeting?"	"We rocked." "We sucked." "It was OK." "Who cares?"

follow-up questions, but to help them bring their existing collaboration skills into the classroom, to refine and develop them, and to place them in the service of the curriculum, not just peer interaction. We can see this as a deep, yearlong project that we are engaged in from Day 1, building a true culture of collaboration.

A Formula for Group Spirit and Interdependence

Did you ever hear that all small groups need to develop along six dimensions in order to develop high productivity and morale? If you nurture these six factors among your students, all kinds of collaborative activity will thrive. You can read about this important formula in the indispensable volume *Group Processes in the Classroom,* by Richard and Patricia Schmuck, now in its eighth edition (2005). You'll learn from the Schmucks (sorry, couldn't resist) that these six group ingredients are

expectations	leadership
norms	communication
friendship	conflict

To grow a strong, interdependent group, these factors must be developed, implemented, and maintained mutually, *by the members.* For maximum productivity down the line, it's better not to impose structures on a new group, but rather to help members consciously and openly create their own ways of being together.

This immediately reminds us why it can be so counterproductive to start a new school year by presenting students with a list of behavior infractions and their consequences. Group theory suggests that it is far wiser to involve students in designing their ideal classroom climate and standards instead. Any teacher-made "consequences chart" creates the opposite of collaboration and mutuality. It doesn't distribute responsibility, enlist initiative, create a friendly atmosphere, or open up communication. Instead it reflects a teacher's less-than-confident expectations: "I have been preparing to meet you students for the first time, and I have been imagining all the things that you might conceivably do wrong." Even worse, the list itself becomes an irresistible menu of misbehavior. (*Hmmm, I wasn't planning on swinging from the light fixtures, but now that you mention it...*)

So how do we put this group dynamics wisdom to work with kids? Take a look at the website, where we show how promoting all six ingredients of group development can create interdependence, both in a class of twenty-five or thirty kids, and also in smaller work groups of four to six students.

Our good friend and colleague Nancy Steineke has written the definitive volume on yearlong small-group development, at least for secondary language arts teachers: *Reading and Writing Together: Collaborative Literacy in Action* (2002). If you still think that having a cooperative class of kids is a luck-of-the-draw deal,

www.heinemann.com/
comprehensionandcollaboration.

you are in for a surprise. If you sincerely wish to take command of your group's dynamics and have a classroom characterized by collaboration and interdependence for 180 days in a row, you must read this book.

*P*redictable Problems

If we do not build this collaborative culture—and sometimes, even if we do— problems can arise. Yes, things can definitely go wrong when kids are working in groups, just as in lectures or lab experiments. We've already noted that Chapter 7 (pages 126–133) offers a set of social skill lessons that directly address and help prevent these difficulties. But right now, let's talk honestly about what can go wrong.

Kids Who Dislike Group Work

When adding new strategies to our teaching, we appropriately worry about motivating *ourselves* to make changes. But kids can be a source of resistance, too. Students generally want school to be predictable, and when we throw them a pedagogical curve, they often balk and try to get things "back to normal." They can accomplish this simply by complaining ("Did you teachers go to a workshop or something?") or by undermining the new activity so that it appears not to work. This resistance is most common among older kids, particularly high-achieving middle and high school students.

There is more happening here than cussedness. When kids moan that they hate to work in groups, we need to listen and learn. Kids most often complain about small groups when we *fail to provide individual, as well as group, accountability.* If this doesn't sound like a problem you have faced, please listen to this story.

We recently had dinner in New York City with our young friend Samantha Friedman. At twenty-seven, Sam has already had two great jobs—first at Christie's auction house and now at the Museum of Modern Art, where she is a curatorial assistant in the drawings department. When we told Sam about this book we were writing, she exclaimed, "Group work? Yuck! I hated that stuff in school." Though we had our own suspicions about the reasons, we asked her to elaborate: "What was unbearable was the disorganization, the feeling that nothing would get done unless I (or someone else) decided to step up and take charge and make a plan. And then everyone got the same grade, no matter what they contributed." Though Sam didn't really mind helping her friends, she worried that in the slapdash process kids gathered information that "was not even verifiable, productive, or trustworthy."

What a classic story of poorly structured small-group work! No wonder Sam disliked this half-baked collaboration. As a talented and responsible student, she'd spent her entire school life being rewarded for outstanding individual efforts. She learned the rules, did her own work, and excelled—alone. Now, she

*S*tudents generally want school to be predictable, and when we throw them a pedagogical curve, they often balk and try to get things "back to normal."

was tossed, unprepared, into a group with other unprepared kids, where she could no longer control the outcomes through the dint of her own efforts. The problem wasn't that Sam inherently "doesn't like" small-group work, but that the experience wasn't structured correctly, and the kids lacked explicit training in interaction and interdependence.

If you set up groups where there is only a single group grade or assessment, you have put out the welcome mat for trouble. Inevitably, some kids will hold back and wait for a Samantha to emerge. And then the Sams who do step forward will end up rightfully feeling exploited. Morale problems cascade, students tattle to you, and the next time you announce a round of group projects, everybody groans. But this is an entirely solvable problem. We teach the social strategy lessons (in Chapter 7) along the way, and we carefully devise systems of individual and group accountability for all the work kids do in groups. Everyone is responsible for, and evaluated upon, their own individual work within the group's goals. For more about individual accountability, see Chapter 12, especially pages 275–276.

Since Sam graduated, in both of her wonderful jobs she has had to work with—guess what?—teams of coworkers. Just like the guys at the Jiffy Lube, Sam's everyday effectiveness depends upon her skills at small-group interaction. Now, because Sam is an extra smart cookie, she didn't suffer unduly from not being taught good group strategies in high school. But how many other kids can get by without experience and training in this vital aspect of life?

"Off-Task" Behavior

Have you ever placed students in small groups and been distressed to see them immediately dive into gossip and chitchat unrelated to the assignment? And then maybe you start worrying: "They are wasting time . . . I never should have done this . . . maybe I should just present this material instead." But before you panic, think about this: what happened the last time *you* sat down for a work meeting with a small group of adults? Socializing, chatter, wedding pictures, snacking, joking—are we right? Turns out that what we label "off-task" behavior in schools is actually a routine human response, one that is not only normal but necessary to the smooth functioning of small-group work.

In the literature of group dynamics, experts identify two kinds of activity: *task work* is related to the official purpose of the group (creating a report, investigating a topic); *maintenance* includes all that socializing, side talk, joking, and goodie-munching. Maintenance activity is sometimes called "social lubrication." If we think of a group as a machine designed to get some work done, socializing is the oil that reduces friction and makes things hum along smoothly. And if you drain the oil by subtracting relationship-maintaining behavior, the team may seize up and grind to a halt. Group dynamics also explains that the need for maintenance

*W*hat we label "off-task" behavior in schools is actually a routine human response, one that is not only normal but necessary to the smooth functioning of small-group work.

is highest at the beginning and the end of a group's life, and lowest during the middle, more task-oriented stages of the work. Thus teachers can expect to see more need for socializing as groups are revving up and again later, when they are closing down and saying goodbye.

So, in school, the question becomes not how we "stop kids from socializing in their teams," but how we *steer* this natural activity. In many schools where we work, respecting the reality of the need for social lubrication, teachers purposely give student teams about two minutes to just chat, to warm up before explicitly shifting to task work. Either teachers or students can generate the day's "maintenance" topic: What animal makes the best pet? What's the best movie you've seen lately? Or, more efficiently, teachers may incorporate an interesting or puzzling content question as the day's small-group warm-up: What have you heard about polar bear extinction? What causes seasons to occur? Talk about how your families recycle. For accountability purposes, our pal Nancy Steineke uses a simple written "membership grid" on which kids briefly note each other's contributions to these start-up conversations (see Daniels and Steineke 2005).

www.heinemann.com/
comprehensionandcollaboration.

Behavior Concerns

As we work in schools around the country, teachers often tell us about the handful of kids in their classes who don't succeed in small-group work and sometimes mess things up for others. This often comes out sounding like, "Well, I have these two boys, Jerry and Buzz…" or "Hey, you haven't met Haley!" When we hear these concerns, we always think to ourselves: aren't teachers the greatest? This is how teachers think: when we run across an idea that might work well for most of the kids in our class, we immediately start worrying about the handful for whom it might *not* click. In any other job, if you had an idea that would work 85 or 90 percent of the time, right off the bat, and could be refined to get even better effectiveness, you'd win the Employee of the Year Award. In teaching, we lie awake at night, not savoring the possibilities, but envisioning how Haley, Jerry, or Buzz might screw things up.

*W*hen we run across an idea that might work well for most of the kids in our class, we immediately start worrying about the handful for whom it might *not* click.

We wish we could tell you that when you start doing small groups "The Harvey & Daniels Way," you'll receive at no extra charge a whole new toolkit of discipline strategies never before known to teacherdom. But alas, that's not how it works. There aren't any secret classroom management techniques—but there are plenty of reasons to believe we can lure our Buzzes, Haleys, and Jerrys to join in small-group inquiries.

ENGAGEMENT. For the kinds of "problem kids" we worry about in the wee hours, small-group activities are part of the solution, not more of the problem. Hey, if you are a disaffected, disengaged kid, the kind of peer-led small-group activity we are describing here is just about as good as school gets. You get to work with a few other kids (ones you may well have chosen yourself), the teacher isn't in your face all the time, you get to speak up and not just listen, and you have choices in what you read, write, do, and discuss. If you are involved in true inquiry circles, you will be pursuing questions or topics that genuinely interest you. And best of all, you get to actually *do something* instead of just sitting there in a lecture or "whole-class discussion." What's not to like?

TRAINING. Sure, if we left those holy terrors Haley, Buzz, and Jerry untrained, they might undermine the effectiveness of whatever group they are in, and perhaps spread discontent abroad. But we are *not* going to leave them untrained. We will give them, along with everyone else, repeated lessons on how to interact, and place them in structures that build mutuality and responsibility—like student-led groups where positive peer pressure drives the work. Luckily, small-group skills are eminently teachable (let us once again point you to the social strategy lessons in Chapter 7). Some kids will acquire them faster than others, and we have to stick to our commitment when things get sketchy. But as we change the terms of how our classroom works, developing an ethos of co-ownership and distributed group responsibility, most kids will eagerly follow along.

Kids Working Alone

This whole book advocates for small groups as a neglected and powerful social structure for classroom inquiry. But that doesn't mean we *always* force kids into teams, no matter what. If you've seen Steph's book *Nonfiction Matters*, you know that we also deeply value projects that kids undertake as individuals.

Some kids just *want to work alone.* This makes sense when a kid has a passion that no one else shares. Cristina, a sixth grader you'll meet in Chapter 11, wanted to explore the occupation of fashion design, but the other four kids in her careers group were interested in science jobs. So Cristina researched mostly alone, connecting with the group just for check-ins and occasional discussions about career planning (and later, used them as runway models for the clothes she sewed). Down the hall in the same school, Audrey was on fire to learn about archery, but couldn't find any partners who shared her interest. Her teacher, Mary Brown, believing that commitment to a topic was *sine qua non* of great inquiries, let Audrey commence her project alone. Soon, a group of boys on the other side of the room who were studying war discovered that Audrey had knowledge of an ancient and deadly weapon—and invited her to sit in. We often see this: kids who start working alone find an affinity with another group, and begin to orbit around it like a moon around a planet—apart, but within the same gravitational field. When another round of inquiries starts, these kids typically join up with a group again.

A tougher decision faces us when a student prefers to *always* work alone. Sometimes these are high-achieving kids who don't want to trust their fate to others. Maybe they've been burned by sharing a mediocre grade with a group and now want to ensure their A. (As we detail on pages 275–276, the teacher can address this by providing careful individual accountability.) It may be "tough love," but we have to say that regularly excusing students from working with others shortchanges their thinking and their preparation for life after school. We wouldn't exempt kids from, say, writing, just because they don't feel like writing. Same with small group work; it is a vital life skill that needs to be practiced—at least some of the time.

Of course, there are some kids who need to work alone. This can be an issue of learning style, or may stem from a disability. At Burley School in Chicago, Bob, a brilliant fifth grader on the autism spectrum simply does better, learns more, and in the end, can share his learning better with others, if he does the work alone.

As we make all these decisions about nudging kids into, or exempting them temporarily or permanently from working in groups, we are responding to kids' needs—first, foremost, and always.

Kids Who Resist

Yes, there are some students who really are resistant, who won't go along, and who seem bent on not cooperating when we set up small groups—or any other classroom structure, for that matter. What about these guys (and girls)?

Let's be honest. Every year, we get some kids for whom school is not, to put it mildly, their current thing. This is especially common in middle and high school, where we may see 75 to 150 different young people a day. Some of these students may come to us with issues not of our making that render them unready or unable to engage in school at this time. So, as dedicated teachers, we make every possible adaptation and invitation to bring these kids in. We try to find out their interests and concerns, we confer with them, we offer alternatives and choices. We carefully recognize and reinforce any signs of engagement, effort, or attachment to the community. With most, we have some success, and kids spend some time overlapped with the work of the group. But some others are able to pass through 180 days of our very best efforts and move along to the next year, the next teacher, seemingly untouched by school. We never won them over, never lured them in, never ignited that latent spark. And that hurts.

But here's the news: they don't all bloom on our shift. That's one of the tough realities of this job. We make this point not to excuse us from trying hard with the most reluctant kids, obviously. But at the same time, we cannot let the unwillingness or unreadiness of a few kids dictate what we do with everyone else in our classrooms.

*W*e cannot let the unwillingness or unreadiness of a few kids dictate what we do with everyone else in our classrooms.

Teachers As Collaborators

Clearly, small-group work has many wonderful benefits for kids, in school and beyond. In "real life," most adults have to work with a small group of other people. That is, most adults except us schoolteachers, who still, after all these years, mainly work alone. (OK, truck drivers work alone too, but they may be the only other lone wolves.) To tell you the truth, we have often suspected that one factor that attracts people (like us, for sure) to teaching careers is our desire to run a Lone Ranger–style operation. Classroom teaching has traditionally been a job where you don't have to work face-to-face with other adults. Most of the day, you can close your classroom door and have it your way, with the twenty-five or thirty kids in your class.

So there's a hearty helping of irony here. Today we teachers, who may have originally been attracted by the autonomy of the job, are now called upon to become experts on collaboration. Our classroom doors are swinging open as more and more adult partners (special educators, coaches, librarians, paraprofessionals) come to work with us, beside us, and among our kids. The Lone Ranger teacher model is quietly dying out. We are part of a team now, and there is a lot to like about that. We are no longer isolated sole proprietors, each operating in our identical cells. We are partners, compadres, teammates. Just as collaboration releases the social power of learning for kids, so the social power of teaching together brings excitement and new possibility to our professional lives.

What We Know About Inquiry

This book is about empowering students to find out: to get answers to important questions about school subject matter, and to questions kids have posed for themselves. Simple enough?

But we have a terminology problem. What do we call this finding-out process? We recognize that this work includes *research*; we know that kids are conducting *investigations*; and certainly, students create and go public with various *projects* along the way. The word *inquiry* embraces all these activities, but means something even more.

Let's start with some every day definitions of inquiry, to get an idea of its unique connotations. And everyday now means Wikipedia, right?

> *Inquiry* is any process that has the aim of augmenting knowledge, resolving doubt, or solving a problem.
>
> —WIKIPEDIA

Now that's pretty straightforward. It reiterates the idea that inquiry is about finding out, and adds connotations of urgency, of resolving some disequilibrium.

What happens when we bring this inquiry process to school? Let's see what else Wikipedia has to say:

> *Inquiry-based learning* describes a range of philosophical, curricular, and pedagogical approaches to teaching. Its core premises include the requirement that learning should be based around student's questions. Pedagogy and curriculum requires students to work together to solve problems rather than receiving direct instructions on what to do from the teacher. The teacher's job in an inquiry learning environment is therefore not to provide knowledge, but instead to help students along the process of discovering knowledge themselves. In this form of instruction, it is proposed that teachers should be viewed as facilitators of learning rather than vessels of knowledge.

Now we are growing a definition. Inquiry-based teaching is problem or question driven; it encourages collaboration; it makes kids into explorers and discoverers; it requires kids to think; and it puts teachers in nonconventional roles.

We created a chart that expands the definition of inquiry and contrasts it with more didactic, information-transmission methods of teaching. Here we pull together ideas from many scholars, but we express special gratitude to Jerome Harste, who has worked for decades to explicate and promote the principles of inquiry-based teaching and learning.

 ## Inquiry Approach *versus* Coverage Approach

INQUIRY Approach	COVERAGE Approach
• Student voice and choice	• Teacher selection and direction
• Questions and concepts	• Assigned topics and isolated facts
• Collaborative work	• Solitary work
• Strategic thinking	• Memorization
• Authentic investigations	• As if/surrogate learning
• Student responsibility	• Student compliance
• Student as knowledge creator	• Student as information receiver
• Interaction and talk	• Quiet and listening
• Teacher as model and coach	• Teacher as expert and presenter
• Cross-disciplinary studies	• One subject at a time
• Multiple resources	• Reliance on a textbook
• Multimodal learning	• Verbal sources only
• Engaging in a discipline	• Hearing about a discipline
• Real purpose and audience	• Extrinsic motivators
• Caring and taking action	• Forgetting and moving to next unit
• Performance and self-assessments	• Filling in bubbles and blanks

There are many ideas here, but we see three key strands. One involves *framing school study around questions developed and shaped by kids,* as much as possible. This doesn't mean our students spend 180 days researching "Why is my skateboard so awesome?" Instead, we draw upon kids' background knowledge and curiosity to evoke deep and real questions about the subject matter we have to teach as well as about the concerns young people bring to school.

Instead of reciting the textbook information about Abraham Lincoln, we patiently invite kids to pose questions while we listen and list: "Did Lincoln really have some weird disease? Was his wife insane? What did he really think of black people? Was he ever a soldier himself? I want to know more about when he was assassinated. Did those guys ever get caught?" And then we build our teaching around kids' genuine curiosity, connecting official curricular topics to their search for answers.

Now, this isn't just catering to students. A recent study by Ivey and Broaddus (2008) showed that kids remember the curriculum much better when their teachers figure out what aspects of it are interesting to them, and *begin there*. And if kids don't have the necessary background knowledge to pose their own questions, we "problematize" the curriculum by posing puzzles that pique kids' interest: "What happens to the world when you buy an iPod? How can we help save tigers from going extinct? Did you know that many of the people who produce sugar today are slaves? What would it take to build a colony on Mars?"

The second big theme of the chart is *handing the brainwork of learning back to the kids.* We've joked about schools being places where young people go to watch old people work. Well, now we are taking kids off welfare. No longer will we coddle them by delivering all the information, explaining exactly how they should structure their thinking, or how they should show what they know. Everybody says kids need a challenging curriculum. Well, here it is. In true inquiry, kids have to take responsibility for things that real learners do. They have to identify worthy problems and questions. They have to use the proper disciplinary tools (microscopes, timelines) and procedures (surveys, formulas), just like real practitioners. They have to work with others, build knowledge, and ultimately, submit their findings to a peer or public audience.

The third strand in our definition of inquiry won't surprise you: *we focus on the development of kids' thinking, first, foremost, and always.* After three chapters of talking about thinking, we don't need to repeat ourselves here. Suffice it to say that in true inquiry-based learning, we move kids quickly along the "continuum of comprehension" from recall and retelling to the higher-level activities of building and using knowledge. And the ultimate manifestation of thinking, to us, is not passing a quiz, but being somehow changed and *doing something* as a result.

The Trend Toward Inquiry

Today, inquiry-based learning is enjoying a bright resurgence, after a few years in the wilderness. In Chapter 1, we explained how the original No Child Left Behind legislation pushed kids back into straight and quiet rows, prized factual recall over deep understanding, and compelled teachers to devote countless classroom hours to test-prep for high-stakes multiple-choice tests. As this testing frenzy wanes somewhat, inquiry is rapidly returning to the center of the national education agenda.

Linda Darling-Hammond, the eminent researcher who served on President Obama's education transition team, has recently published a book on inquiry called *Powerful Learning: What We Know About Teaching for Understanding* (2008). Featuring articles by some of our most prominent education researchers, the book recommends inquiry as the new American pedagogy. Darling-Hammond and her

The ultimate manifestation of thinking, to us, is not passing a quiz, but being somehow changed and doing something as a result.

colleagues call for the "implementation of inquiry-based curriculum that engages children in extended, constructive work, often in collaborative groups, and subsequently demands a good deal of self-regulated inquiry" (p. 13). They argue that in the global economy, for American young people to have satisfying lives—and for our country to remain competitive—"education must help students learn how to learn in powerful ways so they can manage the demands of changing information, technologies, jobs and social conditions" (p. 12). The best framework for this kind of adaptive thinking, the authors continue, is complex, meaningful projects that "require sustained engagement, collaboration, research, management of resources, and the development of an ambitious performance or product" (p. 12).

The Darling-Hammond book is part of an avalanche of new publications promoting inquiry learning. In a *Phi Delta Kappan* article called "School as Inquiry," Chicago researcher Steven Wolk argues: "Telling our students to sit quietly and listen will not turn them into lifelong learners or engaged citizens... inquiry-based teaching can transform our classrooms and spark a love of learning" (2008, p. 115). Wolk goes on to explain that "curriculum is not just the facts and skills we teach, but the knowledge we create together and the understandings and connections that each learner makes from that knowledge. Teaching through inquiry considers our work a failure if students do not leave school filled with questions and the yearning to explore them" (p. 12). He shares stories of schools around the country, including Burley School in Chicago (the subject of this book's companion video), that are moving decisively away from rote learning and toward inquiry circles and related structures.

This move toward inquiry is by no means restricted to elementary teachers and leaders. Jeff Wilhelm, whose work on adolescent literacy is widely influential, has brought new attention with *Engaging Readers and Writers with Inquiry* (2007). Jeff offers one of the shortest definitions of inquiry we've ever seen: "Living the questions." We love that. And he quotes one of our favorite writers, the eminent biologist E. O. Wilson:

> Most people teach biology by starting with the molecule. This is exactly the wrong way to go...It is not how we learn. It is not how the disciplines create knowledge. You need to start with the big issues and questions and problems that drive the discipline. Go top-down and tell the students that you are going to consider the interesting problems that organize the subject. (p. 15)

When we hear a great thinker like E. O. Wilson explaining his own learning, we surely agree with Jeff Wilhelm that "to truly prepare students to be substantive thinkers and democratic citizens, we need to move from the tyranny of information-transmission teaching that dominates American education to inquiry-based teaching" (p. 20).

Now, inquiry may seem like an innovation in some school subjects, but it's long been the standard for state-of-the-art instruction in science. For decades there has been a strong consensus, not just among standards writers and school districts, but among major national organizations like the American Association for the Advancement of Science, the National Science Teachers Association, and the National Research Council, that students should engage in the work of science and not just hear some adult talk about it. As the NRC puts it:

> Students at all grade levels and in every domain of science should have the opportunity to use scientific inquiry and develop the ability to think and act in ways associated with inquiry, including asking questions, planning and conducting investigations, using appropriate tools and technologies to gather data, thinking critically and logically about the relationships between evidence and explanation, constructing and analyzing alternative explanations, and communicating scientific arguments. (1996, p. 20)

Following these principles (which, to us, are totally applicable to all subject areas) science teachers can design experiments that puzzle and provoke, that evoke kids' questions, reveal amazing phenomena, and challenge students to construct scientific knowledge by combining new information with their prior understandings. International comparisons of math and science achievement show that kids taught through inquiry do significantly better on standardized tests than those experiencing the conventional topic coverage model (Weglinsky 2004; McTighe, Seif, and Wiggins 2004; Wilhelm 2007).

*T*he Heritage of Inquiry Learning

Teaching with extended, experiential, and collaborative investigations is not just something we've cooked up in the twenty-first century. Such teaching is actually a long-standing *movement* in education. It traces back to the 1590s, in the academies of Paris and Rome, as students were given authentic problems to solve—such as designing a building or monument. The application of this method to architecture and design became a standard approach and spread through Europe. In 1865, project teaching was introduced to engineering students at the Massachusetts Institute of Technology.

Soon, John Dewey paved the way for inquiry projects with elementary and secondary students. Dewey argued that the public schools should be working, authentic communities and he emphasized the social aspects of learning. He described school as a place where students should practice living democratically and work together to identify and solve problems. Dewey believed that students would learn more about themselves, the world, and about valuable subject matter by working collaboratively with others (1938/1963). Later, at the University of Chicago Laboratory School, he brought to life a place where students often teamed up to develop and carry out inquiries together.

In 1918, Dewey's protégé, James Kilpatrick, published a highly influential essay called "The Project Method: Child-Centeredness in Progressive Education." The

*D*ewey argued that the public schools should be working, authentic communities and he emphasized the social aspects of learning.

article was a sensation because it offered a practical methodology to match Dewey's theories of teaching and learning. Kilpatrick became the leader of a large corps of educators who believed that the most powerful educational structure was "whole-hearted purposeful activity," as when kids engaged in extensive, extended, and life-like inquiries, which he called projects. Even in his own college classes at Columbia University, where he was the most popular professor of the day, Kilpatrick taught congruently with progressive principles—using small-group work, discussion, and summary lectures in classes that typically exceeded six hundred students. As you might surmise, Kilpatrick clashed with the conservative, skills-and-accountability proponents of the time, including the ever-fuming William Randolph Hearst.

*I*nquiry projects turn out to be an enduring idea in American education.

Over the next several decades, the idea of extended, lifelike, student-driven, and experiential projects was incorporated into every succeeding iteration of progressive pedagogy: open classroom, whole language, literature-based instruction, integrated curriculum, the middle school movement, reading and writing workshop, and more. So inquiry projects turn out to be an enduring idea in American education. James Kilpatrick would probably be happy to hear that this movement is still alive ninety years after his seminal essay on the project method.

*I*nvestigating in Groups

Many of the inquiry models going back through the years have featured students pursuing individual questions, and working mostly alone. Nothing wrong with that, of course. Steph shared a model for individual inquiry projects in her book *Nonfiction Matters* (1998) that still resonates today. But when we add teaming to the mix, we reach new levels of energy, authenticity, and depth. Kathy Short, Jerry Harste, and Carolyn Burke made a special contribution when they cogently argued for col-

In inquiry circles kids are pushed to consider new ideas and explain their thinking to others.

laborative inquiry groups in their groundbreaking book, *Creating Classrooms for Authors and Inquirers* (1995). "Because we believe it is through collaboration that students gain new perceptions and outgrow their current selves," they wrote, "we wanted students to form groups where they are pushed to consider new ideas and to explain their thinking to others" (p. 271). The authors describe active, heterogeneous, student-driven groups that worked together, under general class themes, to construct knowledge around their own inquiry questions, and who ultimately shared their thinking in presentations for classmates, using a wide variety of written, oral, dramatic, and artistic forms—and sometimes, taking action in the world.

As you might expect, we are in accord with Short, Harste, and Burke's robust and rigorous definition of what authentic inquiry looks like for small groups of kids. For us, the term *inquiry circles* fits this kind of small-group activity well—though many teachers we work with around the country, including some who have contributed to this book, use other labels, like learning circles, question circles, or group investigations. Well, as long as real, student-driven inquiry is at the core, what's in a name?

*T*he Steps and Stages of Inquiry

So what does inquiry learning look like, not just in theory but in real time, with real students? The world is rife with graphic models of student inquiry, and diagrams portraying the "research process" abound on the Internet. Of course, any paper model is going to be simplistic and potentially misleading, since inquiry is such a complex and varied experience. Still, we can outline some general directions and phases. Our own model of this process draws can be schematically represented like this:

Small-Group Inquiry Model

STAGE	TEACHER	KIDS
Immerse *Invite Curiosity, Build Background, Find Topics, and Wonder*	• Invites curiosity, questioning, engagement • Shares own curiosity • Models personal inquiry • Shows how to ask questions • Demonstrates topic finding • Gathers and organizes relevant materials and resources • Immerses kids in topics to build background • Facilitates small-group formation to ensure heterogeneous groups with compatible interests • Confers with small groups and individual	• Express their own curiosity • Explore, experience, and learn about topics using texts, visuals, Internet, artifacts, etc. • Think about what they know and connect new information to background knowledge and experience • Wonder and ask questions • Read, listen, and view to build background • Respond with questions, connections, and reactions • Meet with teams to set schedules, ground rules, and goals
Investigate *Develop Questions, Search for Information, and Discover Answers*	• Floods kids with resources and materials on a topic or question • Models how to read, listen, and view with a question in mind • Models how to take notes by interacting with text, coding text, and writing in margins or on Post-its • Demonstrates how to determine importance • Helps kids sharpen or change inquiry focus • Facilitates changes in group membership or topics • Confers with groups and individuals • Shows how to infer answers and draw conclusions • Demonstrates how to read for the gist and synthesize information • Connects kids' questions to the curricular concepts and focus questions	• Articulate thoughts and questions that stem from their own interests and experience • Listen, talk, view, and read to gain information • Write, talk, and draw to think about information • Develop questions; then read, listen, and view to answer them • Use text and visual features to gain information • Meet with teams to set and monitor schedules and task completion

Small-Group Inquiry Model, *cont.*

STAGE	TEACHER	KIDS
Coalesce *Intensify Research, Synthesize Information, and Build Knowledge*	• Shows how to infer answers and draw conclusions • Demonstrates how to read for the gist and synthesize information • Engages kids in guided discussions and debates • Shares how to evaluate sources • Teaches interviewing strategies • Facilitates arrangements for out-of-school resources • Confers with groups and individuals	• Engage in deeper reading and research using books, articles, websites, videos, library visits • Target key ideas and information • Keep asking: So what? What about this really matters? • Practice interviewing • Conduct "people" research: interviews, surveys, questionnaires, focus groups • Check sources and determine reliability • Synthesize information to build knowledge • Meet with teams to monitor schedules, complete specific tasks, and plan for sharing
Go Public *Share Learning, Demonstrate Understanding, Take Action*	• Co-constructs expectations for final projects • Shares the widest range of possibilities for sharing/performing • Welcomes kids' suggestions for these demonstrations • Helps kids find real audiences and opportunities to share their knowledge and teach others • Helps students reflect on content and process • Co-creates rubrics to assess and evaluate projects • Responds, assesses, and evaluates projects • Helps kids to share the learning by taking action	• Co-construct expectations for final projects • Demonstrate learning and understanding in a variety of ways: performances, posters, models, essays, picture books, tableaux, poetry • Become teachers as they share their knowledge with others • Articulate their learning process and how learning changes • Reflect on their knowledge building and their cooperative process • Pose and investigate new questions for further research • Consider changes in their own beliefs or behavior • Take action through writing, speaking, community work, advocacy

Let us reiterate that while this representation looks comfortingly linear, the lived experience of inquiry circles is highly recursive; students are constantly shifting back and forth between stages as knowledge develops. Indeed, we could have drawn this model in a circle or flow chart (we tried it), but it would have taken some kind of six-dimensional hologram to reflect the actual complexity of inquiry. Still, the work is generally ordered; after all, you can't make a presentation about information you don't have. But take our word for it, when kids and teachers dig into an inquiry like this, the actual sequence of work is free-flowing, recursive, intuitive, and creative.

As you read the many classroom stories in Chapters 8–11, you'll see how adaptable and flexible this general model can be. At the start of each of those chapters, we will show you an adaptation of our inquiry model, tailored to one of four particular types of investigations: mini-inquiries (Chapter 8), curricular inquiries (Chapter 9), literature circle inquiries (Chapter 10) and open inquiries (Chapter 11).

Conventional Projects Versus Genuine Inquiry

Reading through all these definitions and stages, many of us might shrug with slight amusement and say: "Well, I guess I've been doing inquiry forever!" We'd probably be thinking about our annual research projects or special units, those extended studies that we do every year. Maybe we don't teach this way every day, but every now and then we dust off our unit folders and lead our kids through one of these projects. And we are not alone.

It's not unusual in October to see primary teachers across America launch the annual apple unit, chock full of apple math, Johnny Appleseed stories, apple pie, and apple songs on the bus home from the culminating apple orchard field trip. Intermediate kids head to the library or the Net to grab an encyclopedia or check out a book from a series on states for their annual state reports. In high school, physics students study the motion and forces of amusement park rides. In the lab, they build ramps, smash things together, and use mathematical formulas to calculate the forces involved. Then the unit culminates at Six Flags over Wherever, where the young physicists-in-training investigate firsthand the roller coasters and other torture devices on offer. And, as dutiful participant-observers, the kids ride the rides, too. On the bus going home, they're not singing apple songs, but hunching over their TI-85 calculators and crunching equations.

Sometimes, these special research projects really click. Kids get engaged, excited, committed. Years later, they'll come back and remind us: "Remember my model of the Alamo? Wasn't it awesome? I loved your class!" Sometimes, students exceed all adult expectations, turning up dazzling findings, creating thoughtful products and performances, and occasionally making change in their communities. At their best, these special projects may turn out to be among the more memorable experiences kids have in school.

And yet we know that apple math and formulaic state reports do not necessarily lead to expanded understanding and more in-depth learning. So we have to step back and ask ourselves, Why do our kids seem to remember these projects over time? What are they really getting out of them? Why do some kids come back and tell us how much they enjoyed them?

*W*hy Conventional Projects Sometimes Work

In looking at conventional school projects, there are a few things that seem to jump out and engage kids.

Slowing Down and Going Deeper

We know in our hearts how important it is for kids to slow down and *delve deeply into a topic*. We bridle against the monstrous, overstuffed, insistent curriculum that expects us to teach it in huge, indigestible hunks every day. Even conventional projects give kids an opportunity to explore a topic for more than an afternoon.

Inviting Holistic Performances

*W*e know in our hearts how important it is for kids to slow down and *delve deeply into a topic.*

At their best, conventional projects feature complex, put-it-all-together experiences; they invite students into an extended, authentic, and coordinated performance of thinking and learning. Kids must independently apply the skills and strategies we (and all the teachers before us) have taught them for reading, thinking, writing, researching, and interacting with others. They must select and use tools and structures at their disposal to do research in the real world. And they must plan and schedule their inquiries and take responsibility for all the things that real lifelong learners do—at a developmentally appropriate level.

Working Across Disciplines

We may laugh (just in the family, OK?) at the scattershot aspects of the Johnny Appleseed unit and its look-alikes across the grade levels. But in our attempts to teach thematic units, we reveal our yearning to teach subject matter in all its cross-disciplinary complexity, not the way ideas are normally partitioned in textbooks. Even apples have history in them—and science and sociology and nutrition and much more. Teachers know that the truly momentous and fascinating problems of life (like global warming, endangered animals, or the possibility of peace) do not reside in a single subject area, but require us to draw upon all the disciplines of knowledge.

Providing Opportunities for Collaboration

Often our most successful projects are sociable—they place kids in pairs, teams, task forces, or other peer work groups for at least part of the time. Small-group activity brings energy, richness, multiple viewpoints, and diverse talents to the work. And as we noted in Chapter 3, employers constantly complain that while their new employees may have the necessary literacy and numerical skills, they frequently cannot get along with anyone else, thus rendering their skill level moot. Still, we must honestly admit that most of the projects we see in schools have kids working alone. Maybe that's partly because of today's intense pressure for individual grades, scores, documentation, and accountability.

Small-group activity brings energy, richness, multiple viewpoints, and diverse talents to the work.

Why Conventional Projects Fall Short

Troublingly, and not infrequently, our projects can also fall short. They can collapse in a slow, gradual, and grinding way, where student effort and understanding steadily peter out. Individual kids drag numbly through scores of scribbled note cards and pages of lackluster bibliographies, ultimately coughing up dry, formulaic reports. Research groups can have their own problems—teams may gyrate out of control, with kids gossiping, squandering time, piling all the work on one dutiful classmate, or fragmenting into subgroups who manage to complete even less work than the original whole.

So we have our doubts. We get concerned about the time and effort that goes into these projects. We worry about the variable commitment we see from students. Sure, we've always got a few Alamo kids, but also plenty of slackers and sleepers. We wonder, "What's happening here? Is this worth the effort? How can I make this work every time, not just 'some years'?"

The main reason conventional projects often fall short is that *they haven't been framed and operated as true inquiries.* That is, they fail to embody the key principles listed back on page 56. And then, certain inevitable problems drag them down.

Too Much Teacher Control/Not Enough Student Choice and Responsibility

Though it seems benign, even caring, for teachers to spend their summers planning themes or projects, the most successful investigations don't originate in August teachers' meetings, but when students are involved from the start. With preplanned units, we risk low student ownership and energy, and then end up having to supply extrinsic rewards, incentives, and punishments, all of which undermine motivation. Even when we are conducting curriculum-driven inquiry projects, it works best to let kids develop their own questions about a required topic before we even begin.

One of the distinctive attributes of true lifelong thinkers and learners is that they pose their own questions and conduct inquiries to build their knowledge. Kids need to take responsibility, to undertake all the same activities that "real" learners do. Feeding topics to students is cognitive coddling; they need to find their own. Then, we teachers can "backmap" kids' authentic questions to the required curriculum (see pages 261–262 for a detailed example of this process).

"Boring" Topics

The two of us can sure testify to encountering substellar projects as kids in school.

SMOKEY: Did you ever have to do a state report in school?

STEPH: Oh, sure. It was fifth grade for me, and I drew Nebraska out of a hat, which I knew nothing about.

SMOKEY: I got Alabama. I mean, for a hockey-playing kid from Minnesota, Alabama held zero allure. Now today, as a grown-up who's visited the state, and knows people and places there, no problem. But at age eleven, I had no prior knowledge or curiosity to build on. And everybody else drew a way cooler state: California, New York, Alaska, Hawaii. I was even jealous of Vicki, who got Wisconsin.

STEPH: Hang on! Wisconsin rocks! Remember, I grew up in Wisconsin, the greatest state in the union. Except for Colorado.

SMOKEY: Right, of course. Well, the project was pretty hard for me to connect with. I copied facts out of the World Book. My parents were so ridiculously supportive that we detoured through a corner of Alabama on a family vacation, so I could at least see my subject. We stopped beside the road and I picked up a bagful of those crumbly red rocks that are everywhere in the state.

STEPH: Been there.

SMOKEY: Well, when the time came for my thirty-minute oral report...

STEPH: Half an hour, no way!

SMOKEY: Oh yes, way. So I just burned right through Alabama's principal industries, leading crops, and major cities way too fast. Then all I could think of to fill all the leftover time was to ask the class, over and over, "would you like to see the rocks again?"

> **STEPH:** Ouch.
>
> **SMOKEY:** Yeah.
>
> **STEPH:** The truth is states are fascinating places, all of them. What ruined states was the way conventional school reports treated them—those fill-in-the-blank outlines of the population, the capital, the products, and so on. It is what goes on in each state that captures us. Thoroughbred horse racing in Kentucky, the Grand Canyon in Arizona, the birthplace of the civil rights movement in Selma, Alabama.
>
> **SMOKEY:** Right, and it is inquiry-based teaching and learning that leads kids to discover the amazing aspects of each and every state or topic they explore.
>
> **STEPH:** So let's not knock states, just the way conventional schooling has reduced them to their lowest common denominator!

▼

*W*hen kids of any age are given a patient, thoughtful choosing process, they will lean toward topics of importance and significance.

As teachers, we have found that when kids of any age are given a patient, thoughtful choosing process, they will lean toward topics of importance and significance. But they may get there through initially more superficial choices. In one school where Smokey worked last year, many of the fourth graders initially wanted to do research projects on their pets—there was great excitement about hamsters, gerbils, ferrets, goldfish, turtles, bunnies, cats, snakes, and more. But given time and support to read, talk, and reflect further, they moved on to issues of animal extinction, the testing of cosmetics on animals, and the morality of sport hunting.

James Beane (1997) helps us to understand this dilemma. He warns us not to rely too heavily on "attractive topics." You know the lineup: pets, dinosaurs, sharks, disasters, and, oh yeah, apples. These are subjects that "work," in the sense that kids predictably enjoy them. But just because we can foresee some subjects that kids might have fun with doesn't mean we should string together a yearful of these attractive topics or plan them in advance. When we do that, we unintentionally subtract the powerful experience of coplanning units around kids' real questions about themselves and their world.

And there's a deeper danger: we have to guard against shallowness. If we steer kids toward studying apples, they'll study apples. But if we keep things open, and kids get interested in child labor, they'll study child labor. What's it gonna be?

Lack of Authentic Purpose or Audience

When we set up projects with correct answers and required formats at the end of the trail, we shouldn't be surprised to hear kids say that their projects are "boring." If the only destination for the work is the teacher's in-box and a red pen, we are really just pretending to offer meaningful work. Without an audience, there's no real inquiry needed here, no original work to do, no "ahas" around the next corner. To kids, the work feels more like an assignment than an invitation, and they are just "filling in the blanks"—doing what amounts to a jumbo, multiday worksheet. The same goes for convergent reporting genres or forms; if everyone has to pour their findings into the same template—whether a model, a letter, a sonnet, or a diorama—the subject matter will not always fit the form and the process can feel fake. Better to let (oops, we mean *require*) kids to take responsibility for finding the correct genre for their unique information.

Lack of Models and Modeling

The lack of models has always been a problem. When the teacher doesn't show examples of successful student products—perhaps some collected from previous years—kids have no choice but to *guess* what the teacher had in mind. Doing a research project under these terms is much like trying to put together a jigsaw puzzle without the picture on the box!

But even worse is our failure to offer "live" demonstrations of how research happens. We have to show kids explicitly how we, as proficient adult learners, notice and develop questions, how we search out and evaluate information, and how we put new knowledge to work and share it with others. We can think aloud about how we do research in our daily lives—as when we choose what magazines to read, cereal to eat, or car to buy. If we don't model, we are not teaching research, but merely assigning it. It takes a little courage to demonstrate your thinking "live," to open up your head and show it to students. But if you are already doing think-alouds with text, and write-alouds with composing, it is just a short step to doing "research-alouds." No matter how we start the process, kids simply must see and hear us teachers thinking like scientists, writers, mathematicians, historians—in the classroom, here and now.

Focus on Research Technicalities over Content and Thinking

Perhaps you, like us, can recall doing thematic units or research projects in school that felt mechanical, rigid, and endless. (Or maybe this happened only in the upper Midwest, where we grew up?) The bible guiding these surface-obsessed projects would be a multipage, single-spaced handout provided by the teacher. This daunting document typically listed dozens of stages with point values attached for every step (twenty-five research index cards, three points each, etc.), and ended up feeling more like a schedule of penalties than a guide to action. With older students, such form-over-content projects often crash onto the rocks

*W*e have to show kids explicitly how we, as proficient adult learners, notice and develop questions, how we search out and evaluate information, and how we put new knowledge to work and share it with others.

of attribution—will it be APA style or MLA? How many points do you lose if you put the author's first name first? We are the world's biggest bugs about accurate attribution (just ask our students), but we teach it *at the point of use,* and with a light enough touch to keep the rest of the enterprise alive.

Rigid or Unrealistic Vision of the Inquiry Process

Real researchers do not use index cards anymore. (Well, maybe a half-dozen do, and they probably learned that system when writing their high school term papers.) The scholars we know photocopy, grab chunks of text or charts off the Internet, and bookmark websites. They take notes in personalized formats, using text annotation, double-entry journals, charts, diagrams, doodles, or lists. There's a complex relationship between posing questions, gathering and weighing information, and building knowledge. Patterns for gathering and weighing information are recursive and often highly idiosyncratic. If we teach kids archaic or inaccurately linear research practices, it doesn't enhance our credibility—or give them a useful road map. When we teach the steps and stages of research, we must help kids recognize how it varies, richly and appropriately, among different topics, purposes, and researchers.

Inadequate Text, Materials, and Resources

*T*oo often projects confine kids to a finite universe of possible texts—or maybe even just the textbook itself.

Too often projects confine kids to a finite universe of possible texts—or maybe even just the textbook itself. But for authentic, truly exploratory reading, where following momentary inspiration, checking out hunches, and chasing leads through quick twists and turns are the order of the day, you need lots and lots of great material. The good news: there's been a boom in nonfiction texts for students, and there's tons of good stuff out there. With a great librarian (and whose isn't?) you can quickly assemble a cart of tantalizing readings on almost any conceivable topic. Even more good news: the Internet offers a vast supply of valuable content, both text and visual, that can support young researchers at work. Oh, yeah, and there are also a gillion gigabytes of garbage. We teachers have to demonstrate and monitor Internet research with extra care. (We say much more about web research in Chapter 6.)

Lack of Well-Structured Student Collaboration

When students lack the necessary cooperative skills, dissension may set in, characterized by asymmetrical work loads among members, bickering and blaming, and tattling to the teacher. Not fun. But totally (well, mostly) avoidable. We also know that solitary projects, especially long ones, tend to lose energy, while sociable ones more often have "legs." As we outlined in Chapter 3, these problems are ameliorated when we explicitly implement well-structured collaborative practices. Sociable work generates more energy, brings more background knowledge to the table, allows for classroom differentiation as we make use of different kids' strengths, and provides a richness and variety of views that you cannot get while working solo. It also parallels real life, which for most of us involves various small groups of people—family, friends, and coworkers—with whom we certainly need to work together.

Leveling or Tracking Students

In many districts we visit around the country, well-structured and energizing kid-driven projects like the ones described in this book are already the norm—but *just for the gifted and talented kids*. What's wrong with this picture!? How many times have we heard ourselves say: "The gifted curriculum should be for everyone!" Oh, you've said that too? Then you are probably a gifted teacher! Obviously, the fact that we restrict our richest and most challenging lessons and practices for a fraction of kids reflects some dubious assumptions that schools make about different kinds of students—and about the enduring power of adult expectations to lower or raise kids' "achievement." No news there. Not to put too fine a point on it, but all students need a chance to engage in inquiries like these. Indeed, it is often the students who have been labeled "lower kids," those who are disconnected and struggling, who most need for school to make sense, to be engaging, to give them some way to join in, and maybe, to find a way to shine—before it is too late.

Obtrusive and Unhelpful Assessment Measures

To be honest, some of the projects that we already assign probably happen because we need something big to grade. We need a major hunk of kids' work that we can assign a bunch of points to. When projects are conceived in this way, we can create formulaic or empty exercises. For example, real lifelong readers do not typically make dioramas after reading a great book. Instead they usually find someone to talk to about the book, and when they have talked themselves out, they go and read another book. But in school, where grading pressures are intense, we might slap on a diorama, just to be on the safe side. And we sure as heck know how to grade a project. Hey, we can distinguish a B+ diorama from a B– diorama at a hundred yards! But when projects are done mainly to yield a major grade for the quarter, or some such requirement, their authenticity obviously suffers. In Chapter 12, we offer a host of assessment and grading ideas that allow for thoughtful evaluation of kids' inquiry work without disturbing the collaborative spirit that feeds successful small-group inquiry.

Lack of Seriousness

We've all wrung our hands over kids who, instead of using the time and support offered by their teachers, complete big school projects at the very last minute, staying up the night before the product is due. Maybe those all-nighters include a mom or dad ghost-writing a report for a younger kid—or an older one cutting and pasting off the Internet. Now, it's always tempting to blame this phenomenon on Kids Today, on their lack of a good-old-days work ethic, or (at least for the older ones) on partying too much. But procrastination and last-minute plagiarism are hardly a new phenomenon and usually reveal a lack of engagement along the way, and suggest a poorly designed activity at the core. So here's another reason why collaborative work is so important: kids need social energy to keep caring, feeling responsible, and plugging away. Not to mention team-developed routines and forms for keeping on schedule, dividing up and monitoring the work, and making steady progress toward defined goals.

*T*oo often, projects are done as an add-on, an extra, or a one-time "treat."

Too often, projects are done as an add-on, an extra, or a one-time "treat." As our apple and amusement park stories are partially meant to underscore, schools too rarely sponsor regular, consistent inquiry projects. Frequency matters. Group investigations gain strength and value when they are part of a yearlong commitment, not just scattered special events.

*T*he Teacher's Roles in Inquiry

We have talked a great deal about engaging kids in inquiry circles—giving them choice and handing them the reins. But what about us? What is the teacher's role in inquiry-based learning? We know that adopting this approach means dropping some familiar teacher roles—lecturer, font of all wisdom, sage on the stage—for at least parts of the day. But as we relinquish our regular jobs, what do we do instead? How do we remain active and supportive while giving real responsibility and control to our students? Not to worry, there are plenty of vital tasks to keep us busy.

In inquiry circles, the teacher:

- Exemplifies and celebrates curiosity, which is at the heart of inquiry-based learning
- Models his/her own inquiry process and keeps a research notebook
- Encourages authentic questions
- Offers lessons in comprehension, collaboration, and inquiry (see Chapter 7)
- Shares examples of how inquiry happens in the real world
- Stays alert to inquiry circle topics and searches for relevant texts and resources

- Keeps the curriculum in mind and connects it to group inquiry whenever possible

- Backmaps inquiry circle investigations to the district and state standards

- Helps students locate, organize, and use resources

- Monitors group and individual work plans and schedules

- Regularly meets and confers with groups and individuals about their progress

- Observes groups at work and gives feedback to students

- Supports kids in taking action beyond the classroom

- Responds to and assesses individual and group work

And don't forget school librarians and media specialists. No one knows better than these indispensable folks where to find a great book or a useful website for research. They are also terrific (and sometimes underutilized) teachers. When you launch inquiry circles, invite them in. Talk with them, plan with them, teach with them. Your classroom inquiries will be more productive and efficient, and also more fun when we adults become info-loving teammates!

*T*oday's Growing Inquiry Movement

These are good times for inquiry. Many national groups and movements now espouse some form of inquiry-based learning, and they offer colleagueship for us all. Some of these approaches are codified in books or organizations, some have their own networks of participating schools, and others have bodies of research and practice open for everyone to draw upon. Below are some of the most important organizations or models. Between the two of us, we have been lucky enough to have some personal experience with most.

INQUIRY-ORIENTED INSTRUCTION: CURRICULUM MODELS

Project-based learning

Expeditionary learning

Problem-based learning

Group investigations

Inquiry groups

Study groups

Topic studies

Guided inquiry

Inquiry circles

Literature circles

Question circles

Idea circles

Learning circles

Writing circles

Peer writing groups

Negotiated curriculum

Multigenre projects

Simulations

Junior/senior projects

Now, this is a disparate list. Very disparate. Some are whole institutions or movements; others are just classroom structures shared by many educators. Some are entirely distinctive, while others are mainly different names for the same model. Some hew to pure inquiry and others are more curriculum driven. Some approaches boldly cross subject matter boundaries, while others barely dip a toe in the knowledge pool next door. Some (such as multigenre projects, originated by our colleague Tom Romano) center on one simple and powerful activity, while others (like expeditionary learning) stretch toward being a way of life. A few have a collaborative component, some can be either solitary or social, and others are mainly applied to individual student work. Some have whole organizations, websites, and scrupulously policed boundaries; others are just ideas, floating free for anyone to use.

As far as we know, there is no overall research on these varied inquiry structures, because their approaches are too diverse to combine. But individual models have shown impressive outcomes in well-designed studies. Project-based learning (PBL), which has a quite tightly defined set of ingredients, may have the best research base of all. A 2000 meta-analysis by John Thomas showed strong achievement gains in PBL schools in Massachusetts, Maine, Iowa, Ohio, Georgia, Tennessee, and New York. Another project-based model called Co-Nect, which adds a technology strand to the project approach, has shown strong student achievement gains in multiple schools in Memphis and Cincinnati. Looking more broadly at the PBL model across the country, Thomas also reported improvements in student motivation, problem-solving ability, conceptual understanding, school climate, and teachers' confidence in students.

One especially effective iteration of project-based learning, Expeditionary Learning (EL), has a strong research base and is modeled on the Outward Bound program. In EL schools, students engage in a series of "learning expeditions"—ambitious, authentic, extended, and highly focused group investigations. For example, Smokey was blown away by his visit to the Rocky Mountain School of Expeditionary Learning (RMSEL) in Denver, where a diverse student body works through a full year of learning projects that parallel the curricular inquiries we describe in Chapter 9. When the middle school kids at RMSEL study the civil rights movement, they first spend weeks digging into the history and literature of the period, developing their own questions about the dynamics, people, and settings of the era. And then they travel to Memphis and other civil rights landmarks to seek answers to their questions.

You could say this book is about *projects that work*. It's about combining what we know about the research process, about thinking, and about people working together, to create a structure that consistently supports kids to build knowledge that matters in their lives. It's about reversing the disadvantages of conventional projects and making them into true inquiries where kids work deeply, powerfully, and joyfully. Our job is to build upon kids' curiosity, to act as though their questions really matter, and to transform our classrooms from lecture halls to researchers' workshops. As we look around at inquiry-based learning today, we see a coalescing of research, practice, models, leadership, and advocacy. The moment is favorable—and change is at hand.

SETTING THE SCENE FOR SMALL-GROUP INQUIRY

Preparing Your Active Learning Classroom

When we walk into a school that promotes active learning and collaborative inquiry, we can feel it right away. A group of fourth graders scans a fold-out, cross-section illustration of the Titanic. Four first graders huddle over a Big Book on natural disasters, jotting and drawing their questions about volcanoes, earthquakes, and tsunamis on a large poster. Several fifth graders crowd around the computer to hunt for the most cost-effective way to purchase malaria nets for children in Africa. A gaggle of middle school kids interviews the cafeteria manager to determine how much food is being thrown away each day at lunchtime. A roomful of seniors listens attentively as a group of classmates, teachers, and outside experts hold a symposium on global warming.

Throughout the building, teachers also brim with curiosity, modeling their own inquiry process, pursuing their own authentic questions, and doing research right in front of the kids. Students and teachers read, write, and talk with each other. Teachers meet in study groups, book clubs, or inquiry circles of their own. Everyone is engaged in active learning—posing questions, finding answers, and taking action. In these schools, learning often reaches beyond the classroom, as kids gather information from the world—and bring information to it. In schools like these, thinking is not a spectator sport.

The Active Use of Knowledge

David Perkins of Harvard's Project Zero is one of our favorite educational researchers. Listen to this:

> Learning is a consequence of thinking. This sentence turns topsy-turvy the conventional pattern of schooling. The conventional pattern says that first students acquire knowledge. Only then do they think with and about the knowledge they have absorbed. But it is really just the opposite: Far from thinking coming after knowledge, knowledge comes on the coattails of thinking. As we

think about and with the content we are learning, we truly learn it. Knowledge does not just sit there. It functions richly in people's lives so they can learn about and deal with the world. (1992, p. 8)

Active learning—reading, writing, drawing, talking, listening, and investigating—leads to acquiring knowledge, coming to understanding, and putting new knowledge to work in the world. Kids should not just be *remembering* what they learn in school, but *using* it in their everyday lives. As teachers, one of our most important jobs is to foster the active use of knowledge. We teach kids to think and work together so they can acquire knowledge and actively use it.

As Holly Occhipinti's fourth graders in Antioch, California, engaged in a curricular inquiry about African American history, the whole class studied the concept of slavery and then broke into inquiry circles. Through a circuitous route, their slavery study led one group to ask the question, Is there slavery today? As they read to find out, they discovered the disturbing answer and went on to pursue an in-depth study of contemporary child labor. Astonished and outraged, Allyson, one of the group members, created and wore a sandwich board with "Ask Me About Child Labor" printed on one side and a plea for action on the other. Then she simply paraded around the playground for several recesses that week, answering questions and inviting interested people to sign the petition running down the left side of the sign. Both kids and teachers stopped to talk with Allyson; they learned a lot, and many became passionate advocates against the practice themselves. Now that's taking action for you! (See Chapter 8 for more of Holly's inquiry project.)

So how do we make this kind of deep work possible? What does the learning, understanding, and active use of knowledge look like in everyday classrooms? How do we teach so that kids fold newfound knowledge into their daily lives and use it effectively?

Allyson's child labor sandwich board.

Principles That Guide Us

When we commit to helping kids develop and use knowledge, we carefully set the scene. We create a culture where everyone can think well together. As we know, any culture is made up of beliefs, attitudes, habits, routines, rituals, systems, processes, materials, and artifacts. Ten key elements are important when we work with kids. We consistently see these same elements being skillfully addressed in the classrooms of veteran inquiry teachers like the ones who have contributed to this book. In inquiry-based classrooms we:

1. Set up an engaging environment.

2. Gather great text and resources.

3. Hone our teaching language.

4. Provide for rich interaction.

5. Differentiate instruction for everyone.

6. Teach with the big ideas in mind.

7. Promote authenticity and relevance.

8. Think about purpose.

9. Foster passion, curiosity, and fun.

10. Help kids take action.

1. Set Up an Engaging Environment

Room arrangement is central to life in the active learning classroom, from pre-kindergarten through high school. Desks in clusters or tables fill the room so kids can easily talk to one another, read and work together, and learn from each other. We create comfortable meeting spaces for whole-class instruction. Proximity to the teacher during whole-class instruction is paramount. Kids need to be up close and personal so they can listen, share their thoughts, and turn and talk to each other. No back rows for hiding!

Clipboards act as portable desks for note taking and drawing. Carpeting or carpet squares on bare floors enhance comfort, sound control, and productivity. Even sixth graders can sit on the floor! And older, too-cool-for-the-floor teenagers can pull up chairs in a semicircle or gather in a U-shape around tables. We arrange large areas where inquiry circles and other small groups of kids can spread out and work together, as well as small spaces where kids can read quietly and work independently. Cast-off, overstuffed couches are a welcome retreat where kids can curl up with books and magazines. Soft lamps can take the edge off of those constantly buzzing fluorescent lights. We want our classrooms to resemble warm, receptive coffee shops and bookstores rather than hospitals or prisons. (See Burley School's vibrant classroom spaces on our companion DVD.)

Materials and supplies are vital as well. If we want kids engaged in thoughtful work from the minute they set foot in the room each day, we need to make that easy for them. Clipboards and notebooks are easily accessible. Labeled baskets of books are conveniently placed throughout the room, as are bookshelves where some titles and covers can be seen as well as spines. An array of sharp pencils, crayons, paints, markers, and pens reside in cans and cubbies scattered around the room. Blank paper, lined paper, charts, index cards, and Post-its of every imaginable size and shape are within easy reach. No more midclass refrains of "I forgot to bring a pen" or "Can I go sharpen my pencil?" We eliminate the opportunity for kids to waste time procuring resources. Kids who forget stuff do *not* lollygag back to their lockers—we put them directly to work instead. We create a culture of abundance, not scarcity, and flood the room with resources that are within arm's length.

WHAT ABOUT MIDDLE AND HIGH SCHOOL? Does all this sound a little elementary? Maybe you're wondering: how am I supposed to create secondary-level analogues of these warm and well-supplied learning spaces when the architecture of my teaching world is so different? Many middle and high school teachers constantly move from one bare, antiseptic room to another and aren't allowed to customize a single special place for their 150 learners. Can we just pause and say: "Man, this is tough!" Room hopping is one of the most mis-guided "efficiencies" of the factory-model secondary schools that we are still quite insanely constructing today.

Some heroic secondary teachers drag all the stuff they need with them as they crisscross their building over seven or eight periods. Smokey remembers fol-lowing Kath Bergin around Glenbard West High School in west suburban Chicago as she rolled a cart packed with all the materials she needed for rich, interactive teaching. Since Kath's classes were scattered on different floors, she had to ride the elevator to each destination during six-minute passing periods. (One positive side effect: she became close pals with all the students in wheel-chairs as well as the injured football players.) At each destination, kids organized to help her unpack and repack, and Kath got the transitions down to a science. But much as we may admire her stamina, most of us are not about to become another "Cart Martyr," as one of Kath's pals dubbed her. Who among us has the persistence, the organization, or the horsepower?

But just because we share classrooms does not mean we give up on creating energizing workplaces for our students. No way! Instead, we meet with the col-leagues who use the same room and work out a deal where everyone gets to bring the tools and create the spaces they need. (For obvious reasons, it is impor-tant to hold this meeting in the shared room itself.) Such negotiations can be easier than they sound. In his second year of teaching, Smokey shared a class-room with a colleague who simply didn't care about the look of the space, and who cheerfully delegated it to him to do the "decorating," as she called it.

As we sit down with the other people teaching in Room 302 (who may actu-ally be from different departments), we arrange for a sharing of space, walls, shelves, floors, corners, even sections of the whiteboard. If I want the kids in a circle and you want them in straight rows, we agree to have our kids reset the room to the preference of the teacher coming in next. If we use common supplies and materials—paper, clipboards, paper clips, markers, staplers, dictionaries—we work together to gather them and make them available to all students. If we need special materials for our classes only, we take responsibility for locating them, and store them on our share of the shelves.

Sitting with our colleagues, we have a natural opportunity to have conversations about instruction and space that may move us all forward. Do we really want individual student desks in this room, set up in rows? Collaborative groups like inquiry circles work so much better with movable chairs, which allow for quick and flexible regrouping. This arrangement can also help us manage noise levels: it's much quieter when kids can hold discussions knee to knee instead of shouting across pulled-together desks. How might all of our teaching change if

we requisitioned tables and chairs instead, and set up a two-zone classroom—a chairs-only large-group meeting area on one side, and work tables on the other? Kids could move the chairs back and forth, depending on the work that's under way. What about that cold blue lighting? Does anyone have any old floor lamps at home they could donate? Beanbag chairs?

But what if you are truly stuck in an inflexible situation, where because of school rules, security concerns, the fire marshal, or staff norms, you simply cannot add or leave any stuff in the room? This is the time to remember that the most important ingredients of a classroom climate are the human ones: how we act, speak, and live together. We know absolutely sensational secondary teachers who can weave a web of cognitive richness around their kids, even when the walls are bare.

Kids need varied and comfortable spaces to work alone, in inquiry circle teams, and as a whole class.

These resourceful teachers don't arrive in their barren classrooms empty-handed, however. If you have watched as many movies as we have, you know that master spies always have a special suitcase packed and sitting beside their door. The same applies to teaching in strange and empty rooms. You need a Go-Bag. See below for a baseline set of materials with which you can always survive—the whole kit weighs less than a laptop.

THE ACTIVE LEARNING TEACHER'S GO-BAG

- **Post-it notes** of several shapes and sizes so kids can capture, record, categorize, and compare their thoughts, questions, connections, and responses to the days' lesson, sticking them directly where meaning is being made.

- **Three-by-five index cards,** another great teaching tool, just right for short writing-to-learn exercises. Perfect for sharing or passing thoughts around the room, creating gallery walks, serving as exit or admit slips. Make a deck, shuffle, and deal out ideas to share.

- **A piece of your current personal reading**—a book, article, or magazine that you can read aloud or talk about with your class, so you are constantly modeling your own curiosity, learning, and thinking.

- **A "one-page wonder"** to share—thirty copies of a sensationally interesting short article, story, poem, graph, or image, tied to the curriculum and guaranteed to evoke kids' interest right now.

- **Your personal learning log or journal,** with at least two sections:

  - Your own jottings, musings, inquiry questions, to-do lists, and other entries that you can share to show kids your own thinking and writing process.

  - One blank page for each student in each class. Donald Graves says you can't teach any student until you know at least ten things about his or her life. We agree. On these "kid pages," as you get to know each student better, you jot down what you've learned (has a black Labrador; struggles with spelling; grandmother lives with her; is interested in Abraham Lincoln; plays soccer).

2. Gather Great Text and Resources

*O*ur big job is to immerse kids in an ever-increasing variety of text and resources and teach them how to find material that will engage and hopefully enlighten them as they search for information.

In active learning classrooms, we flood the room with text and resources that spur wonder and excitement. Kids need text they can and want to read in school every day. In order to focus on content, topics, and issues, we use a multisource, multigenre, multimedia curriculum. We pump nonfiction, but we also encourage our kids to read across genres. We love books, but also send students to the Internet. We subscribe to magazines, but also fill the room with artifacts and objects of interest. The more varied and abundant the resources, the better.

So while we love books, we go way beyond them. Magazines, newspapers, graphics, videos, artifacts, objects, websites, and blogs offer a wonderful way to spur thinking, answer questions, find information, and satisfy curiosity in the inquiry-based classroom. Our big job is to immerse kids in an ever-increasing variety of text and resources and teach them how to find material that will engage and hopefully enlighten them as they search for information.

So while one goal of our collection efforts is breadth and variety, we're also extra careful to build our collection of resources in areas of interest. Over time, we may see patterns in kids' interests and questions; the same topics come up perennially. So if our high school kids always want to learn about gangs, we are on special lookout for materials on that topic; same for animals with primary kids, extreme weather with intermediate grades, the future with middle schoolers.

BOOKS, MAGAZINES, AND NEWSPAPERS. Text matters, big time. Schools ought to offer the most direct route to learning by engulfing kids in rich, varied, and intriguing books, magazines, and newspapers of all sorts. We fill up the room with compelling text that kids simply can't *not* read! As kids move into middle and high school, they should be reading some of the same material as thoughtful, curious members of the adult community. This means daily newspapers, magazines, and most especially, the current trade nonfiction books that grown-ups are buzzing about. Eighth-grade teacher Doug Livingston begins every English class with kids reading and talking about the newspaper for ten to fifteen minutes. He reports that they can't get enough of it, and even those reluctant readers climb aboard with the city beat, the sports page, or the movie reviews.

We stay on top of newly published books of every genre for our students by subscribing to magazines and journals that review and recommend them—*Reading Teacher, English Journal, Language Arts, The Horn Book, Booklist, School Library Journal, Journal of Adolescent and Adult Literacy,* and the like. Russell Baker once said that Americans love fat books and thin women. Despite her objections, Steph has to admit there is some truth to this. We love books, long ones too. (Forget the skinny women part.) But too often, all we serve up to older kids are long chapter books, when in fact most of what gets published in America is *short* nonfiction. We have to match school reading with real-world reading, which absolutely means more short nonfiction in school.

We need a constant flow of magazines and newspapers to our classrooms. (See our magazine bibliography on the website.) Packed with current issues, ideas, and concepts, they spur discussion and debate and often generate new questions and further research, and they have the added bonus of preparing kids for the kind of articles we adults read every day. Many of the inquiry circles in this book emerged from reading a short nonfiction article or relied on short articles to get information during the inquiry itself. With Anne Goudvis, Steph has published *Toolkit Texts,* three volumes of such articles for grades 2–7 (2007). Smokey and colleague Nancy Steineke are preparing two volumes of these "one-page wonders" for middle and high school teachers (2010). (See our list of compelling short text collections in the Appendix.)

VISUALS, GRAPHICS, AND VIDEOS. Information comes in all shapes and sizes. Of course we get information from text, but also from visual and graphic features. Illustrations and photographs play a prominent role in inquiry-based learning. Sometimes it is possible to get our questions answered from the visuals without even reading the text, making nonfiction the most accessible genre, particularly for our younger readers, English language learners, and less-developed readers. Nothing prompts a question quicker than an image of a spewing volcano. Nothing spurs an inference faster than a hungry Komodo dragon stalking a wild pig. And such powerful images are so much easier to find today with websites like Google Images, not to mention the sites of the world's great museums, historical societies, and cultural institutions of all kinds. (Also see our Internet bibliography on the website.)

Great as electronic images are, we still love the old-school paper versions, too. Large-format text—Big Books, posters, coffee-table books, calendars—all

www.heinemann.com/
comprehensionandcollaboration.

*B*ringing intriguing objects and artifacts into the room adds to our kids' engagement, teaches them to think, and builds content knowledge.

help to inspire questions and provide information. Don't miss opportunities to find and save these. Head to garage and stoop sales for old books, magazines, and posters. Out-of-date photographic calendars are a gold mine. People just throw them away at the end of the year and bookstores often sell them at a deep discount. Posters abound at fast-food restaurants, which are usually happy to save them for a passionate teacher. Think creatively to scare up resources!

Visual features such as maps, charts, and tables are rife with information. They appear in the newspaper every day on topics of great interest to kids—flow charts of the best summer movies, graphs of the most popular Halloween candy, comparative maps of the shrinking polar ice cap. Clip them to share with your students. Diagrams, cutaways, cross-sections, overlays, distribution maps, and thought bubbles visually inform researchers of important information. Bring them in, share with students, and teach kids how to read and understand them. Once kids have learned how to read a distribution map, they will be much more likely to pay attention to one when they come across it in their own research. Once they have seen that bar graphs are not all that confusing, they may take time to get information from them as they read on their own.

Of course, images don't have to be static; today, videos abound on the Net. When Smokey led a class of sixth graders through a round of inquiry circles, online videos were one of the main sources the kids used—especially early in the process, for a quick shot of background knowledge. The group researching global warming began its study by sitting down at a classroom computer and watching a cautionary video narrated by Leonardo DiCaprio. The group studying the French language went straight to the Web for movies shot in French and subtitled in English. The chuckling boys studying nuclear weapons got a sobering attitude change when they played the History Channel documentary on the destruction—and casualties—of Hiroshima. And all these kids had to do was walk across the room, belly up to a computer, and find and play a free video.

We recognize that videos are a huge source of information today, and a central ingredient of every young person's life. What kid could live without TV, YouTube, music videos, news clips, and downloadable movies? Obviously, we teachers need to draw more heavily on this rich resource. But many schools lag far behind in the use of video material with instruction. Or if they nominally have access, valuable videos are often blocked by whatever censoring software the school has installed to protect kids from inappropriate content. We need to get past this. For almost any topic we might take up in school, there are countless free videos somewhere on the web that can help provoke curiosity, build upon kids' knowledge, and provide information. For just one example: the History Channel offers half-hour or longer videos on, well, almost everything historical. Check it out at www.history.com. For more

www.heinemann.com/
comprehensionandcollaboration.

instructional video ideas, take a look at the website for some of our favorite websites, many of which include video resources.

OBJECTS AND ARTIFACTS. Bringing intriguing objects and artifacts into the room adds to our kids' engagement, teaches them to think, and builds content knowledge. Shari Tishman writes that "closely examining everyday objects sparks students' curiosity and leads to increasingly complex thinking" (2008, p. 44). In her research study, Tishman asked a teacher to examine a darning egg with her middle and high school students. A common tool as recently as the 1950s, a darning egg is a wooden egg-shaped object that provides a solid surface for mending holes in socks. The teacher guided the discussion by asking kids to make careful observations about the unfamiliar object and think expansively about it. They began to talk to each other and ask questions about it. As the discussion ensued, they made nuanced observations, posed generative questions, and made inferences about the darning egg. Soon they were considering the context of the society in which people used the tool and comparing it to their own lives and times. Tishman says the key reason to use objects to teach thinking is that "objects naturally invite high level thinking and provide an authentic context in which to cultivate it."

Harvey and Goudvis (2007) suggest that teachers bring in unfamiliar objects to teach inferential thinking to elementary-age kids. The teacher might pass around a strange object—a round apple corer, for instance—and ask kids to infer what it is by observing it closely, touching it, and noticing its attributes (sharp on one side, for example). As kids struggle to identify the object, the teacher brings forth an apple as an additional clue. Those kids who haven't yet figured it out almost always get it when the apple appears. This is how inferring in reading works. The more clues we pick up on, the more reasonable our inferences become. For more on this, see Tanny McGregor's book *Comprehension Connections* (2007), which includes lessons that use objects and artifacts to teach kids to connect, question, and infer with concrete objects before they consciously try those strategies in text.

Smokey owns a two-pound triangular chunk of Adolph Hitler's granite desktop from his chancellery office in Berlin. This war souvenir was retrieved by Smokey's great-uncle Jerry Keith, who was among the troops who stormed the fuhrer's office in the closing days of World War II. When teaching U.S. history, Smokey always passed this chunk of polished stone halfway around the circle of students before telling them what it was. There was usually an audible gasp at that moment. Suddenly the object comes alive. Some students would then refuse the stone when it was passed their way; others looked down at their hands wondering "what did I just touch?" while still others wanted to get the stone back and hold it again. Primed by this experience, the kids were eager for an in-depth study of Hitler's life, personality, and deeds.

ONLINE RESOURCES, MEDIA, AND WEBSITES

SMOKEY: We're going to write about the Internet now, right?

STEPH: Yeah, is that a problem?

SMOKEY: Let me ask you a question.

STEPH: Uh-oh.

SMOKEY: When was the last time you set foot in a library? Like a real bricks-and-mortar library?

STEPH: Well, every day, when I am in schools with kids . . .

SMOKEY: Well, of course, school libraries. But for my own research, my own questions . . . I can get everything I need off the Internet now. I haven't set foot in a regular library in a long time. Except to vote.

STEPH: Hmm, I was going to call you some kind of techno-yuppie, but now that you mention it, I'm totally hooked on the Internet myself. And that is pretty strange for a person who has loved libraries and librarians throughout my whole childhood and adult life. But you're right. I don't get in the car and drive to the library nearly as frequently as I used to.

The Internet has completely transformed the practice of research, information-gathering, and inquiry since we two dinosaurs were kids. And even since today's kids were kids! The available online resources seem to expand daily in a dizzying array of alternatives. The Web is the obvious go-to resource to jump-start any inquiry project—and often, for digging deeper and deeper. But the Web is not an unmixed blessing. The Internet is also full of digital junk, misleading information, and disreputable sources.

Because the Web is potentially so useful to student researchers, so central to the work of inquiry circles, and also because it is so fraught with dangers and difficulties, we devote a whole chapter to it (see Chapter 6).

3. Hone Our Teaching Language

The British linguist and educator James Britton reminds us that "language floats on a sea of talk." Everything that we eventually want kids to be able to do in school must be, and can only be, built on a deep and wide foundation of oral language. There are no shortcuts: you've got to talk to grow, talk to learn, talk to read, and most definitely, talk to write. We silence or curtail kids' talk at their cognitive peril. Indeed, as educators, one of our most basic duties is to invite kids' spoken language, plenty of it, on a wide range of topics, for a whole range of purposes, and across scales of formality. But we don't merely solicit an uproar. As we elicit kids' talk, we extend, channel, shape, and expand it. Language is the most powerful teaching and learning tool we possess.

It all begins with the example we set. What we say or don't say when teaching has far-reaching consequences for our students—both their learning and their lives. When we catch ourselves using phrases like these:

"Who knows the answer to this?"

"Not quite; anyone else?"

"That wasn't exactly what I was looking for."

"You've almost got it."

*W*e want kids to adopt and adapt our teaching language as their learning language.

we are revealing some pretty obvious assumptions about learning: that the teacher is the font of knowledge, that she controls the conversation, that the goal of learning is to regurgitate the one right answer, and perhaps, that remembering information is the most prized kind of thinking.

Wholly different assumptions are conveyed when we use language more inclusively, openly, and tentatively—and when we challenge kids not just to recall, but to think. Ritchart and Perkins (2008) share a story of skillful teacher language that illustrates this quite well. Some first graders in Australia became interested in a mine collapse in Tasmania which was all over the news. They had many questions, so their teacher facilitated a discussion about what they thought they knew about the incident. Every time one of the kids made a comment, she responded by saying *What makes you say that?* The kids shared their thoughts in response to her question. Soon, students began to justify their answers without her prompt of *What makes you say that?* They seemed almost to hear her words in their head, so rather than waiting for her to ask them, they went right on and explained why they had said what they said.

So our teaching language can prompt thinking. Questions like, *What makes you say that? Can you say more about that? What makes you think that?* and *How did you come up with that?* push kids to expand their thinking, justify their thoughts, and come up with big ideas. One of our favorite books, Peter Johnston's *Choice Words: How Our Teaching Language Affects Children's Learning* (2004), shares specific teaching language that invites everyone in, opens up questions, and spurs kids to think. In her related book, *Comprehension Through Conversation,* Maria Nichols (2006) shows how a teacher's use of language and ability to scaffold kids' conversations can help enhance comprehension. When students hear this kind of thoughtful, inclusive language from their teachers, they tend to use it with each other. And this is just what we seek—for kids to adopt and adapt our teaching language as their learning language.

4. Provide for Rich Interaction

In active learning classrooms, kids interact with text and resources in a variety of ways. They hold their thinking while reading by jotting and drawing their thoughts on Post-its, graphic organizers, and in the margins. They talk to each other throughout the day in book clubs, inquiry circles, pair shares, and in large groups as teachers have them turn and talk to one another during mini-lessons. They interact with images, videos, objects, and artifacts. And they interview knowledgeable people and interact with specialists in the field as they engage in inquiry.

Interaction is central to inquiry-based learning. When learners interact with the teacher, the text, and the resources, with each other and with outside specialists, learning sticks and understanding thrives.

Enter Jack Anderson's sixth-grade classroom on the first day of a unit study on Native Americans. Luz writes a question on a Post-it as she examines a splintered wooden spatula. Richard places a withered quiver over his shoulder and withdraws an imaginary arrow. He jots an inference on his Post-it: *Big enough for about five arrows.* And so it goes from around the room. Each small group of kids handles and scrutinizes an Indian artifact, jots down questions and inferences, and joins in a conversation about what they noticed.

First-grade teacher Anne Garcia begins an insect study each year with photos of insects from a Big Book. She has kids turn and talk about what they wonder about the image and then suggests they draw and/or write their questions on a piece of paper. Fourth-grade teacher Holly Occhipinti launches a study of pre–Civil War slavery by going to Google Images and printing disturbing photographs and illustrations of various aspects of slavery. She divides the kids into groups, each with an image, and has them jot their questions and inferences on Post-its and place them on the image. Many teachers we know across the grades launch curriculum topic studies by having kids interact with images, objects, and artifacts.

Throughout this book, you will find examples of teachers modeling how to interact with text, and kids recording their thinking in text, on images, and with artifacts. You will also notice that kids spend a great deal of time talking to each other. Nothing enhances understanding more than talking to someone about your thoughts and questions. Interaction is at the very core of this book. To understand what they read and research, kids must interact with the text and the resources, their teacher, and most of all, each other.

5. Differentiate Instruction for Everyone

Well-structured small-group inquiries can provide extraordinary opportunities for kids with special needs not just to join in, but to shine. Indeed, inquiry circles can be a crucible of inclusion when we commit to heterogeneous membership,

See Lesson 3, "Think and Wonder About Images," p. 118.

diverse along every dimension—gender, learning style, special needs, home language, and more. Diversity is an asset. It makes groups stronger when one student is a solid writer, another likes to draw and illustrate, someone else is a tech whiz, this kid is a reliable record keeper, and yet another can conduct an effective interview. Each person can be a vital part of the group's work without having to read the same materials, do the same task, or have the same learning goals. Special educators Patrick Schwarz and Paula Kluth (2007) call such individualized contributions to a common project "curricular overlapping."

One size does not fit all. So we always consider how our instruction, materials, and assessments can be adapted to students with varying reading proficiencies, learning styles and needs, and language backgrounds. Instruction occurs in a variety of groupings—large groups, small groups, pairs—and with individuals.

These methods of differentiation make sense for all kids. But we keep a special eye out for our English language learners and adjust our speaking, listening, and comprehending challenges accordingly. We make information as concrete as possible, using photographs, drawings, charts, artifacts, maps, and the like. Such visual aids help make concepts and ideas clear, providing English language learners multiple entry points into English instruction. We offer readings in kids' first language whenever possible. *Toolkit Texts* (2007), the short nonfiction pieces that Steph and Anne Goudvis created, have Spanish translations of every article.

Just as we differentiate our instruction, we vary our text. It's essential to offer readings at a wide range of levels, on many varied topics. The monthly National Geographic Kids' magazines offer a spectrum of reading levels, beginning with *Young Explorer* for kindergarten and first grade, *Explorer Pioneer* for second and third grades, *Explorer Pathfinder* for fourth and fifth grades, and *Extreme Explorer* for middle school. We love *Pioneer* and *Pathfinder* in particular because the two have exactly the same articles every month—same photos, same titles— but *Pioneer* is written in more accessible text. If you have both in your classroom, your less developed readers can read *Pioneer,* and those who need a bit of challenge can read *Pathfinder* and then discuss them together.

TEXT SETS. As kids participate in inquiry circles, we support them by creating "text sets"—multiple selections on the same topic, but at different reading levels. We are always building collections of articles and other texts on the same or a related topic, making sure that we have both accessible and more challenging choices within the set. For their work with high school kids, Nancy Steineke and Smokey have assembled five-piece text sets on native–settler contact, the Tuskegee Airmen, John Brown and abolitionism, global warming, invasive species, the Second Amendment, and other topics.

*I*nquiry circles can be a crucible of inclusion when we commit to heterogeneous membership, diverse along every dimension—gender, learning style, special needs, home language, and more.

For the intermediate and middle grades, there is a commercial series particularly designed for textual differentiation. The National Geographic Theme Sets feature four texts, each on a common theme covering a huge range of science and social studies topics. For example, under the theme "Cells at Work," there are six texts each on blood cells, muscle cells, skin cells, and bone cells, each at a different level but with the same large concepts and themes. This series is ideal for small-group curricular inquiry because students can read about similar topics and themes, but at different reading levels.

Teachers often wonder where these reading sets come from. Clipping articles from newspapers, staying up to date on recently published trade books, and scouring the Net for online articles become part of your daily routine. At Burley School in Chicago, Ben Kovacs created a set of articles on different kinds of orphans to prepare kids for reading *Bud, Not Buddy.* Ben used Info-Bits, a subscription web service available through his school district, as well as other web resources to create a broad, kid-friendly, and multi-leveled set of readings. We are always on the lookout for texts of varying difficulty on key topics in our curriculum. We get in the habit of seeking articles on a common topic—one easy, one medium, and one difficult. This allows us to put every kid in front of material they can read about the subject at hand. Our most developed readers can investigate topics right alongside our less developed readers, and each member can make a contribution. This is one of the beautiful things about inquiry circles. Kids can investigate the same topics even if they read at different levels.

Yes, there is some effort involved here, but once you have created a text set, chances are you will be able to use it several times. We maintain and refresh these sets by replacing one article at a time, as we run across better or newer information. And we don't limit ourselves to text alone when we build these sets; we are always on the lookout for a striking image, a good video, an interactive website, or a cool blog to include as well. Helping kids find appropriate text and resources at their level and of interest to them is one of our top priorities as teachers in inquiry-based classrooms.

6. Teach with the Big Ideas in Mind

Many of us came of age in classrooms that look very different from those we talk about in this book. Classrooms peppered with desks in rows; no talking; teacher lectures; daily quizzes on history dates, vocabulary lists, and math facts. But we know that in-depth, robust learning requires much more than regurgitating what the teacher says.

True education is not about memorizing facts. Most of us can state that $E=MC^2$, but may not be able to explain it at all. We know that Pearl Harbor was bombed on December 7, 1941, but may still have misconceptions about what

If we guide kids to think about and discuss the important fundamental concepts and themes that can turn up almost anywhere in literature or content, they will derive a greater understanding of the issues.

happened. To really learn, understand, and gain knowledge that we can put to work in our lives, we have to think about the big ideas behind these dates and facts; we have to read and talk about the implications of the complex issues that surround these events and concepts; and we usually have to do further research for a more complete understanding.

To lead kids to deeper understanding, we teach with the big ideas in mind. If we guide kids to think about and discuss the important fundamental concepts and themes that can turn up almost anywhere in literature or content, they will derive a greater understanding of the issues. Sometimes these big ideas are part of the content standards—how symbiosis affects coral reefs, or why people emigrate. Frequently, these ideas emerge from kids' questions about what they are learning. Other times, we may have thoughts of our own about what is worth further discussion. Often these big ideas are not written out explicitly in the text; we have to infer them. Themes like jealousy and betrayal in literature, the impact of climate change in science, or how war changes human beings in history— these are the big ideas that we want our kids to wrangle with.

As part of her group's career inquiry, Cristina conducts a phone interview with a fashion designer.

Kids' questions are often the best segue into underlying themes and big ideas. While hearing Tomie dePaola's *The Art Lesson* read aloud to his kindergarten class, Tanner asked, "Why is he so good at art? He is only in first grade." Steph suggested the kids turn and talk about that. After a short time, she asked them to share their thoughts. "Because he loves to draw so much" and "because he practices all the time" were the responses. Steph synthesized their comments into two big ideas that were not explicitly stated in the text: passion and practice. "When we love something a lot and practice a lot, we get really good at it," Steph emphasized, as she wrote the words *passion* and *practice* on a chart titled "Big Ideas in *The Art Lesson.*" Then she had kids talk about their own passions and how practice made them better soccer players, dancers, artists, and so forth. But Steph didn't stop there; she continued to wrap the notion of passion and practice into the school day whenever possible, so that kids were frequently reminded of these two ideas, giving them a better shot at understanding and actively using this new knowledge.

Questions for Content-Area Reading

When reading in the content areas, we often share a sequence of three types of guiding questions that help us root out the big, important ideas—the **definition question,** the **consequence question,** and the **action question.** Definition questions ask what is happening. Consequence questions explore why it matters. Action questions probe what can be done.

The Definition Question

- What is it?
- What is happening"
- What is going on?

The Consequence Question

- Why does it matter?
- What difference does it make?
- Why should I care?

The Action Question

- How can we get involved?
- How can we help?
- What can we do about it?

For example, if we view a magazine cover of a red-eyed tree frog peering out from under the title *Two Thousand Amphibian Species Threatened,* we immediately ask the definition question—*What is happening to these amphibians?* and continue to read with that question in mind. Once we discover the answer, we follow up with the consequence question—*Why does it matter if a bunch of frogs die?* As we read, think about, and discuss this idea we are likely to develop a better understanding of the consequences and may be moved to take action. So we ask an action question—*What can we do about this?* and research possible actions. Perhaps in a history textbook, we come across the subhead, "The Bill of Rights." We encourage kids to ask the definition question—*What is the Bill of Rights?* Once they find the answer, we remind them to consider the consequence question, *Why do they matter?* Ultimately they may take up the action question, particularly if they notice that someone's rights have been violated. These three guiding questions lead kids to surface big ideas and underlying themes, and inquiry circles are a perfect place to delve into these issues, hash them out, and even take action.

7. Promote Authenticity and Relevance

Authenticity reigns supreme in inquiry-based classrooms. We make sure that what our kids are learning inside school is applicable outside. We emphasize the kind of reading we adults do every day—newspapers, magazines, Web articles, editorials, essays, memos, and so on. We advocate book clubs and lit circles just like those in our neighborhoods. Kids choose inquiry topics based on real questions and interests. We engage them in authentic research such as Web searches, interviews, surveys, focus groups, and visits to the library. We invite specialists to visit and serve as mentors for our kids. There's no better way for them to learn than as apprentices to knowledgeable, skilled professionals. We teach kids how to work with others and we support them to work in small, collaborative groups just as they will in future careers. We show kids how we ask questions and research information to make informed decisions every day. And we teach kids to take action based on their learning, using their knowledge to answer questions, facilitate change, or make a difference just as we adults do in our daily lives. When learning is authentic, kids climb aboard.

We encourage authentic questions from both students and teachers. When we were in school, the teachers had the questions and we were supposed to supply the answers. Authentic questions are those that we do not know the answer to, that are worthy of further research, and that really matter. Authentic questions

- prompt thinking
- don't always have one right answer
- may have many answers

- cause us to ponder and wonder

- dispel or clarify confusion

- challenge us to rethink our opinions

- may clear up misconceptions

- lead us to seek out further information

- are subject to discussion and debate

- may require further research and conversation

—ADAPTED FROM HARVEY AND GOUDVIS 2007

Relevance is a close cousin of authenticity. The two often go hand and hand. When learning is authentic, it is almost always more relevant. When learners can relate to what they are studying or investigating, learning is more seamless and enjoyable. Students who are truly interested in a topic and view it as relevant to their own lives are more likely to work at it for longer periods of time and enjoy doing so (Hidi and Renninger 2006).

8. Think About Purpose

We read, listen, and view for many different reasons. When reading in inquiry circles, our purpose is usually to answer questions, find out information, gain knowledge, and even act on it. When reading for a standardized test, our purpose is to pick out the right answer and fill in the right bubble. In book clubs, we read to connect to characters and themes so we can talk about them and better understand one another. We might read poetry for amusement, renewal, transformation, or to fill ourselves up. And nothing goes further to nurture our soul than curling up in front of a crackling fireplace with a great book!

The purposes for reading run the gamut from learning and questioning to just plain enjoyment. Sometimes these purposes overlap; other times they are quite different. We need to keep purpose in mind as we share how reading happens for us and consider how it happens for our kids. Certain practices apply when we are reading to learn that do not apply when we are reading strictly for enjoyment. During a nonfiction study, we often advise kids to stop, think, and react to information as they are reading to learn, coding the text as they go. Whereas, when we see a fifth grader in an overstuffed chair curled up with a good novel, we sure don't interrupt and ask him to jot down his questions! When kids fall in love with any book, we offer a thankful prayer to the reading gods and just let them read.

AESTHETIC READING AND EFFERENT READING. The famous reading theorist Louise Rosenblatt talks about two distinct reading stances, *efferent* and *aesthetic.* Efferent reading is reading to learn. When we read efferently, we are

*W*hen kids fall in love with any book, we offer a thankful prayer to the reading gods and just let them read.

reading to "take away" pieces of information or to synthesize big ideas. It is the stance we usually take when we are reading informational text. When we read fiction or literature, Rosenblatt says, we take a different readerly stance. "In aesthetic reading," she explains, "the reader's attention is centered directly on what he is living through during his relationship with that particular text" (in Probst, 2006). For instance, in a great fiction read, we might imagine ourselves in the story, sailing across the ocean, hearing waves slapping the gunnels and seagulls squawking above. As the sensory images fill our minds, it is highly unlikely that we would stop and write a Post-it about it! When reading aesthetically, we fall into the storyworld of the book. Indeed, when we settle down with a good piece of fiction, it is often our conscious purpose to get lost in a gripping narrative.

Nonfiction reading—efferent reading—is a whole different animal. Getting lost is not a goal when reading nonfiction! Sure, there are great nonfiction books and articles that can transport us into another kind of absorbing, pleasurable world. But usually the purpose for reading nonfiction is to find information, grab it, and put it to work. Much of the reading that kids do in inquiry circles is like this. They read trade books, magazines, newspapers, and Web articles as they research information. When readers are seeking information, they need to stop frequently, think about, and react to the text. In most nonfiction resources, there is simply too much information for a reader to process without stopping and jotting notes. As readers gather information, they need to read with a pencil in hand and a pad of Post-its at the ready. In active learning classrooms, kids' nonfiction texts burst with Post-its or margin notes of their connections, questions, inferences, and important ideas. Annotating informational text gives readers a much better chance of learning, understanding, and remembering what they read.

When kids are reading fiction, we still encourage them to keep a pad of Post-its and a pencil close at hand in case they need them. But we do not recommend that they constantly record their thinking, as it is likely to interfere with their reading. They might stop and jot when they are confused, have a question or topic to discuss in their lit circle, or need to practice a new strategy. But writing about reading should enhance engagement and understanding, not bring it to a halt. With fiction, we have found that some of the most thoughtful responses come *after* reading, from both talking about and writing about the ideas in the text and various connections to it.

As kids get older, the forms of annotation they use can become increasingly sophisticated. When Smokey taught the Second Amendment in a New Hampshire high school, he showed kids a letter that Harvard University sends to freshmen each year. "Throw away that highlighter in favor of a pencil. Make your reading thinking intensive," says the university. "Develop your own system of codes you can use to mark texts" (2006). Smokey then offered students a sample system that included these codes:

See Lesson 5, "Annotate Text: Leave Tracks of Thinking" p. 120.

✓ = I knew that

X = This contradicts my expectations

★ = This is important

? = I have a question

?? = I am confused or puzzled

! = This is surprising or exciting to me

L = I learned something new

Combining these new codes with their regular habits of underlining and jotting notes in the margins, the kids attacked the articles Smokey had brought. During the subsequent discussion, they had tons of ideas to debate and ponder. All they had to do was glance down at their annotations to grab a topic, a question, or a response.

Whatever the grade level, marking text with Post-its and annotations makes readers more aware of their thinking and encourages them to stop, think, and reflect along the way. But we never just mark text for its own sake: the purpose of all reading, regardless of genre, is understanding and engagement!

9. Foster Passion, Curiosity, and Fun

Einstein said: "I have no special talent. I am only passionately curious." Interesting, considering the source. Some might disagree. But Einstein meant it, and he wrote extensively about passion and wonder and their role in learning. As teachers, we are insatiably curious about kids' thinking and about life in general. We live in a way that surfaces our musings and wonderings. We celebrate curiosity in the classroom and out. We let kids know that nothing matters more than their questions. Passion and wonder are contagious; as we model and share our passions and questions, kids are inspired to join us with their own ideas and inquiries.

When renowned quantum physicist Richard Feynman received his Nobel Prize, he said: "Getting the Nobel is a pain in the rear. I do physics not for the glory of the awards and prizes. But for the fun of it. For the sheer pleasure of finding out how the world works, what makes it tick" (1999). Can we use the f-word in a professional book? Feynman did physics for F-U-N! For finding out and for the joy of it. Fun needs to be at the heart of teaching and learning. We really won't learn, understand, and remember much if we aren't having some fun as we go. Feynman talked about his "puzzle drive," that compulsion to find out about the world, to ask questions and hunt for answers. We share our "puzzle drive" with kids to help them surface their own.

Teachers in classrooms that nurture curiosity create an irresistible urge to wonder. We set up an environment that disposes our kids to curiosity. You can't help but wonder in a room that is filled to bursting with great text, stirring images, unusual artifacts, globes, maps, animals, and magnifying glasses—not to mention a crew of friendly, fascinating classmates.

When kids live in this kind of climate, they are not only eager to come to school each day, but they may find it a little harder to get on the bus in the afternoon.

Teachers in classrooms that nurture curiosity create an irresistible urge to wonder.

10. Help Kids Take Action

Maybe you saw the news reports about Brittany Bergquist, a thirteen-year-old student who created an organization called Cell Phones for Soldiers. It all began when Brittany was studying ancient history in school. Not the ever-popular ancient Egypt, awash with images of slimy brains dripping out of mummy noses, mind you, but rather ancient Mesopotamia, which can be watching-grass-grow dull for your average seventh grader. Brittany's thoughtful teacher, however, was dedicated to making ancient history relevant, so she explained that what was once Mesopotamia is now Iraq and Iran. She assigned newspaper reading as nightly homework, asking kids to bring in articles that pertained to contemporary issues in that region.

As Brittany perused the paper one night, she found an article about a young American soldier who, upon his return from a year in Iraq, was greeted with a huge cell phone bill for calls he had made from Iraq to family and friends back home. Outraged, Brittany decided to act. She enlisted the support of classmates and her teacher and organized a bake sale to pay his cell phone bill. The media got wind of this, publicized it, and suddenly, miracle of miracles, the phone company erased the bill!

But Brittany didn't stop there. What about other soldiers across the country who might face the same shock upon their return to the States, she wondered. Through research and action, she and some classmates discovered a green non-profit organization that offered five dollars to individuals who recycled their old cell phones. So Brittany and her friends began a cell phone drive, collecting old cell phones and turning them in for cash to pay the phone bills of soldiers. The media picked up on this and soon the cell phone company took up the cause as her partner. A group called Cell Phones for Soldiers was born, and money was raised for soldiers in Iraq and Afghanistan to receive free minutes to call home.

This is a terrific story of an amazingly impressive young teen, her thoughtful teacher, and a team of kids who took action—an exemplary model of actively using knowledge and applying it to something that matters. The organization Brittany and her class created is still vigorously operating today at www.cellphonesforsoldiers.com.

You might be saying, let's get real! How often does this happen? How many kids, no matter how admirable, start something like Cell Phones for Soldiers? How many of us adults, for that matter? The truth is, we believe many more kids *would* take action based on their learning if we were modeling our own curiosity and teaching them to actively use knowledge every day in school—if we were teaching them to work together and think about big ideas and ask questions from the first day of kindergarten.

Kids investigating global warming show how some people turn their back on the problem.

6

Surfing and Searching: Internet Research in School

We adults often nervously joke that young people can run rings (or nings) around us technologically. Well, it's no joke—or exaggeration. Today's students operate fluidly in a digital universe where we teachers, at least us senior ones, aren't quite at home. These kids arrive in our classrooms as the most experienced researchers we have ever taught; they've long since learned how to find information fast, defeat protection schemes where necessary, and put information to work. We may not love the world they are digging around in, and we may doubt their ability to evaluate what they find, but there is no denying that these kids are veteran researchers. Come to think of it, today's students are also the most experienced authors—whoops, we mean content creators—we have ever taught. They are not just consumers of the Internet; through blogs, websites, wikis, emails, and social networking sites, they are creating it every day, leaving their tracks throughout the digital world. And these kids are just starting their lifelong cyber-journey. As technology guru Will Richardson predicts:

> "Our students must be nomadic, flexible, mobile learners who depend not so much on what they can recall as on their ability to connect with people and resources and edit content on their desktops, or even more likely, on pocket sized devices they carry around with them. Our teachers have to be co-learners in this process, modeling their own use of connections and networks and understanding the practical, pedagogical implications of these technologies. (Richardson 2008)

When we initiate inquiry circles, our kids will depend upon the Internet for all kinds of information. The Web is the go-to tool for answers, images, and interaction. But even as online resources expand exponentially, making us info-seekers drool over the possibilities, the complications, confusions, and uncertainties of Internet research also seem to be multiplying daily. To sort all this out, with a special eye on small-group research, we've asked our colleague Andrew Hess, technology whiz for the Mamaroneck Public Schools in New York, to create a guide for all of us who are surfing and searching with kids.

Student Inquiry and Collaboration in a Networked, Digital World

—CONTRIBUTED BY ANDREW HESS, MAMARONECK SCHOOLS, NEW YORK

In your own life, you know how the Web has transformed the way you access information and communicate with others. Your computer (maybe even your cell phone) has become your mailbox, encyclopedia, newspaper, and perhaps your radio, telephone, photo album, movie theater, or conference room. You email friends for information, check the day's news, and look up a fact in Wikipedia. You may offer advice and stories on message boards, share vacation photos and videos on an image-sharing website. You might even talk "face to face" with friends and family around the world, participate in virtual worlds like Second Life, or craft a video that you upload onto YouTube.

While much of the Web has become part of your life, you may still feel like an outsider in this ever-changing and evolving digital world, a "digital immigrant" struggling to keep up with the new media. Our students, however, are "digital natives," growing up immersed in this sea of digital, multimedia, networked information (let's just call it "the Web"). They expect to be able to use these tools.

Regardless of whether you are immigrant or native, there's no denying that online media and all of its related tools (e.g., digital cameras, cell phones, editing software) are fertile ground for inquiry and collaboration. When kids do searches in Google or Wikipedia, they are engaging in authentic inquiry, finding information that satisfies their curiosity. When they IM a friend, post to a blog, send a video with their cell phone, read a tweet, or participate in a virtual world, they are taking part in communities that span the world.

As promising as these new electronic media are for inquiry and collaboration, they have also raised legitimate and thorny issues about how much access students should have in school: Should cell phones be allowed? Should the school filter blogs? YouTube? Email? Are online resources distracting entertainment or valuable research tools? We can ask kids to leave their media tools at the door, but by doing so we risk making schools less relevant for them as a place of learning. Our challenge is to make student inquiry and collaboration *within* the classroom as compelling, dynamic, purposeful, and authentic as it often is *outside* the classroom. To do that we need to provide the technology supports—the infrastructure, hardware, and software—and teach the necessary technical skills. We need to offer the instructional support to connect technology use to student learning goals. And we need to teach both the traditional and the emerging information literacy skills that will enable our students to be thoughtful consumers and effective producers in this online multimedia landscape.

What does it look like when the technology, instructional support, and literacy skills are brought together to support student inquiry and collaboration?

Let's look at two examples here—a second-grade class of weather researchers and a senior class delving into the 2008 presidential election process. Afterward, we'll consider what it might look like across the grades.

INQUIRY: *Second-Grade Meteorologists*

PRIMARY

—CHATSWORTH AVENUE FACULTY, CHATSWORTH AVENUE SCHOOL, MAMARONECK, NEW YORK

When Chatsworth Avenue School second grade here in Mamaroneck began planning for a weather unit, the teachers wanted to provide the resources and opportunities for each student in the class to "become a specialist" in a particular kind of weather, such as clouds, hail, tornadoes, and hurricanes. Many of the teachers had taken district workshops on technology integration and so already had some ideas on how to bring online resources into the unit. Long before the unit was due to begin, the teachers started planning with the technology coach and the computer TA. Together, they collected a library of preselected websites, galleries of weather photos, and *Unitedstreaming* video clips. The coach set up a website with these resources and a simple how-to sheet so that students could access the site at school and at home.

Students balance web sources with traditional texts to triangulate and validate information.

Since the classrooms did not have equipment to share all these resources with the whole class, the teachers booked extra time in the computer lab and the library, which had projectors and large screens. The computer TA set up the computer lab with dual headphones, so that students could listen in pairs to the videos, a great way for them to debrief with each other as needed.

The websites, image galleries, and videos provided a rich library of information, which made it easy for kids to follow their curiosity and wonder. The vivid images provided by the photo and video galleries made the weather phenomena real for the kids in a way that would otherwise have been hard for them to experience.

Access to information was important, but the classes also needed to learn how to manage this information. To help kids navigate and read these sites, the coach taught mini-lessons: one on navigating websites, and another on using the students' understanding of nonfiction text features to analyze the features of web-sites, discovering similarities as well as unique elements such as links, animated images, and banner ads. The students viewed the photo and video galleries, searched Web pages for answers to crosswords, took notes, and brainstormed questions. They kept track of questions they had answered, new questions that were raised, and questions that persisted. The coach contacted a local meteorologist, who agreed to email the classes and answer the questions that the students couldn't find answers to (e.g., "Why don't you ever get hurricanes and tornadoes at the same time?" Answer: "Often, hurricanes do spawn tornadoes."). It's worth noting that, although the whole grade was involved in the planning for the unit, teachers tailored the scope of the work to the needs of each class.

Finally, students selected compelling images, wrote about different aspects of their chosen weather element, and created a set of nonfiction picture books. Students then published their picture books; some classes published hard copies, while other classes also put them on the class website and encouraged families and other classes to email responses.

INQUIRY: *Presidential Debates*

HIGH SCHOOL

—ELIZABETH CLAIN & CAREN LEE, MAMARONECK HIGH SCHOOL, MAMARONECK, NEW YORK

The presidential election that captured the attention of the country in the fall of 2008 also opened the opportunity for a compelling social studies project. The challenge for the students: to develop a deep understanding of the issues at the heart of the election and the positions of each of the candidates. Elizabeth Clain, chair of the high school social studies department, and her colleague, Caren Lee, built students' interest and background knowledge in their government classes by offering a timely choice for summer reading: either Barack Obama's *Audacity of Hope* or John McCain's memoir (written with Mark Salter), *Faith of My Fathers*.

Elizabeth and Caren also encouraged students to follow the campaigns over the summer by watching the Democratic and Republican nominating conventions and following media coverage. Students were steered to the *New York Times*, CNN, National Public Radio, and the *Wall Street Journal*. Over the summer, they were asked to print or clip at least four articles about the election that they found interesting; they were also encouraged to clip articles that were confusing, so misconceptions could be clarified in subsequent class discussions.

In September, the government students argued the merits of the presidential candidates and their memoirs with passion and specificity in literature circle discussions of the candidates' books. Throughout the fall, Elizabeth noted with delight several indicators of students' mounting and genuine interest in the upcoming election. Many students opted to read *both* candidates' memoirs, citing a need to understand rival positions. A sizable throng of students showed up at school on a

Friday night with pizza, popcorn, and cupcakes to watch the final Obama/McCain debate together.

Finally, to maximize students' involvement in the election, Elizabeth and her colleagues in the department scheduled student debates, to be held in schoolwide assemblies. Four teams (two for each candidate) were created. Each team had a campaign manager, and a staff who researched and prepped the candidates. To research the issues and the candidates' positions, the teams read articles online and scoured the candidates' websites. To develop their debate skills, they watched debate footage online. The teams met regularly with faculty to deepen their understanding of the issues, refine their arguments, and develop their presentation skills.

As the project developed, so did the students' excitement and commitment. As the debates neared, the students' efforts broadened into a more all-encompassing campaign experience; the teams prepared posters and posted them around the school. They also studied the features of political ads and produced their own ads for each candidate. The school's video teacher saw the students' devotion to this project and began documenting the work, ultimately producing a short documentary video that was aired at the school debates, then again later at a teachers' conference day and on the local cable TV station.

The students, several of whom were approaching voting age, keenly felt the relevance and purpose of the project. As Elizabeth put it, "The kids took it and ran with it. We provided the framework, a debate presented to the whole school. The kids showed tremendous initiative and dedication, arguing strongly for what in some cases went against their personal beliefs."

The heart of this project was developing a rich understanding of the issues and positions surrounding the election. At each step technology and online resources supported this goal by providing access to information and opportunities for student expression. Elizabeth felt that the ability to share the latest media offerings with her class as part of their research (the district technology coordinator helped her access speeches and download YouTube videos) made the project incredibly topical and relevant for her students. She also felt that the commercials and short documentary set the stage at the assemblies, communicating to the school as a whole the importance of the project and of the students' work.

Whether in a classroom of primary or senior students, technology offers several key benefits for student inquiry. Online resources provide the easiest access to a wealth of information that enables students to learn about compelling and relevant issues in their lives. Digital information is both multimedia and hyperlinked, creating a rich web of information, ideas, and documentation. Online tools also support communication with others, offering opportunities for collaboration both within the classroom and worldwide. And finally, digital multimedia tools enable students to craft powerful work—authentic messages that can be shared with real audiences.

> *O*nline resources provide the easiest access to a wealth of information that enables students to learn about compelling and relevant issues in their lives.

All of these classes used the Web and online media in several ways, from the initial immersion to the final publishing of their work. How you incorporate online media into your class may be low-tech and limited to one activity, or be technologically sophisticated and woven throughout the unit. Your considerations will include your access to technology, your support network, your own technology comfort level, the content area, the time frame for the unit, and your grade level. At the heart of these considerations, of course, are the content-area and information literacy learning goals for your students.

Research and Electronic Information Literacy

What are the important information literacy skills your students need when using online resources? Researching online involves the same information literacy skills students have always needed. They need to reflect on their questions, research options, and project needs. They must access and manage useful information. They need to synthesize that information and develop their own ideas. Big 6 and Super 3 (both at www.big6.com) offer good frameworks for these research skills.

But using electronic information effectively shifts the emphasis to certain literacy skills, particularly skills that involve collaboration and the thoughtful use of information. Ask yourself these key questions about your students' ability to use electronic information:

- Can my students understand information that comes from a variety of media?
- Can they use new information technologies thoughtfully and ethically?
- Can they collaborate in their learning?
- Can they communicate and share their ideas through a variety of media?
- Can they participate authentically in real-world issues?

Two organizations have outlined standards to guide thoughtful and effective use of electronic information: the American Association of School Librarians' *Standards for the 21st-Century Learner* (http://www.ala.org), and the International Society for Technology in Education's *National Educational Technology Standards* (http://www.iste.org).

In order to teach these skills to your students, you must first provide them with access to information in a way that is appropriate to their grade level.

Access to Information

To pursue online inquiry into their chosen topic, students need access to rich, appropriate information. This is one of the great benefits as well as great challenges of the Web. On the Web, the world is your students' oyster. But this wealth of information also threatens to send your students swimming in an ocean of information they can't manage. Your students need support and skills in order to navigate the waters.

Searching the Web risks exposing kids to inappropriate images, sites they can't understand, and frustration as they try in vain to learn about their topic. Providing younger kids with preselected websites and media ensures that they can make choices within a manageable collection of information. Students in higher grades can learn more advanced search skills—they can select from a larger collection of sites, learn basic keyword search skills while searching within particular sites, and, ultimately, learn how to conduct full-on searches using search engines. For some safe and supportive websites, see the website.

www.heinemann.com/
comprehensionandcollaboration.

Evaluating Information

Finding information means little if students cannot evaluate the usefulness of the information. The Chatsworth students learned how to find appropriate information by scanning sites for answers to questions and by discussing which site, or where within a particular site, they might find the answers to their questions.

See Lesson 23, "Checking Our Sources," p. 138.

Evaluating information for higher grades involves drawing on multiple and multigenre sources. Students need to determine how appropriate a particular site is to their task and how divergent information among sites can be reconciled. Here are three key questions for consideration. At the end of each consideration are two sites that kids might compare.

- Is this source **accurate** and **authoritative?**

  Do you recognize the source? Do other, trusted sites refer to it? Does the information make sense to you? Can you verify the information from other sources? What does the URL tell you? (If you are not sure, you can use online tools, such as www.alexa.com *and* www.easywhois.com, *to check the site's authorship.)*

  Compare: www.wto.org *and* www.gatt.org

- Is it **up to date?**

  Timeliness will matter in differing degrees for different topics. Look at the bottom of the site. Is the site dated? If so, is it current?

  Compare: www.cnn.com *and* http://cmp.ucsf.edu/

- *Can I identify bias in this source?*

  Sites are rarely completely neutral. Who is the author? What is their stake in the information? Is the subject controversial? Can you identify the purpose of the site—is it informational, editorial, satirical? Does the purpose of this source match the purpose of your project?

Compare: www.thekingcenter.org *and* www.martinlutherking.org
(*A word of caution:* shockingly, www.martinlutherking.org is a hate site with disturbing language and imagery, definitely not for the young ones.)

Many sites—some created especially as case studies for site evaluation, some serious, others not so serious—offer great opportunities for honing your students' evaluation skills. Try your hand at evaluating the sites below:

- Dihydrogen Monoxide Research Division (www.dhmo.org)
- The Official City—Mankato, Minnesota, Home Page (http://descy.50megs.com/Emankato/mankato.html)
- The Pacific Northwest tree octopus (http://zapatopi.net/treeoctopus/)
- Ladies against Women (www.ladiesagainstwomen.com/index.html)
- RYT Hospital (www.rythospital.com/2008/)
- dehydrated water (buydehydratedwater.com)
- Pets or Food (http://petsorfood.com)

A great resource—for you and your students—for learning how to evaluate sites is the University of California at Berkeley Library's Finding Information on the Internet: A Tutorial (http://lib.berkeley.edu/TeachingLib/Guides/Internet/FindInfo.html).

Finally, to help kids evaluate the authenticity of sites, just google "fake web sites" and choose from a number that pop up. One or our favorites is Phil Bradley's site http://philb.com/fakesites.htm which gives multiple examples of fake sites to aid students in evaluating internet resources.

Access to Communication

We've been considering the opportunities for online information access, but the opportunity to communicate online with people beyond the walls of your classroom is also a major benefit of the Web. Your school website and email are great ways to reach your school community. Primary grade kids can cocreate and send whole class emails. Higher grades can email in small groups or individually.

Email is not the only way to communicate electronically, of course. Video-conferencing is easier than ever with programs like Skype (www.skype.com). Several elementary classes in our district have had Skype videoconferences with other students in the district and, in one case, discussed their Africa research projects with an expert in South Africa.

So how do you find partners for collaboration? Many of the contacts we've found for classes in our district have come from friends and colleagues. If you don't know offhand of people your class can collaborate with, whether it's another class in your district, a class in a far-off country, your community, or a specialist in a subject area, there are several strategies for making contact. Mine your school's staff first. Sometimes the most knowledgeable people are right down the hall. Parents are also a wonderful resource for expertise. Contact museums and universities. Put out requests on discussion boards or email lists. There are also several sites especially for connecting your class with classes around the world (e.g., www.epals.com; www.iearn.org).

Technical Considerations

For students who are researching online, it makes sense to write and organize their work on the computer as well. The Chatsworth second grade weather researchers weren't quite ready for full-on computing, so the teacher modeled it as they worked together to write their whole-class email messages. As students begin to use the computer for more tasks, they will need basic skills in keyboarding, word processing, and file management in order to reliably save and manage their work. This is a mundane but critical consideration; you don't want your students to go through the heartbreak of misplacing or accidentally erasing weeks of work.

Once they have these basic skills, older students can take notes electronically, copying and pasting URLs and selections from websites into a document. If they

are working with multimedia, they need strategies for keeping track of this information. They can save images into a personal photo gallery and keep an electronic bibliography of where they found the information. This bibliography can provide a crucial check for accuracy when needed.

Another consideration is whether your students have the resources and technical skills they need to produce their work. Can they create a background image or pullquote for their magazine article? Can they insert an image into their Word document, PowerPoint slide show, or Web page? Can they create a hyperlink? Can they edit audio for their podcast or video for their documentary?

It is important to consider when to introduce new technical skills, since rushing to finish their projects at the same time that they are learning new technical skills can be overwhelming for students. One strategy for avoiding this scenario is to build students' technical skills gradually over the course of the year. For example, in the beginning of the year students can produce short videos using images, title slides, and narration. Later they can learn how to select clips from videos. And by the end of the year students can shoot their own footage and make thoughtful decisions about which of these options belong in their videos.

Also keep in mind that there are both low- and high-tech options for your students' work. For example, if kids are creating an oral presentation, they can print images and paste them onto poster board; compile a PowerPoint slide show to present orally or with recorded narration; or create a video of images, titles, and narration (perhaps even with music and sound effects). In short, the choice of medium should support, not interfere with, your students' message.

Finally, remember that students don't necessarily have to be responsible for all of the technical work. When a kindergarten class here wanted to produce a *Magic School Bus* video on sharks, the computer TA and coach were responsible for filming, editing, and uploading the video to the class website. The class learned the necessary genre conventions by viewing *Magic School Bus* videos. They learned how to storyboard their video. They made decisions on the angles and movement for shots so the cameraperson could get the shot they wanted. And, finally, they previewed the video during the editing process and, with the technology coach at the keyboard, made decisions about the order of video clips, transition styles, titles and credits, and so on. And these kids were only kindergartners. Oh, to be a student in the twenty-first century! When we remove the complex, technical challenge, kids' productions soar.

Internet Responsibility and Safety

As mentioned, copying and pasting is a great way to work with electronic information, but it raises legitimate concerns about plagiarism. It is easier than ever for students to copy and paste images and blocks of text into their work. Citing sources and respecting intellectual property are basic elements of responsible online use. How to address issues around intellectual property will vary for different grade levels. The focus in lower grades can be on becoming aware of where they are finding information and on the importance of giving credit for other people's work. Many students are surprised that this is true not just for text, but also for images and other media. For great lessons on attribution for secondary students, see Barry Gilmore's *Plagiarism: A How-Not-to Guide for Students* (2009).

Older students can learn more advanced skills, such as using proper citation formats and understanding copyright. Creative Commons (www.creativecommons. org), discusses a range of rights management for creative work, offers a provocative opportunity for students to consider the social and ethical issues around information use. Flickr (www.flickr.com), a photo-hosting site, is one of many sites that use Creative Commons.

Another critical issue is safety. If you expect your students to be online, you need to help them use it safely. How to protect them can be a daunting task; there is a lot of media hyperbole on the dangers of the Internet, but there *are* some real dangers. Also, with the Web changing so rapidly, it's hard to know how to prepare your students for what they will encounter online. However, some basic understandings and decision-making skills will help them respond appropriately to whatever comes along. These skills are not so different from those we teach kids about face-to-face encounters. They include protecting their privacy, avoiding online predators, avoiding inappropriate sites, giving credit for others' work, treating people with respect online (for example, avoiding cyberbullying), and, most important, communicating with a trusted adult about their online experiences.

This is an area where you can look for support in your school. In our district, computer TAs, the technology coordinator, and the technology coach all have regular discussions on responsible Internet use and Internet safety with classes from elementary school on. NetSmartz (www.netsmartz.org) is a good resource to learn more about Internet safety and responsibility.

One caveat. We recognize that in this era of tight budgets and limited resources, some schools and districts have been forced to eliminate technology specialists altogether. If you're in a school that just lost funding for the tech specialist (or didn't have one in the first place), never fear. Your school is likely to be filled with a lot of tech-savvy folks, both adults and kids. So make friends with those techies. You can learn a lot from them.

Twenty-first Century Learning Tools for Real Outcomes and Audiences

Ultimately, your students' inquiry circles will lead to some sort of outcome. If their inquiries address an authentic issue and are directed at a real audience, then the format of their work is an important consideration. What outcomes will best demonstrate their learning and understanding? Should they write a brochure or newsletter? Make a photo exhibit? Publish on a website or blog? Give an oral presentation? Produce a public service announcement or radio or TV broadcast? Often the end result comes from the inquiry itself: for example, a public service announcement about the dangers of malaria and ways to deal with it, a blog to discuss current political issues. Fortunately, your students likely have both online access and a host of media tools available, which gives them a wide choice of online multimedia products to demonstrate and share their newfound knowledge.

Blogs

The possibilities for the kinds of online work that students can produce are vast. New online tools offer expanded possibilities for student projects and also create new opportunities for collaboration. For example, because blogs (such as http://www.edublogs.org) make it easy to publish articles as well as post comments on the articles, the nature of the writing changes; instead of a finished work it becomes an ongoing dialogue between writer and reader. The distinction between researching, synthesizing ideas, and publishing becomes blurred as the students' published work continues to be food for further understanding and further investigation. What might have been "printed and handed in" is now simply the latest version, open to further comments and revisions by project participants and readers.

Blogs also make it easy for teachers to manage student work. Their user-friendly interface makes it simple for you and your students to put words, voice, and images online. Built-in blog tools such as tags, search bars, and archives organize the work for you. And especially important, blogs have built-in security. You can moderate student writing, set limits on who views your students' work, and filter outside comments (see http://weblogg-ed.com for more on blogs).

Podcasts and Videos

Blogs are not the only online media tool that creates new ways to share student work. Students may not have access to a radio station but, if they have access to the Web, they can publish their own podcasts. Video-hosting sites, like YouTube, make it easy for students to produce and share their video projects. Because of concerns that students might access inappropriate videos on YouTube, other video-hosting sites have sprung up to ensure that students can access videos within a safe environment (http://www.teachertube.com, http://edublogs.tv).

Social Networking

A recent National School Boards Association survey found that 80% of young people who are online are networking (2007). Social web technologies have emerged as yet another way for kids to communicate and share content. Networking sites for every age group and interest connect people all over the world—teenagers on Facebook and My Space, younger kids on parent approved, teacher endorsed sites such as Imbee www.imbee.com and Whyville www.whyville.net. A recent visit to Imbee, a networking site where kids blog, trade cards, share photos and information about themselves showed kids blogging about a national science challenge and supporting a Toys for Tots online event. Whyville is an online virtual world where kids must manage money, eat properly, and learn to communicate effectively. Both sites educate kids about online safety and connect them with other kids through chatting, playing, and learning together.

Virtual Field Trips

In this world of decreased school funding and shrinking educational budgets, onsite field trips are sadly on the wane. However, virtual field trips are quickly filling the void. They allow teachers to bring the world right into school without ever leaving the classroom. With many to choose from, virtual field trips offer one more tool in inquiry based teaching and learning. Rather than a trip to the local zoo, teachers and kids can visit mission control at NASA's Jet propulsion lab http://virtualfieldtrip.jpl.nasa.gov, explore over fifty global destinations at National Geographic Expeditions online www.nationalgeographic.com/xpeditions or tour the many art, history or natural history exhibits at the Virtual Smithsonian www.//2k.si.edu. Just Google *Virtual Field Trips* for an extensive list of possibilities.

Google Earth

Another exciting opportunity for student engagement is provided by Google Earth (http://earth.google.com). In essence a virtual globe of satellite images, Google Earth is a powerful tool for understanding a wide variety of geography-related topics from canyons to stars. Google Sky shows myriad ways to explore the universe. Google Ocean maps the ocean floor. And Google Street View allows panoramic street-level views of spots all around the world. That alone makes Google Earth useful, but because it also includes geographically tagged photos, Wikipedia entries, and other kinds of information, Google Earth becomes a kind of geographical information portal, an encyclopedia of the earth.

Now consider that Google Earth makes it easy to tag locations in Google Earth and save their tags in a file. You can even use Google Earth as a sort of geographic organizer, bookmarking and annotating locations, linking to sites and images, in effect creating an annotated virtual tour of the globe. In this way, students in one fifth-grade class here created Google Earth presentations of their states project. Their tours were both compelling and interactive, enabling them to adapt their presentation to respond to the audience's comments and questions. (For more information on using Google Earth in education, see http://edweb.tusd.k12.az.us/dherring/ge/googleearth.htm.)

Putting It All Together

Regardless of the type of outcome your students choose for their work, they need to understand how to communicate effectively in their chosen format. If they are giving an oral presentation, can they use voice, text, and images persuasively? If they are creating a podcast or a documentary, do they understand the particular genre conventions and can they use them in their own work? In lower grades, it may be enough for students to understand that their work is an authentic product, addressing a real issue, and directed at a real audience. Students in higher grades can begin to make their own decisions about which type of media product is most appropriate for their project, and can reflect on the choices they made in crafting their work.

Key Considerations

Students have never had more access to information, nor have they ever had more possibilities for expressing themselves to an interested public outside the classroom. All of these choices for online research, collaboration, and publication may seem overwhelming, but they needn't be. Your students will drive much of this work. Your job, regardless of your students' topics or grade level, is to keep your eye on several key considerations:

- Learn how inquiry, comprehension, and collaboration can be supported online.
- Seek out technology support in your school so that infrastructure, hardware, software, and technology instructional needs are met.
- Keep the technology focus on student learning goals. Focus on keeping the online work relevant and authentic.
- Teach responsible and safe online practices.
- Scale the technology tasks to match your students' abilities.
- And have some FUN!!

Key Lessons in Comprehension, Collaboration, and Inquiry

Our many years of working side by side with students has totally convinced us that kids want to know. High school seniors and kindergartners and all the young people in between want to find out what's going on and how it affects them. Though the bigger kids may conceal it with coolness, they are burning to learn about the world, particularly when they have some choice in the matter. With inquiry circles, we unleash that urgent need-to-know. But also, kids need structures within which to wonder, explore, and share.

Teachers ask us again and again, How do you get kids to follow their questions and read to find out information? How do you help them sustain their interest? How do you get them to work together collaboratively? How do they stay on top of their research? This chapter outlines the specific lessons we teach in comprehension, collaboration, and inquiry. It follows the instructional approach called the Gradual Release of Responsibility, which scaffolds kids with modeling and guided practice as they move to independence. In a few pages, we will offer twenty-seven practical lessons that help kids become thoughtful, independent readers, thinkers, communicators, and researchers. But first, let's talk about why modeling and practice matter so much.

The Importance of Models

When Steph's son Alex was twelve years old, he auditioned for and landed the role of one of the young princes in Shakespeare's *Richard III*, a momentous event for a young lad who at six years old climbed to the top of the schoolyard slide, pulled his plastic sword from its scabbard, and called out triumphantly, "We few, we happy few"—the immortal lines from *Henry V*.

One problem with landing a role in an adult play revealed itself quickly when Steph learned that rehearsals would take place nightly at 6:00 p.m.—sometimes lasting until midnight. The thought of this sixth-grade boy rehearsing night after night concerned Steph, and she began to reconsider. But when he locked himself in his room and refused to come out, she acquiesced. She did, however, extract a promise from Alex: when he was not on stage rehearsing his scenes, he would do his math homework faithfully every night. And as far as she knew, he complied.

Rehearsals lasted about four weeks and the play itself another five, about the same span as the first quarter of school. At parent conferences, no one was more stunned than Steph when the D in math jumped off the report card. Later when she confronted Alex, he shrugged and said he would do better next time. "But you promised to do your homework every night when you were not on stage rehearsing your scenes," Steph exclaimed.

"I was busy," Alex responded.

"Hello??!!! You were busy!! How could you possibly be busy when other people were up on stage rehearsing their scenes? That's when you were supposed to be busy all right, busy with *homework!*"

"I had to watch them," Alex answered.

"What are you talking about?" Steph asked.

"I learn more from watching really good actors work than I learn from rehearsing my own scenes!" Alex implored.

And even though he nearly flunked sixth-grade math that quarter, Steph begrudgingly had to admit he made sense. We learn by watching and doing. Watching talented, knowledgeable, experienced people ply their craft and share the process behind it and then practicing ourselves is the key to learning and understanding. But way too often in conventional schooling, we tell kids what to do without *showing* them how and giving them time to practice.

*W*atching talented, knowledgeable, experienced people ply their craft and share the process behind it and then practicing ourselves is the key to learning and understanding.

*M*odeling Our Own Thinking

Imagine learning to dance when the dancers around you are all invisible. Imagine learning a sport when the players who already know the game can't be seen. Bizarre as this may sound, something close to it happens all the time in one very important area of learning: learning to think. Thinking is pretty much invisible. To be sure sometimes people explain the thought behind a particular conclusion, but often they do not. Mostly thinking happens under the hood with the marvelous engine of our mindbrain. (Perkins 2003, p. 1)

Harvard professor David Perkins is right. Thinking does not reveal itself front and center. It lurks offstage, behind the curtain. It is the job of all teachers to raise that curtain and make our thinking visible and concrete for the eager audience of students that sits before us each day.

So just like Alex watching master actors work their scenes, we ask our students to watch us as we make our thinking visible for them, sharing our questions, our inferences, our reactions, our curiosity, our process of inquiry. This works in all subject areas. Kids need to see how historians look at documents, how scientists draw conclusions, or how mathematicians approach difficult problems. So we model that familiar repertoire of thinking strategies—activating background knowledge, making connections, asking questions, inferring, visualizing, determining importance, and synthesizing information—to let kids see what's happening in our "mindbrain." We also model the social strategies thinkers use to communicate and learn from each other. And we model the inquiry strategies and processes we employ to find information.

In real estate, the mantra is *location, location, location.* In teaching it is *model, model, model.* When we open up our heads and make our thinking process visible, students have a better shot at understanding, remembering, and actively using knowledge. Modeling our thinking and sharing our thought process is central to the instruction in this book. In all cases, whether we are teaching a comprehension strategy, a social skill, or an inquiry technique, we model how the process happens for us and we give students time to practice what they have seen us do.

*T*he Gradual Release of Responsibility

The teaching and learning in this book is framed around the instructional approach known as the Gradual Release of Responsibility (Pearson and Gallagher 1983). We provide explicit instruction through modeling and guided practice, and then invite students to try it on their own during collaborative and independent practice.

To get a better handle on how the gradual release approach works, let's take a look at a sports example. Steph plays a little tennis, so imagine a tennis lesson for a moment. She wants to learn how to serve a tennis ball. The first thing the pro does is watch her serve to assess her needs. As she hits three serves hard into the bottom of the net, he agrees that she could use a serving lesson! So he shows her how to serve a tennis ball by serving the ball himself several times. As he serves, he explains two or three processes that help him serve—throwing the ball up, stepping into it, and following through. This is the *modeling phase.* Once he has modeled how he serves, he asks her to give it a shot as he stands closely by. He may hold her arm as she swings through to give her an idea of what the follow-through should feel like. This is the *guided practice phase.* After she has tried a few serves with him, he leaves her to practice on her own for a few minutes—the *independent practice phase.* Or he might suggest she practice with a partner who plays at about the same level—the *collaborative practice phase.* When he returns, he watches her again. He sees that she is getting only about 50 percent of her serves in and notices that she needs to throw the ball up a little higher to improve the serve. So he steps in to model again, but this time he asks her to simply watch how high he is throwing the ball since that is what she needs to work on (more *modeling*). After modeling himself he joins her and literally serves the ball with her, by throwing up the ball as she swings through (*guided practice*). He leaves

The Gradual Release of Responsibility

TEACHER MODELING

- Teacher explains strategy.
- Teacher models strategy.
- Teacher thinks aloud to show thinking and strategy use.

GUIDED PRACTICE

- After explicit modeling, teacher gradually gives students more responsibility for task engagement and completion.
- Teacher and students practice the strategy together in shared contexts, interacting, and constructing meaning through interchange.

COLLABORATIVE PRACTICE

- Students share their thinking process with one another.
- Students work in small groups and pairs and reason through text together.
- Teacher moves from group to group, checking on how things are going.

INDEPENDENT PRACTICE

- After working with teacher and other students, students try practicing the strategy on their own.
- Student receives regular feedback from teacher and other students.

APPLICATION OF THE STRATEGY

- The student uses the strategy in authentic situations.
- The student uses the strategy in a variety of different genres, settings, contexts, and disciplines.

(From Fielding and Pearson 1994. Adapted by Harvey and Goudvis 2005)

her to practice again and this time she gets a greater percentage of serves in (*independent practice*). The next time he returns and watches her, he decides not to model, but instead heads to the opposite side of the court to volley with her. He doesn't try to rip the ball past her backhand when she serves to him; he keeps the ball in play. This is still *guided practice*, but it is not as closely guided as when he is literally serving the ball with her.

When they finish volleying together, the pro suggests that Steph play a game with the person on the next court—*application*. Getting into a game is always important, but just being in the game does not guarantee proficiency. When playing the game, we attempt to apply what we know and continue practicing. The next time the pro checks in with Steph, he notices that she keeps serving to her opponent's powerful forehand, so he shows her how to put a little spin on the ball when she serves so that she can move the ball around the court, *modeling* again. So gradual release is not a linear progression. It is a responsive, recursive, dynamic process that allows us to design instruction that meets the needs of the student at the time.

And gradual release does not just cover instruction. We practice gradual release with text selection as well. When we launch a new strategy, we choose the most accessible text available: the easiest book, the friendliest website, the most familiar video. We begin with accessible text so the learner can concentrate on the strategy or process without having to worry about reading that is too hard. And we subscribe to gradual release through the year, giving our kids more independence in both academic and social learning as we build a community of learners and thinkers.

In the past few years, we have come to understand that modeling should be short and sweet. Kids' waving hands, whispered comments, or downright blurt-outs have sent us this message loud and clear. If all we ever did was think out loud about a piece of text or a social skill, kids wouldn't listen for long. So we model for a few moments, just long enough to get our point across, and then we quickly engage the students in guided practice, inviting them to participate as we create meaning together. The guided practice phase is where the Gradual Release of Responsibility is most robust. Teachers scaffold instruction as needed and then slowly remove themselves as appropriate, dipping back in when necessary and then out again. Whether teaching reading strategies, social skills, or research techniques, most of our instructional time is spent in guided practice because that is where we can best support kids as they move toward independence. And independent practice is key. The amount of time kids spend actually doing the work makes all the difference.

*I*ntroducing the Lessons

Recently Steph sat in Brad Buhrow's second-grade classroom and watched a small inquiry circle investigating the history of writing and signatures. They all had been taught to stop, think, and react to their reading, to read, listen, and view with a question in mind, to think about new information, to talk to each other about their topic, to work together, and to do research. Four second graders sprawled on the floor surrounded by books, magazines, paints, and paper worked for nearly an hour, reading, writing, drawing, and making hand prints as examples of first signatures. Completely engaged and focused, they continued uninterrupted while Brad met with other students. But if kids haven't been taught to think when they read or if they have not been taught to work together, things can go south fast! So we build on their natural curiosity and drive, provide them with wonderful text and media, and then explicitly teach them strategies and mini-lessons for reading and understanding, for working together, and for doing research.

The following twenty-seven key lessons in comprehension, collaboration, and inquiry are *generic*, meaning they can apply to many teaching situations and levels. You'll notice we favor the Gradual Release of Responsibility Model throughout. The lessons strike a balance between whole-group modeling, small-group and individual practice with teacher support, and independent investigation and knowledge-building. Still, you'll naturally want to adapt our language and procedures to your students, the content they are tackling, and your own teaching style.

To be sure you can see how these general lessons play out in a wide range of classroom practice, we've provided Lesson Link icons throughout the book. Most of these lessons appear in one form or another in the classroom inquiries we share. In this chapter, you'll find the basic, bare-bones versions of key lessons in comprehension, collaboration, and inquiry. But in the many classroom stories stranded throughout the book, we have flagged spots where teachers have created their own versions of one of these basic lessons. There you will see how these generic lessons can be reshaped to a particular classroom and moment.

These are actually more than lessons. They are really practices and processes that we teach in all grade levels and across the curriculum. We don't model just once how to read with a question in mind and then pray our students remember to do it in chemistry as well as English. We don't teach kids one time only to "disagree agreeably," then clap our hands together and say, "Done with that." All of these lessons can and should be taught over time at every grade level in different subjects, disciplines, and contexts. And once taught, many kids will need to keep practicing what they learned as they participate in inquiry circles.

As you scan these lessons, you will quickly see how easily they can be adapted across grade levels. However, those of you who teach early readers will notice that many of these lessons are best taught to your kindergartners and first graders through listening and viewing. Visual literacy is key in small-group inquiry with young children. In many cases, they will be more comfortable drawing their responses than writing them. And they may need more structure as they begin working together in small groups. For instance, sitting knee to knee and eye to eye as they meet with a partner, taking turns talking in small groups, and keeping their bodies facing forward and turning their heads only as they turn and talk during a whole-class lesson.

If you're a secondary teacher with concerns that some of the lessons appear to be a bit elementary, no worries! Each lesson comes with tips for grade-level adaptations as well as other pertinent suggestions. So if a lesson seems like it was created for younger kids, review the tips section for secondary suggestions. Primary teachers, if a lesson seems too high school for your kids, check out the tips for early-reader adaptations. Above all, we trust you to adapt these lessons, and all instruction in this book for that matter, to the needs and desires of your kids.

Activate and Build Background Knowledge

See this lesson in action on page 171.

➡ **TIP:** Stress learning over knowing! We teach the term misconception even to very young kids and let them know that misconceptions are a natural part of the learning process. Secondary students need to understand this too. Have them jot down their new learning in a notebook and encourage them to share when they learn something new or reverse a misconception.

WHEN *and* **WHY:** Nothing colors our learning more than what we bring to it. We model this lesson at the beginning of the inquiry process so kids remember to think about what they know as they read, listen, and view and thus can connect new information to their background knowledge to better understand it.

INITIATE: Begin by selecting a good read-aloud text on a rich topic. Next, have kids turn and talk to a partner (pair share) about what they think they know about the topic. After rehearsing their thinking in the turn and talk, kids are more comfortable sharing their thinking and may even have cleared up a misconception.

TEACH/MODEL: Before reading the text aloud, create an anchor chart with two columns: What We Think We Know and What We Learned. Then think aloud about what you think you know. When you read on and learn something different, share how great it is to learn something new; then strike through what you thought you knew in the first column and add what you learned in the second column. Invite kids to share what they think they know and you record their thoughts on the chart.

GUIDED PRACTICE: Read on in the text together, clear up misconceptions, strike through the inaccurate information on the left side, and write the new information in the What We Learned column. Teach the term misconception. Stress the importance of learning over knowing, so kids are less likely to freak out about being wrong. In fact, celebrate in a big way when kids reverse a misconception, because it shows that they have learned something new, which is our goal!

WHAT WE THINK WE KNOW	WHAT WE LEARNED
Spiders have 8 legs	
~~Spiders are insects~~	Spiders are not insects
~~All spiders spin webs~~	Some spiders spin webs
Spiders eat flies	Spiders eat other bugs too

INDEPENDENT PRACTICE: Have kids read on for themselves in a nonfiction text at their level. Hand out a think sheet labeled What I Think I Know/What I Learned (see the website), for kids to fill in as they read for information and answer questions, clearing up their misconceptions as they go. As kids work, confer with individuals or small groups. Make sure that young children feel free to represent their thinking by drawing.

Listen to Your Inner Voice

See this lesson in action on page 179.

See this lesson in action on page 179.

→ TIP: For secondary kids, use the same two-column form: What the Text Is About/What It Makes Me Think About. They can jot and write a brief summary of the information in the first column and their thoughts in a bulleted list on the thinking side. Remind primary kids that they can draw their thinking on Post-its if they choose.

WHEN *and* **WHY:** Early in the inquiry process, kids need to be able to monitor their comprehension or they run the risk of simply reading without thinking and missing important information.

INITIATE: Begin by talking to kids about the difference between summarizing or retelling the text and thinking about it. When we retell or summarize, we list the events in order or come up with some bits of important information. We distinguish this from our own thoughts, which might not even include any retelling of the story. For instance, we might read about a child who loves art and connect that to our own love of riding horses. We want kids to be able to do both—understand what the piece is about and also what it makes them think about.

TEACH/MODEL: Share that when learners read, listen, or view, they have an inner conversation with the text. They listen to their inner voice, the voice that says, *I don't get this part* when they are confused, or says *I never knew that before* when they learn something new. Read a piece of text aloud, then stop and share your own inner conversation and jot down what the text makes you think about on Post-it notes or on an overhead transparency of the text. Include connections, questions, inferences, and reactions as you model your inner conversation.

GUIDED PRACTICE: Read on a bit, then stop and invite kids to turn and talk about their inner conversation. Encourage them to jot what the text makes them think about as you continue reading. Create a chart with two columns: What the Text Is About and What It Makes Me Think About and have them put their Post-its on the thinking side. Then discuss what the piece is mostly about, and write the summary on the summary side.

> It's really scary when animals become endangered.

> Are polar bears disappearing because of global warming?

> Reminds me of ice fishing in the winter time, FREEZING!

INDEPENDENT PRACTICE: Have kids jot or draw their thoughts on Post-its as they read, listen, and view during independent work time.

Think and Wonder About Images

See this lesson in action on pages 153, 171, 177, 240.

➡ **TIP:** High school kids need opportunities to infer and question from images too. Google Images is a great source for historic and scientific photos of all kinds. But use caution—some of the images are inappropriate for kids. Large photographic calendars and nonfiction Big Books are a terrific source of images. We often begin a curricular unit by sharing images and having kids interact with them in this way.

WHEN *and* WHY: Paying attention to images is important throughout the inquiry process because as kids are doing research, they can gain a lot of information from images. Visual literacy is key when reading informational text.

INITIATE: Bring in some large, compelling images and have kids turn and talk about what they notice or wonder about these photographs.

TEACH/MODEL: Share a Big Book with elementary kids or find some compelling photographs for older kids. Model how you notice information, make inferences, and ask questions from the photos. For instance, if you see a snake with a diamond-shaped head, you might infer that it is poisonous. You might look at a World War II photo and ask where the soldiers come from. An image of a mosquito may spur a question. Place the Post-it notes with your learnings, questions, and inferences on these images to show how you pay attention to images as you do research. Talk about how much you can learn when you "read" images as well as text.

COLLABORATIVE PRACTICE: Engage kids in the process. Have them get together in small groups. Hand out large images on a topic they are studying or on any topic of interest. Ask them to view the images and then jot their questions and thoughts on Post-its. Then have them share their thoughts in their groups.

> Why does a mosquito bite itch?

> How did WWII start anyway?

> I think it must be poisonous.
> head

INDEPENDENT PRACTICE: As they read independently, remind kids to pay attention to photographs and illustrations and jot down what the images make them think or wonder about, or what they can learn from the images.

Use Text and Visual Features to Gain Information

See this lesson in action on page 245.

See this lesson in action on page 245.

TIP: With younger kids and English language learners, the Feature/Purpose anchor chart should include visual representations of the features, so if you write map in the feature column, you should draw or place an actual map next to the word. With older kids, focus more of your time interpreting features and analyzing them. The point of this lesson is to get kids to pay attention to and learn from text and visual features.

WHEN *and* WHY: At all stages of inquiry projects we want kids to think about and learn from the text and visual features as they research their questions and read for information.

INITIATE: Explain that nonfiction has two distinct types of features—visual and text—and that we need to pay attention to both types when reading. Choose a range of different readings texts with both visual and text features—nonfiction trade books, magazines, newspapers, and so on. Make sure these include a variety of both visual features, like maps, graphs, and charts, and text features such as bold print, subheads, and titles.

TEACH/MODEL: Flip through the texts and point out which features are visual and which ones are text. Turn to a page and model how you make sense of a graph, distribution map, chart, or other visual feature. Point out a text feature such as a subhead, title, or bold print. Create a Feature/Purpose anchor chart. Think aloud about the purpose of a feature; then write the feature in the left-hand column and the purpose in the right-hand column.

FEATURE	PURPOSE
Photograph	To show something
Caption	To tell about the photo
Label	To name something
Graph	To compare amounts

GUIDED PRACTICE: Hand out some nonfiction texts on a wide range of topics and at a variety of levels; encourage kids to go through them and find a feature. Ask them to turn and talk to a partner about the purpose of each feature and then have them share their features and purposes with the class as you record their responses on the Feature/Purpose anchor chart.

COLLABORATIVE PRACTICE: Pass out a two-column Feature/Purpose graphic organizer. (See the website for this resource.) As the kids read in their inquiry circle, have them jot down the features and their purposes. At the end of the period, invite them to share these elements, their purposes, and most importantly, what they learned from the features.

COMPREHENSION LESSON

Annotate Text: *Leave Tracks of Thinking*

See this lesson in action on pages 149, 179, 183, 209.

➡ **TIP:** When working with library books or textbooks that cannot be marked up, kids use Post-its instead of writing in the margins. Post-its are especially handy for our earliest readers, since they can also draw their thoughts. The 3x5 size works very well for the youngest kids. We teach older students to use the whole range of text-marking tools—Post-its, codes, underlining, and annotation—so they can really "attack" the surface of texts and dig out meaning.

WHEN *and* WHY: As kids do research and read for information, they need to leave tracks of their thinking so they can learn, understand, and remember what they read.

INITIATE: Annotation is a powerful reading tool. Explain that we need to make our reading "thinking intensive" and interact with the text while we read by jotting our thinking. Share an analogy. Talk about the tracks animals leave in the snow after a storm. When we wake up in the morning after a snowfall, we can tell who has been there from the fresh tracks, even though the animal is long gone. Explain that we need to see the kids' thinking even if they are no longer reading. Readers need to leave tracks in the margins, just as animals do in the snow or on the beach.

TEACH/MODEL: Explain that *annotating* means writing down your ideas as you read. Tell them, "Nothing matters more than your thinking when you read." Let kids know that instead of highlighting, you are going to jot your thoughts because when readers do that, they remember why they wrote something and are better able to understand. Mention that tracks like these give readers a place to hold their thinking. At the overhead projector, think aloud through a piece of text and jot connections, questions, important information, and inferences in the margins. Share some text codes—a ★ for an important information, a **?** for a question, and so forth. Show how you notice when you find an answer or how you might need to research further if your question is not answered.

GUIDED PRACTICE: Engage kids in the process by handing out a copy of the same article you have been modeling with. Read a paragraph, then stop and give students time to jot their thoughts and codes in the margins. Encourage them to turn and talk to a partner and discuss their thinking tracks. Create an anchor chart of various text codes that you come up with together.

TEXT CODES

✓	for something known
L	for new learning
? or Q	for a question
??	for confusion
★	for important information
!	for exciting or surprising information
R	for a connection (Reminds me…)

COLLABORATIVE PRACTICE: Encourage kids to leave tracks of their thinking as they continue to read and respond to articles in their inquiry circles.

Ask Questions and Wonder About Information

See this lesson in action on pages 146, 160, 172, 196, 213, 247.

➡ **TIP:** Our youngest readers can draw their questions and mark them with a **Q** or a **?**. You may have to confer with them to find out what they wondered. You may also want to script what they wonder and read it with them. With older kids, you can conduct your read-aloud using a projected copy of the text, and use marginal notes, rather than Post-its, to flag your questions and later the answers. You can also model two main types of questions, self questions and world questions. Share a question that is related to you personally and one that is more global in nature so that kids learn to distinguish between them.

WHEN *and* **WHY:** Right at the beginning of the inquiry process, we stress that asking questions is central to inquiry-based learning. Questioning propels readers ahead.

INITIATE: Begin this lesson by sharing your own curiosity. Make sure kids understand what it means to be curious. Let them know that you are insatiably curious about their thinking, too.

TEACH/MODEL: Share that thoughtful readers have a lot of questions and that the most important ones are not the teacher's or the book's questions, but the reader's questions. Think aloud with a nonfiction article on an interesting topic. Jot your questions on Post-it notes as you read. Model different kinds of questions, such as questions that clarify confusion (What does this word mean?) or ask about the content (How are they going to solve this problem?). Mention that reading ahead often answers your question. Model continuing to read and finding an answer. Mark your Post-it with an *A* and move it the spot where you found your answer. Show how some questions get answered and others don't.

GUIDED PRACTICE: Give kids the article and continue reading. Encourage them to jot their questions on Post-it notes or annotate right on the page. Have them talk to a partner about how questions get answered. Create an anchor chart with their responses.

WAYS TO GET OUR QUESTIONS ANSWERED

Read on	Think about what you know
Do further research	Reread
Ask someone	Make an inference
Go online	

INDEPENDENT PRACTICE: As kids read and do research, remind them to jot their questions and notice whether they get answered. If so, they should move the note to the spot in the text where the question got answered and mark it with an *A* for answer or, if they are annotating directly on a page, they should code the spot where their question was answered with an *A*. Have kids review their questions when they finish and note those that were answered. Encourage them to think about those that weren't answered and decide whether getting an answer is important. If it is, they should check out the chart and try an alternative way to get their question answered.

Stop, Think, and React to Information

See this lesson in action on pages 149, 172, 178, 211, and on the website.

➡ **TIP:** Secondary kids can annotate right on the page. Rather than writing down inner thoughts, they can simply code the text with an *L* when they learn something new, ★ for surprising, **!** for important, **?** for a question, and similar short codes. They may jot marginal thoughts when they need to but will primarily just code the text. We ask kids to stop, think, and react to images and videos as well as text. Whenever kids are presented with information of any sort, we expect them to interact with it.

WHEN *and* WHY: When kids are reading for information, they often have trouble deciding what is important to remember. Before we ask them to pick out important information, we teach them to simply stop, think, and react to new information. This awareness of new learning will help them understand what they are reading and sift out the most important information later on.

INITIATE: Explain that when we read nonfiction, we are reading to learn information and that we almost always learn something new. Tell students that nonfiction readers merge their own thinking with the information to understand it. If they are unfamiliar with the word *merge*, talk about how traffic merges onto a freeway. Share that readers put their thinking together and merge it with the words and ideas to make sense, just as cars merge into traffic.

TEACH/MODEL: Share that when you read nonfiction you have to stop, think, and react (STR) to information. Read a paragraph from a nonfiction piece and stop when you learn something new. Share what you hear your inner voice say, something like, "Wow, I never knew that sharks don't really like to bite people." Then mark a Post-it with an **L** for learn, jot down your learning, and place the note near the spot in the text where you learned the new information.

GUIDED PRACTICE: Ask kids to turn and talk about the voice they hear in their head when they meet new information. Then have them share with the class some of their language of new learning—*I never knew; I didn't know; No way*—whatever they come up with. Explain that those phrases are signals that the reader is learning something new. Hand out a sheet of paper with six 3 x 3 Post-it notes attached to a clipboard. Continue reading aloud to them. Engage them in the process by continuing to read and having them stop and mark an **L** on a Post-it note or in the margin when they learn something new.

> **L**
> I knew dogs could be smart. I just never knew how smart. They can sniff out survivors in collapsed buildings.

> **L**
> In ancient China only boys were educated.
> **No Fair!**

> **L**
> Amazing! Over half of the world's gold is in South America.

INDEPENDENT PRACTICE: Send kids off with their inquiry circle texts and have them jot their new learning on Post-its. Remind them to **STR—stop, think,** and **react** to new information, whether in a book, on the web, or on a video.

Notetaking: *Read with a Question in Mind*

See this lesson in action on pages 159, 162, 173, 191, 205, 213, 240.

➡ **TIP:** Differentiate for early readers by having them write or draw their question on a sheet of blank paper rather than the two-column form. All kids, regardless of their grade level, should be encouraged not only to read, but also to listen and view with a question in mind—videos, photos, slides etc.

WHEN *and* WHY: From the beginning of the inquiry process this strategy is needed to help kids gather information with focus and purpose.

INITIATE: Explain that reading with a question in mind is a very helpful strategy to get exactly the information we need. Share a time when you wondered something and then went off to read to find the answer. Explain that you ended up taking notes on (or highlighting) just about everything, lost your way, and didn't find the answer. Let the kids know this happens to all of us at one time or another.

TEACH/MODEL: Share with kids that keeping your question in mind as you read will help you notice the information that answers your question while screening out ancillary information. Model taking notes using a form with two columns: Notes and Thinking. At the top of the form write your question and then show how you read with that question in mind. Explain that the Notes column is for factual information that relates to your question and the Thinking column is for your reactions, connections, inferences, and so on. Read a short piece of text and stop as you encounter information that relates to your question. Jot that information in the Notes column and any thoughts in the Thinking column. As you read, keep returning to your question and talking about whether or not the information you read addresses your question. Remember to write thoughts in the Thinking column so they can see how you merge your thinking with the information.

QUESTION: WHY ARE SO MANY FROGS DISAPPEARING?

NOTES	THINKING
• 1/3 of all amphibians are threatened	• I bet humans are to blame.
• Been around for 350 million yrs.	• Leave it to humans to mess them up.
FACTORS	
1. destruction of native habitats	• Shocking
2. Climate change 3. pollution 4. fungus	• Why does it matter?
Serious when a species goes extinct	• Will frogs become extinct?

GUIDED PRACTICE: After you have modeled for a few minutes, give kids a copy of the article and the form and have them work while you continue modeling. (See the website for this form.) Ask them to keep the question in mind so they will notice when it gets answered. Make sure they understand that sometimes you can read an entire article and not get an answer. Usually, though, you will have more information to infer an answer than you had before you read.

COLLABORATIVE PRACTICE: Hand out more two-column forms and encourage kids to use them as they research their question in inquiry circles. Remind them to jot down their thinking as well as the facts related to their question. That is what keeps them engaged as they read and respond.

Drawing Inferences from Images, Features, and Words

See this lesson in action on pages 173, 243.

→ **TIP:** For secondary kids, you might introduce inferring with a discussion of body language—for instance, ask them what they can infer when they see someone in the cafeteria off at a corner table, huddled over his lunch with his hood up. Foster a discussion about what they can infer from the way kids walk, what they wear, the way they talk, and other clues. As you move through the lesson, graphs, tables, and charts are a great place to teach inferring with older kids.

WHEN and WHY: When kids are engaged in research, we teach them to infer since much of the information they encounter will require inferential thinking to expand understanding.

INITIATE: Explain what it is to infer by playing a version of charades. Make a face that looks frightened and ask kids what they infer. Act as if you are crying and ask what they infer. If they say scared the first time and sad the second, explain to them that they are inferring. They are taking what they know, their background knowledge, and merging it with clues. Encourage them to try this with a partner.

TEACH/MODEL: Write this inferring equation on chart paper: **BK + TC = I** (Background Knowledge plus Text Clues equals an Inference). Share how you take what you know and merge it with text clues to draw a conclusion about something. Explain that when the information is not written in the text, you often have to infer to get an answer. Photos are a great place to demonstrate inferring. You might show a photo of a moth whose wings are spread and painted with two large spots that look like eyes. Share how you infer that these are to keep away predators, because you know that moths could be eaten by bigger creatures. Or you might share a distribution map that shows where avalanches occur and explain that, since you know most avalanches occur in mountains, you can infer that the areas that have the most avalanches are mountainous. Write your inference on a Post-it marked with an **I** for infer and place it near the clue that helped you infer.

I

I infer those holes in the praying mantis knees are like ears.

Halloween

Snickers   Hershey bar   M&Ms   Reese's

Kids eat more Reese's than anything else

COLLABORATIVE PRACTICE: Engage kids in the process. Have them go through nonfiction texts and look for photos, text and visual features, and words, jotting down their inferences and then talking to a partner about them.

INDEPENDENT PRACTICE: Ask kids to keep their research questions in mind as they read and view their texts. Remind them to think about the inferring equation, because it is much easier to make a reasonable inference if you think about what you already know.

Synthesize Information: *Read to Get the Gist*

See this lesson in action on pages 180, 211.

➡ **TIP:** Rather than writing, primary kids can turn and talk about the gist, based on the three criteria in the lesson. With older kids, show how you try not to read more than your hand can cover before you stop to bracket and jot the gist, since that is about as much information as we can digest at a time. With practice, kids can write more complete summary responses that include both the gist and their thinking.

WHEN *and* WHY: Throughout the inquiry process, kids encounter a ton of information. They simply can't (or shouldn't) remember it all. We need to teach them to stop frequently and synthesize the information before moving on or they run the risk of merely running their eyes across the page and getting lost.

INITIATE: Explain that it is difficult to sift important information and come up with the gist. To make this explicit, share a common story such as *The Three Bears* and summarize the events. Then share the bigger idea(s) in the story—*perhaps it's not a good idea to go wandering into people's houses when they are out*—making a distinction between merely summarizing the events and getting the gist. Share that to synthesize, you need to **1)** Think about the information, **2)** Decide what is important, and **3)** Shape it into your own thought.

TEACH/MODEL: Reading for the gist requires us to think about the information and pull it together, or synthesize it, into a big idea. Model with an article on the overhead or whiteboard, showing how you read for the gist. Begin by previewing the article, first paying attention to the title, subheads, visuals, captions, and so on to get an idea of the article's focus. Share what you think the title suggests about the big ideas. Now, read and stop frequently, shaping the words and ideas into your own thought and capturing the gist. Bracket a paragraph and jot the gist in the margin next to it.

WOMEN OF THE NEGRO LEAGUES

A woman nailed a single off of Satchel Paige

Famous pitcher Satchel Paige was on the mound one day in 1953. A nervous second baseman stepped to the plate. Paige wound up, hurled the ball, and the batter cracked a base hit into center field.

This was no ordinary hit. The second baseman was no ordinary ball player. She was Toni Stone. Stone described the base hit off Paige as "the happiest moment in my life."

Three women played side by side with men in the Negro Leagues. Many white women played professional baseball, but they played in an all-women league. Toni Stone, Mamie "Peanut" Johnson, and Connie Morgan were African American women who played in the men's league. (They weren't allowed to play in the women's league. It was open only to white women.)

Not allowed in white leagues
African American women played in mens league

Reprinted with permission.

GUIDED PRACTICE: After modeling, read a paragraph and have kids bracket and jot the gist on their own copies. Move about, looking to see how it's going. Have them turn and talk about what they noticed as they synthesized the article.

COLLABORATIVE PRACTICE: Have students practice with articles they are reading in their inquiry circles. Confer with them as they are working together in their small groups.

Turn and Talk

See this lesson in action on pages 178, 183, 207.

➡ **TIP:** With primary kids, demonstrate how they should sit on the floor, keeping their bodies facing forward, and just turn their heads and talk to a partner. This posture minimizes the distraction of turning all the way around to talk to someone. Turn and talk is not something we do once a day, or once in a lesson. In inquiry-based classrooms teachers encourage such quick kid–kid talk every few minutes to make sure ideas are being processed.

WHEN *and* **WHY:** We teach this pair discussion structure early in the year to engage kids in purposeful interaction from Day 1.

INITIATE: Explain that there is no better way to understand information we read, hear, or see than to talk to someone else. Share that when we actively process information, we almost always learn, remember, and understand better.

TEACH/MODEL: Round up another adult to model how you talk to each other about a piece of text. If no adults are available, invite a student to practice with you and then model together for the class. Ask kids to notice what the two of you are doing. Read a piece of text silently (have the observers read it also), and then talk with your partner about it. Demonstrate how you look each other in the eye, listen attentively, ask follow-up questions and other active listening behaviors.

GUIDED PRACTICE: Have kids report out what they saw you doing. Record their responses on an anchor chart titled Turn and Talk Guidelines. Add any they missed that you think are important. Then suggest a kid-friendly topic and ask them to turn and talk. Give them about thirty seconds, then have them regroup and share what they discussed and what they learned both about and from each other. When you ask kids to turn and talk, you can vary the prompts. Some are open-ended thinking prompts such as *Turn and talk about what you are thinking; turn and talk about what you are wondering.* Others are more specific: *Turn and talk about the main character; turn and talk about the senator's position on this bill.* We generally tend to ask more open-ended thinking prompts, but we also pose some specific topics, particularly if we think our students are missing something important.

TURN AND TALK GUIDELINES

Use eye contact	Disagree politely
Listen attentively	Share connections
Ask follow-up questions	Express reactions

COLLABORATIVE PRACTICE: Turning and talking is one structure that cannot be practiced independently! So as you facilitate guided discussion either during a lesson or when kids are back in their work spaces, continue to ask them to turn and talk frequently. As with all strategies, kids become more proficient with practice.

Home Court Advantage: *Showing Friendliness and Support*

See this lesson in action on pages 227, 247.

See this lesson in action on pages 227, 247.

➡ TIP: This lesson was originally developed in high school, where put-downs are a special concern. Yes, it sounds corny—but it works. And even the little ones comprehend the metaphor of this lesson— so many of them are on soccer teams! In place of showing the newspaper article, you can simply question them about their experiences playing at home versus away.

WHEN *and* **WHY:** We use this lesson for group-building early in the year or at times when bickering or disunity have occurred. Thanks to Nancy Steineke for introducing us to this powerful lesson.

INITIATE: From the sports pages of the newspaper, clip out the standings for a local baseball, football, or soccer team—the ones that include home and away game outcomes. Make copies for kids or project them on a screen.

TEACH/MODEL: *"OK, guys, take a look at these standings from today's paper. What do you notice about home games versus away games? Turn and talk with a partner for a minute."*

Kids will report back that teams generally win more home games than away games.

"Why do you think that is? What would be some reasons? Get back together and jot down a few ideas you have."

Kids typically will return with ideas like these:

Fans cheer you	You know the field/court
Nobody boos	Feel comfortable
Same place we practice	Your friends are watching
No distracting fans	

As a whole group, prioritize the suggestions and make a consensus list. If kids don't bring it up along the way, be sure to highlight the issue of put-downs.

"Is anyone in here on a team? What do you do when one of your teammates makes a mistake?"

Students may offer ideas like, "We say, 'Nice try Bob' " or "We don't laugh or boo."

"Exactly. And in the classroom we are a team also, we are all on the same side. You never put down a teammate. If you hear a put-down in here, you can just quietly say 'home court' to remind people we are a team. OK?"

INDEPENDENT PRACTICE: Invite kids to make posters that depict the idea of home court advantage. They can place the term at the center and elaborate around it with drawings and specific sayings people can use with teammates ("Good effort, Janie" or "No put-downs"). Hang posters around the room and refer to them periodically.

Creating Group Ground Rules

See this lesson in action on pages 162, 189, 217.

➡ **TIP:** You obviously must review the consequences for appropriateness. If kids propose paddling miscreants, not OK. But if one group wants to keep laggards out until they catch up, while another wants to put them to work as a recorder, both are defensible and potentially constructive solutions. For primary kids, we'd do this lesson as a whole class, rather than asking groups to develop separate ground rules.

WHEN *and* **WHY:** Use this lesson when a new group is just forming for an inquiry project.

INITIATE: *"We have already made a list of things that make meetings and discussions more effective and more fun. Now you are launching into different inquiry projects with your own groups, so you may need some special guidelines just for your particular team. You'll be doing more than just discussing: you'll be researching, interviewing people, doing experiments or surveys, and creating writing or charts, videos, artifacts, or performances. That's a lot of work! So it's a good idea to talk now about how you will work together and solve any problems that arise, before you begin your projects."*

TEACH/MODEL: *"Get into your groups and brainstorm for a few minutes. What would be some important rules to have as your team works together?"*

Allow five or six minutes for kids to talk. Regather the class and list suggestions on a chart as kids volunteer. Expect to hear comments like these:

- Show up prepared, having done your work
- Do what you promise
- Bring all materials
- Join in the discussions and work time
- Help other people in the group
- Work hard

Comment on the entries, letting kids know which ones sound useful and enforceable. There will probably be overlaps with the discussion skills chart already developed, existing classroom practices, or your classroom constitution, if you have one. Work for a long list, maybe eight to twelve items.

"Now you have two jobs. First, you need to decide what rules you want to adopt; some may be from this list and others may be just for your group. You don't want tons of rules—maybe just three or four important guidelines for your project. When you have decided, write them down on the Ground Rules form I've given you. (See the website for this form.)

"Finally, you have to decide what would be appropriate action if a member isn't following a particular guideline. How do you get someone to change their behavior? What will you ask people to change if they aren't contributing what the group needs?

"I will come around and help you while you work on your guidelines and action steps. Each group can have its own rules, but I have to approve them for you, so be sure to hand me the completed form when you are done."

Making and Using a Work Plan

See this lesson in action on pages 162, 221, 232, 254, 265, 275, 285.

➡ **TIP:** With primary kids, you will most likely need to meet with each of the small groups separately to hash out some of these plans. You can create a planning sheet that looks at steps in the inquiry process rather than calendar dates—for example, ask questions, find out answers, write and draw information, share learning. Our youngest kids want and need to share their learning frequently, perhaps daily—not necessarily with the whole class, but at least with a partner.

WHEN *and* **WHY:** To succeed with small-group inquiry and to guarantee individual accountability, kids must identify different tasks, divide up the work, monitor their progress, and make adjustments as conditions require. We help students create a work plan shortly after any long-term project is launched, and we help them revise it along the way.

INITIATE: Make a calendar covering the school days and classroom times available for work on the inquiry projects. If you are setting dates for certain segments of the work, put these on the calendar also (e.g., "Presentations on March 24 and 25, 10:30–12:00"). Hand out copies to all kids along with work plan forms (see the website for this form).

TEACH/MODEL: *"Now that you have gotten a start on your projects, I want to help you plan your work over the days ahead. I have made a blank calendar that shows all the time we have for these projects in class. We may also be using some out-of-class time to pursue parts of these inquires, so let's look at this calendar together now and talk about your schedule."*

"I have also given everyone a blank work plan where you can write down your own specific jobs and deadlines. Right now, everyone take five minutes to start jotting some notes: what are your own special inquiry questions, what tasks do you have to do, and how will you schedule them? Then you can begin talking in groups about how your plans fit together. I will come around and help you."

GUIDED PRACTICE: As kids work, confer with individual students to help them develop their plans and schedules. (This is a key way that we ensure individual accountability in small-group projects.) Help kids figure out how their tasks will fit together, who may partner with whom for certain jobs, and so on. Review or make copies of each student's work plan.

TEACH/MODEL: Let kids know that they should use their work plans as a touchstone all the way through the project. Formalize this by doing official "midcourse corrections" (Lesson 17) once or twice during longer projects.

Practicing the Skills of Effective Small-Group Discussion

See this lesson in action on page 220.

TIP: For your youngest learners, read a nonfiction piece out loud to one small inquiry group and have them write or draw their thoughts during and after the reading. Facilitate a fishbowl discussion as other class members watch. Stop the discussion after a few minutes and ask others what they noticed the fishbowl group did well; have them jot their thoughts on an anchor chart. Add any important things you noticed that they didn't catch. And now for the fun—give each group a chance to share a bad example with the class.

WHEN *and* WHY: From the beginning of the year, kids must join in sustained, focused, and balanced small-group discussions. This means kids must listen carefully, take turns, and monitor their own participation. Since few of us are born with these skills, we must teach them explicitly, early, and often.

INITIATE: *"We are going to be working a lot in groups this year, and we need to get really good at talking to each other. So let's practice discussing."*

TEACH/MODEL: Find a short, high-interest article or story and have everyone read it, using their best comprehension strategies to mark the text with their thinking, reactions, and questions. Then ask a volunteer group of kids to fishbowl a small-group discussion about the article.

"The rest of you, your job is to observe carefully and make notes on what the fishbowl kids are doing well. What do they do to make their discussion fun and interesting?"

Typically kids will notice that members

get right to work	ask questions
listened to each other	share the airtime
take turns and don't interrupt	support their opinions
build on others' ideas	disagree, but in a friendly way

GUIDED PRACTICE: Now, ask kids to meet in their small groups and prepare to role-play a *bad* discussion, using the same article. (Kids love doing this.) Invite several groups to perform their version, since different distracting, annoying, or off-task behaviors will emerge. Expect to see behaviors like these:

not being prepared	being mean
interrupting	dominating the discussion
getting up and walking around	disrespecting others' ideas
sleeping, gossiping	shuffling papers, tapping pencils

COLLABORATIVE PRACTICE: Create a classroom chart that makes explicit the ingredients of successful small-group work by having kids fill in both positive and negative examples for each social skill category, as on page 47. They can continue to add to this chart through the year.

Written Conversations

See this lesson in action on pages 38, 218.

━━▶ **TIP:** For young kids and those with special learning needs (and, really, for everyone), legalize drawing as a fine way to join in written conversation. To launch a whole-group debrief, say: "Will each group please share one highlight, one thread of their discussion? Something you spent time on, something that sparked lively discussion, maybe something you argued about or laughed about."

WHEN *and* **WHY:** Kids need to be *discussing ideas* all the time. But out-loud talk is not the only alternative. In this variation, kids hold a sustained silent discussion by exchanging a series of one-minute notes that are passed around a small group. This form of discussion equalizes air time, invites deeper thinking, and leaves tangible evidence of kids' thinking.

INITIATE: Identify a "debatable" topic for discussion—maybe specific questions that have come up in inquiry groups, or a whole-class subject relevant to all. The best topics for written conversations are open-ended, with no right answer, have a value or interpretive or judgment dimension, and are subjects that reasonable people can disagree about.

TEACH/MODEL: Kids sit in their small groups and each writes his or her name in the upper-left-hand margin of a large piece of paper. Explain two rules:

"First, be sure to use all the time for writing. I will tell you when to stop and pass your paper. Second, don't talk, even when passing notes. We want to keep all the energy in the writing. OK? Write for just a minute or so. Write your thoughts, reactions, questions, or feelings about today's topic."

Keep time by walking and watching. When most students have filled a quarter of a page, it is time to pass. This may be more like two or three minutes.

"Pass your papers to the next person in the circle. Now read the entry on the page, and just beneath it, answer for one minute. Tell your reaction, make a comment, ask questions, share a connection you've made, agree or disagree, or raise a whole new aspect. Use all the time for writing and keep the conversation going!"

Walk the room, looking over shoulders to get the timing right.

COLLABORATIVE PRACTICE:

"Pass again, please."

Repeat this process three or four times total. Kids read all entries each time and may respond to one or all. Since there will be more text on the page, allow more time for each successive pass.

"Now pass one last time, so that you get back the paper that you began with. Now read the whole conversation you started."

As soon as kids are done reading and start talking, invite them to continue the conversation out loud. You can keep it open or announce a more focused prompt ("Do you think that blacklisting could ever happen again in America?"). In a few minutes, you can call kids back for a short and highly focused whole-class discussion.

Midcourse Corrections: *Reflecting and Replanning*

See this lesson in action on pages 219, 242, 275.

➡ **TIP:** With older kids, you can use the chart from page 44 to help with the group skills debriefing. Have your primary kids reflect on how the process is going so far. Are they working together in a positive way? Are they using what they learned in the fishbowl to practice working together? Have they answered their questions? Are they having trouble finding answers?

WHEN *and* WHY: When kids move to extended inquiry projects, regular debriefing and replanning become especially important, since changing questions, surprising information, or people's behavior in the group can change the working conditions on any given day. This also helps prevent procrastination or slacking among the older kids.

INITIATE: *"Today, we are going to practice stopping to reflect on how our inquiry projects are coming along. Each of you is working both as an individual and as a team member, so we need to look at both roles. In your work plan [see lesson 14], you have jotted down plans, goals, and deadlines. We can use these to check on how things are going."*

TEACH/MODEL: Prepare a chart with the questions listed below.

"First, let's think about your work as individuals. Take out your work plan, your research notebook, and any materials you have been working on today. Take a few minutes to look through everything, and then write about these questions in your research notebooks (see Lesson 20):

> How is my part of the project going?
> Am I finding the information I need?
> Are my goals or topics changing?
> Do I need help from someone?
> Will I be able to meet the calendar deadlines I have set?
> If there are problems in any of these areas, what steps can I take to move ahead?

"Now, make some notes about how your group is doing in a two-column chart in your notebook. On the left, jot down some specific things that the group is doing well. On the other side, list some areas where the group needs to make changes, reschedule, or help each other."

GUIDED PRACTICE: *"Now, turn to your group and take turns sharing your responses, first about your own individual work. Members, listen actively, look for ways to help each other or revise work plans. When you have heard from everyone, talk about your group reflection charts. Celebrate the things you are doing well, but then try to find at least one problem or weakness and make a plan for how you'll improve on it in your next meeting. I'll come around and help you, and later we will all get back together and share what we have learned."*

Next, gather kids as a whole class to elicit instances of problem solving, revising plans, helping others, or committing to a new direction or time line.

I Beg to Differ: *Disagreeing Agreeably*

See this lesson in action on page 218.

See this lesson in action on page 218.

➡ **TIP:** For your youngest learners, bring in a colleague and model how you use respectful language when you disagree with each other: "That is really interesting, Steph, but I don't agree with you. I'm thinking . . ." Then have kids practice the language. Make a big deal about it when you notice someone using respectful language in a classroom disagreement. Share with the rest of the class what you heard and how effective you thought it was.

WHEN *and* **WHY:** When kids investigate their burning issues in small groups, disagreements are inevitable—about whose source is better, whose interpretation is right, or who is carrying their fair share of the load. So, before they begin (or when trouble arises), we show kids how smart people can debate and disagree, and still remain the best of friends.

INITIATE: *"Have you ever heard the expression 'I beg to differ'? What do you think that means?"*

Invite volunteers to define the term.

"Turns out that 'I beg to differ' is an old English expression that means, basically, 'I disagree, but I don't want to hurt your feelings. May I have permission to state my contrary view?' That's really polite, isn't it?"

TEACH/MODEL: *"Today, we are going to learn how to argue! Doesn't that sound like fun? We are going to look at some arguments and try to figure out what social skills effective arguers use, so they can explain their side of an issue without being mean or hurting people's feelings."*

Now you need a sample of an argument. This could be:

- A fishbowl role-play, done by you and a few kids (or other teachers), in which you first portray a really dysfunctional, unmannerly debate, and then a congenial and constructive one.

- Some video clips from a TV discussion show (CNN and MSNBC feature panels of opposing experts almost all day long; the Sunday morning news shows always end with a roundtable of pontificating pundits). You should easily be able to find segments of loud, rude, ad hominem arguing, as well as some examples of patient, civil give-and-take.

- A read-aloud from an article, trade book, or picture book in which people disagree disagreeably, and hopefully, learn to discuss things more constructively.

Whichever demonstration you choose, kids can work on it the same way.

GUIDED PRACTICE: *"Now we have heard some arguing, haven't we? Some of this was pretty crabby and mean, and some of it polite and useful. So what made the difference? Get into your groups and make a list of things you can say or do that allow you to disagree, but still be friendly and polite."*

19

Model Your Own Inquiry Process

See this lesson in action on pages 145–150, 158, 248.

➡ **TIP:** This activity works for all ages. Sharing your curiosity and demonstrating your own inquiry is a powerful model for your students. The purpose here is to give kids an idea of how the inquiry process works and how it differs based on the question. It is great for them to begin with an easily answered question, so they can experience some of what happens when they do research.

WHEN *and* WHY: At the very beginning of an inquiry project, share how you do research and go through the inquiry process so kids have a model from which to draw.

INITIATE: When you begin teaching the research process, share your insatiable curiosity! Begin all inquiry projects with a celebration of the nature of curiosity. Talk about your own "puzzle drive" and how curiosity drives you to learn more.

TEACH/MODEL: Explain that research is not a four-letter word. Research is an important process that adults go through every day to make choices and decide how to act. We do research when we buy a new car, when we decide on a pet, when we go and cast a vote. Create a list of things you wonder about and share them with your students. Share a time when you got an authentic question answered and take the kids through that inquiry, so they can see what you did to get your question answered. As you share your inquiry process, talk about different ways you found information—these might include reading, going online, asking a specialist, and doing further research—so they will understand that there are many different ways to discover answers to questions. Also explain that some questions—called Quick Finds—are easily answered by jumping online or asking a knowledgeable person, while others require much more research to find answers.

GUIDED PRACTICE: Have kids come up with at least three authentic questions they wonder about and create their own wonder list. (Most kids will be able to come up with at least one if you request three.) Then have them talk to a partner about their questions.

WONDER LIST

- What causes pain? Why do some people feel it more than others?
- How can we get someone to pay attention to our falling down school?
- Allergic reactions—How can a bee sting kill a person? How can nuts get you all puffed up? How can animal hair make you sneeze?

COLLABORATIVE PRACTICE: Have students check their wonder lists and see which questions they think might be Quick Finds and which will take further research. Have them code their Quick Finds with a QF and explain that you will also build in time for them to research more complex questions. Invite them to search for answers to their Quick Find questions.

Create Research Notebooks

See this lesson in action on pages 146, 204, 287.

➡ **TIP:** Intermediate kids often call their research notebooks "wonder books." With the primary grades, we create construction paper booklets for kids to draw in and label with their thoughts and questions. They also enjoy keeping recipe boxes, which we call "wonder boxes," filled with index cards on which they've written or drawn their topics and/or questions. In this way they can easily find their questions and remember them as they are searching for answers. When they find answers, they can write or draw them on an index card to store in their wonder box.

WHEN *and* WHY: As students begin small-group inquiry, they need to create research notebooks for the purpose of holding thoughts, questions, and notes related to their inquiry.

INITIATE: Plan for a day to launch research notebooks. Make sure all kids have a notebook on that day. Spiral notebooks with pockets inside covers help to store collectibles—articles, photos, maps, charts, and so forth.

TEACH/MODEL: Explain that researchers keep notebooks while engaging in inquiry so that all of the information they gather can be located in one place, making it easy to find information when needed. Share your own research notebook and explain that you use it to organize your thoughts, questions, and findings as you engage in inquiry. Explain that we write something down so that we can remember it and use it later. Share that it is easy to lose track of things related to your inquiry and that the notebook solves that problem (unless you lose the notebook!). Tell them that you hold all of your findings and notes in your research notebook; flip through it so that they can see what it looks like. Mention that you read through your notebook frequently to discover information that may not be obvious at first blush. Then demonstrate how you create a list of things you wonder about in your research notebook and share that these wonderings may lead to further inquiry.

GUIDED PRACTICE: On a chart, co-construct a list of the kinds of things that are included in a research notebook. Begin by jotting down several things you keep in yours—questions for research, topics you are interested in investigating, project ideas. Have kids turn and talk about what might be included in such a notebook. Invite them to share their thoughts as you record them on an anchor chart. Here's a typical list:

RESEARCH NOTEBOOK CONTENTS

Topics	Quotes from books, teachers, kids, outside specialists	Interesting findings
Project ideas		Bibliographic information
Drawings, sketches, doodles	Observations	Written drafts
Diagrams	Interview guidelines	Photographs, maps, postcards, and other visuals
Charts	Interviews	
	Notes from research	

COLLABORATIVE PRACTICE: Kids jot their initial questions and thoughts in their notebooks and bring them to their inquiry circles. They share some of the entries, giving others a chance to see the variety of writing and drawing that goes into the research notebooks.

Explore and Use Multiple Sources

See this lesson in action on pages 154, 256.

➞ TIP: Although this may seem quite elementary, all of our kids can benefit from learning about available resources, becoming familiar with them, and then deciding whether they are useful or not. For cost effectiveness alone, it's not a bad idea to ask intermediate and middle grade kids to check with a teacher or librarian before they print a whole packet of information from the Internet that they can neither read nor understand.

WHEN *and* WHY: As kids begin small-group inquiry, they need to be aware of the many resources available to them.

INITIATE: Explain that when doing research, it is important to take advantage of the widest range of resources. It is not enough to simply depend on a single website or textbook. Real researchers "triangulate," information by reading and comparing several sources then present kids with a wide range of materials on the topic under study.

TEACH/MODEL: This is always a fun day. Invite the school librarian in to fire kids up about the many ways to get information. Begin with print materials—books of course, but also magazines and newspapers. Show visual as well as text features—graphs, charts, maps, photographs, and so on. Big Books and large photographic calendars are terrific for younger kids. Share reliable Internet resources, blogs, and web pages. (See both our magazine and list of URLs on our website.) Videos are among the best resources to engage kids, get them excited about their inquiries, and give them information. Take a moment to talk about indexes and tables of contents. Both help us find information quickly.

GUIDED PRACTICE: Together go through some trade books and show how you determine whether they are appropriate for you. Share how you put a text back if it is too hard. No sense spending time with a resource you cannot read and understand. Talk about "printer flu," which gets a grip on us when we go to the Internet and print out page after page, even though we are hard pressed to understand them. Encourage kids to read through online material first and to print only if they are able to read and understand it.

INDEPENDENT PRACTICE: Flood kids with resources on topics they have chosen. Have some pore over the print materials; send others to computers with a list of reliable websites to explore. Another group might go to the school library to learn what is available to them. Continue to confer with individuals. Be ready to share resources that relate to their inquiry projects. Smokey's students in New Mexico dubbed this lesson a "Reading Frenzy" because they got to feast on so many sources at once.

Choosing Topics to Investigate: *Free Focused Writing*

See this lesson in action on pages 160, 174, 196, 204, 248, 265.

➡ **TIP:** When we ask kids to list three topics, most kids will come up with at least one! And some will think of many more. Topics are contagious, and kids who have trouble finding a topic may discover one as they listen to other kids share theirs. We encourage our early writers to draw their topic lists and share what they wonder orally as we record their thoughts for further research.

WHEN *and* **WHY:** This lesson is important at the beginning of the inquiry process to help kids discover topics that truly interest them and that they have energy to pursue further. Sometimes students have already chosen topics; sometimes topics come from the curriculum. But when we are offering a broader personal choice, we need to show kids how we find exciting, sustainable inquiries.

INITIATE: Explain that research works best when we choose topics we know something about, care about, want to learn more about, and may want to teach someone. Also share that just jotting ideas can be an act of discovery because as we write, we often find subjects and questions to pursue in further research.

TEACH/MODEL: Explain that we all are specialists in something. A specialist is someone who knows a lot about something, cares a lot about something, wants to learn more about it and share the information. At the projector, create a list of three topics that you know something about, care about, and, most of all, wonder and want to learn more about. Tell the story behind each topic and then choose one to elaborate upon through free focused writing. Free focused writing is writing spontaneously on a topic of choice from your background knowledge. Quickly draft a one-pager about your topic right in front of the kids, including some interesting information you know as well as some questions you discover as you write. Read through your free focused writing and share anything you wonder about your topic that might be suitable for further research.

TOPIC LIST
- reading and writing
- skiing
- Tibet

I am passionate about tibet. Having been one of the lucky few to visit this magical place I can't stop thinking about the plight of Tibetans. Tibet is a Himalayan Country that borders India, Nepal, and China. The Chinese

government next door claims Tibet for its own. The Chinese government has occupied Tibet since 1959. My respect for the China govt. is greatly diminished by this situation. Tibet deserves freedom! I wonder if they will ever achieve it.

GUIDED PRACTICE: Have kids come up with a list of three topics they know, care, and wonder about. Once they have jotted down their topics, have them share with a partner and choose the one to write about that most intrigues them.

INDEPENDENT PRACTICE: Give kids time to write freely on the focus topic of their choice. After they have written a page or so, have them share with a partner and then jot down any questions that emerge from their writing. These questions give kids a good place to start their research.

Checking Our Sources

See this lesson in action on page 102.

See this lesson in action on page 102.

➡ **TIP:** Any time a student encounters a source that dramatically illustrates a particular reliability defect—such as misleading statistics or conflicting information—build a mini-lesson around it and use it as an example for everyone.

WHEN *and* **WHY:** When gathering information, kids must determine what materials are accurate, fair, and reliable, and weed out stuff that is inaccurate, biased, or simply untruthful.

INITIATE: For the younger kids, you can read aloud two contrasting pieces about a topic and have them talk about what seems right and not-so-right in the two versions. For older students, find and copy four short articles on the same topic (a half page each is a good length) that embody different points of view or levels of trustworthiness. We might use a set on global warming for instance that includes an international scientific report, a rant by a climate change denier, a press release from Exxon, and a commentary from the Sierra Club.

TEACH/MODEL: *"In your projects, you are gathering tons of materials, and you always have to decide what to trust, right? Today we are going to look at four different articles about one topic and see if we can develop some procedures for validating our sources. Then you can use these guidelines as you continue researching."*

GUIDED PRACTICE: Have students read and annotate the four pieces, then gather in small groups and talk about different ways of knowing whether a source can be trusted or not. Kids are likely to come up with ideas like these:

- Does this information come from a respected author or organization?
- Is this information credible?
- Is it up to date?
- Do other articles or Web pages confirm the information? If not, what is different and why?
- Is the material biased? Does the author have an axe to grind?
- If there are different sides to this topic, does the author cover them all?
- When I trace the links, ownership, or other materials in this source, what do I learn?

An important topic to discuss with kids, if they don't bring it up themselves, is blindly accepting ideas just because they come from a big, well-known institution. Without nurturing cynicism, we want kids to become skeptical of *all* claims. Think of all the governments and organizations that have intentionally distributed false information.

INDEPENDENT PRACTICE: Winnow down the list to the most useful criteria, co-create a checklist that kids can have handy as they read, and then monitor its use as you meet with groups and individuals.

Organize Group Findings: *Create Question Webs*

See this lesson in action on page 209.

WHEN *and* WHY: As kids work together in inquiry circles, they need a place to keep track of group information collected throughout the process.

INITIATE: Share how hard it can be to keep group information organized while pursuing answers to questions. Question webs help us stay on top of what individual members are learning by offering a place to make thinking visible and hold it over time.

TEACH/MODEL: Similar in form to other semantic webs, question webs differ in that the group inquiry question is at the center of the web. The spoke lines that emanate from the center are used to add information that relates to the question. Individual group members continue to add lines radiating out from the center as they come up with more information related to the question. Invite one of the inquiry circles to model with you. Create a large poster-sized question web and list the inquiry circle members at the top. Write their question at the center. Share one piece of information related to that question and write it along one of the lines along with your name. Write the source of that information next to your name. Find a spot in the room to hang the question web where kids can easily add to it. Tell them that when they have information related to that question, they should write the information on the web, sign their name, and add the source. This is a great way to keep track of important information that might otherwise get lost in the shuffle.

> **TIP:** Question webs are not the only way to hold group thinking. Older kids may have a common inquiry notebook where individuals can make entries. Primary kids might jot their information on Post-its and then place them on a large poster with the question written at the top. The structure can be adapted for different grades and students. The important thing is that you facilitate a place to keep track of group thinking, save it and make it visible.

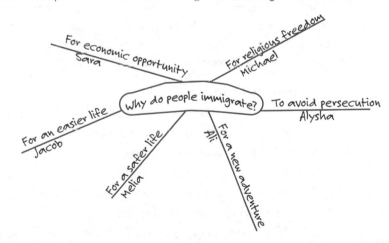

GUIDED PRACTICE: Have each inquiry circle create a question web, writing their names at the top and the group question at the center.

COLLABORATIVE PRACTICE: As kids research their question in their inquiry circles, they should post information related to it on the question web and notice whether the answer is emerging.

Demonstrate and Practice Interviewing

See this lesson in action on page 258.

See this lesson in action on page 258.

→ **TIP:** Our youngest learners love to interview people. It is helpful if the class comes up with a few very simple questions before kids practice interviewing with a partner. Explain that a follow-up question is one that builds upon the interviewee's response. Successful interviews engage the subject and follow the person's train of thought. Model how you ask a question, listen carefully, and then ask a follow-up question.

WHEN *and* WHY: About midway into the inquiry process, teach kids how to interview specialists in the field to gain more information. We usually do this over two days, demonstrating interviewing on the first day and having kids practice interviewing a partner on their inquiry topic on the second day.

INITIATE: Tell kids the most important thing they can learn about interviewing is to listen carefully.

TEACH/MODEL: Find a colleague to demonstrate how to conduct an interview. Sit in chairs facing each other with kids observing closely. Ask them to notice what you do as you interview, because you will ask them to reflect afterward. Explain that your objective is to learn as much as possible because you may not get another chance to interview this person. Show how you jot down some specific questions before the interview, but that you remain flexible and concentrate on the interviewee's response. Come with a list of generic questions in case the subject is not very talkative and open up your notebook to jot responses quickly. Show how you ask both personal (Why do you love to swim?) and universal (Who is the world's fastest swimmer?) questions. Depending on your purpose, you may ask more of one kind than the other.

GUIDED PRACTICE: Have kids turn and talk about what they noticed you doing. Have them think about what questions they might add to those you already discussed. As kids come up with additional questions, jot them down in your notebook. Once kids have gone home for the day, create an anchor chart titled Interview Questions, list the questions you co-created with the kids, and post it in the room. Also make individual copies of these.

Interview Questions

- How did you develop your interest or expertise in this field?
- How did you learn more about this interest?
- Who helped teach you what you know?
- What knowledge about this field do you have from personal experience?
- What are the big issues or problems in the field today?
- Whom do you admire in your field?
- What are you working on now that is interesting to you?
- Is there anything I should have asked you but didn't?

Co-construct Interview Guidelines

See this lesson in action on page 258.

WHEN *and* WHY: After seeing the demonstration interview and practicing partner interviews in Lesson 25, kids can now identify steps and stages in a successful interview.

INITIATE: Ask kids to think about what they learned from interviewing a partner and then turn and talk about the experience.

TEACH/MODEL: Construct a set of interview guidelines together with your students. Begin by sharing one of your own—start with the importance of listening carefully. Then have kids talk about that guideline and evaluate whether they did it successfully in their practice interviews. Record it on an Interview Guideline anchor chart.

GUIDED PRACTICE: Have kids turn and talk about what they noticed you doing during your demonstration interview as well as what they found themselves doing when they practiced. Then have them share their thinking and add it to the chart. Comments that may come up include these:

➡ **TIP:** Intermediate and even some middle grade kids may struggle to jot information as they conduct an interview. Suggest a friend join them and jot down the responses during the interview—or ask permission to tape the subject. Primary kids will be more successful if you attend the interview with them and jot down the answers, but still let them take the lead in asking questions.

INTERVIEW GUIDELINES

- Listen carefully to the subject—you may find surprising information.
- Ask follow-up questions to take the interview deeper.
- Ask mostly open-ended questions. Yes and no questions get short answers and can even cut people off from talking.
- Ask both specific and universal questions. Both can spur rich talk.
- Let the interviewee do most of the talking.
- Take charge when the interview goes astray. Ask one of the questions on your question list.
- You can't write everything down. Jot down key words and short notes that will help you jog your memory later.
- Record important information as soon as the interview is over so you don't forget it.
- Video your interview (with permission of your subject) for a reliable record.

COLLABORATIVE PRACTICE: Make copies of these guidelines so kids have them at their fingertips when needed. Have them try their first real interview with a low-stakes individual, such as another adult in the school or a parent. Once they have practiced with that person, they should feel more comfortable when they interview an outside specialist.

Response Options: *Take Learning Public*

See this lesson in action on pages 163, 175, 194, 197, 205, 214, 222, 246, 259, 266.

➡ **TIP:** You'll need to explicitly model a variety of response options for primary-grade kids. As they plan their presentations, talk to them about what they learned and what they would like to teach someone. Discuss ways that they can share their learning.

WHEN *and* WHY: Near the end of an inquiry project, we help kids pull their information together, take it public, and present it.

INITIATE: Tell kids that there are many ways to share information, from simply telling someone what you have learned to creating a more extensive project. It is our job to share the widest range of possibilities for demonstrating learning and understanding. These presentations need to be authentic, relevant, and meaningful.

TEACH/MODEL: Share a memorable story or several stories of presentations that left a big impression on you. Explain why. The inspiration might have been a captivating speaker, a thoughtful poster, a written document, or an example of someone who took action based on their learning. Explain that when someone presents information to you, you hope to go away thinking about the presentation, having learned something, and perhaps even having some lingering questions. Also share that the presentations and projects you remember are those that have some sort of real-world application, like the kids who studied malaria and found a group that encouraged donations for malaria nets, or the group who wrote health articles and published a journal for doctors' offices. Share the widest range of possibilities for projects that are authentic, meaningful, and useful in the real world. This automatically eliminates dioramas, book reports, and other inauthentic responses.

GUIDED PRACTICE: Have kids jot down at least three ways that they could share their information, demonstrate their understanding, and create a project that teaches something. Then ask them to share with a partner. Ideas like these are contagious; they will come up with more after sharing. Also invite kids who have already decided on a type of presentation to share what they have in mind. Create an anchor chart of the many response options that emerge.

RESPONSE OPTIONS FOR SHARING LEARNING

- Teaching others
- Posters
- Letters
- Picture books
- Journals and diaries

- Magazines and newspaper article
- Essays, editorials
- Poetry anthologies
- Tableaux

- Reinactments
- Musical performance
- Drama
- Murals
- Book reviews

COLLABORATIVE PRACTICE: Have students meet in their inquiry circles and discuss their final presentations. Using some of the collaborative strategies they've learned, they need to come to a consensus on their plan. Once they have decided, they should check it out with you.

PART

3

FOUR MODELS OF SMALL-GROUP INQUIRIES

Mini-Inquiries

We can't count the number of times we have waltzed into a classroom to model the inquiry process, only to hear groans and moans when we utter the word research. "I hate research" is, sadly, a common refrain among the older kids in our schools. Maybe this is not so surprising when you consider the dull drudgery that conventional schooling often dubs research. You know the type: mandatory animal reports in second grade, country reports in fifth grade, and term papers in high school, all of them sounding remarkably like encyclopedias, differentiated only by the name in the upper-left-hand corner.

Research is not a four-letter word, literally or figuratively. Research is not a boring endeavor reserved only for school reports. Authentic research is a process we go through every day, not just once a semester to produce a term paper. We do it when we buy a new bike, choose a brand of cereal, or head off to the polls. Research is central to making informed decisions in daily life. Research is a vibrant, dynamic process that we engage in to find specific information to learn about the world and deal with daily life. Research can and should be F-U-N!

Getting Started with Inquiry

Many books on literacy instruction focus heavily on teaching kids to ask questions. Teachers ask us all the time: "When do they get to answer all of these questions?" Our response: every single day, with what we call mini-inquiry. The purpose of asking questions, of course, is to find the answers. Mini-inquiry projects—short-term small-group research that lets students search for and find information relatively quickly—give kids a wonderful opportunity to ask questions, find some answers, and satisfy their curiosity.

A powerful benefit of mini-research is that it offers the perfect avenue for getting started with small-group inquiry. As kids ask mini-research questions and search for answers, we can teach them important literacy, collaboration, and inquiry strategies. And there is much for us to teach and for kids to practice if we want them to work in small groups, think deeply, investigate questions, and demonstrate their learning and understanding. Taking students through the mini-research process

Small-Group Inquiry Model Adapted for Mini-Inquiry Projects		
STAGE	**TEACHER**	**KIDS**
Immerse *Invite Curiosity and Wonder*	• Invites curiosity, questioning, engagement • Shares curiosity and models personal inquiry • Models how to ask authentic questions • Teaches kids to collaborate by turning and talking • Facilitates small-group formation to ensure heterogeneous groups with compatible interests • Confers with small groups and individuals	• Express their own curiosity • Wonder and ask questions
Investigate *Develop Questions, Search for Information, and Discover Answers*	• Models how to read, listen, and view with a question in mind • Shares ways to get questions answered • Helps kids think about where to find information • Supports kids to work together and figure out roles • Confers with groups and individuals	• Develop questions; then read, listen, and view to answer them • Searches through multiple resources and media to find answers • Divide the workload
Coalesce *Synthesize Information and Build Knowledge*	• Supports kids to find information and answer questions • Shares how to evaluate sources	• Target key ideas and information • Synthesize information to answer questions • Continue to work together and share responsibilities
Go Public *Demonstrate Understanding and Share Learning*	• Builds in time for kids to share findings • Supports kids to share the learning	• Demonstrate learning and understanding by sharing the answer to their questions and teaching others • Share additional information related to their question if they choose to • Pose new questions for further research that may emerge • Take action if motivated

builds familiarity with the nature of inquiry and gives kids a head start on effectively using research and collaborative strategies so they can employ them in the longer, in-depth inquiry circles we describe in the following three chapters. See chart above for a mini-inquiry adaptation of our inquiry framework.

Getting started with small-group inquiry requires just a few basic precepts:

• Teachers model their own curiosity and occasional skepticism, sharing their authentic questions, and keeping a research notebook of their own.

- Teachers share a variety of ways to get questions answered.

- Teachers explicitly demonstrate their own inquiry process by showing kids how they go about researching a question, finding an answer, and acting in response to their findings.

- Teachers model several lessons during mini-research that will be foundational later on when kids are doing their own more in-depth inquiry projects.

- Teachers invite kids to be curious.

- Kids ask questions, search for answers, and share their new learning.

As you will see, mini-inquiry can be simply jumping online to answer a quick question or may mean spending several hours over the course of a week to investigate a concept. Either way, the questions most often posed in mini-inquiry are what we call Quick Finds (QFs)—questions that are answered in a relatively rapid and easy way. One bonus of encouraging kids to answer these Quick Find questions is that they often get more interested in the topic as they research it. So mini-inquiry sometimes evolves into a more in-depth research project, particularly if the learner gets stoked about the newfound information.

In this chapter we share examples of primary through secondary mini-research projects that take as little as fifteen or twenty minutes or as long as four or five hours. Keep in mind that mini-inquiry will not provide an in-depth, complex understanding of a large concept or essential question, but it does give us a bit more information about a question, helps to satisfy our curiosity, and often fuels our desire to find out even more. And from a teacher's point of view, it offers the best natural opportunity to teach some important aspects of the research process in a relatively short period of time, so kids are better prepared for longer, in-depth inquiry projects later on.

Model Your Curiosity and Record Questions in Your Notebook

See Lesson 19, "Model Your Own Inquiry Process," p. 134.

One morning Steph gathered thirty fifth graders in front of her. "I know this sounds terrible, but I didn't used to recycle as much as I should," she confessed. "It's true. I'm embarrassed to admit it, but it was such a pain to separate all of the items into different bins—one for aluminum, one for paper, and one for plastic." The kids looked as if every last drop of respect they had for Steph had disappeared along with the Coke cans and plastic bottles. She went on to explain that recently the recycling company had left a flyer titled "Recycling Without Sorting" on her front door. She flipped through and discovered that she would no longer have to sort plastic, glass, or paper items because of a new process called single-stream recycling. The recycling company would provide one large recycling bin for all of the family's recyclables. So the very next day, Steph happily dumped paper products, plastic bottles, and aluminum cans all into the same recycling bin.

See Lesson 20, "Create Research Notebooks," p. 135.

"But you know what? I'm curious by nature and I can't stop wondering whether this is a good idea. It seems too easy. I wonder if this single-stream recycling is as good a method of recycling as sorted recycling. I really want to find this out. I'm going to write that question in my notebook," Steph said as she opened a spiral notebook. "I jot down and record questions and thoughts in my research notebook so I won't forget them. A curious fifth grader I knew called these notebooks 'wonder books' [Harvey 1998], but whatever you call them, they give me a place to hold my thinking. When my curiosity gets the best of me, I jot down what I wonder and then follow up later by doing some quick research. It is my curiosity that drives me to answer my questions and find out information. Richard Feynman, a very famous scientist, referred to this curiosity as his 'puzzle drive.' It is my puzzle drive that spurs me to solve puzzles and search for answers to my questions. And it is writing those questions down that reminds me to do the research."

She added the new recycling question to her wonder list and then shared some other questions from her research notebook.

- Are washing detergents all equal when it comes to cleaning clothes regardless of the price? Is Tide more expensive just because it is Tide, or is it better at cleaning the clothes? (A)

- How does a Toyota Highlander Hybrid handle in the snow? The brochure doesn't have any pictures of it in snow. How will it perform in the mountains in a big snowstorm? (A)

- What exactly are credit default swaps? I have heard that they are the root of the recent recession.

- Is horse racing bad for horses? I have heard about some horses that died while racing or at the end of the race. I wonder why?

- Will it hurt my car to use a lower, cheaper grade of gasoline in the engine? The manual recommends premium gas. Does that mean I have to use it?

- Is recycling without sorting as environmentally sound as separating recycled items? How does it work? Does it take more energy in the long run?

Share Different Ways to Answer Questions

See Lesson 6, "Ask Questions and Wonder About Information," p. 121.

Steph explained that she had already found answers to a few of these questions in her notebook, and others she still needed to research. "There are different ways to find answers to our questions. I went online to learn about the Highlander Hybrid. After a Google search, I found a website called ToyotaNation.com where people who own the cars talk about their performance—not the people who sell the cars, but people who own them. I think you can count on getting better information when someone is not trying to sell you something. It turns out the Highlander Hybrid is a terrific green car for energy savings, but not so good in a lot of snow. One Highlander Hybrid owner wrote on that site that his Hi Hy was like a boat anchor in the snow, meaning it could hardly move in snow. I called a local Toyota dealership and asked about this. They said if I wanted a really good snow car, I ought to look at their Toyota 4-Runner. So I got my question answered: the Highlander Hybrid is a fabulous green car, but not so good in snow, which means it's not for me, since I am looking for a car that is good in the mountains in winter. I haven't chosen one yet, because I still want a green car. So I am still looking. Does this make sense to you?" The kids nodded.

"Now, other times, it helps to ask a specialist or an expert for information. To answer the laundry detergent question, I interviewed a man who worked in the detergent industry and I learned there is a key ingredient in detergents known as a *surfactant* that allows water to get clothes cleaner. The more surfactant in the detergent, the cleaner the clothes. Surfactants are expensive, however. Tide, it turns out, has more surfactants than most detergents, making it better at getting clothes clean, but also more expensive. However, this man also explained that some brands, particularly the Kirkland brand at Costco, have the same number of surfactants but are cheaper than Tide. So if I want to save money but still get clothes as clean as Tide does, I might change to the Kirkland brand of detergent. That's an example of how talking to a specialist can help us get information. So I marked both of these questions with an *A* for answer and then jotted down the answers in my notebook so I would remember the information."

After her explanation, Steph asked the kids to turn and talk about their thoughts and reactions to the inquiry process she had just explained. After several shared, she handed out research notebooks to each of them. Holding up her own, she said, "Like mine, these research notebooks are a place for you to hold your thoughts and questions as you

Questions and musings from Cassie's research notebook.

I Wonder 100

1. are there really other lifeforms out there, or is that just a myth?
2. if there are other lifeforms out there, are they intellegent and wonder about us too?
3. how did the first people learn to talk?
4. what were Africans thinking on the ship "Amistad", on the journey?
5. what came first, the chicken or the egg?
6. what is the purpose of life?
7. how does grass cause stains?
8. when did the first person say a word in english?
9. how do the buttons work on a remote control?
10. how long can a person say ahhhh...?
11. how much carbon dioxide does a coke can contain?
12. what is the highest amount a ___ cycle can have?
13. where did rabies come from?
14. what was Monet's first painting?
15. what does Isabell (my kitten) think while I'm gone?
16. on the inside, what is the difference beetwen wheat and white bread?
17. how can a lightbulb burn out if running on electricity?
18. how long will the Leaning Tower of Piosa lean?

Cassie

See Lesson 20, "Research Notebooks," p. 135.

wonder about anything you are curious about. Take a moment to jot down several things you wonder about, maybe three or four questions that you want to find out about, just like I did with the laundry detergent and the hybrid car. Once you have a few questions written down, turn and talk and share them with a partner. We will keep these notebooks as we go through the inquiry process, adding our thoughts, questions, notes and findings."

Curiosity is at the heart of inquiry. We discover much information simply by being curious, keeping track of our questions, and taking the time to find answers. As teachers, we model our curiosity every day. We share a question or two that we have and record them in our notebooks. We share our "puzzle drive" so our kids will catch it and jot their wonderings in notebooks as well. A page from fifth grader Cassie's notebook explodes with curiosity about a universe of topics and shows the broad spectrum of things kids wonder about every day. See Cassie's list on the previous page.

One of the first words we teach in inquiry-based classrooms is *curiosity*. We model our own insatiable curiosity about life and the world. And above all, we celebrate our students' curiosity.

Demonstrate Your Own Inquiry: Single-Stream Recycling

To show kids how research really works, we make our own inquiry process visible by modeling how we go about asking questions and finding out information. We can do this using either a mandated curriculum topic or a personal question of our own. Whichever we choose, we start our mini-inquiry with small questions that can be answered relatively easily.

We take kids through mini-research to encourage them to pursue their own questions and to show them some of the important aspects of the inquiry process. In the mini-inquiry process, the final product is often simply locating and sharing information or even making a decision based on newly discovered data. Answering authentic questions and then acting on them is what grown-ups do every day.

After explaining how she researched and found information about the Hybrid in snow and the most cost-effective detergent, Steph took her kids through the process more explicitly as she unpacked how she would go about answering her most recent question about recycling. "I am a better recycler since I began the single-stream recycling, but I still wonder if it is as good for the environment as regular recycling. I'm skeptical. Being skeptical means that you have some doubts. For instance, if sorting single-stream recyclables uses more energy than the extra amount of energy recycling saves, I might decide to stop recycling without sorting. So I decided to investigate to find out for sure. Skepticism pushes me to ask questions and find answers."

Steph began modeling her own inquiry process by flipping through a recent *Newsweek* article on recycling. Although she gained some new information, she

> *O*ne of the first words we teach in inquiry-based classrooms is curiosity. We model our own insatiable *curiosity* about life and the world. And above all, we celebrate our students' curiosity.

didn't find an answer to her specific question. She explained that it was great to learn more information about the benefits of recycling and that incorporating this new information about recycling would build her background knowledge of the topic. But she was on a mission to get her specific question answered, so she needed to take a different tack. She decided to go online, and gathered the kids in front of a computer screen. She Googled *recycling,* only to find hundreds of sites. She showed how she narrowed her search by entering *recycling without sorting.* A number of articles came into view, all extolling the virtues of single-stream recycling.

And then, voila, as if by magic, a video and an article titled "Recycling Without Sorting: Engineers Create Recycling Plant That Removes the Need to Sort" popped up on the screen (*Science Daily* 2007). Steph explained that this title indicated she might get some important information directly related to her question. So they watched together—stopping, jotting their thoughts, and discussing throughout. Sure enough, the video explained the entire single-stream recycling process from start to finish. It mentioned that a recently developed technology now allowed new recycling plants all over the country to take the sorting out of the public's hands through a new recycling technology. In this process, trucks dump the unsorted mess of paper, plastic, and metal onto a conveyor belt where magnets, air blowers, and optical scanners separate the items, making it possible for the plant to resort and recycle the different products.

The article went on to explain that 30 percent more families are recycling now that sorting is no longer required. "What do you all think? Turn and talk about that," Steph suggested. The kids burst with enthusiasm as they chattered away. Steph's curiosity nudged their own and, in light of the fact that so many more people were participating in single-stream recycling, most of the kids were immediately sold on the idea. Steph noted that they could get more information about this topic if they read the accompanying article. So she printed it and passed it out to the kids, suggesting they read it, mark it up, jot their thinking in the margins, and find two or three kids to talk to about the article when they finished reading it.

After they finished reading and discussing, Steph asked kids to share anything they learned or wondered about. Students jumped in with tons of thoughts and ideas about recycling, how they might use the recycling tips to get more people in the neighborhood to recycle, and how their own family recycled. A couple of kids mentioned that the article raised some questions in a section headed "Pros and Cons." They noted that some people thought that single-stream recycling was not as good as sorted recycling, because the recycled materials were in some way degraded or diminished. As a result of their further reading, several kids rethought their position. Steph celebrated their skepticism and explained that the more we learn, the more we wonder. In this instance,

See Lesson 7, "Stop, Think, and React to Information," p. 122.

See Lesson 5, "Annotate the Text: Leave Tracks of Thinking," p. 120.

from what she had learned so far, she believed that the pros of single-stream recycling outweighed the cons. So for the time being, she was convinced that she would become a more committed recycler because of the convenience of single-stream recycling. However, she added that the jury was still out and that she would continue to search for more information that might change her mind in the future.

"This is so interesting; now that I know a little bit about single-stream recycling, I am really interested in this issue and want to know even more. And even though I find single-stream recycling very convenient, I always need to be willing to change my mind in light of new evidence and information," Steph said.

Co-construct Meaning to Capture and Hold Thinking

After Steph modeled her own inquiry process on single-stream recycling, she asked the kids to share out what they noticed her doing. As they did this, Steph recorded their responses on a chart to make the collective thinking visible. This anchor chart remained posted for all to see so they could return to it for guidance when they engaged in their own small-group inquiry projects.

HOW WE FIND OUT INFORMATION...

- We are curious.
- We write our questions in notebooks.
- We care about finding answers to our questions.
- We are skeptical.
- We ask specialists and experts.
- We read articles and books.
- We go online.
- We narrow our online search with specific words.
- We are awake to new information about our topic and continue to gather information.
- We change our minds in light of new evidence.

What's great about a lesson like this is that everyone learns about both the content *and* the process. After doing the research, Steph and the kids knew a lot

Co-constructing Anchor Charts, K–12

Gone are the days when we headed off to the Teacher Store in August and bought premade charts to decorate the room. We are teachers—not interior decorators! Also, gone are the days when secondary teachers left their walls bare, making it impossible to track ongoing thinking or projects across days and weeks. Anchor charts are for all teachers! They capture ideas and provide graphic representations of the collective thinking that comes to life in our classrooms when kids and teachers take their thinking public. Anchor charts visibly connect past teaching and learning to future teaching and learning. We hang them in the room so kids can refer to them as they practice what they have learned.

When we co-construct anchor charts with our kids, we solicit their responses, synthesize them, and add them to the chart. And although our thinking does not dominate the conversation, we are not afraid to weigh in with our own thoughts and opinions, particularly if we notice something missing. Teaching and learning in inquiry-based classrooms is a process of co-constructing meaning. Everyone builds knowledge, kids as well as the teachers.

more about single-stream recycling. But they also got a good idea of how the inquiry process works. Steph made her thinking visible in a number of ways:

- She shared and modeled her curiosity and her skepticism—thinking dispositions that drive further research.

- She demonstrated how she determined importance while reading in the effort to answer her question.

- She showed how she moved on to other sources when her question was not answered.

- She shared how she finally answered her question and how that answer would guide her as she moved forward.

- She recorded what she learned about the process on a chart.

- And above all, she pointed out how interested she now was in the issue of single-stream recycling, because the more we know about something, the more we care and wonder about it! This newfound interest spurs her even now to follow this issue closely and be open to changing her mind in light of new evidence.

We model the inquiry process and make our thinking visible for a number of reasons. Three important ones rise to the surface. When we go through the inquiry process ourselves:

- We show our kids that we value this kind of work. If it is important enough for us to do, it must be important for them too.

- We can teach the process by modeling it. There is no better way for kids to learn than by watching and doing.

- We learn something through our own inquiry that shows kids how our curiosity drives us even as adults, and enriches us in the process. You never stop learning!

Mini-Inquiry Projects

In the remainder of this chapter, you will see several mini-inquiry projects at different grade levels. As you read through them, you will recognize some of the inquiry techniques that Steph modeled so far in the chapter. You'll notice kids asking questions about topics that pique their interest, reading for information, jumping on line to find answers, and working together in small groups. You will see teachers conducting some of the lessons that we described in Chapter 7, "Key Lessons in Comprehension, Collaboration, and Inquiry." We have found that practicing these research strategies in mini-inquiry projects first leads to more successful extended inquiry circles later on.

INQUIRY: *Gak! It's Ipecac*

MIDDLE

HIGH SCHOOL

*W*e want to change "look it up" from an epithet to an adventure.

—Smokey Daniels, Best Practice High School, Chicago, Illinois

Did this ever happen to you as a kid? You suddenly had a burning question about the world that you posed to some adult, maybe a parent or teacher. Perhaps you asked something like, "How come we never see the far side of the moon?" And the grown-up gazed back at you with what seemed like annoyance and said, "Why don't you go look it up?" It almost felt like a putdown—like, hey, don't bother me, kid, I am in the middle of something important here. Now, as grown-ups ourselves, we might suspect that the adult's response was just a cover for not knowing the answer. But in our classrooms today, we want to change "look it up" from an epithet to an adventure. We want to turn that interaction around, so that when kids pose spontaneous inquiry questions, we drop everything and help them find answers (or at least scratch that curiosity itch) right away. That means sometimes we happily interrupt the flow of our lesson to show kids that curiosity rules, and that their questions really matter. As you'll see in this example, mini-inquiry can be as simple as asking a straightforward question and finding the answer in a dictionary or on a website, but that doesn't lessen its impact.

Smokey was working with some high school students in Chicago, helping them to polish their literature circle skills. During this day's small-group meetings, kids were reading a wonderful short-short story called "This Is How I Remember It," by Betsy Kemper. In this nasty-lovely tale, three mischievous children surreptitiously taste the forbidden red berries from a bush in the woods. Suddenly their moms appear, drag the kids into the house, and force a thick purple liquid down their throats, which causes them to vomit up the possibly poisonous berries. (Kids always love this story for the sensory details of multicolored projectile vomiting.) As the six different literature circles were meeting, one group grabbed Smokey and asked, "What is this purple stuff the moms gave the kids? Why does it make you throw up? We never heard of it." Smokey was surprised, since syrup of ipecac was a staple in his family's medicine cabinet—and because he had once given it to his daughter after she gobbled a bottle of baby aspirin.

"It's called ipecac," Smokey said. "Do you want to find out about it? Do you think it would help you understand the story better?" The kids gave an enthusiastic "Yeah!" and sprang to the classroom computers. Kids looked up from other groups and Smokey asked: "Are you guys also wondering about the purple stuff?" Seeing many nods, he said, "This group is going to look into it and report back in a few minutes. So just enjoy your discussions, and we'll let you know when they are ready to fill you in."

The investigating group quickly found some information and also a big surprise. From a handful of websites, they were easily able to answer their "What is it?" question: ipecac is an emetic (which means a substance that makes you throw up) made from the dried rhizome and roots of the ipecacuanha plant. The active ingredients are two alkaloids that act both on the stomach lining and the medullary chemoreceptor trigger zone to induce vomiting. It has been used for many decades as a home remedy for poisoning; parents were advised to immediately give ipecac to a child who had ingested any poison, so that the toxic substance would be vomited out. The kids also found an I-Tube video of a college kid who drinks four bottles of ipecac on a dare and then vomits violently on-screen. Isn't technology great?

The surprising finding came from the American Academy of Pediatrics (AAP) website, which says ipecac is unsafe and is no longer recommended for use at home. Oh, yes, it does make a person vomit, quite reliably. But the vomiting is not effective in purging the poison from the victim. Research done in 2003 showed that poisoning outcomes were no better with ipecac—and that it has several potentially dangerous side effects. So now the AAP recommends that parents not use ipecac, but rather call the local poison control center if they think their child has ingested a harmful substance.

The group reported the ipecac facts to the whole class, who listened, as you might expect, with rapt attention. This whole process, from question to answers to sharing and back to work in the groups, took no more than five or six minutes. But everyone built their background knowledge, and it also helped students place the story in the late 1950s, where it in fact was set. The kids who pursued this inquiry project not only reinforced their questioning and research skills, they also were energized by the process of finding immediate answers to their questions and putting that information to work right away.

INQUIRY: *Why Do Mosquito Bites Itch?*

See Lesson 3, "Think and Wonder About Images," p. 118.

—STEPH HARVEY, FROSTWOOD ELEMENTARY, HOUSTON, TEXAS

Steph once came across three second graders reading a book on insects. One had just placed a Post-it on a rather creepy, close-up photo of a mosquito penetrating a human arm, just the kind of image that makes kids squeal with delight or disgust ("Ewww, gross!"). We are reminded that questions emerge from images and text features as well as from text. *Why does a mosquito bite itch?* a kid wondered. A great question for mini-research, and another potential Quick Find. QFs often lend themselves to online research. Now, a Quick Find answer is unlikely to lead to in-depth understanding of a concept or an issue. It is doubtful that these kids would understand the complex arrangement of a mosquito's digestive enzymes with one click of a mouse. However, they could very well get a basic idea of what causes a mosquito bite to itch.

So after a brief discussion with Steph about how they might answer their question and a determination that it was probably a QF, they went to Askkids.com and typed in the very same question. The answer popped up at Kidshealth.org and they wrote it on a larger Post-it: *The female mosquito has a special part of her mouth that she uses to suck blood, and her saliva (spit) thins the blood so she can drink it. In fact, it's the mosquito's saliva that makes the bites itch!*

During sharing, this mini-research group showed the image to a chorus of *oohs* and *ahhs*, then revealed the answer. Mini-inquiry could end right there with the answer to an original question. Or kids might get hooked and want to learn more. As kids shared their findings, questions came fast and furiously: Do male mosquitoes bite? How does the saliva cause itching? And more. A number of kids expressed a desire to learn more about mosquitoes. So Steph encouraged them to write down anything else they wondered about mosquitoes in their notebooks and go from there. They read more of the article at Kidshealth.org, and with Steph's help found some mosquito texts at their reading level. Suddenly, they were off to the races with a slew of mosquito questions and an urge to find out more. The initial investigation took about a half hour. Their subsequent mosquito research had them reading, writing, and talking about mosquitoes for several days. No more filling in bubbles and blanks during independent work time. These kids were reading more than ever and emerging as mosquito specialists, all bubbling up from one question about one image.

See Lesson 21, "Explore and Use Multiple Sources," p. 136.

Tackling Longer Mini-Inquiries

Like the other teachers featured in this chapter, Bodo Heiliger recognized that he could teach some of the important steps in the research process by starting small and then leading kids through a mini-inquiry project. But unlike those spontaneous Ipecac and mosquito bite inquiries, Bodo devised a plan that would allocate five 60-minute class periods over the course of the week to his kids' more extended mini-inquiry projects. Following the Gradual Release of Responsibility instructional framework, Bodo guided his fourth graders through some basic steps in the inquiry process, teaching some important research strategies at the start and then releasing the kids to do research in their own small collaborative groups. He confined the students' inquiry to issues and questions that arose from a single issue of *Time for Kids* magazine, so they could get their arms around their first small-group inquiry projects. Bodo was convinced that through this mini-research experience, his kids would gain a new appreciation for how much their questions matter. And he hoped that they would be better equipped to tackle the more in-depth group research projects that would follow, both in his classroom and beyond. So, in Bodo's own words, here's an in-depth look at how fourth graders handled a week-long mini-inquiry project. .

INTERMEDIATE

INQUIRY: *From Cheese to Magazines*

—BODO HEILIGER, ALEXANDRIA COUNTRY DAY SCHOOL, ALEXANDRIA, VIRGINIA

The way a child's mind operates is simply a miracle. I have recently come to appreciate how amazing kids' questions are and that what really matters is being available to help students discover information and find answers. Their natural curiosity is stunning. I confess that in the past I sometimes felt overwhelmed by the sheer volume of kids' questions. Unable to answer or unwilling to take the time, I frequently fell into the "go look it up" trap, rather than indulging their curiosity. I have recently come to appreciate how amazing kids' questions are and now understand how much we all learn when we join together, investigate and search for answers. From Day 1 of the school year, I had focused on teaching kids to think. They had learned and practiced how to monitor comprehension, activate background knowledge, make connections, ask questions, make inferences, determine important information, and summarize and synthesize while reading. I decided that we could build on these thinking strategies to support kids as they did research as well. You really can't do research without thinking carefully about what you read, hear, and see. And kids soon discovered that using these strategies flexibly helped tremendously as they engaged in the research process.

Mini-inquiry projects not only provide kids with the tools to do independent research, but also validate and honor their questions, their pursuits, and their findings. And it is the celebration of their wonder and curiosity that makes all of the difference. As they engaged in mini-inquiry projects, students came to me daily with information they found. They voluntarily shared articles, ideas, and issues. They looked things up, hopped online, and read widely and wildly in pursuit of answers to their questions. And what amazed me most about this mini-inquiry project—apart from the students' sheer pleasure and engagement—was how well it helped them transition to larger and more in-depth research projects later on.

I followed the Gradual Release of Responsibility instructional approach as we moved through this project, beginning with my modeling my own question on the first day, guiding them to find answers, supporting them to work together on the second and third day, and then sending them off for collaborative practice, teamwork, and sharing findings on the final two days of the inquiry. Here's an overview of our lesson sequence.

Day 1: Introduction to Mini-Inquiry Projects

- Teacher introduces researching and note taking by modeling with a teacher-created question in mind: When and how was cheese invented?

- Present findings.

Day 2: Modeling How to Find and Research a Question

- Using *Time for Kids,* teacher models how to read while questioning the text.

- Teacher and kids co-create a question for research: Who is the Dalai Lama and what does he do? Model researching and note taking with a question in mind.

- Present findings.

Day 3: Working in a Group to Come up with a Researchable Question

- Students work in groups and read *Time for Kids* while recording their questions about the text.

- Students determine which of their questions interest them the most and can be answered by reading a variety of texts.

Day 4: Researching the Answer and Preparing the Presentation

- Establish ground rules for collaborative work.

- Students research additional resources and take notes with their question in mind.

- Students prepare a poster, skit, paper, or other presentation.

Day 5: Presentation and Reflection

- Present findings.

- Celebrate the research!

- Reflect on the process.

Day 1: Introduction to Mini-Research Projects

I have always found that the way you introduce any project can make or break the entire experience for students. I contend that if you show enthusiasm for watching paint dry, kids will sit down next to you and watch (at least for a few minutes)! The first day of any project inspires or discourages the students and sets the stage for excellence or mediocrity. To foster the former, I begin this project with all the students sitting around me at the easel, and I ask them the following questions while recording some of their answers on chart paper.

> **"I'm thinking of some questions that are always asked by kids, but rarely answered by anyone. Why is the sky blue? Why is the grass green? Why is blood red? Where does dust come from? What are eye boogers? Have you ever had any questions that have never been answered?"**

"I have so many every day!"

"I always wondered why my feet stink."

"Why does hair fall out?"

"Why do muscles get all bulked up when you lift weights?"

"Has anyone ever told you to look up the answer? If so, have you ever looked it up? Why did you or didn't you?"

"Mr. Heiliger, I asked you a question about the plague and you told me to look up different types of Black Plague remedies, but I didn't because I didn't have time and I kinda forgot."

"All the time, but I never look it up because I'm too busy."

"My mom always tells me to look it up. When she does that, I just don't care about the answer anymore."

"There are so many questions we come up with every single day and rarely take the time to answer. During this next week, we are going to work together to answer those questions. You are going to come up with questions that are important to you, and you're going to find the answers to them! What's awesome is that we don't know what the questions will be! You're going to come up with them."

Kids always become excited about the unknown, and having the ability to create their own questions helps to inspire them. However, to begin the project, we need to do a quick whole-class investigation on some topic that will be of great interest to the majority of students and will serve as a model for them. To come up with a good question, I reflect on the personality of the class as well as a subject I am interested in learning more about. I have found that each class, every year, establishes some sort of personality and becomes completely enamored with something or someone. This past year was no different; these kids were fascinated by *cheese*, of all things. Perhaps it's a funny word or overly used in cartoons, but this love of cheese became the basis for our whole-class question: How and when was cheese created? I've found it particularly useful to come up with a question that most kids would never

What kids learned about cheese (without using the Internet).

When and how was cheese invented?

Source	Notes

"Cheese" Colliers 1993	• 5,000 years ago (3,000 B.C.)
	• 5,000 B.C.
	
	• Made from animal's milk
	  – horse, cow, reindeer, buffalo, goat, sheep
	
	• Process
	  – take out whey
	  – add bacteria
	  – add dye for color
	  – mix for 15-90 min.
	  – add thickener
	  – put in animal's stomach
	  – cut curds into cubes
	  – leave to dry
	  – press it
	  – add salt

Book of Knowledge 2001	
"Dairy" Colliers 1992	
Comptons 1994	

www.heinemann.com/
comprehensionandcollaboration.

*See Lesson 19, "Model Your
Own Inquiry," p. 134.*

think they'd be asked to research. This question on cheese was perfect. To read about our one-day cheese investigation, and how it set the kids up for finding individual mini-inquiry topics the next day, please go to the website.

Day 2: Modeling How to Find and Research a Question

During the first day's lesson, we talked about how to come up with a question (the origins of cheese) and then research with that question in mind. The second day focuses on using an issue of *Time for Kids* (March 28, 2008) to help generate questions.

I tell the students that we are going to read through a couple *TFK* articles together and come up with a question. Then we are going to work in two stages. First we will research that question and keep track of our thinking by taking notes. Then, after our whole-class question creation and discovery, kids will break into groups to come up with their own questions. Throughout the year, students read *TFK* and write down tons of questions on their Post-its as they read. Because they are familiar with both *TFK* and questioning, I encourage the students to write down their own thinking while I read and share mine. We don't get past the first article on Tibet and its struggle with China before we have at least twenty "researchable" questions:

Who is the Dalai Lama?	Why don't we [the U.S.] do anything to help?
Why did China invade Tibet?	What's it like to live in Tibet?
Why don't the Tibetans fight back?	What is Buddhism?
What's happening in Tibet today?	How is Buddhism different than Christianity?

It is important to discuss all the questions because the school's Internet service is down today of all days! So we need to figure out which questions can be answered in a library without Internet access. We decide that it would be a struggle to answer a question such as, "What's it like in Tibet today?" and "Why don't we do anything about it?" without the Internet, because printed sources are unlikely to reflect the current situation in Tibet. I explain that while time-sensitive information is best dealt with on the Internet, we can often get more information about a topic that is not current from books. I chose the Dalai Lama question because I am interested in learning more about him. So, I say to the class:

> *"I'm extremely interested in the Dalai Lama and I am delighted that someone came up with a question about him. Do you think we can find the answers in the library? I really don't know much about him and would love to learn more. Is it OK if we, as a class, agree on the question, Who is the Dalai Lama?"*

I rarely have much dissension with a whole-class decision like this, but if there is, I always let the kids know they will have the chance to research a different question later. Prior to the lesson, I collect as many books on Tibet and the Dalai

See Lesson 8, *"Notetaking: Read with a Question in Mind," p. 123.*

Kids' researchable questions about Tibet.

Lama as the library has to offer. I begin reading the book *Tibet: Through the Red Box* (by Peter Sís) while constantly reflecting on the question and asking myself if the information helps me answer it. Toward the end of this beautiful Caldecott-winning book is a story about the Dalai Lama—exactly what we need. There is a sidebar with a complete description of who the Dalai Lama is and how he came to power. I write down every important fact that helps us answer our question. Once we exhaust this book, I grab an encyclopedia. Interestingly enough, we find only one extra fact to add to our research. The students are amazed that we were able to find more information in a picture book than in an encyclopedia. I spend a minute talking about how picture books often provide us with valuable information, plus they have the added bonus of beautiful writing and pictures. I bring closure to today's lesson by asking both a content and a process question:

"What did you learn today about the Dalai Lama?"

"There have only been fourteen Dalai Lamas."

"He is the leader of Tibet."

"Dalai means 'ocean of wisdom' and Lama means 'master or teacher,' so the Dalai Lama is a teacher or master with an ocean of wisdom."

"He lived at Potala, which is a palace with a thousand rooms with huge towers or spiritual wings. But now he is in exile in India."

"What did you learn about researching today?"

"Picture books are more fun to research with."

"Encyclopedias have a ton of information, but not always more than a picture book. Plus encyclopedias are not as interesting."

"If a book like Through the Red Box does not have a table of contents or index, then you might have to read through the entire book to find what you're looking for. That takes a little more time, but it was an interesting story."

At the close of the period, I tell the students that tomorrow they are all going to do this kind of research in a small group, pursuing a topic of their own choice.

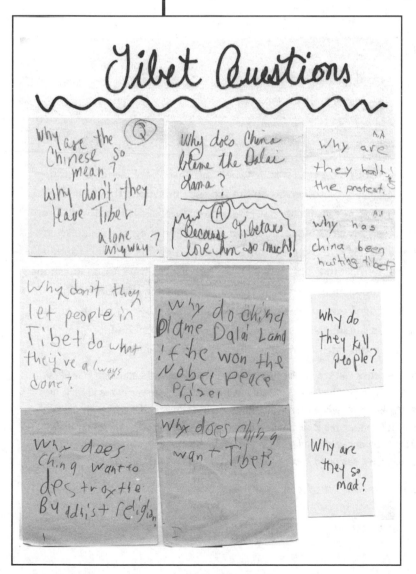

See Lesson 6, "Ask Questions and Wonder About Information," p. 121, and Lesson 22, "Choosing Topics to Investigate," p. 137.

Day 3: Working in a Group to Come Up with a Researchable Question

The days when I release the kids to go off on their own are always exciting because they show me whether my teaching worked. To begin today's lesson, I gather the students around me and we reflect on what they've learned over the past two days about researching. After a review of the reading-with-a-question-in-mind strategy and working in groups, I break the students into the same heterogeneous groups from the first day and have them read through the entire *Time for Kids* while focusing on coming up with questions that really interest them. I give the students about thirty minutes to read through the articles in the magazine and chat with each other while I circulate, listening to their thinking.

"Can glaciers reform?"

"Are protests ever peaceful?"

"How do scorpions sting?"

"How come the middle states seem to have more harsh weather than other places?"

"Why are some people allergic to things while others are not?"

"How can people get cars out of floods when they are covered in water?"

"Why does China blame the Dalai Lama if he won the Nobel Peace Prize?"

Once all the groups have read through the magazine or are close to finishing, I tell them that they will need to decide on the top four questions they believe they can answer with resources in the library. (The school Internet is still down.) I tell them they can choose their top questions and if they cannot agree, we'll discuss their choices as a class. I give the groups five minutes to decide on their top questions. I then have them sit in a large circle so we can discuss the chosen questions as a whole class to determine which ones can be answered in the library. This helps all groups recognize what types of questions can be answered at the library and which may need outside resources such as newspapers or the Internet.

I always preface this decision-making task with this statement:

"I know that because you are all working in a group, your favorite question may not be chosen by the whole group or may not be a question you can answer in the library. In life, there are moments when your ability to be flexible will help the entire group. OK, who has a question they think cannot be answered in the library, and why? Any question that cannot be answered today in the library, let's keep track of it, so when we have the chance, we can go to a more current source to find the answer."

"What's happening with the flooding in the Midwest can't be answered because we would need a newspaper or the Internet, which we do not have right now."

"How many schools are peanut-free can't be answered because we don't have the Internet."

"So those are good questions to research later on, if anyone is interested. Now, what question or questions have you chosen to research today?"

GROUP 1: "We decided on the question, Do allergies ever start at an older age?"

After every group's question, I ask the class,

"Does everyone think they should be able to find the answer in the library? Where should they look? Okay, group 2 . . . "

GROUP 2: "What causes massive flooding?"

GROUP 3: "Is it our fault global warming has started?"

GROUP 4: "What is a scorpion's stinger and how poisonous is it?"

GROUP 5: "Apart from the fighting, is Tibet a nice place to live?"

"Wow, each group has such a different topic from the others. Tomorrow, you are going to research the answers to your questions. I'm excited to see what you all find out!"

Some of the groups had two questions they could not agree upon, so I intervened and gently steered them toward the question I felt would yield the most information as they pursued their answers.

Inquiry questions from the Allergies group using annotation codes.

Day 4: Researching the Answer and Preparing the Presentation

See Lesson 8, "Notetaking: Read with a Question in Mind," p. 123, Lesson 13, "Creating Group Ground Rules," p. 128, and Lesson 14, "Making and Using a Plan," p. 129.

Today, the groups will seek answers to their questions. Before sending them off to research I call them into a circle to review how to take notes on the researching template, and how to respectfully work together as a group to find the answers. Depending on the dynamic of a class, a teacher can assign roles for each member of the group. However, I usually allow the students to figure out the best method for their group to work together. I explain the idea of consensus, that we need to listen to everyone's ideas, but if we cannot agree on a process, we can always take a vote. I make it clear, however, that we need to keep in mind the feelings and thoughts of everyone in the group as we go through this collaborative process. If conflicts arise that cannot be resolved, I let them know that I may assign roles and jobs (timekeeper, reporter, illustrator, manager, etc). This doesn't happen often, though, because most fourth graders take pride in working something out without the teacher's involvement. After the discussion about collaborative work process, I send the groups off for approximately ninety minutes to research and prepare the presentation—the time will be determined by the topics and amount of available information.

Once each group has researched the answers to their questions, I explain the sharing phase of the inquiry. The instructions are simple and the choices are wide: each group must prepare some sort of presentation to explain their findings and create a powerful visual to go with it.

Mini-Research Projects...What question do need answered?

? What is a scorpions stinger?

Source	Notes
BOOK Title: World book Author: ~ Publishing Company: World Book Inc. City: Chicago Year: 1994 Pages Used: 210	• a curved organ • at end of tail • made of two glands. • give out poisen from 2 pores. • Stings are rarely deadly to humans
WEBSITE URL: ~ Author: ~ Page:	Interesting fact The bigger the better (The bigger the scorpian, the less poiseness flourescent when under UV light stings as a whip.

Two-column form to support kids as they answer a question.

See Lesson 27, "Response Options: Take Learning Public," p. 142.

Day 5: Presentation and Reflection

I invite kids to present their findings in any way they choose, as long as there is some visual component. For this inquiry presentation, most groups decide to create a poster and present their findings through skits. One group comes up with a song to help enhance their presentation. It's important to leave the door open to all the different ways in which students can make their learning visible. Songs, lectures, posters, skits—there are countless ways to show learning. This freedom allows for maximum creativity and excitement. My only requirement is that each group's presentation allow the audience to clearly understand its research. The last step of the project is to reflect with the children on what they learned about the research process and how this will help them when they have questions in the future, especially as they move into more in-depth research. Some of their responses:

> "It's sooo important to research with a question in your mind! It makes it so much easier! You don't have to take so many notes, because you just write notes about your question."

> "I now know that it's not that hard to find answers, even without the Internet! I'm going to do it more often!"

> "The library is a great place to get information. The Internet is probably better for current stuff."

> "When we get to the bigger projects, we could probably break down our paper into several different questions and then research them one by one."

> "You should remember to use more than one source to get your information."

> "It's fun to be allowed to present our research in a fun way."

> "This was awesome."

> "It's fun to research!"

This whole project was a response to my inability to answer all the questions my students posed. By brushing off their questions with flippant responses, I squashed much of their enthusiasm and interest. Now, when kids ask me questions I cannot answer, I find time during the day for them to search for the answer—right away, if possible, no waiting. I am certainly aware that there isn't enough time in a day to answer every question because many uncontrollable forces dictate much of our class time. However, if you provide kids with small chunks of time in class, they'll feel validated and often will begin to find time on their own outside of school. Too often children rely on adults for the answers to questions. We want students to feel a sense of independence and a desire to head to the library and use the Internet to complete their own inquiry projects. Our job is to foster this desire. Kids love researching when they're interested and invested in the topic and when they know their interests are valued. As Albert Einstein stated, "The important thing is not to stop questioning." As teachers, we have the power to squash students' curiosity or foster it so they never stop wondering.

> Parts
>
> Alexa = Narrator
> Emma P. = Gabby
> Emma B. = Ashley
> Charlotte = Teacher
>
> Narrator Hello and welcome to our play. Our question is "What is a scorpian stinger?"
>
> Teacher Good morning children!
>
> Children Good morning Mis. Carter!
>
> Teacher Today we are going to start off with science.
>
> Narrator While the other kids were getting out their books Gabby and ashley got ready for their science presentation.
>
> Ashley Hello. I'm Ashley and this is —
> Gabby Gabby.
> Teacher What will you be sharing about this fine morning?
> Ashley Scorpion's
> Gabby Stingers!
> Ashley Did you know that like the stinger is a curved organ? Totaly!!
> Gabby At the end of it's tail.
> Gabby It's made of 2 glands.
> Ashley And scorpians give out poisen from 2 pores inside the glands

> Narrator Pores are a tiny opening in a skin gland.
>
> Gabby Don't worry though stings are deadly rarely to humans.
> Ashley Oh thank heavens! If I died it would be a waste of fabulousnus. Ya see these shoes? It would be a waste of 50 bucks.
> Narrator Well okay....
>
> Gabby When the scorpian stings it's tail is like a whip.
> Ashley A cool fact is like the bigger the scorpian the less poisen.
> Gabby It also lights up when it's under a UV light.
>
> Ashley Gab THE END !!!!!
>
> Teacher Well I sure learned a lot today about scorpians.
> Narrator This is Narrator saying
>
> Song! Scorpian scorpian does whatever a scorpian does, can he sting, yes he can and he stings with his tail like this Wachhhh
> (Emma)

Script of final presentation skit.

Starting small with mini-inquiry projects makes a lot of sense. It gives us the opportunity to model important research strategies and gives kids a chance to dip their toe in the inquiry waters. Every bit of research does not require an extended time for gathering information or a formal presentation of findings. We don't need a concrete product at the end of every project. Sometimes, acquiring new knowledge and sharing it with others is the goal and the most important result. When kids have a chance to answer questions as well as ask them, they grow as thinkers and gain knowledge and insight in the process. As P. David Pearson reminds us, "Today's new knowledge is tomorrow's background knowledge." (Pearson 2005). Building a store of knowledge and integrating it is what education is all about.

For two more examples of mini-research in action, check the website for: "The Lotus Seed" with Debbie Miller and "Sharks" with Barb Smith.

www.heinemann.com/comprehensionandcollaboration.

Curricular Inquiries

We've already made the case that traditional instruction, relying upon textbook reading and teacher lectures, doesn't have much sticking power for kids. Sure, it seems quicker to simply tell students the causes of the Civil War than to send them off to investigate on their own. But will students remember the textbook/lecture version? And how can students learn to do historical thinking if they only hear the conclusions and never experience the disciplined process through which historical interpretations are made? When we slow down, go deeper, and set students up to experiment like real scientists, investigate like historians, and solve problems like mathematicians, they experience how those specialists actually reason, investigate, and come to understand.

So sometimes, instead of deploying our kids in the standard six rows of five and presenting the information, we select chunks of curriculum and teach them using well-structured small groups. We hand kids the reins of responsibility, equip them for thoughtful investigation, and guide from the side. We are still "covering the material," but doing it in a challenging, sociable, hands-on way.

Even as we acknowledge the value in this approach, we may still worry. Going deeper takes significant time, which means we have to be selective—featuring certain content and skimming or even (yikes) omitting some. Do you see that five-hundred-pound gorilla sitting over there? The official curriculum! Most of us have state or district mandates that require us to teach specific topics, concepts, and processes every day, week, and year. Much of this mandated curriculum is valuable and potentially interesting to kids. But for true understanding, we know we must go deeper; we can't "cover" everything. So what matters most?

What Content Is Most Worth Teaching?

In a world of strict time limits and urgent deadlines, how do we determine which chunks of school curriculum are most worth kids' time and ours? Our first test is always the same: Is it interesting to kids? Well, duh! This idea of capitalizing on what kids care about isn't exactly new—indeed, the instinct resides in the DNA of most teachers, even if we often feel we dare not act upon it. In a fascinating 2008 study,

Gay Ivey and Joan Broaddus showed that to maximize students' content-area learning, teachers needed to figure out what topics within their field were really interesting to students, and then *begin with those.* Once students are hooked, it is easier to lead them into the less immediately tantalizing corners of a discipline. This study was especially important since it concerned middle-grade English language learners.

The "backwards design" movement, led by Grant Wiggins and Jay McTighe (2005), helps us identify curriculum that warrants our slowing down and digging deeper. They offer four "screens" for determining what curriculum is vital to teach—and, implicitly, what other topics can safely be deemphasized. The first screen: *Is the topic potentially interesting to students?* Now where have we heard that question before? Next Wiggins and McTighe advise us to wonder: *Does the topic lie at the heart of the discipline?* In other words, is this subject matter vital, central, essential to one's understanding of the field as a whole? Is it the kind of topic that, without having studied it, we cannot really call ourselves knowledgeable in the field?

The next screen is: *Does the subject require uncovering?* Though we often use the term *covering* to indicate that we have taught or delivered information, it can have another meaning. Sometimes the key ideas in a subject field are covered up—not obvious, counterintuitive, or subject to widespread misconceptions. These are topics where, if you don't take time to teach them, kids may go through life with flawed understandings or wrong assumptions about a whole domain of knowledge. We can't have that.

Finally, kids in middle and high school are always asking us, "Why do we have to learn this?" or sometimes more pointedly, "When will I ever use this stuff?" These plaintive queries are taken seriously by Wiggins and McTighe's fourth curriculum screen: *Does the subject connect with everyday life? Does it have practical, immediate applications to the world we live in?* This test obviously dovetails with and reinforces our focus on relevance and concern about kids' interest and engagement.

So now we have a pretty useful formula for deciding what parts of our overstuffed curricula we should devote time and energy to. Curricula worth teaching involve topics that kids wonder about, that might be a little puzzling, that have real-life implications, and that are genuinely key to understanding the field.

What Content Is Best Suited to Small-Group Inquiries?

Once we have identified especially vital and valuable parts of the curriculum, we can decide which of them can be framed as small-group inquiries. Teachers have found most success with these criteria:

- Students have already posed questions or shown curiosity about the topic.
- The topic is rich and complex.

- Interpretation and analysis are required.

- There are different facets or subtopics to be explored.

- Thoughtful learners can disagree and debate.

- There is a values, social, or moral dimension.

- There are decisions to be made, objects to be created, positions to supported, or actions to be taken.

- There can be multiple outcomes, understandings, or solutions.

- Investigations lead to even more questions, problems, or puzzles.

These considerations don't screen out very much, do they? There are countless topics in every subject field that meet several or all of these criteria. Kids can undertake investigative small-group work on polar bears, trips to Mars, grammatical structures, geometric formulas, photosynthesis, and more, more, more. See the following chart to adapt our small-group inquiry framework to curricular inquiries.

Small-Group Inquiry Model Adapted for Curricular Inquiry

Content and concepts are determined by state standards, district curriculum, and/or teacher planning.

STAGE	TEACHER	KIDS
Immerse *Invite Curiosity, Build Background, Find Topics, and Wonder*	• Plans instruction and teaches with central curricular concepts and focus questions in mind • Gathers and organizes curricular materials and resources • Immerses kids in multiple sources to build background knowledge • Invites curiosity, questioning, engagement • Models own curricular inquiry • Conducts think-alouds with text and materials related to the curricular topic • Demonstrates how to ask questions about curricular topics • Facilitates small-group formation to ensure heterogeneous groups with compatible interests • Confers with small groups and individuals	• Express their own curiosity • Explore, experience, and learn about topics using texts, visuals, Internet, artifacts, etc. • Read, listen, and view to build background knowledge about the curricular topic • Talk, write, and draw in response to instruction • Wonder and ask questions • Meet with teams to set schedules, ground rules, and goals

continues

Small-Group Inquiry Model Adapted for Curricular Inquiry, *cont*.

STAGE	TEACHER	KIDS
Investigate *Develop Questions, Search for Information, and Discover Answers*	• Continues bringing in resources and materials on a curricular topic to build background knowledge • Models how to read, listen, and view with a question in mind • Models how to take notes by interacting with text, coding text, and writing in margins or on Post-its • Points out how kids' learning relates to the broader curricular concepts • Engages kids in guided discussions and debates around a curricular topic • Facilitates changes in group membership or topics • Confers with groups and individuals	• Articulate thoughts and questions related to curricular topics that stem from their interest and curiosity • Listen, talk, view, and read to gain information about the topic • Engage in literature circles with curriculum-related short text • Develop questions related to the curricular topic; then read, listen, and view to answer them • Write, talk, and draw to share learning about the topic • Meet with teams to set and monitor schedules and task completion
Coalesce *Intensify Research, Synthesize Information, and Build Knowledge*	• Shows how to infer answers and draw conclusions • Demonstrates how to read for the gist and synthesize information • Connects kids' questions to the curricular concepts and focus questions • Shares how to organize and evaluate sources • Facilitates arrangements for out-of-school resources • Confers with groups and individuals	• Engage in deeper reading and research using books, articles, websites, videos, library visits • Target key ideas and information about the topic • Conduct "people" research, interviews, surveys, questionnaires, focus groups • Check sources and determine reliability • Synthesize information to build knowledge • Meet with teams to monitor schedules, complete specific tasks, and plan for sharing
Go Public *Share Learning, Demonstrate Understanding, Take Action*	• Co-constructs expectations and rubrics for final projects • Shares the widest range of possibilities for demonstrating understanding of the topic and its relationship to the broader curricular topic • Helps kids share their knowledge and teach others about the topic • Responds, assesses, and evaluates projects • Supports kids to share the learning by taking action • Helps kids to notice lingering or new inquiry questions • Encourages kids to reflect on social and thinking processes	• Co-construct expectations and rubrics for final projects • Demonstrate learning and understanding in a variety of ways—letter writing, posters, models, essays, picture books, tableaux, poetry • Become teachers as they share their knowledge with others • Reflect on their knowledge building • Reflect on their cooperative process • Pose and investigate new questions for further research • Consider changes in their own beliefs or behavior • Take action through writing, speaking, community work, advocacy

$\mathcal{S}$mall-Group Inquiry Under a Curricular Umbrella

Shortly, we'll show you how a half-dozen teachers from elementary grades through high school select certain chunks of the required curriculum and depart from tell-and-test instruction. Instead, they lead students on lively, sociable inquiries that investigate big ideas so deeply that kids enjoy, remember, and often act upon them.

These teachers view the district curriculum as an overarching umbrella for self-selected inquiries into a topic related to the curricular content. They teach with big ideas and essential questions about the curriculum in mind. As kids pursue topics of choice in their inquiry circles, the teachers help them connect their learning to the broader curricular concepts. In this chapter, you will see teachers at a variety of grade levels facilitating inquiry circles beneath the curricular umbrella and adapting the small-group inquiry model to curricular inquiry. (See chart on pp. 167–168.)

In all the inquiry models in this book, teachers work to connect kids' research projects to academic content whenever they see the opportunity. However, in curricular inquiry, teachers offer projects specifically to enhance understanding of the curricular content. In this chapter, notice kindergartners asking and answering questions about Antarctica as their teachers relate their learning to some of the bigger curricular concepts. Watch fourth graders delving into African American history, fifth graders studying bodily systems, and eighth graders exploring civil rights. In every case, the teachers work to relate the kids' specific topic or question to the larger curriculum concepts.

INQUIRY: *Antarctica*

PRIMARY

—Kristen Elder-Rubino (Teacher) and Melissa Oviatt (Librarian),
Columbine Elementary School, Boulder, Colorado

Young children love the weird, the strange, the odd, the unusual—the more exotic the better. And you can't get much more remote than Antarctica, with its amazing animals, ferocious winds and weather, and striking geography. Antarctica is part of the Boulder Valley Schools science and social studies curriculum, and the lucky kids who have the opportunity to explore this vast iceberg of a continent are kindergartners. Teacher Kristen Elder-Rubino and librarian Melissa Oviatt team up, as they do throughout the year, to collaborate on this curricular study that culminates with kids asking and then investigating their own authentic questions in small groups and pairs. This introduction to nonfiction reading, writing, and thinking takes place in "researcher's workshop," where kids can apply the strategies they learn as they investigate a self-chosen topic within a district-mandated unit.

Curricular inquiry circles offer an ideal opportunity for teachers and librarians to work together. During this Antarctica inquiry, you will see that Kristen and Melissa both work with the kids, teaching and conferring with them throughout the study, sometimes in the classroom and sometimes in the library. Everyone wins in this type of collaboration, especially the children.

The district curriculum often includes long lists of standards. As Kristen and Melissa discuss overall goals for the unit as well as specific lessons and instruction, they focus on three district standards that combine science, social studies, and geography:

1. A location's physical environment and climate influence all living things.

2. All living things have the same basic needs and are interdependent.

3. People use maps, globes, and other geographic tools to locate and analyze information about the Earth's physical characteristics.

When learners can make connections between their own experience and new information, they learn, understand, and remember more. Knowing this, Melissa and Kristen also focus on comparing the children's own environment to the climate and conditions of Antarctica. This theme of comparison continues through the year as the class explores other habitats and cultures, such as the continent and countries of Africa.

Content Focus

Kristen and Melissa use the following focus questions to frame their topic study.

1. How does the climate in Antarctica influence all living things?

2. How do animals adapt to such a harsh environment?

3. How do scientists brave difficult conditions to find answers to their questions?

During the study, Kristen and Melissa make a point of linking what kids are learning to these overarching focus questions on animal adaptations, the continent itself, and how scientists observe conditions and conduct research.

Process Focus

Kristen and Melissa design several distinct parts of this topic study. With kindergartners, visual literacy is key, so teaching children to listen and view to learn is central to the process. They focus on teaching kids to:

• learn information by viewing photographs and videos

• listen to information during read-alouds

• merge their thinking with the information and connect what they already know about the topic to new information

• brainstorm questions to be answered

• draw, write down, and talk about their learning in myriad ways

Kristen and Melissa flood the room with nonfiction texts on Antarctica and immerse the kids in visuals of all types. They believe strongly in the power of nonfiction as a source of information for all children, but particularly young learners who are not yet decoding. Nonfiction is stuffed with visual features, pictures, photos, graphs, charts, maps, and the like, making information accessible even when kids can't read the words.

Collaborative Planning

Melissa and Kristen meet a number of times to plan the study before they launch the unit with the students. Their combination of library and teaching skills is a bonus. In their planning meetings, they focus on finding great materials and resources. They design lessons that use those resources and dovetail with district standards and the focus questions. They plan their schedules, taking advantage of the fact that there are two of them. Two heads are better than one, and with kindergartners, four arms are better than two! The teaming approach makes huge sense because they can better differentiate to meet the needs of the class. One can gather small groups for focused instruction while the other works with the remaining kids. They can watch the social interaction more closely and devote more time to work on collaborative strategies with small groups. The instruction can take place in the library as well as the classroom, sending the message to very young children that libraries are for investigation and research.

Building Background with Maps, Globes, and Images

To launch the study and build the kids' background knowledge, Melissa and Kristen bring kids into the library to closely examine several different globes and maps of Antarctica. Kids burst forth with questions: "Why is Antarctica all white?" "What's the blue around it?" These landlocked kindergartners observe photos of the land, snow, oceans, and mountains of Antarctica simultaneously, so they can begin to connect the more abstract information on the maps and globes with actual geographical features. Terms like *snow*, *ice shelf*, *ocean*, *mountains*, and *icebergs* are written on a content word bank. Then kids create a large content word wall, illustrating these different concepts next to the appropriate word. A large, blank map of Antarctica also hangs on the wall, and over time kids add physical features to it as they learn about these. Next the kids gather in the library to list "what we think we know about Antarctica." Kristen and Melissa emphasize "what we think we know" for a reason—they want to make sure that kids are ready to change their thinking when they encounter new and more accurate information. As the kids eagerly share their background knowledge, Kristen records it on a large chart. In response to the common misconception that polar bears live in Antarctica, Kristen reads the book *There Are No Polar Bears Down There* by Trish Hart. This lets kids know how important it is to rethink misconceptions and embrace the new!

See Lesson 3, "Think and Wonder About Images," p. 118.

See Lesson 1, "Activate and Build Background Knowledge," p. 116.

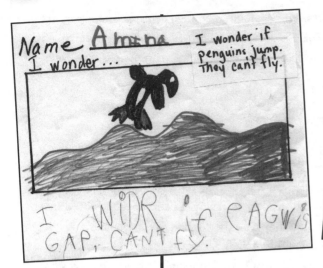

Learn and wonder word frames.

See Lesson 7, "Stop, Think, and React to Information," p. 122.

See Lesson 6, "Ask Questions and Wonder About Information," p. 121.

Constructing New Information and Keeping Track of Thinking

As the class begins reading *In Antarctica* by Marilyn Woolley, a nonfiction book chock full of information about the geography and animals of the snowy continent, Kristen and Melissa model how to draw and write about the information, using the language "I noticed" and "I learned." Still sitting up close, kids try this with a piece of paper with the words *I noticed, I learned,* or *I am wondering* attached to their clipboards while Melissa and Kristen confer with individual children, sometimes scripting a thought for a child or helping them write down the sounds they heard using invented spelling. Each lesson begins with Kristen and Melissa noticing, viewing, and discussing information; then the kids spread out at tables and on the floor with baskets of books at a variety of reading levels. They read, view, and discuss the new information as they work, becoming increasingly independent in their ability to put the information into their own words and illustrate it. At the end of each session, they gather in a circle to share the amazing information they learned that day.

Reading to Ask and Answer Questions

As the topic study progresses, Kristen and Melissa model comprehension lessons designed to help children ask their own questions and find the answers. They record strategies for answering questions on an anchor chart.

How Do We Answer a Question?

We can . . .

Read

View

Talk to someone

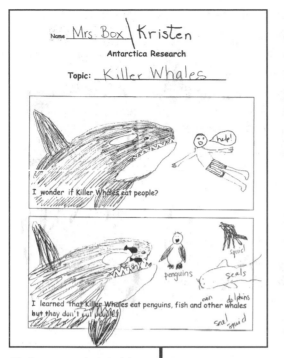

Name Mrs. Box \ Kristen

Antarctica Research

Topic: Killer Whales

I wonder if Killer Whales eat people?

I learned that Killer Whales eat penguins, fish and other whales but they don't eat people.

Kindergarten teacher's model of asking and answering a question.

Kindergarten Post its of facts about penguins.

See Lesson 8, "Notetaking: Read with a Question in Mind," p. 123.

See Lesson 9, "Draw Inferences from Images, Features, and Words," p. 124.

They model how they ask a question—do killer whales eat people?—and how they record the answer on their Antarctica research form (reproduced here). Then kids answer the question by finding the information in a nonfiction trade book and writing and drawing their question and answer on an 11x17 research form. The teachers make sure to show other ways of gaining information throughout the study, including using the Internet and asking people in the field.

Children learn to link the question with information from pictures or text. When they have questions and answers about animals, for instance—leopard seals, or orcas, or penguins—they put their questions and answers on large cutouts of these animals posted in the library (see the penguin with its Post-its). Seeing their store of facts about the animals prompts more questions and further research.

Making Predictions and Inferences During Reading

Reading Helen Cowcher's *Antarctica* prompts the kids to think beyond the text—predicting, inferring, and speculating about animal behavior and the events in the book. At ambiguous points in the text, kids make predictions and draw inferences using their background knowledge, and Kristen charts their thinking to document the conversation. Kristen shapes their thinking as the kids use what they have already learned about life in Antarctica, combining their background knowledge with information from the text to make inferences. At the end of the story, children come up with a number of lingering questions about how people live and do research in Antarctica, prompted by the book's final question, which they paraphrase as, "When people come to Antarctica, will they help or hurt the animals?"

Researcher's Workshop

After these lessons, questions abound. The kids are knowledgeable enough now to have some pretty good questions. Kristen has listed them on a chart, which they continue to add to. Kids can't wait to do more research to answer some of their questions. Now, Kristen helps the children divide into pairs and small inquiry circles based on their curiosity about one of these seven kid-created questions:

See Lesson 22, "Choosing Topics to Investigate," p. 137.

WHAT WE WONDER ABOUT ANTARCTICA

1. Isn't it too cold for people to live there?
2. Can the people get near the animals?
3. Do they hunt the animals for food?
4. How big are killer whales?
5. Where do researchers live—in tents? in houses?
6. How do they stay warm in such a cold place?
7. How do they get to Antarctica? How long do they stay?

Now the classroom is awash in enthusiasm, markers, large poster paper, and scissors. Louis and Amina have chosen question 6, and confer with Kristen about their plans for their project. Having seen photographs of scientists taking measurements outside, they are struck by the heavy, protective clothes. Their goal is to create a life-size mural of a scientist—complete with mittens, hats, goggles, boots, and other gear—to answer the question, How do scientists keep warm and survive in Antarctica? Given the go-ahead, they escape to the hallway to get started.

Kenny, Alyssa, and Jack are startled to find information that details how animals are protected in Antarctica, complete with a chart of how far away people must be when viewing animals, whether they are on foot or in vehicles. "How far would that be in this classroom?" Alyssa wonders. Kenny grabs the chart and a yardstick and together the three of them, with help from Melissa, pace off the distances and mark the floor. They get a very real concept of how far away people are required to stay from animals in an effort to protect them. They create their own chart and hang it outside in the hallway. Kids come and see for themselves as a member of this group stands by to offer any additional information or explanation.

An inquiry circle of five kids chooses to create a map of Antarctica. Spread out on the floor over a quite large outline of the continent, they add to the mural in a variety of ways. Some create animals, science stations, or ice mounds out of construction paper and paste them on the map. Others draw with markers right on the map. Still others write and draw information on Post-its, which they place on the map. They talk about what is still missing and add more information. The map becomes a stunning, artful record of their new knowledge about the continent at the bottom of the world.

See Lesson 27, "Response Options: Take Learning Public," p. 142.

One group poses a question—how big are killer whales? Are they the biggest of all whales? They know whales are big, but how big? So, with the help of their teacher, they begin checking sources of information that add to their knowledge. Once they have answered their question, they share their information on a poster with a painting they have done of a killer whale. While doing their research, they discover that killer whales can grow up to thirty feet long and are bigger than an elephant. So this team creates a poster comparing a killer whale and an elephant, which gives them a really good understanding of how big killer whales are, because the kids have a sense of elephant size.

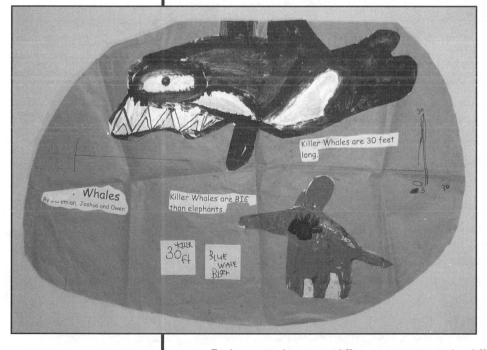

An artful comparison of the size of a whale to an elephant.

Each group chooses a different question and a different way to share their learning. Kristen and Melissa devise lessons to teach the children a variety of ways to share their information and ideas and take their thinking public. They share response options from former kindergartners as models. They model how they make a poster themselves. They take the kindergartners to visit first and second graders who show them how they create posters, self-published books, mobiles, and so on. They tour the school hallways and point out the different features—illustrations, captions, labels, close-ups, maps—that older children have used to demonstrate their learning.

We celebrate the diversity! There is no one right way—researcher's workshop provides flexibility so that kids who are ready to work independently can have at it, while children who need a bit more support can confer with a teacher to guide them more carefully though the process. The key is to support kids with the level of structure that makes sense for them and to provide the widest possible variety of response models from which to choose. The point is for all of them to find a way to express their learning and understanding that makes sense for them.

When they have completed their projects, groups share them with other classes, usually in the library. After the other kids observe and listen to the kindergartners present their learning, they write or draw their comments and questions for the presenter on large Post-its, respectfully sharing what they learned from the presentation. The pre-senter is usually over the moon about these responses. Back in the classroom, each child creates his or her own small map of Antarctica—adding and drawing features, animals, and information learned over the course of the study—a great way to assess everyone's learning and thinking!

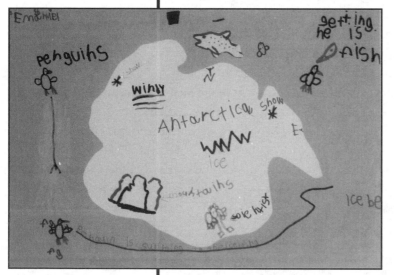

A map created by a student with information gleaned from the Antarctica topic study.

INQUIRY: *Slavery and Child Labor*

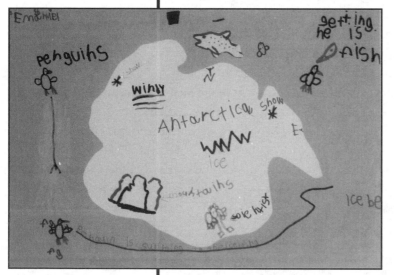

INTERMEDIATE

—Holly Occhipinti and Michelle Schirmer, Oakley Elementary School, Oakley, California

January is African American History Month, and in most American schools, this ush-ers in a unit on Martin Luther King and other figures in black history. The Oakley Union School district is no different, and fourth-grade teammates Holly Occhipinti and Michelle Schirmer wanted to give kids a genuine appreciation of Martin Luther King and the African American experience. They hoped that as kids began to study slavery before and during the Civil War, they would make connections to related contemporary issues around the theme of slavery and discrimination, helping them to recognize how historic events and ideas thread their way through time and impact our lives even many years later.

See Lesson 3, "Think About Images," p. 118.

Poster of slavery image with kids' questions and inferences

Ascertaining Background Knowledge

Holly and Michelle knew that one of the best ways to engage kids in a new inquiry study is to have them interact with compelling images, whether these show polar bears struggling to swim from one shrinking ice floe to another, capture meteors careening through space, or depict aspects of human slavery. So to prepare for the unit, Holly went to Google Images (http://images.google.com), clicked on *Images* in the upper-left-hand corner of the screen, and typed in *Civil War slavery* to find a plethora of striking images that represented different aspects of slavery.

Some were stark and disturbing: handcuffs; the filthy, crowded interior of a slave ship; a whiplashed, scarred human back. Others were more confusing, especially for kids who lacked background knowledge about the topic: a slave auction, an abolitionist speaking in church, a copy of the Emancipation Proclamation. But Holly believed that all of these images would intrigue the kids and draw them into the topic. She printed them and pasted them onto large, individual posters with space ready for kids to place Post-its after jotting their thinking. On the first day of the unit, the posters were set up around the room.

Holly and Michelle began by gathering both of their classes around them and leading a short discussion about their expectations. At this point, their primary objective was to ascertain how much background knowledge the kids had about slavery and the African American experience. They let the kids self-select into groups of five or six, and then suggested that they move from one poster to another, view the image, write their thoughts on Post-its, and place them on the posters near the images. They hoped this interactive viewing would prompt lots of thoughts and, most importantly, lots of questions.

Kids wandered group by group from one poster to another and jotted their thinking on Post-its with their

See Lesson 11, "Turn and Talk," p. 126.

names or initials. Holly and Michelle understood that it is imperative that we know the baseline background knowledge of individual kids as well as the whole group when we launch a curricular inquiry project. When they read the Post-its later, they found that about 60 percent of the kids had some background knowledge about these images and could connect them to slavery. About 10 percent had a great deal of background knowledge, and about 30 percent of the kids had practically no knowledge at all about slavery, the Civil War, or the historical African American experience.

At the conclusion of the forty-five-minute period, Holly and Michelle gathered the kids back together in a large group and had them turn and talk about their thoughts and questions. After a vibrant discussion, Holly and Michelle asked: "Knowing what you know about your teachers, why do you think we would put these images out in the classroom for all of you to view?" One child who had the background knowledge to understand what these images represented suggested that perhaps they were going to be studying slavery. Holly and Michelle concurred and explained that they were embarking on a study of African American history and that they wanted everyone in the class to get educated about slavery and the African American experience, so they could better understand why we now honor Martin Luther King and other historic black figures. They hoped that when they finished this inquiry, everyone would better understand where Dr. King's dream came from and why he was so passionate about equality for all. "Education is the only way that we can begin to understand," Holly stated emphatically.

Thinking About Information and Building Knowledge

See Lesson 7, "Stop, Think, and React to Information," p. 122.

Holly and Michelle now had a good grasp of the knowledge base of both individual students and the class as a whole. They recognized that the next step was to build all of the kids' background knowledge so they could learn more and ask more thoughtful questions, which would lead to a more fulfilling inquiry. The next week found Holly and Michelle continuing to build background knowledge by sharing information in many different forms and having kids interact with it. They gave each student a a research notebook with pockets to collect and hold all of their work. They showed a video on the Declaration of Independence and the Constitution. Kids gathered with clipboards as the teachers stopped the video at various points and had them turn and talk and jot their thoughts, stopping, thinking, and reacting to the video just as they would a piece of text a teacher might read. In their discussion, they found that even though the Constitution called for equality, it was written by white men, many of whom were slave owners. In fact, the kids discovered that the original Constitution did not guarantee equality to all, not to African Americans, not to Native Americans, not to women. Kids were stunned by this discovery, and a thoughtful discussion of the nature of constitutional amendments ensued. The kids learned that it was the amendments that attempted to secure equality for all. Holly and Michelle were delighted that the kids' questions had prompted such a big idea. What a bonus that these kids now had a better understanding of the Constitution as a result of their interaction with the images and the video.

Asking and Answering Questions

To follow up, Michelle conducted an interactive read-aloud with *Now Let Me Fly* by Dolores Johnson, a powerful picture book about the life of a woman who was captured as a child in Africa and became a slave on an American plantation, where ultimately her family was broken apart when members were sold to other plantation owners. This fictional account provides a quite thorough, albeit frightening, overview of the tragedy of human slavery. Michele modeled her thinking, shared her inner voice, and then asked kids to write down their reactions as she continued reading the story. By the time they finished their discussion, they had synthesized their thinking into a big question: How and why did slavery begin in the United States?

To help them keep that question in mind, Holly wrote it at the top of a chart. She then followed up with a section from a nonfiction title, *Daily Life on a Southern Plantation 1853*, by Paul Erickson, which she believed would give kids quite a bit of information related to their big question. She made copies so kids could jot their thoughts and questions right on the pages. After Holly modeled reading a few paragraphs with that question in mind and annotating her thinking, she sent kids into their inquiry circles with instructions to read the piece together, keeping that question in mind, have a discussion about slavery, and jot their thoughts and questions in the margins. Each group struggled to comprehend the idea that humans were sold. When they discovered that there was an actual slave trade, where people made money by selling

See Lesson 2, "Listen to Your Inner Voice," p. 117.

See Lesson 5, "Annotate Text and Leave Tracks of Thinking," p. 120.

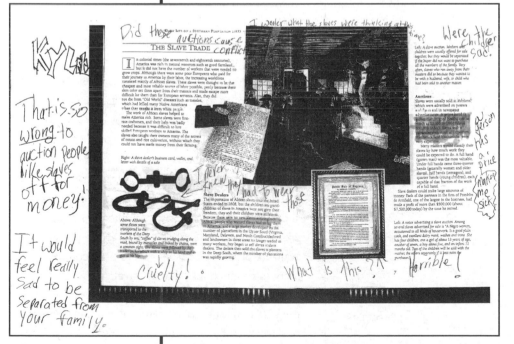

Kylee's responses to the "Slave Trade" article.

other people, they were appalled (see Kylee's annotations reproduced here).

To gain further understanding, one group went online to find more images. Another focused on maps of free states, slave states, and agriculture. Each group read anything they could get their hands on. As they talked, read, and viewed to answer why slavery had happened, they slowly began to understand that some Africans betrayed and sold other Africans for money, that ship captains were paid a good deal of money to transport Africans to America, and that plantation owners bought slaves so they could increase their own wealth by using an unpaid labor force. The kids came to realize that money was at the center of the issue of slavery. This was a big idea that almost none of them had understood before this exploration. When we teach with the big ideas in mind, kids learn to uncover them.

Demonstrating Understanding: Summarizing and Synthesizing Information

LESSON LINK

See Lesson 10, "Synthesize the Information," p. 125.

From that point on, kids continued to immerse themselves in Civil War slavery topics and themes, reading, talking, and viewing extensively. Haley's reaction to the video is shown here. Thinking that it might be helpful for the kids to have a more personal experience with the time and the circumstances of slavery, Michelle and Holly had them form picture book literature circles where they read and responded to books about kids in slavery—books like *Minty: A Story of Young Harriet Tubman* (Alan Schroeder), *Henry's Freedom Box* (Ellen Levine), *Almost to Freedom* (Vaunda Micheaux Nelson), *Nettie's Trip South* (Ann Turner), and *Journey to Freedom: A Story of the Underground Railroad* (Courtni C. Wright). (See responses to picture book literature circles on the following page.)

Holly and Michelle are big fans of picture book lit circles for a variety of reasons. First, most fourth-grade lit circle groups can finish a thirty-two page picture book rather quickly and thus start talking about the entire book soon thereafter. Second, even though they are short, many picture books give kids plenty of big ideas and themes to think about. And finally, book groups often end up reading every one of the available picture books since the time commitment is so much less than a novel.

Throughout that week and the following one, the kids continued to expand their understanding of slavery. Holly did a think-aloud with Bettye Stroud's *The Patchwork Path*, a book that explains how Underground Railroad conductors sewed codes into quilts that helped slaves escape. Fasci-

Thinking about Minty

Minty is too young to be in the fields, she's only eight years old. At what time do they eat. I think that an overseer might be a name of a chief.
— Yorge Mondragon #16

I'm learning about minty having a hard time being a young slave. minty wants freedom for her and her family. Who wouldn't?
— Yorge Mondragon #16

1/18/08 What is minty? ester gadol might be mintys only girlfriend. Minty felt sad when they throwed mintys friend.

I think minty said loneliness. where Does minty sleep? where will minty go if she escapes? ~maybe shell find a house to sleep~
— Yorge Mondragon #16

may be will sleep in a warm place. If I was minty I would give Freedom to all slaves! Minty is H.T !!
— Yorge Mondragon #16

Name **Kyle** #11

The Journey to Freedom ~A Story of the Underground Railroad~ by Courtni C. Wright (Kyle)

Choose a sticky note that represents your deepest thinking and place it in the box. Then expand on your thinking.

why was the male slave more money? Is it because he is more stronger? why

Text (Quote or describe what was happening in the text): The slave owner read a wanted poster to the slaves and said don't you try to run off now.

Question: Why were the mens laves 500 dollars and the woman and children only 350 dollars?

Thinking: was it because the men were stronger and able to carry more stuff?

Was your question answered? NO If not was there enough evidence in the text to support your thinking? NO What was the evidence?

Picture book literature circle responses.

nated with the codes and quilts, one small group designed and drew their own quilt squares and wrote brief comments to demonstrate their understanding (one of their quilt squares is shown below). Another group wrote letters from the perspective of a slave who could read and write (see Kylee's letter on the following page).

"The Underground RR"
By: Mariana Peña

The Underground RR was not an actual railroad. It wasn't underground either. The meaning is "secret". Slaves would escape from their plantation and go north to freedom. After 1850 they couldn't just go to another state they had to go to Canada. Sometimes it was in underground tunnels though. The RR used codes to get to a safe house. A safe house is a house that the people that own the house keep fugitive slaves. Some of the codes are a quilt on the porch or a lantern in the window. That's what I think is fasinating about The Underground Railroad.

So what did these lessons, readings, responses, and experiences have in common? What was the shared thread running through all of them? The answer: interaction—interacting with images, videos, texts, the teacher, and, most importantly, with each other. Holly and Michelle's goal of building background knowledge about slavery

January 8, 1742

Dear Sally,
It's hard not to have a sister anymore. I hate to say I told you so, but if you hadn't tried to escape, you would still be here where you're safe with me. Tonight I am kitchen duty all by myself. I'm thinking about poisoning the master's dinner, so I can escape! Today I got whipped for giving the master his tea too late. I'm lucky one of the old house servants taught me how to read and write, otherwise I couldn't write to you at all. Oh no masters coming, gotta go bye!

Sincerely,
KyLee

Kylee's letter from the perspective of a literate slave.

succeeded because they modeled their own thinking and learning and fostered student-to-student interaction. It was interaction that led kids to the discoveries they made and the insights they gained. Their content knowledge soared because their teachers filled the room with great resources that engaged the kids, caused them to think deeply, and encouraged interaction.

Child Labor: A Related Inquiry Emerges

By the end of the second week, to take stock of where they were, Holly and Michelle gathered the whole class together for a guided discussion. The conversation focused on many aspects of slavery, but the discussions were more thoughtful because the kids were better able to personalize the slavery experience, having read so many books from the perspective of children in slavery. They co-constructed an anchor chart where they listed personal feelings and experiences they would have if they were trapped in slavery: sadness, hunger, poverty, confusion, fear, anger, hopelessness, emotional and physical pain, loneliness, invisibility, and cruelty all came into play.

After giving them the opportunity to share these emotions and feelings publicly, Holly asked them, "Now that you have talked to each other, heard stories, read books in lit circles, watched videos, written responses, and generally built a lot of knowledge about slavery, what do you still wonder about it? Do you have any lingering questions?" Eric blurted out, "Is there still slavery today?" Murmurs of "That's what I was wondering, too" and "Darn, he took my question!" filled the room. Both Holly and Michelle noticed that there didn't appear to be a single child who did not wonder about this. These thoughtful teachers were gratified, because one of their goals with history topics is for kids to relate historic information to contemporary issues.

A truly great thing about curricular inquiry is that kids are far better prepared to ask deep, expansive, important questions because they have built the necessary background knowledge around a topic. You simply can't ask a very good question about something you know little about. But when the whole class studies a common topic in an interactive way—working in small groups, jotting thoughts about the text, viewing images and videos and responding to them—they really learn about it. Now that this group of fourth graders had a pretty thorough grasp of Civil War–era slavery, they could connect it more seamlessly to contemporary life.

See Lesson 11, "Turn and Talk," p. 126.

And so began their related inquiry to discover the answer to their biggest question so far—is there slavery today?

The next day, Michelle and Holly facilitated a discussion on human rights. Michelle began by asking kids to turn and talk about what rights slaves had. After a few moments, kids concurred that slaves had no rights on plantations or even under the Constitution, that slaves were considered to be the property of their owners. Holly unfurled a large poster with the title "What Are Your Rights?" She asked them to turn and talk about that question. The general consensus on rights was unclear. Although the kids knew they were not property, they really didn't know exactly what their rights were. After all, they were kids! What rights did they have? Mostly they knew what they couldn't do: they couldn't vote; they couldn't drive; they couldn't drink alcohol; they couldn't even leave school in the middle of the day without permission.

So Holly chose to read *For Every Child: The Rights of the Child in Words and Pictures*. Published in association with UNICEF, this book presents fourteen of the fifty-four principles adopted at the 1989 United Nations Convention on the Rights of the Child. Those rights include a child's right to a name, to survival, and to education. They also include the right to protection against exploitation, abuse, and the forcible separation from a parent. In sum, the convention on children's rights declared that kids had the right to be safe.

As she read the book aloud, Holly had the kids stop, think, and talk. As they shared their personal stories, several kids expressed their own lack of safety. Some began to reflect on rights they did not have because of family income levels or broken relationships. When one child shared, "I feel I should have the right to deny foster care," the students were able to talk about how helpless they feel as children in a world controlled by adults. Obviously, this saddened Michelle and Holly, and they hoped that their investigation would give some kids more tools to control their own lives. After reading the book aloud, Holly and Michelle asked the kids to write down what they believed were their rights on Post-its and place them on the large chart (pictured on next page).

The book mentioned that there are kids in the world who are not allowed to go to school because they have to work. The fourth graders seemed puzzled, so Michelle asked them, "How many of you have heard about child labor? What do you think that is? Turn and talk about that." Holly and Michelle soon discovered that the kids knew next to nothing about child labor, although several did believe that child labor was some sort of slavery since kids were forced to do it and not allowed to go to school.

"Since you are all so interested, we are going to study how slavery looks today. It doesn't necessarily look like it did during the Civil War, but I think you are right that there is still slavery. And it will help us a lot to understand slavery now if we think about slavery back then," Holly added. The next day, the teachers followed up by having the small groups choose among three articles on child labor from *The*

See Lesson 5, "Annotate Text: Leave Tracks of Thinking," p. 120.

Comprehension Toolkit (Harvey and Goudvis 2005) and *Toolkit Texts* (Harvey and Goudvis 2007). The kids read and annotated the articles and then discussed them in their inquiry circles. Spirited discussion ensued—and the students were outraged. (See an annotated article from *Toolkit Texts* on the next page.)

"There is slavery today. Child labor is slavery!" Martha announced as the kids nodded in agreement.

"It seems as if we are getting an answer to our big question about whether there is slavery today. So what other questions do you have, now that you know

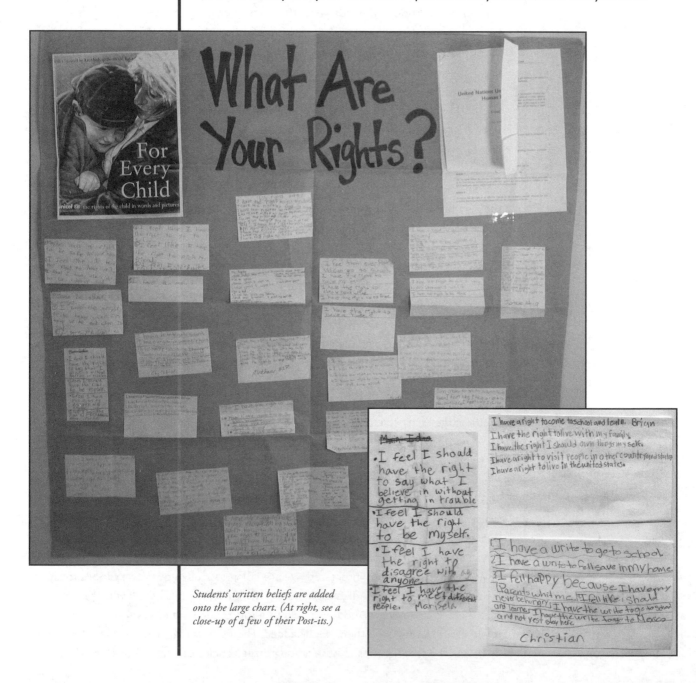

Students' written beliefs are added onto the large chart. (At right, see a close-up of a few of their Post-its.)

this kind of child slavery exists today?" Holly prodded. Questions poured out and Holly recorded them on an anchor chart:

> When and how will child labor stop?
>
> Can we stop child labor?
>
> Why do adults let it happen?
>
> Why do humans get treated like this?
>
> How long have children been working like this when they should be in school?
>
> Who teaches kids to do what they do when they work?
>
> Why doesn't the government stop this madness?
>
> Why is there such a thing as child labor?

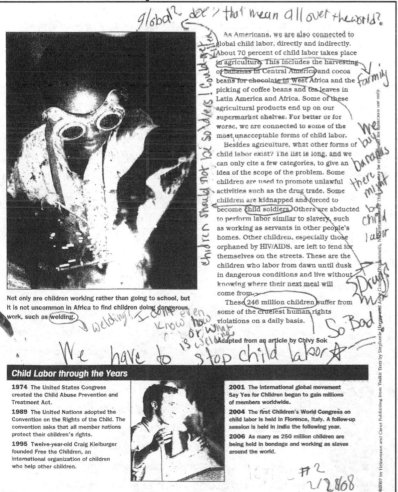

global?, doe's that mean all over the world?

children should not be soldiers I could write

family

We buy bananas there might be child labor

Drugs

So Bad

welding! I don't even know how dangerous is or what welding

We have to stop child labor

As Americans, we are also connected to global child labor, directly and indirectly. About 70 percent of child labor takes place in agriculture. This includes the harvesting of bananas in Central America and cocoa beans for chocolate in West Africa and the picking of coffee beans and tea leaves in Latin America and Africa. Some of these agricultural products end up on our supermarket shelves. For better or for worse, we are connected to some of the most unacceptable forms of child labor.

Besides agriculture, what other forms of child labor exist? The list is long, and we can only cite a few categories, to give an idea of the scope of the problem. Some children are used to promote unlawful activities such as the drug trade. Some children are kidnapped and forced to become child soldiers. Others are abducted to perform labor similar to slavery, such as working as servants in other people's homes. Other children, especially those orphaned by HIV/AIDS, are left to fend for themselves on the streets. These are the children who labor from dawn until dusk in dangerous conditions and live without knowing where their next meal will come from.

These 246 million children suffer from some of the cruelest human rights violations on a daily basis.

Adapted from an article by Chivy Sok.

Not only are children working rather than going to school, but it is not uncommon in Africa to find children doing dangerous work, such as welding.

Child Labor through the Years

1974 The United States Congress created the Child Abuse Prevention and Treatment Act.

1989 The United Nations adopted the Convention on the Rights of the Child. The convention asks that all member nations protect their children's rights.

1995 Twelve-year-old Craig Kielburger founded Free the Children, an international organization of children who help other children.

2001 The international global movement Say Yes for Children began to gain millions of members worldwide.

2004 The first Children's World Congress on child labor is held in Florence, Italy. A follow-up session is held in India the following year.

2006 As many as 250 million children are being held in bondage and working as slaves around the world.

36

Holly and Michelle suggested that kids form groups around a question that interested them, either from the anchor chart or of their own choosing. Five groups coalesced around the following questions:

> What are the basic rights needed for survival?
>
> What are the necessary human rights?
>
> Why might someone be denied basic human rights?
>
> Why is there slavery today?
>
> What can we do about modern slavery?

Holly and Michelle reminded each group to keep their own question in mind, as well as the final question on the list: What can we do about modern slavery? Pointing out that the active use of knowledge is the goal of studying, questioning, and learning, they stressed that the culmination of thoughtful inquiry may well involve taking action.

Over the next week as kids worked together in inquiry circles to research and answer their questions, Holly and Michelle continued to share texts, materials, and websites of interest and to facilitate discussions about books, videos, and images with the whole class when they came upon resources they thought all kids should hear or read. They shared a study of child labor done by the International Labor Organization (known as the ILO study), which found that there are 246 million child laborers worldwide. Kids wrote their reactions and questions to the ILO study. Holly and Michelle modeled and then facilitated child labor/slavery role plays so each inquiry circle could engage in a role play related to its study. Each day at the end of the period, the inquiry circles came together to share new ideas and questions with the whole class. Sharing sessions provide great opportunities for new learning. During one sharing session, Kylee explained that she saw a connection to Civil War slavery. "I just realized something. Child labor is all about the money! That's what we learned about Civil War slavery. Slavery happens because people want money. Child labor happens for the same reason." Michelle and Holly, recognizing Kylee's connection as an important insight, guided a discussion to make sure that all the kids had a chance to think about what Kylee had said. Curricular inquiry gives teachers the chance to shine a light on big ideas as they emerge from kids' thoughts and questions.

Taking Action

After the kids got a serious handle on child labor and modern slavery and answered their own questions, Holly and Michelle co-constructed an anchor chart with the class to address the larger question for all to consider: what can we do about modern slavery? Having learned about the realities of child labor in the world, these fourth graders were ready to do something about it. The teachers shared several different ways to take action.

Activism—Doing something specific

Awareness—Educating others

Aid—Contributing your own resources

Holly and Michelle called these three components an "action path" and gave specific examples of all three. Then they suggested the kids work together to decide by which path they would actively use the knowledge they had gained. Most chose to offer aid. One group decided to have a bake sale and donate the money they earned to a foundation they located on the Internet that supports efforts to oppose child labor throughout the world (International Labor Rights Forum, www.laborrights.org). Another group planned a car wash to raise money and donate it to the same organization. And, as we recounted in Chapter 5, yet another group made sandwich boards explaining the problem of child labor and asking passersby to learn about the issues, to think and care about exploited children.

But even after taking these actions, the kids wanted to do more. Join us at the website and see how these fifth graders connected to the wider community of concerned people fighting child labor and created a quilt to benefit impoverished children with direction from a nonprofit group called morethanwarmth.org. Their work with More Than Warmth represented an extraordinary culmination to a thoughtful, in-depth, self-selected curricular inquiry that resulted in a need to take action.

www.heinemann.com/
comprehensionandcollaboration.

INTERMEDIATE

INQUIRY: *Health and Body Systems*

MARY PFAU, DRY CREEK ELEMENTARY SCHOOL, CENTENNIAL, COLORADO

Immerse: Engage Kids, Activate, and Build Background

To get kids fired up about doing a small-group inquiry under the curricular umbrella of the human body, fifth-grade teacher Mary Pfau began the unit by bringing in newspaper and magazine articles with medical themes. For a couple of days, with the kids gathered around her, she simply read articles and guided a discussion about them, having kids turn and talk throughout the reading. The topics included AIDS in Africa, a Denver Bronco football player with a torn ACL, and the eradication of chicken pox. Mary hoped that sharing these authentic articles would make these health issues relevant and would reel the kids into the human body unit. Several days in, she modeled on the overhead projector how she took margin notes right on an article, jotting down her inner conversation as she read.

For homework, she asked kids to read and bring in an article that had a medical slant. Kids scoured newspapers and magazines both in school and out and shared articles about frostbite, the complexity of the brain, health benefits of chocolate—you name it. Mary copied three articles for the class and let each child choose one, read it, and take notes in the margins just as she had modeled. When they finished reading the article and jotting their thinking in the margins, she had them find someone in the room who read the same article and discuss it. This activity was essentially a mini–literature circle. Read an article, jot down your thinking, and talk to someone—exactly what adults do when reading to learn and research information. We call this process read, write, and talk (Harvey and Goudvis 2005), and it provides a terrific way for kids to interact with text and with each other every single day.

By midweek, kids began to view themselves as medically inclined. They began to think about their daily lives in medical terms. Case in point—one of the kids twisted a knee on the playground during lunch recess, hobbled in, and asked Mary if she knew the difference between pulling a muscle and tearing an ACL. After tending to his sore knee, Mary suggested he hop on the Internet and find out. Kids couldn't get enough of viruses, bloodborne diseases, muscle spasms, and of course, the routinely gross stuff like snot and farts. By week's end, a bunch of kids had decided that they wanted to be doctors, nurses, or EMTs. Recall for a moment your own fifth-grade human body unit—that laborious textbook chapter and one worksheet after another asking you to label and correctly spell the body parts. By the end of the first week were you chomping at the bit to learn more? Not likely. It's a wonder we have any doctors at all in light of how deadly conventional schooling made medicine.

Mary's purpose during that first week was twofold—definitely to get kids pumped about the topic, but also to build their background knowledge. This is part of the first immersion phase of curricular inquiry: build background so learners can connect new information to what they already know. Too often, we try to teach material that kids are not able to process because they do not have enough background knowledge to understand the concepts. But the previous week's extensive reading, writing, and talking about health issues had built Mary's kids' background knowledge—and they had a gazillion questions after that immersion in medical content. They were right where Mary wanted them, pumped to investigate more. When we make connections to new information, we understand it better and we ask more informed questions.

Form Inquiry Groups Based on Interest

The fifth-grade human body curriculum called for kids to understand and describe the roles, functions, and interrelationships of the seven bodily systems: digestive, respiratory, circulatory, skeletal, muscular, nervous, and reproductive. The following week Mary handed out a survey and asked kids to indicate their system preference in order, jotting down on the form what they wanted to learn more about and what they wondered. After collecting their surveys, Mary synthesized their interests and divided kids into four inquiry groups based on their preferences.

- *Muscular-skeletal system.* The surveys indicated that these kids were primarily interested in issues of health and fitness in relation to this system.
- *Circulatory system.* This group was curious about the heart, lungs, and blood diseases.
- *Nervous system.* This group coalesced around issues related to the brain and spinal cord.
- *The history of medicine.* This group was a bit of an outlier. Their surveys indicated they wanted to study epidemics and plagues in the Middle Ages. So Mary went with that, keeping in mind how she could nudge them to systemic considerations and contemporary illnesses as well.

Mary realized that these inquiry groups did not cover every bodily system the curriculum mandated. But she was undaunted—she would simply fill in the gaps and teach the other systems and their interrelationships throughout the study. She would teach with the big ideas in mind and stay focused on the overarching concepts of the roles, functions, and interrelationships of the seven bodily systems. And she would highlight when a student or group wrote or said something that related to these larger systemic concepts. Mary knew that these inquiries would not only engage the kids, but would lead to more learning and understanding of the overarching body system concepts as well.

In addition, Mary recognized that this inquiry project was about more than learning content, although that was a very important goal. She would also model lessons and foster discussions on constructing guidelines for social interaction and on reading for information, taking notes, and doing research. From Mary's perspective, the outcomes for kids included being more knowledgeable about bodily systems and their relationship to human health as well as being more capable, independent communicators and researchers.

Develop Group Ground Rules

See Lesson 13, "Creating Group Ground Rules," p. 128.

Once kids were assigned to groups, Mary had them meet to come up with some social guidelines for group interaction. Students talked to each other and jotted down some suggestions. Then they came together as a class, where they discussed and debated the guidelines, decided on some ground rules, and co-constructed an anchor chart with Mary. Mary posted the chart on the wall and they reviewed it each day before meeting in their small groups.

INQUIRY CIRCLE EXPECTATIONS

1. Be respectful, participate, and be prepared.

2. Be enthusiastic and motivated. You are learning and sharing new and fascinating information!

3. Positive, thoughtful workers attract others.

4. Actively participate in research, discussion, and listening.

5. Be a responsible group member.

6. Don't "hog" the spotlight! Let everyone have chances to share.

7. Disagree agreeably.

8. Prepare! Read, think, and share.

For her part, Mary organized the inquiry ahead of time by

- flooding the room with trade books on health and the human body
- continuing to gather medical articles that might be of interest to various groups
- searching the Internet for accessible health-related websites to recommend
- reviewing and then highlighting textbook pages that were accessible and helpful
- bringing in plastic models of the human skeleton, the circulatory system, and various organs, such as the heart, lungs, and brain

Investigate: Read to Gather Information and Develop Questions

The second phase of a curricular inquiry project involves helping kids to choose their own inquiry question within the required topic, then read and do research to build knowledge and answer the question. Steph joined Mary at the beginning of this phase. As they talked together, Mary identified a problem. She explained that when the kids took notes, they wrote down way too much. Some simply copied what they found on the Internet or in books and articles, rather than synthesizing the information. And often those who did synthesize the information wrote too much that was unrelated to their question. They seemed to just take notes aimlessly without any direction. Together Steph and Mary decided to explicitly teach reading and researching with a question in mind.

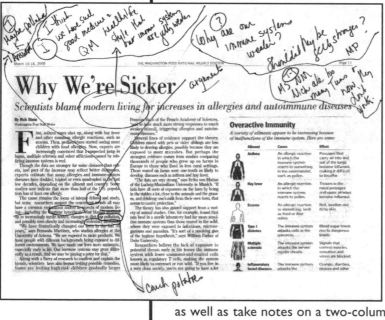

Steph modeled with an article from the *Washington Post* titled "Why We're Sicker." She explained that she was going to annotate her thinking on the article as well as take notes on a two-column form headed Notes/Thinking. (See her annotated copy of the article.) When she saw the title of the article, she had immediately wondered, Why are we sicker than we used to be? Steph explained that it seemed to her we should be healthier than we were in earlier times, because of the advances of modern medicine. So this really confused her, and she wondered how this was possible. She wrote her question on the top of the form and explained that she would read with that question in mind and try to jot only notes related to that question. In that way, her question would guide her note taking. The Notes column would represent the facts and information in the

See Lesson 8, "Notetaking: Read with a Question in Mind," p. 123.

article that related to her question and the Thinking column would reflect her thoughts as she read.

This two-column Notes/Thinking form is one of our favorite ways to help kids narrow their focus as they take notes. It seems to scaffold them to screen out less pertinent information. And we feel very strongly about the thinking side of the form. In conventional schooling, we only asked kids to write down the facts, ignoring the thinking behind their note taking. We now know that when they write down their thinking as they take notes, they are more likely to learn and remember the information.

As Steph read with her question in mind, she came to learn that modern life itself seems to be at the root of our increase in allergies and immune system disorders. Ironically, many researchers now believe that our obsession with keeping things clean has led to diminished immune systems that allow allergies and immune disorders to proliferate. After the lesson, Steph suggested that the kids go back to their groups and generate questions about their topic. She asked them to jot down their questions, read and research with that question in mind, and take notes on the Notes/Thinking form.

QUESTION
Why are we sicker than we used to be?

NOTES	THINKING
• Allergies are on the rise in Europe and North America.	• What exactly is "modern living?"
• Hay fever, asthma, etc. are increasing in E & NA.	• Everyone is constantly cleaning stuff.
• Have not seen a significant increase in 3rd World countries.	• Why are allergies increasing so much in US & Europe.
• Hasan Ashard, allergy expert says the rise in allergies is epidemic.	• Why not in Africa & South America and parts of Asia?
• Modern living is how we live today (Answered)	• My kids' allergies are worse than mine. Wonder why?
• We have caused people to be immune because we spray all that antibacterial stuff etc.	• Maybe that's why my kids" allergies are worse.

Inference

★ So it sounds like our obsession with keeping things clean may have lead to more sickness.

Mary had surrounded each group with text sets related to the chosen bodily system. Steph and Mary moved about the room to observe the various groups. Steph stopped at the nervous system group first and listened as they pored over brain books and articles and had an energetic discussion about the brain. Katherine was recording all of the questions that came up in the group.

> The brain is still a mystery. Why is it so difficult to figure out how it works?
>
> How does the brain make dreams and why?
>
> What are migraines exactly?
>
> Do kids struggle with migraines as much as adults?
>
> What exactly is artificial intelligence?
>
> How do computers and brains act differently?
>
> Could a computer admire a painting?

Quentin asked the last question and commented that in the movie *I Robot*, a computer chose to save the stronger man, and a human chose to save a child in need. So he felt that human judgment and empathy (his words, not ours!) were part of what differentiated computers from humans. Recognizing that these kids were soaring on their own, Steph moved on to the circulatory group. She noticed that it looked quite small, however. One of the group members, Kelly, told her that two of the boys were at the computer. Steph headed over to see what they were up to and, surprise of surprises, it had nothing to do with body systems, health, or even body parts! She stood quietly behind them as they engaged in a lively discussion of the previous night's NBA scores.

"So what are you guys up to?" Steph asked, as Dylan tried quickly to get off the website.

"Researching," Cody answered.

"What are you researching?" Steph asked. They looked at each other and neither could answer. "Okay, let's talk about what you are interested in," she suggested.

"Blood diseases!" Dylan answered as Cody nodded.

"And the NBA," Steph added as they smiled sheepishly.

"We were actually wondering about something before we came over here, but the rest of the group wasn't interested," Dylan said.

"And what was that?" Steph asked.

"We saw this show on the Discovery Channel about malaria and we wondered why there is malaria in some places but not here," Dylan said.

"We had a lot of questions about malaria," Cody said.

"Well, guess what, you can have your own small inquiry circle on malaria then. It fits really well under the circulatory system, because it is related to the

Question: Why do some mosquitos carry malaria and others don't	
Notes/Info from the text	**Thinking**
malaria - infectious disease caused by a parasite • Flu like symptoms - chills-fever breathing problems.	• What is a parasite? *QF • I think it might be a bug. Something bad.
• Transmitted by a mosquito bite and blood cells - 4 types only one is life threatening	Why do some mosquitos carry different types of malaria
Infected - mosquitos cause malaria in humans but if a regular mosquito bite you they get infected.	- one reason certain mosquitos don't carry malaria is because they haven't bite a infected human.
	Why do mosquitos carry malaria in other countries
www.imc worldwide.org	
Fact one million people die every year from malaria most occure in Africa south of the sahara desert	

blood, isn't it?" Steph encouraged.

And so it began, Dylan and Cody's investigation into malaria. This was a pretty small group of two, but we need to practice flexibility when engaging kids in small-group inquiry, because for kids to take their research seriously and work hard, they have to be interested in it. And the truth was, both of these boys were big jocks. Neither would choose school reading if they could throw a football or debate NBA statistics. But they seemed genuinely interested in malaria, which was half the battle.

And so they began reading with their question in mind. The more they read, the more they learned, and the more they wondered. One question led to another, and when they learned that malaria kills more than a million people a year, mostly women and children, they immediately wondered the most important question of all—what can we do to help? (See Cody and Dylan's malaria notes.) Lo and behold, that's when I found them back at the NBA website, but this time legitimately! They had been directed there when they asked the action question— "What can we do about this?"

The NBA had partnered with an organization called Nothing But Nets, which has as its mission to cure malaria by getting bed nets to African families to protect them from infected mosquitoes. Serendipitously, at that site, they came upon an article by their very favorite writer in the world, Rick Reilly of *Sports Illustrated* fame. They devoured his essay, marked it up with their thinking, and ended up at the Nothing But Nets website, where they found an educational video about what to do to help out. For as little as ten dollars per person, they discovered that we can buy a bed net that protects one child for four years!

Knowledge is powerful. Cody and Dylan were now unstoppable. They knew the other kids in the class would not be able to resist once they saw the video and heard the pleas for help. Kids climbed aboard, shared the information with their families, and actively raised money for bed nets for families in Africa in an effort to stop the spread of malaria.

See Lesson 27, "Response Options: Taking Learning Public," p. 142.

Coalesce and Take Learning Public

Each of the four inquiry circles ultimately wrote a variety of feature articles about their findings. They used writing workshop time to craft them and Mary did mini-lessons on nonfiction feature article writing during this time. Finally, they decided to gather all of the articles together and publish a magazine focused on health and medical issues. They looked at professional journals as models for their own publication. Cody and Dylan wrote an article about malaria—the causes, its effects, and what we can do about it, as shown below. Others wrote about artificial intelligence, migraines in childhood, allergies, and other topics. The result was their own "Journal of Health and Wellness." Several kids got the idea of distributing these journals to doctors' offices for their waiting room reading! We love this. Nothing better than taking a school project and putting it to work in the real world.

Cody and Dylan's malaria feature article.

Malaria: Nets Save Lives
If you go to Africa or Asia, be sure to throw on some bug spray. Why? Because if you get bitten by a mosquito you have a good probability of bringing malaria back to your country. And if you bring malaria back to your country, not to many people will want to be near you!

What is Malaria?
Malaria is a dangerous, infectious disease found in different parts of the world, mostly in Asia, Africa and South America. You get malaria from a mosquito bite. Surprisingly, only female mosquitoes can give you malaria. They carry it in their saliva. If you get bitten by an infected mosquito in one of these countries, you have a good chance of getting malaria. Malaria actually has two hosts. Infected mosquitoes can give it to people by biting them or mosquitoes can get malaria when they bite an infected human. So it spreads really fast.

When Malaria Started
Malaria started as far back as 2700 BC in China. It got its name in the middle ages. It comes from the Latin meaning bad air. A mosquito bit an animal that had malaria. So the mosquito became a carrier and bit a human and infected the human with malaria. The people didn't worry too much about it, until the man passed away a month later. Malaria is still dangerous today and there is still no vaccine, but there are ways to reduce the risks of malaria, like taking medicine before you go to a place with a lot of malaria, wearing bug spray and sleeping under a net.

Hot Spots of Malaria
If you ever wonder why people in Africa, Asia and South America get malaria and we in the United States don't? It's because countries on those continents are much poorer than the United States. And they don't have all of the medicines and stuff to prevent malaria before you even get it. They also have a higher mosquito population, the climate in those places is hot and wet near the equator and that kind of climate breeds more mosquitoes. Africa suffers the most from malaria. More than one million people die a year from malaria and 90% of those are African children.

How to Prevent Malaria
The best way to prevent malaria is to sleep under a mosquito net which doesn't let mosquitoes get into your bed when you are sleeping and to wear plenty of bug spray. For only $10 you can donate to an organization that is supported by the NBA called Nothing But Nets. They have sent more than two million bed nets to Africa. You can save lives with just $10 by buying one bed net for a family who cannot afford their own nets. Go to www.nothingbutnets.org and read all about it. WE bet you will want to donate $10 to help save lives! .

Cody and Dylan
April 2008

INQUIRY: *Sugar and Civil Rights*

—SARA AHMED, BURLEY SCHOOL, CHICAGO, ILLINOIS and LYNETTE EMMONS, NATIONAL-LOUIS UNIVERSITY, CHICAGO, ILLINOIS

MIDDLE

HIGH SCHOOL

Usually, curriculum-driven inquiry projects originate with requirements from the state, school district, or department. But some very authentic and memorable experiences arise when a teacher brings in a topic about which she herself is passionately concerned, and invites the kids to investigate it right along with her. That's what happened when Sara Ahmed came back from a vacation in the Caribbean. Lynette Emmons of Chicago's Center for City Schools at National-Louis University collaborated with Sara on the following account.

Sara's Chicago classroom could be an archaeological excavation site, it is so filled with layers of student-made posters, charts, and illustrations created during different research projects throughout the year. Kids' self-made question lists and writing are posted everywhere. The room is arranged so that students can easily go back and forth between working alone to meeting with small groups or discussing with everyone in the learning community area. Here the "furnishings" include a rug, an old couch, books in boxes and on stands, beanbag chairs, and lots of cushions for kids to sit on.

At this time in the school year, the curriculum says that the kids should be embarking on a study of civil rights. But, after a very disturbing personal experience, Sara has already had civil rights on her mind. She had recently vacationed at a resort in the Dominican Republic, and while visiting there became very uncomfortable about the extreme poverty she saw all around her. As Sara started asking questions, she learned that in the Dominican Republic there are old sugar plantations called *bateyes* where very poor Haitian migrant workers live, and sometimes work. A human rights group called the Health Justice Collaborative describes these plantations (www.bateyrelief.org):

www.heinemann.com/
comprehensionandcollaboration.

> From their founding the Bateyes lacked basic necessities such as clean water, latrines and electricity. Falling sugar prices in the late 1980s and decreases in US quotas designed to protect US farmers led to a severe decline in the sugar industry. In 1999, sugar mills were leased to private companies in contracts lasting 30 years, which has so far led to a corporate focus on meeting production goals with little investment in the estates and factories, leaving them in severe decline. This transition has contributed to increasing unemployment, poverty and joblessness in the Bateyes.

A United Nations report also documented the high poverty, scarce educational opportunities, and high rates of AIDS/HIV infection for both children and adults in these poor communities (United Nations Economic and Social Council 1998). The report also noted that the Dominican national government seemed committed to economic policies that concentrate wealth in a tiny elite, leaving most of the population in miserable living conditions.

Sara came home from the Caribbean wanting to know more about this situation and the plight of the people involved. As she says, "Sometimes in life, issues find you and you have no choice but to react to them." But she also realized that this could be a great inquiry project for her students—looking at the idea of civil rights in a faraway place—something strange and distant, yet very real and important. She also thought this would be a great way to model for her students how our real-world experiences should make us stop and question what is going on around us. And finally Sara wondered, Shouldn't it also make us want to do something about it?

To start the inquiry, Sara knew she had to build the students' background knowledge. So she got a globe and maps and began with the Dominican Republic's location, physical features, resources, and people. She gathered assorted books and materials that helped create interest in what was going on in this new-to-the-kids country. She showed numerous photographs from her trip and talked about her experience. She wanted kids to concentrate on two big questions about the plight of the *bateye* people: First, how did this happen? And second, who was responsible?

See Lesson 6, "Ask Questions and Wonder About Information," p. 121.

But the kids zoomed past these goals. As Sara's knowledge building was unfolding, the kids began to ask their own questions. They began to make a list of all of the questions they had about the Dominican Republic, its people, and their production of sugar cane. Sara put down all of their questions on chart paper, valuing each one. Implicit in these questions were personal connections kids were making. Brenda announced that the impoverished *bateye* kids could have been them. Jason wondered if the Haitians in the plantations were impoverished because they were people of color. Kids decided to find out if the *bateye* people were discriminated against mainly because they were Haitian, or because of the tone of their skin.

See Lesson 22, "Choosing Topics to Investigate," p. 137.

Based on these newfound questions and connections, the students were eager to dig in, read, and learn. Sara helped the kids put their questions into five categories: government, health, education, wealth, and lifestyle. The next goal was for the students to choose which of these topics they were most interested in and form small inquiry groups for the duration of the project. Now, each group's task was to begin to ask additional questions around their specific topics, identify the most important ones, and gather more information.

The small groups jumped right in, scanning the Internet, reference books, maps, and what newspaper articles they could find. But there was a problem. There weren't many resources on the topic. There was very little published or posted about the *bateyes*, and the kids were surprised. Did this mean nobody cared? Sara used this opportunity to open a deep conversation about why a lack of information might exist in a case like this. The kids immediately made the connections to Chicago's local media, thinking about which events get reported and which are ignored.

But the kids wanted information *now*, so Sara helped them brainstorm a way around the apparent dead end. She introduced the students to the Bateye Relief Alliance, and it was from this website that the kids discovered a photographer who had posted several images from his research on the topic. The students now had a connection to a researcher whom Sara could e-mail with kids' questions about the *bateyes*. The United Nations report was another helpful find: pretty hard reading, but if the kids worked together, they could dig out the important parts about wealth, poverty, and disease.

As an end product of the small-group inquiries, Sara asked kids to prepare a monologue or Reader's Theater performance based on the research done in each group. In these performances, kids had to take on the voices of real Haitian and Dominican people. The students became the health workers, children, parents, aristocrats, the dictator, and the members from the Bateye Relief Alliance. With their own inquiry questions and their sources in hand, students synthesized their learning by writing their character monologues or dialogues. As a form of rehearsal, the students interviewed each other and answered tough factual and interpretative questions in character. By the day of the culminating performance, the students had both built knowledge and developed empathy for their subjects.

When the other seventh-grade class filed in to be the audience, they got an eyeful. Images of the photographer's photographs and ones from Sara's vacation flashed behind students as they presented their powerful monologues.

All this had stemmed from one teacher's curiosity and uneasiness about the world. What a good message for kids: that by inquiring into our own discomfort, we can make a difference in the world. Over just a few days, the students moved from complete unawareness of the *bateyes* (and perhaps the Dominican Republic) to feeling a deep investment in the future of a group of fellow humans a thousand miles away.

See Lesson 27, "Response Options: Take Learning Public," p. 142.

HIGH SCHOOL

INTERMEDIATE

www.heinemann.com/
comprehensionandcollaboration.

When we say that inquiry circles can be applied to almost any subject matter, we mean it. Check out the website for a small-group curricular inquiry on exponential functions from a Chicago high school math class.

If we want classrooms full of kids who are engaged, thoughtful, collaborative learners, they must have ownership of what they study and investigate. Inquiry circles—under the umbrella of the curriculum—offer a wonderful way for kids to contemplate and question information, to work together, and to do authentic research to find answers. In curricular inquiry, kids learn the research process for sure, but also the content of the district-mandated curriculum. Of the four models of inquiry described in this book, curricular inquiry probably fits most seamlessly into the school day and year, because we all have to "do" the curriculum. And as you have seen, the curricular inquiries in this chapter are a far cry from the ubiquitous apple units, formulaic state reports, and annual term papers that we remember from days gone by. When kids drive inquiry, they not only enjoy themselves, but learn a ton as they go!

CHAPTER 100

Literature Circle Inquiries

The school activity known as literature circles (now interchangeably called book clubs) began spreading back in the early 1980s. This invention was something like the storied collision between peanut butter and chocolate—something unexpectedly delicious was created when two tasty but previously separate ingredients were combined. The two big trends in education at that time were collaborative learning (anyone ever attend a Johnson & Johnson workshop?) and independent reading, which was boosted by a best seller called *Hooked on Books* by Daniel Fader and Elton McNeil (1969). When teachers put these two ideas together—kids reading self-chosen books and then discussing them in small, peer-led groups—shazam! Lit circles were invented.

One cool thing about the origins of lit circles was that, in many places around the country, kids invented them. It turns out that if you leave students alone in a classroom with multiple copies of good books, they will often form small book discussion groups spontaneously. It just makes sense to pick a book with a few friends, read, and discuss it. Creation stories like these abound, from Kathy Smith's fifth graders in Arizona to Becky Abraham Searle's middle schoolers in Illinois, and in dozens of other spots.

As far as we know, Jerry Harste, Kathy Short, and Carolyn Burke were the first to enter the strategy into the professional literature with their admirable and still eminently useful *Creating Classrooms for Authors* (1988, 1995). Ralph Peterson and Maryann Eeds offered their inspirational take on literature discussion groups in 1990 and more recently in the updated *Grand Conversations* (2007). And Smokey's groundbreaking 1994 book *Literature Circles: Voice and Choice in the Student-Centered Classroom* (revised in 2002) showed teachers how to adapt the structure to their own classrooms and teach kids the collaboration skills needed for this challenging, interactive strategy. Over the years, a host of other teachers and authors have added to this literature, which now includes dozens of titles.

So we can define literature circles as *small, peer-led reading discussion groups.* In their original form, they were typically used when kids were reading chapter books or novels. Groups of students would choose a book to read, divide the text into three or four sections, and then meet every few days to discuss the reading as it unfolded. While this whole-book model is still very prevalent, teachers now use the lit circle structure not just with novels, but with poems and plays, with short chunks of text, and with nonfiction across the curriculum. These days, we often have short, one-time meetings to discuss text we have read right in class; sometimes we have conversations in writing as well as out loud. In short, the use of book clubs has exploded past its original application and become an everyday tool for teachers looking to involve kids actively in talking about text of any kind.

WHAT'S NEW AFTER TWENTY-FIVE YEARS OF LITERATURE CIRCLES?

www.heinemann.com/
comprehensionandcollaboration.

1. De-emphasis on role sheets. Instead, capturing kids' responses using Post-its, text annotations, bookmarks, journals. For details see the website.

2. More use of drawn or graphic responses to text.

3. More explicit teaching of social skills.

4. Not just novels. More use of short text—picture books, stories, poems, articles, charts, graphs, cartoons.

5. More nonfiction text, from articles through adult trade books.

6. Reaching out across the curriculum: book clubs in science, social studies, and so on.

7. Sparking or supplementing out-loud discussion with written conversations.

8. Multitext literature circles (jigsawed text sets, theme sets, multigenre inquiries).

9. New forms of assessment. Fewer book reports, and more critical book reviews. More performances (reader's theater, tableaux, drama, song lyrics, etc.).

10. Moving from books to topics and from literature circles to broader inquiry circles.

Literature circles have been a nice success story. By some estimates, *millions* of American schoolkids are engaged in something called literature circles every day (Daniels 2002). Our national literacy standards, promulgated by the National Council of Teachers of English and the International Reading Association, say that kids should be doing "Book Clubs, just for fun" regularly in their classrooms (NCTE 1996). A growing body of research (www.litcircles.org/research.html) has shown that literature circles can enhance the reading achievement, attitudes, and work habits of students at all grade levels. And the strategy itself, nurtured here in American schools, has spread around the world; Smokey hears constantly from teachers in Europe, the Middle East, and Asia where kids are doing book clubs with their classmates. The most recent report, from international educator Teresa Kubasak, included photos of a class of Iraqi refugee teenagers meeting in literature circles in Damascus, Syria.

But there have been difficulties as well. The most prevalent was the overuse of "role sheets," a set of tools adapted from generic cooperative learning activities and designed to give each group member a specific job like Questioner, Word Wizard, Literary Luminary, or Illustrator. In classroom use, these role sheets often become mechanical, hindering rather than empowering lively, spontaneous book talk. Smokey has been crusading against role sheet abuse for years; he teaches kids to instead use Post-its, journals, bookmarks, or drawings to harvest their responses as they read (Daniels 2002).

Also in the olden days of lit circles, when the kids finished a book club book, teachers would typically assign a project or book report—put on a skit, rewrite the ending, or create a new cover. While these activities were occasionally fun, they more often felt mechanical, with kids just going through the dutiful motions. As we tried to analyze why these end-of-book projects so often flopped, we started examining our own behavior. As adult readers, we had to admit that when we finish a book, we generally don't sit down and make a diorama about it...

▲

SMOKEY: I do. I make dioramas all the time. My house is just filled with all the dioramas I have made about books I have read.

STEPH: You are such a liar. I've been to your house a million times and I've never seen a single diorama, not one.

SMOKEY: Well, maybe I keep them in a special room. You should see my diorama of **The Poisonwood Bible**, it has the cutest little snake in there.

STEPH: Will you please stop?

SMOKEY: And the one about **Macbeth** is really awesome. I found some great miniature witches at Michael's, and there's a tiny cauldron...

STEPH: Sure, uh-huh.

SMOKEY: You have no sense of humor.

STEPH: When people are funny, I do.

SMOKEY: I was just trying to emphasize how silly it can be when we make kids do these projects that are so artificial.

STEPH: Yeah, that's for sure. But you scared me there for a minute. I'm thinking, holy moly, maybe he is crazier than I thought.

▼

When they finish a book, real readers usually *talk about it*—with anyone they can find. And once they have talked themselves out, they go and find another book to read. So, since we want school to be as lifelike as possible, we backed off on cute but artificial lit circle projects, even as we sought better ways to extend the learning. On the next page is our small-group inquiry model adapted for literature circle inquiries.

Small-Group Inquiry Model Adapted for Literature Circle Inquiries

STAGE	TEACHER	KIDS
Immerse *Invite Curiosity, Build Background, Find Topics, and Wonder*	• Shares own engagement with books • Helps kids choose books and discuss them in small, peer-led groups • Shares how books can change us and leave lingering questions • Models a personal inquiry stemming from a book • Shows how to develop inquiry questions from reading • Helps groups to identify a topic or question for further study • Confers with groups and individuals	• Choose, read, and discuss books in small, peer-led groups • Think about what they know and connect new information to background knowledge and experience • Are aware of their own wonderings and reactions as they read and talk • Discuss and jot down potential beyond-the-book inquiry questions as they read • Discuss possible inquiry topics when books are finished
Investigate *Develop Questions, Search for Information, and Discover Answers*	• Helps students to hone and refine beyond-the-book inquiry topics • Floods kids with resources and materials on a topic or question • Models how to read, listen, and view with a question in mind • Models how to take notes by interacting with text, coding text, and writing in margins or on Post-it notes • Demonstrates how to determine importance • Helps groups to sharpen or change inquiry focus • Facilitates changes in group membership or topics • Confers with groups and individuals	• Listen, talk, view, and read to gain information about their chosen topic • Write, talk, and draw to think about information • Develop questions and read, listen, and view to answer them • Use text and visual features to gain information • Meet with teams to set and monitor schedules and task completion
Coalesce *Intensify Research, Synthesize Information, and Build Knowledge*	• Shows how to infer answers and draw conclusions • Demonstrates how to read for the gist and synthesize information • Engages kids in guided discussions and debates • Shares how to evaluate sources • Teaches interviewing strategies if needed • Facilitates arrangements for out-of-school resources • Confers with groups and individuals	• Engage in deeper reading and researching—books, articles, websites, videos, library visits • Target key ideas • Keep asking: So what? What about this really matters? • Practice interviewing • Conduct "people" research—interviews, surveys, questionnaires, focus groups • Check sources and determine reliability • Synthesize information to build knowledge • Meet with teams to monitor schedules, complete specific tasks, and plan for sharing

continues

Small-Group Inquiry Model Adapted for Literature Circle Inquiries, *cont.*		
STAGE	**TEACHER**	**KIDS**
Go Public *Share Learning, Demonstrate Understanding, Take Action*	• Co-constructs expectations for literature circle extension projects • Offers the widest range of possibilities for sharing/performing • Welcomes kids' suggestions for these demonstrations • Helps kids find real audiences and opportunities to share their knowledge and teach others • Helps students reflect on content and process • Co-creates rubrics to assess and evaluate projects • With students, responds, assesses, and evaluates projects • Supports kids to share the learning by taking action	• Co-construct expectations for literature circle extension projects • Demonstrate learning and understanding in a variety of ways: performances, posters, letter writing, essays, picture books, tableaux, poetry, editorials • Become teachers as they share their knowledge with others • Consider changes in their own beliefs or behavior • Take action through writing, speaking, community work, advocacy • Reflect on their knowledge building and cooperative process • Join in another cycle of literature circles, being alert for new or lingering questions and inquiry topics

As we looked deeper into our own responses, we realized that books often leave us *changed*. When we read a book, a book of consequence, we end up a slightly different person from the one who opened the first page days before. Usually the change is subtle; we have gained some background knowledge, expanded our understanding of a time, a place, some events, a topic. Or perhaps, as we enter the lives of fictional or historic people in a book, we end up understanding life a little better—how families work, or how people abuse power, or how to deal with loss. The next time we find ourselves talking with friends about one of these topics, we may notice that our thinking has been informed or influenced by that book we read a while back. Obviously this lingering effect is less common with formulaic "beach books," which we can essentially read without generating any brain waves at all (which is the whole *raison d'etre* of beach books, when you think about it).

At other times, books change us overtly and powerfully. We come flying out of the back of the book activated, revved up, concerned, with a need to change something or take action. This is especially common with current nonfiction text. After reading Eric Schlosser's *Fast Food Nation: The Dark Side of the All-American Meal*, we may swear off cheeseburgers forever (or at least for a week). After reading Hampton Sides' *Blood and Thunder: The Epic Story of Kit Carson and the Conquest of the American West*, we may emerge historically reframed, with a whole new understanding of the European theft of a continent from its native peoples, and shocked at how "traditional" histories (like school textbooks) leave out so many important details. With books like these, we emerge wanting to learn more, and sometimes, to *do something*. We have lingering questions, new questions. Is some fast food better than others? Just how many other genocidal "long walks" affected tribes other than the Navajo?

So these days, when we do literature circles with kids, we don't assign an arbitrary or superficial project at the end of each book. Instead, we ask, "Has this book changed you in some way? Where does this book take you next? What do you want to find out or do as a result of having read this? Do you have any lingering questions?" We help young readers dig into their own thinking to discover how the book has affected them, what questions linger, what new curiosities have been provoked. When we teach this way, kids' extensions from the book are far more significant and meaningful than any diorama. Instead of mechanically constructing an object to be graded, they become true inquirers.

*L*it Circle Inquiries in Practice

In the following pages, we'll visit several classrooms where you can watch creative teachers extend literature circles in new directions, toward lively inquiry circles. If you are a teacher who has already done some kind of book clubs with your kids, this may sound like a natural next step. If you haven't already tried lit circles, these stories may leave you eager to try out this well-proven, well-structured form of collaboration with your kids.

PRIMARY

INQUIRY: *Frog and Toad and Friendship*

—STEPH HARVEY, BROMWELL ELEMENTARY DENVER, COLORADO

Join Steph as she works with a first-grade lit circle to help them define their inquiry.

"Toad's nicer," Jenna declared.

"Uh-uh," Jake shook his head. "Frog is."

"I think they are both sometimes nice and sometimes not so nice," Sophie added.

Jenna, her nose buried in the book, raced to a page where Toad was giving his jacket to Frog. "See, Toad gave Frog his jacket because Frog spent so much time helping him find a button. That is really nice, to give away a jacket!" she commented.

Jake, without looking up, ripped through the pages and halted when he came to a picture of Frog writing a letter to Toad, who had expressed sadness at the fact that he never got any mail.

"That is really nice, to write Toad a letter so he gets some mail," Jake offered.

"They're friends! That's why," Callie chimed in.

And so it went, six first graders meeting in a lit circle and discussing the gut issues in Arnold Lobel's *Frog and Toad Are Friends,* just as their parents might do on a winter evening in their living room in their own neighborhood book club.

For those of us grown-ups who join them, book clubs offer a direct route to staying connected to books and to each other. And often, we head off to work the next morning brimming with lingering questions and issues from the previous night's discussion. But the book club is over, done with. And the next time we meet, we will be on to another book, another author, and another discussion. Nothing wrong with that! Wide reading stimulates our brains and our imaginations. But this is where school comes in handy. School doesn't go away. In-school lit circles can pursue books further than neighborhood book clubs can, because kids can easily continue to explore the ideas in the book the following day or even the following week!

The next day, Steph met with these six *Frog and Toad* kids to explore their thinking. "So, after having read these great *Frog and Toad* stories, what are you still wondering?" Steph asked.

"I want to know the difference between frogs and toads," Jorge said.

"Me too," Jake added.

"Hmm, that's interesting. So even though this is a made-up story about a frog and toad, you would like to learn more about real frogs and toads. Anybody else want to join these two as they learn more about real frogs and toads? Samuel, great! While I am checking with the others, take a minute to talk to each other about some things you think you know and some things you wonder about real frogs and toads."

Steph turned to the three remaining group members—Jenna, Sophie, and Callie. "And what are you three wondering about after reading these great *Frog and Toad* stories? Blank stares greeted her. Steph waited a moment and when no one responded, she prompted, "Well, I noticed in your lit circle conversation yesterday that you were having a great discussion about who was nicer, Frog or Toad."

"They were both nice. They are best friends," Callie jumped in.

"What makes you say that?" Steph asked.

"Because they treat each other nicely . . . most of the time," said Callie.

"Friends do that," added Jenna. Sophie noted that she was really good friends with Callie and Jenna and most of the time she tried to be nice to them.

Noticing that they might be onto an interesting inquiry about friendship, Steph nudged, "So I am wondering, what do you think makes a good friend? Would you three like to talk about that for a moment?" All three nodded and began to pore over the *Frog and Toad* books looking for evidence of friendship as Steph went off to check in with the "real" frog and toad group.

"We have lots of questions," Samuel smiled as Steph joined them.

"Great! I have an idea. I am going to give you this great big notebook and you can find a place on the floor where you can all fit around it. Then you might try writing or drawing anything you wonder about frogs and toads, any questions you have about them. I think that's a good way to begin since you already have a lot of

See Lesson 22, "Choosing Topics to Investigate," p. 137.

See Lesson 20, "Create a Research Notebook," p. 135.

questions. Writing them down is the best way to remember them all. What do you think?" Wide smiles spread across their faces as Steph handed them the oversized notebook to get started. "And maybe later on, you can do some research to find answers to some of your questions," Steph added.

Steph returned to Sophie, Jenna, and Callie, who were still debating which character was nicer. Steph asked Callie about her earlier comment on friendship and they began to talk about what it means to be a friend. "How about I give you one of these large notebooks to write down anything you wonder about friendship and what it means to be a friend?"

"I have an idea," said Sophie. "Maybe we can teach other kids how to be a good friend."

"Wow, what a great idea—teaching other kids about friendship. That's one of the main reasons we read—so we can share what we learn with others. I bet you already have some good ideas, but I am thinking you can really learn more from these *Frog and Toad* books. Frog and Toad are good friends, and the stories here show that. I have some other *Frog and Toad* books that might help you think about friendship as well. Maybe you three can reread some of these stories with a question in mind—what does it mean to be a good friend? You can have an inquiry circle on friendship! What do you think?"

All three nodded in agreement.

"OK, I will write that question on a Post-it, and you can write it at the top of this notebook page if you like. Then you can jot down or draw some things you learn from the books as well as some ideas you already have about how to be a good friend."

Suddenly, two very interesting and very different inquiry studies sprang forth. Inquiry circles emerge naturally from literature circles. Lit circles are the kindling that can light up thinking and ignite inquiry. They fire up young minds with questions, issues, and ideas kids care about. They stoke kids to investigate their thoughts far beyond the initial conversations and discussions.

To support these kids to dig deeper, Steph headed off to the library with each group and engaged the librarian in a search for relevant text. One hallmark of inquiry circles is that diverse readers can participate in the same group, because they can all read text that is just right for them. Avid readers can choose more challenging text on the topic; less-developed readers can read more accessible text. It is our responsibility to point kids in the right direction as they search for text related to their topic. In this way, all kids can contribute to the inquiry regardless of their reading level.

When initiating small-group inquiry, there is no better way to get started than by asking kids to write down what they wonder about their topic. It is through their questions that they discover what matters to them and what they want to investigate. After much research and discussion, the friendship inquiry circle decided to create a self-help book of sorts, a manual on how to be a good friend. They shared it with the class and made several copies for the classroom and the school library.

See Lesson 8, "Notetaking: Read with a Question in Mind," p. 123.

See Lesson 27, "Response Options: Take Learning Public," p. 142.

The "real" frog and toad inquiry circle chose to teach others about the differences between frogs and toads. On the day of their presentation, they led the class in an activity. They handed out Post-it notes and Jorge passed around a football and a basketball. They then asked the class to jot down which was more like a frog and which was more like a toad. The kids looked bewildered but took a stab at it. When they finished jotting, the boys revealed a poster-size image of a frog and a toad. They invited each classmate to come up to the poster and look closely at the animals' skin through a magnifying glass. As they viewed the image, several kids blurted out, "Toads are like the basketball and frogs are like the football!" The boys had made their point graphically and kinesthetically, and it is likely that no one in that class ever forgot that frogs have smooth skin and toads are bumpy!

INQUIRY: *Bullying*

INTERMEDIATE

—MIKE LAEHR AND SUE FISHER, CLOUGH PIKE SCHOOL, CINCINNATI, OHIO

Mike Laehr tells how he and his teaching partner, Sue Fisher guided their fourth graders through a lit circle inquiry around the theme of bullying.

Kids in my fourth-grade classes engage in lit circles of every shape and size. They read novels, trade nonfiction, picture books, and short articles. They come together in rousing conversation and are frequently so caught up in their text talk that they don't want their lit circle to come to an end. One thing I have noticed is that these lit circle discussions often lead to lingering questions and a need for further inquiry.

During the spring last year, a lit circle group chose to read Janell Cannon's picture book *Crickwing*. It is the story of a cockroach who is the brunt of much teasing because of a crooked wing. Soon Crickwing, having been victimized by larger bullies, morphs into a bully himself as he taunts and threatens an army of tiny leafcutter ants. The story ends on a high note when Crickwing sees the light and saves the day. But the conversation that ensued in the literature circle was darker, and focused primarily on what it feels like to be bullied. This bullying discussion spilled over to the rest of the class. Some other kids picked up *Crickwing* on their own, and soon bullying became the topic in the room.

My teaching partner Sue Fisher and I have long noticed that the end of fourth grade seems to be a particularly ripe time for bullying to emerge. So in response to that perennial concern and the conversation sparked by the lit circle kids, we decided to take up the issue with the entire class and see what happened.

Day 1: Interactive Read-Aloud

We begin our bully inquiry with an interactive read-aloud of *Oliver Button Is a Sissy* by Tomie dePaola. Nothing like a short, theme-filled picture book to hook kids and get them thinking. The big ideas and brevity of picture books give us a great jumping-off point for spirited discussion. The material in *Oliver Button* is easy enough for all of our students, yet is packed with meaningful ideas.

I hand out small booklets I have made in which the students can write their thoughts about self-selected passages from the book. Having taught strategies since early in the year, I know their annotations are likely to include connections, inferences, and other reactions. The story begins with Oliver being called a sissy because he "didn't like to do things that boys are supposed to do." Instead of playing football, Oliver liked to take walks, read, sing, and dance. As I read aloud, I immediately notice the pencils and pens flying across the pages. I let the students write for a minute and then ask them to turn and talk to each other about what they are thinking, just in these first couple of pages.

We quickly transfer our thinking to a chart; questions, connections, and inferences emerge. Saraya asks, "What are boys supposed to do? Why aren't they allowed to read?" Andy adds that Oliver is "just trying to find himself." When we read the part in which Oliver's father calls him a sissy, the whole class is feeling sorry for Oliver, and Marc infers that the story is about rejection. As we read the rest of the story, students share their thoughts about Oliver's feelings—anger, sadness, embarrassment, determination. We stop to talk at critical points in the story.

When we have finished the story, I tell the students to read over what they have written and add any new thinking to their booklets. I also ask them to draw a picture of what they visualize when they think about this story (an example is shown here). I move about the room conferring with kids. At the end of the period, I collect their booklets and go over them that night, looking for evidence of thoughtful reading.

See Lesson 2, *"Listen to Your Inner Voice," p. 117, and Lesson 11, "Turn and Talk," p. 126.*

Saraya's thinking in response to Oliver Button.

Day 2: Share the Thinking by Writing and Talking

The next day we "circle share" what we have written about Oliver Button. After reviewing their booklets and listening to their sharing, I search for at least one line from each student and put it on an overhead so we can share the thoughts with the whole class. Here are a few examples of their thoughtful reading:

"His dad calls him a sissy. Ouch." —RYAN

"I like to read. Am I a sissy?" —ZAC

"I would never want to go to school ever, ever again." —ELLY

"Never give up on what you like to do. Don't let anyone discourage you." —KOBY

I use the overhead to showcase the students' thinking. The comments reveal how boys in particular are frequently challenged to prove their "manhood" and toughness. Projecting their names in this way celebrates all of our kids, even the quiet students who may be hesitant to share in a group.

Day 3: Read, Write, and Talk About a Nonfiction Article on Bullying

Sue and I agree that it's time for the kids to get some real, factual information about bullying. We find a *Time for Kids* nonfiction article titled "The Bully Battle" that gives some startling and frightening statistics about bullying in American schools. We create a two-column thinksheet with the article printed on the left side and space for kids to write on the right-hand side. I call the class to the rug and explain that we are going to look at a nonfiction article about bullying, and that I would like to know their opinions about the article. As I model at the overhead with a transparency of the thinksheet for a few minutes, it is obvious

Name Danielle   April 24 2008

WORLD REPORT EDITION *Cover Story*
The Bully Battle
Are nasty, mean kids making your life miserable? Take action!

print this story

Now I'm thinking....
Now I'm wondering....
Now I'm feeling....

Christian champ, 10, a fifth-grader in Prescott, Arizona, got his first taste of bullying in kindergarten when a second-grader pushed him off a swing. Since then—Christian has learned how to deal with bullies—people who tease, hurt or threaten others. In fourth grade, when a bully cursed at him, tried to hit him and started swinging a shoe, Christian followed his father's advice. "First I ignored the bully," he explains. "Then I told the teacher."

How can you hurt a kindegarten? I would be scared.

People don't like to be pushed or teased for getting good or bad grades or be made fun of for how they look. Sadly, about 1 in 7 schoolchildren is a bully or a victim of one. Five million elementary and middle school students in the U.S. are bullied each year, according to the National Association of School Psychologists. Each day, bullies' teasing leads some 160,000 fearful kids to skip school.

why for getting good grades (jealousy)
I think it's more than this.
Ooch! This tells me these kids don't know what to do.

The Big, Bad Bully
A recent study of bullies found that most often the popular kids, the ones liked by both kids and teachers, are doing the teasing. "Most bullies are the kids that other students look up to, the ones everybody wants to hang out with," says Dorothy Espelage, an assistant professor of psychology who co-authored the study.

I didn't Name them there terrafied.
Amazing! they must be afraid to lose their popularity

Psychologist William Pollack agrees that too often a bully's behavior is encouraged and not stopped. Some bullies become popular ringleaders with other kids, but not all bullies are the cool kids, he says. Some are troubled students who may have been bullied themselves.

Terrible!
Do the teachers understand the problem?
Bullies aren't cool at all.

Taking The Bully By The Horns
Schools across the U.S. are fighting back against bullying. Last week 6 states observed Safe Communities = Safe Schools Awareness Week. From October 15 to 21, about 300 communities held antibullying and antiviolence activities for kids. The week was coordinated by Safe Schools, Safe Students, an Arizona-based group founded by Rod Beaumont. He says the purpose of the awareness week is to make people realize that bullying and other types of school violence are not something that can just be ignored.

Why does schools have to have bullies? Why even have them at all? Have there always been bullies?
I agree

The organization arranges bullying-prevention workshops. Many of them are led by a huge, leather-wearing, tattoo-covered man called the Scary Guy. He challenges kids not to use mean words and not to push or shove others for at least seven days. "I was a bully my whole life," the Scary Guy admits, "but now I'm not." *He changed!!! Wow!*

great idea!

The workshops teach kids that words can hurt just as much as physical violence. Rebecca Sassoon, 10, of New York City, knows this well. When Rebecca was 7 years old, she was bullied by three boys in her class for being too smart. "I got things right on tests, and they didn't, they teased me," she recalls. "I used to go home after school and cry."

Jealousy!!! You can never be too smart Maybe the three boys are jelous of her getting good grades because they don't!

That's terrible what they do to kids these days.

See Lesson 5, "Annotate Text: Leave Tracks of Thinking," p. 120.

from the first paragraph that my class is not going to have any problem jotting or talking about their thinking as they continue reading. When Danielle reads in the article that five million elementary and middle school kids are bullied each year, she writes, "I think it's more than this. Ouch! This tells me these kids don't know what to do. I don't blame them. They're terrified." Sara writes, "Well, yeah, words can hurt." She expresses her own concerns about middle school and the need for teachers to be more aware of this ever-increasing problem. The talk is so lively and spirited and the feelings so strong that I decide to do a quick survey of my own. At lunch, I jot down the questions and make copies for the students and then hand out the surveys for homework that evening.

- Have you ever been bullied? Explain what happened.
- Have you ever bullied someone else? Explain.
- Have you ever **seen** someone else being bullied? Explain. Tell what you did about it.

Day 4: Review and Display Survey Findings

See Lesson 24, "Organize Group Findings: Create Question Webs," p. 139.

I collect their surveys and find some sad results. All but one of my twenty-seven students say that they have been bullied. And nineteen students admit that they have bullied someone. Most students believe bullies act that way because they think it is "cool." Others say that bullies learn that behavior from their parents. Still others say that it is a way to get attention. We graph the findings from the surveys on a bar graph for all to see and discuss what we have learned so far. Saraya asks "So why do people bully anyway?" Together we decide that this is an essential question in our bullying inquiry. Later that day, I create a question web with the question Why Do People Bully? In the center. I draw lines out from the central question and encourage kids to search for additional information and answers to that question as they engage in their bullying inquiries. Each day the web grows, as kids come up with new learning related to the central question, share their findings and sign their name to their contribution and add the source.

www.heinemann.com/ comprehensionandcollaboration.

Day 5: Inferring Big Ideas in Poetry and Song

A few years ago, our wonderful literacy coach and mentor, Tanny McGregor, introduced us to the song "Rachel Delevoryas," written and performed by Randy Stonehill (1992). The song naturally lends itself to our bullying inquiry, as you can see from the lyrics.

RACHEL DELEVORYAS
—By Randy Stonehill

Rachel Delevoryas
With her thick eyeglasses and her plain Jane face
Sat beside me in my fifth-grade class
Looking so terribly out of place
Rachel played the violin

And classical music was out of style
She couldn't control all her wild brown hair
Her nervous laughter and her awkward smile and
    It was clear that she'd never be one of us
    With her dowdy clothes
    And her violin
    And a name like Rachel Delevoryas

But I'd pass by her house in the evening
Going to play with my best friend Ray
And the music floating from her window
Spoke the things that Rachel could never say

Rachel Delevoryas
Was eating her lunch as the boys walked by
"Rachel is ugly" she heard them shout
She sat on the schoolyard bench and cried and
    It was clear that she'd never be one of us
    With her dowdy clothes
    And her violin
    And a name like Rachel Delevoryas

And every year the hedge got higher
As it grew around Rachel's house
Like the secret wall inside her
That she built to keep all the heartache out

Rachel Delevoryas
Moved back east with her family
Now she's dressed in a beautiful gown
Standing on stage with the symphony
Rachel plays the violin
But every night when the lights go down
I wonder if she still remembers those days
And cruel little boys in this one-horse town and
    It was clear that she'd never be one of us
    With her dowdy clothes
    And her violin
    And a name like Rachel Delevoryas

See Lesson 7, "Stop, Think, and React," p. 122.

See Lesson 10, "Synthesize Information: Read to Get the Gist," p. 125.

Before class I copy the lyrics to the song on a chart. Next to each verse, I leave room to record the students' thoughts. I love to incorporate music into my teaching of thinking, so we listen to the song and stop at the end of each verse to talk and write about our thinking. I also give each child a small booklet containing the words to the song and room to write down their thoughts, feelings, and reactions.

Comments burst forth and we record them:

"She's just being herself!"

"She lets out her feelings through music."

"Why does she have to go through all this?"

"I can feel her pain."

"Calling someone 'ugly' is like a different kind of racism."

The end of the song brings audible sighs of relief as Rachel succeeds beyond anyone's wildest dreams. Avery gleefully points out the line, *It was clear that she'd never be one of us.* "She's not one of them," he pronounced. "She's better."

After much discussion, I know the students are ready to write more extensively. Their assignment is to draw what they are visualizing on the front cover of their booklets and to add any thoughts they have beyond our discussion. (One of their booklets is shown here.) The following day, we circle-share our writing and visualizations. I am absolutely floored when Matthew shares his thoughts:

Elly' response to Rachel Delevoryas.

B. I. (Big Idea)…Bullies…Is the hedge a metaphor? Yes…for protecting her feelings. When I heard this, it made me feel the pain too. Can't someone understand how she feels? No. They are too busy. They just pay attention to themselves. They don't think that words can hurt, but they do hurt her. They hurt her a lot. She builds a wall, like a castle of protection around her heart to keep the bully's words from hurting her. The problem is that the wall also keeps her locked inside. It cuts her off from people. What will Rachel have to do to tear down the wall? Maybe she will have to stand up for herself or see that there are some people in the world she can trust.

Days 6 and 7: Expand Our Thinking About Bullying by Going Beyond Personal Experience

I want my students to be aware of the many kinds of bullying and to expand their thinking to a broader scale, beyond the personal experience. So I put up a bulletin board titled "Bullies in Literature." I simply tell the students that, when they find an example of bullying in their independent reading, they should write down the title of the book, the page, and a short quote from the book. I put out some strips of blank construction paper for the kids to write on.

Zac writes about Voldemort from *Harry Potter*. Koby, a voracious reader, gives an example from Sharon Creech's book *Ruby Holler*. Brandi has five examples on the board from Eve Bunting's *Cheyenne Again*, a book about the forced schooling of Native Americans. She mentions that white men in the book are really bullies. Matthew posts a chilling quote from the Karen Hesse's *Witness*, a book about the Ku Klux Klan. He expresses that Klan members are extreme bullies. In fact, they all demonstrate an interest in learning about extreme bullies and what happens when they are left unchecked. Some of their bulletin board contributions are shown here.

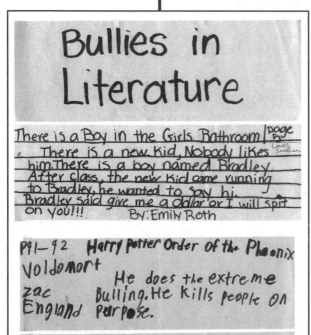

Quotes from independent reading that kids cite as examples of bullying

Day 8: Form Inquiry Circles

I gather the students on the rug to see how they might feel about doing some independent research into "extreme bullying." From reading they have done, they come up with four examples that involve what they believe to be extreme bullying:

The Ku Klux Klan

The Trail of Tears

Nazi Germany

Women's Suffrage

Although they choose these topics, their background is limited. It is clearly time for more in-depth inquiry. They join together in four inquiry circles of about six or seven kids each. Some choose their group based on interest and curiosity about the topic. Others choose their group based on who they want to work with. I allow this, but remember to help them learn that working with anyone can be rewarding. My only instruction is that they have to present some kind of project to the class a week later. That night, after school, I tape up some construction paper with a title for each group and the heading "Questions."

Day 9: Researching the Question

See Lesson 6, "Ask Questions and Wonder About Information," p. 121, and Lesson 8, "Notetaking: Read with a Question in Mind," p. 123.

The next day, each inquiry circle fills the group's chart with questions (the Trail of Tears poster is shown here) and then sets off to do research—always with their questions in mind. They bring in books, magazines, and information they have found on the Internet. The students cannot wait to get together to share what they have learned.

> # Trail of Tears
> ## Questions
> **Ryan:** Why do people attack Sacagawea's tribe?
> **Elly:** Why don't the Cherokees have a choice to move or not?
> **Elly:** Who are the Cherokees and why must they go west?
> **Danielle:** Why did some tribes raided the Hopi village and steel food and blankets?
> **Sarah:** Why DiD the indens get tereted so Bad?
> **Danielle:** Why was Andrew Jackson so mean?
> **Danielle:** Why did Andrew Jackson take away some-ones land that was not even his?

The Following Week: Research Continues

Every day, students are asking to stay inside to work during recess. When I come into the room after recess, they are spread out on the floor with their books or sitting at the computer searching for more information. Students are asking for permission to go to our library to find more information. Our librarian is thrilled to see students so excited about learning. Some students can't wait to share what they are finding. Sarah expresses outrage that Andrew Jackson was behind the removal of the Cherokee Nation from Georgia. Michael and Anne-Marie can't understand why our government couldn't stop the Ku Klux Klan from their racist actions, and the boys investigating Nazi Germany are horrified by the pictures of the concentration camps.

See Lesson 27, "Response Options: Take Learning Public," p. 142.

Presentation Day: Take Learning Public

All four of the inquiry circles present their information and demonstrate their understanding in different ways:

- The KKK inquiry circle members have mounted their information on black poster board ("Black represents evil," Michael tells us). They share their information about the history of the KKK, and we learn that the KKK threatened, intimidated, and even killed African Americans as well as other groups of people.

- The Trail of Tears group carries protest signs that say, "Treat the tribes better" and "We want peace for the settlers." The kids have written a letter of protest to Andrew Jackson (reproduced here). They also have a map showing the routes the Cherokees were forced to march. In addition to pictures depicting the suffering that the Cherokees endured, they have a copy of Andrew Jackson's message to Congress about the removal of the Cherokees.

- The inquiry circle investigating the Nazis has put together a descriptive poster listing all of their original questions plus a few new ones. These students have written a paragraph to answer each question and included pictures to support each paragraph. They close their presentation with the most meaningful question, "Why should people know about the Holocaust?"

The Nazis

What were the ghettos like?

The ghettos were run-down sections of the cities. They had walls and fences to keep the Jews inside. They were very crowded and there was very little food. Diseases spread fast and there was no medicine. A lot of people died of starvation. The ghettos must have been terrifying and terrible for the Jews.

What was Hitler's plan?

Hitler's plan was to get rid of all the people that he thought were inferior. He wanted to start a race of German people that he thought were better than everyone else. He planned to get rid of all Jews, Black people, and the handicapped.

Why did the people follow Hitler?

The Nazis had a special State Police. They would arrest anyone who would stand up to them. The Nazis also used many ways to convince people that the Jews were bad. Teachers taught about it in schools. There were posters and radio ads, and children's books that showed Jews as monsters. People began to believe the lies.

Who were the Nazis?

The Nazis were members of the National Socialist Party in Germany. The party was formed by a group of men and led by Adolph Hitler. They forced their ideas and hatred on the people in Germany and other countries.

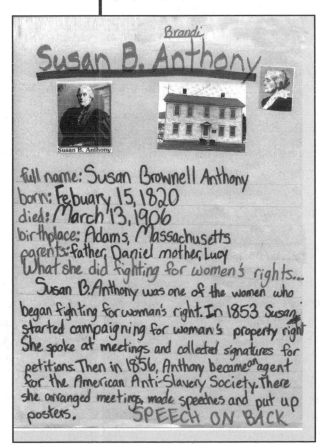

Brandi

Susan B. Anthony

Susan B. Anthony

full name: Susan Brownell Anthony
born: Febuary 15, 1820
died: March 13, 1906
birthplace: Adams, Massachusetts
parents: father, Daniel mother, Lucy
What she did fighting for women's rights...
   Susan B. Anthony was one of the women who began fighting for woman's right. In 1853 Susan started campaigning for woman's property right She spoke at meetings and collected signatures for petitions. Then in 1856, Anthony became an agent for the American Anti-Slavery Society. There she arranged meetings, made speeches and put up posters.   SPEECH ON BACK

- The kids in the women's rights group dress up as the women they have researched (Sojourner Truth, Elizabeth Cady Stanton, and Susan B. Anthony). They share a book they have created that includes details of the women's lives along with speeches and quotes. Then each stands and presents a speech. Shelby holds the class spellbound with a presentation of Sojourner Truth's "Ain't I a Woman" speech, given at the Women's Convention in 1851.

So what did these children gain from this inquiry into bullying? They have learned that, if they have been bullied, they are not alone. If they have ever bullied someone else, they have learned more about the harm that can be done by their words and actions. Maybe they have learned to be more caring and accepting of other people's differences. Hopefully, they have learned that they ought to stand up and help those who cannot help themselves. And they have learned that bullying left unchecked can result in extreme bullying, which must not be allowed. As the group of boys who studied Nazi Germany wrote,

> It is important that we can understand how it happened and make sure that it can never happen again. We have to treat all people equally. We should stand up for people that aren't being treated fairly. If we treat other people the way we want to be treated, we can keep something like this from ever happening again.

INQUIRY: *Native–Settler Contact*

—DIANE TITCHE, MURRAY LAKE ELEMENTARY, LOWELL, MICHIGAN

Diane Titche teaches fifth grade in Lowell, Michigan. This year, she is trying literature circles for the first time. She has heard from other teachers that they usually assign kids some kind of project—a poster, report, or skit—immediately after their reading and discussion are done. But after attending a weekend workshop with Smokey and Nancy Steineke in Santa Fe, Diane decided instead to engage her kids in extended small-group inquiries into questions raised by their literature circle books.

This meant that as student groups met to discuss sections of their chosen novels, she would help them to notice what they were wondering about, what questions they were developing along the way. By the end of their books, each group would identify one big lingering question or topic of interest, and then launch an investigation of it. This shift from project-style book reports to ambitious inquiries would not just allow kids to explore new ideas that surfaced in their reading, but would also move them beyond a single novel into the whole universe of nonfiction, multiple genres, the Internet, and "people" research.

Building Background Knowledge and Curiosity

Diane tries to correlate her language arts instruction with curriculum themes and with the fifth-grade social studies content, which is taught by a colleague. This year, she knows that her students will be studying American history, and particularly the contact between white settlers and native peoples in different regions across the country. After some initial class discussion, Diane discovers that her kids don't have much solid information about Native Americans. So, she decides to start by growing her students' background knowledge with a series of readings about settler–native contact. (See the website for more on how Diane builds kids' background knowledge in this way.)

INTERMEDIATE

MIDDLE

www.heinemann.com/
comprehensionandcollaboration.

Listen to Diane as she takes over in her own words:

After all this knowledge building, the kids were chomping at the bit to pick their books. After careful research, I had selected five titles on settler–native contact at a range of reading levels, from fourth through seventh grade. Lit circles are always a great way to differentiate instruction in the classroom; with five book choices, I can be sure that my developing readers and kids with special needs as well as my avid readers will all be both interested in and able to read their books. These were the five options:

Indian Captive: The Story of Mary Jemison by Lois Lenski. Set in the Midwest and New York in 1758. A fictional account of a true story of a young girl captured and raised by Seneca Indians.

Blood on the River: James Town 1607 by Elisa Carbone. The story of the settlement of the James Town colony as told through the eyes of a young page of Captain John Smith's. Includes both positive and negative images of Native Americans.

Sign of the Beaver by Elizabeth George Speare. Set in 1769 in the Maine wilderness; tells the story of a young boy who maintains his family's new home on his own, with the help of a Native American boy and his tribe.

Crooked River by Shelley Pearsall. Based on a true story, set in 1812 on the Ohio frontier. The story of a thirteen-year-old girl whose father holds an Indian, accused of murder, prisoner in the family's attic until his trial. The girl struggles with her doubts about the "certain" guilt of the Indian and ultimately must decide whether she should go against everyone in her town and try to save the Indian from certain execution.

My Heart Is on the Ground by Ann Rinaldi. Takes place in 1880 at the Carlisle Indian School in Carlisle, Pennsylvania. The book is the fictional diary of Nannie Little Rose, a Sioux Indian girl who is sent to the Carlisle Indian School to "cleanse" her of her Indian past and make her more like a white person.

Choosing Books and Forming Groups

We took more than an hour of class time to choose the books. The process included book talks by me, a book pass, and "voting," where each student marked a ballot with his or her top three choices. I assured the kids that they would get one of their top three choices. (For more on the choosing process, check the website.)

On Friday morning, the kids bounded in, desperate to find out whether their book groups had been set up. I read off the book groupings, to a wonderful chorus of exclamations in the background (*"Yes!"* "All right!"). I had the groups get together in meeting spots scattered around our room. They used the rest of our time on Friday morning to come up with a schedule for their readings and meetings and a set of ground rules for how they would operate as a team.

www.heinemann.com/
comprehensionandcollaboration.

See Lesson 13, "Creating Group Ground Rules," p. 128.

See Lesson 16, "Written Conversations," p. 131.

See Lesson 18, "I Beg to Differ: Disagreeing Agreeably," p. 133.

First Group Meetings

There was definitely an air of excitement in the room as reading time approached, and the kids were anxious to meet in their groups and get going. I wanted to be sure they had a strong foundation for starting their discussions, so instead of letting them plunge into out-loud discussion, I began by having them do a write-around, or written conversation. I explained that in their "written silent discussion," they could share any thoughts they had about the book so far. I gave them some options to consider if they weren't sure where to start. The options included:

Writing about the main character—what was their impression of the character so far?

Writing about the events in the book so far—what did they think about what had happened?

Sharing their predictions about what they thought would happen next and why.

Describing challenges they encountered while reading (thinking about themselves as readers).

They set right to work, and wrote for three to four minutes before I told them to swap their writing. They passed their journals several times. After the final pass, I invited the kids to simply shift into out-loud conversation, continuing the discussion they had begun in writing. A buzz of voices filled the room as kids took up my invitation. I circulated, listening in on conversations and helping groups that needed a little nudge. When I came to the group reading *Crooked River,* I stopped to listen in on their conversation and was reassured by what I heard. I was delighted to hear that they were disagreeing agreeably, a lesson I had taught earlier in the year.

▲

KYLE: *I feel sad for the girl. Her dad treats her like a slave, and the girl is thinking about killing herself to be with her mom. So her dad is mean and evil but her mom was nice.*

MICHELE: *It did not say that the girl was going to kill herself to be with her mom. But it did say she missed her mom and she wanted to be with her. But it did not say that she wanted to kill herself.*

HANNAH: *Yeah, she didn't want to die. It said that right in the book. And it didn't say that her mom was nice, but I know that she is better than her dad. I would be really mad if my dad put a murderer in our house, wouldn't you? But I don't think that he is actually a murderer. Why would a dad be so mean to his kids? I think that maybe he is just mad that his wife died. Either that or he needs help (serious help)!*

EMILY: *Kyle, how do you know her mom was nice? Yeah, I agree with Hannah that her dad needs serious help!*

▼

www.heinemann.com/
comprehensionandcollaboration.

*See Lesson 17, "Midcourse
Corrections: Reflecting and
Replanning," p. 132.*

Across all the group, kids were totally into their books, had plenty to talk about, were supporting their comments with excerpts from the text, and were using their social skills well, trying not to interrupt each other. I even felt that I could see kernels of future inquiry questions in the conversation, here on the very first day.

A few days later after kids had read another quarter of their books we held a second round of book club meetings. (Read about these on the website.)

Reflecting on Collaboration Skills

Today, I wanted the lit circle groups to reflect on their collaborative process over the first two meetings. I asked them to talk in their groups for a few minutes about what went well and what needed improvement, and then we gathered to list both pluses and minuses. The kids were quick to mention some positives:

"When someone misunderstands something, we can help them."

"We get to learn the way other people think."

"Having the question charts helped give us focus."

"We were really 'into it!'"

"Group members help us understand."

"It makes the book more fun because you get to know what everybody else thinks about it."

"The book is less confusing when we share our thinking."

I had a more difficult time getting them to share even a single negative, until I reminded them that sharing group problems is not the same as "ratting" on your friends. Rather, it is a way to look at things that get in the way of good, productive discussions and figure out how to solve those problems. After hearing that, hands went up with problems—and suggested solutions.

"People get off task." It is the responsibility of everyone in the group to gently remind those who aren't on task to regain their focus. The first person who notices the problem should always speak up. After that, the consequences in the group's ground rules should be applied if needed.

"Someone from another group came over during our first meeting and distracted us." The unanimous solution: we should nicely tell that person that we are discussing our book and they should be with their group discussing their book.

"We spent too much time arguing." I asked the kids if they could remember our previous discussion about what to do if group members can't agree. Nick right away said to look in the text for evidence to support your thinking. I told him that was great, but asked again what would happen if their thinking was inferential and they couldn't agree whose inference was "right." Rachael immediately raised her hand and said, "It's OK to agree to disagree, and maybe they'll be able to end their argument after reading more."

See Lesson 15, "Practicing the Skills of Small-Group Discussion," p. 130.

"We spent too much time spent trying to figure out one little part of the book." The kids decided that if they thought the part of the book was really important to the overall story, then it was OK to spend a lot of time discussing it. However, if the majority of the group thought that part of the book was not so important, it was probably best to move on, and come back to it later if they found out something that made it more important.

"I didn't get a chance to talk." This was an easy fix; kids quickly realized that if this was a problem in their group, they were forgetting to use the rules of polite discussion that our class regularly follows. They agreed to try to remind each other when the conversations became too dominated by one or two group members.

The best (and most endearing) part of their meetings today was how many kids were "copying" the positive behaviors we discussed during our debriefing. This was exactly what I'd hoped for.

Looking for Big Questions

I began the next day by talking to the whole class, looking for "big issues" and developing a question that each group agreed they wanted to investigate. Then I briefly conferred with each group individually, but still in front of the whole class, thinking that if everyone heard what the other groups were thinking, it might help each group develop its own questions. I asked them what their proposed topics or questions were, probing for their thinking. I invited kids from other groups to join in with suggestions and refinements. Then I turned the groups loose to work, and visited each for a few minutes.

As I coached individual groups, I stressed that they should find a question that was not only of burning interest, but also "researchable." They needed to figure out *how* they could go about researching their question. I suggested they brainstorm terms and phrases they might use to search the Internet. I also encouraged them to think about how they would enlist the help of our librarian as they did research.

After some work time and lively conversations, all the groups finalized their inquiry questions, as follows:

Blood on the River: "How did women get the right to vote?"

Sign of the Beaver: Where did white men get the idea that Indians were savages?

Crooked River: What causes hatred and prejudice against one certain group of people?

Indian Captive: What were/are the customs and traditions of the Seneca Indians?

My Heart Is on the Ground: What is the history of the Indian schools run by white people, and why did some Indian parents choose to send their kids to these schools?

These questions covered a wide range, from fairly narrow factual questions to broader issues with universal significance. I felt that each of these topics was potentially researchable, and the kids seemed fired up.

See Lesson 14, "Making and Using a Work Plan," p. 129.

I asked kids if they were ready to "divide and conquer." We had talked about this strategy before, but to refresh their memory, I asked, **"What do we mean by divide and conquer?"** They responded with comments like these:

"We can make a plan to split up the work."

"We don't have to be working together on one Internet search. We can each search for something different."

"We don't all have to read everything we find. We can divide up the reading, then tell the rest of our group what we read about."

Next I asked, **"And how can you be sure that everyone knows what their job is?"**

"We have to talk it over."

"We let everybody volunteer for what part they want to do."

"We have to write down our work plan and give it to you, right?"

They were right on track.

We decided on a plan to correlate the tasks with our schedule. The kids decided to use reading time that afternoon and all the next week to conduct their research and search for answers to their questions. Then, during the following week's reading time, they planned to work on a way to share their learning and thinking with others, scheduling presentations at the end of that week. This amounted to about seven hours of class time to complete these inquiry projects. Given all this input, I sent kids back to their groups to negotiate jobs and to revise their written work plans and schedules.

Onward to Investigation!

Over the next week, the kids went to work on their questions. They researched on the Internet. They went to the library. They spoke with other people in the field. Each day, I moved around the room, meeting with groups and coaching them through their research. Different issues emerged for each group. Some needed help finding appropriate information, so we talked about narrowing Internet searches or finding the right books in the library. Others needed suggestions about how to find accessible Internet articles, so I pointed them to websites I had researched that had text closer to their grade level. Some needed my support with a social strategy. My role was to help facilitate their inquiry groups in whatever way I could.

(Visit the website to see how Diane coached groups through their research.)

Planning to Share the Learning

I always want my kids to "go public" with their learning in some way. For these inquiry projects, I wanted them to move beyond the typical simple book reports that kids can crank out almost without thinking. Having attended an "Assessment Live!"

www.heinemann.com/
comprehensionandcollaboration.

See Lesson 27, "Response Options: Take Learning Public," p. 142.

www.heinemann.com/
comprehensionandcollaboration.

workshop with Nancy Steineke, I was already aware of some more engaging and thoughtful ways for kids to show what they know. Based on her book (Steineke 2009), Nancy had showed us a dozen "paper-free" reporting structures (found poetry, reader's theater, song parodies, etc.), and I described a number of these alternatives to the kids. They were immediately attracted to the idea of tableaux, a series of frozen scenes based upon carefully crafted captions read aloud by a narrator. Since there was a groundswell for tableaux, I thought we'd better practice them.

(Read about the initial stages of kids' rehearsals on the website.)

Rehearsals and Presentations

After kids completed the research phases, they spent parts of several days scripting and blocking their tableaux. They worked on their presentations, making lists of props and costumes needed, and rehearsed. After all this preparation and rehearsal, showtime arrived. The picture shows the *My Heart Is on the Ground* group's tableaux for their first caption.

> *"If Indian parents did not agree to have their children taken to the school, they were taken by force."*

After a big round of applause, the group took questions from classmates. Landon asked if the girls knew what kinds of diseases the kids at the school died from. Anna mentioned a few different sicknesses, and Kenzie added that the children also died from trances. The kids asked what that meant, and Kenzie explained that some native

kids would go into a deep trancelike state, be mistaken for dead, and be buried alive. We were stunned. Then Michelle asked why Indian parents would send their kids to the school if they didn't want them to go. Kenzie said if parents didn't give up their kids, they were usually forced to send them anyway, often at gunpoint. I added some information about other tactics used by the whites, such as withholding food and resources from reservations where families refused to send their kids. Kenzie also mentioned that some parents sent their children so they could learn to read English—and understand the treaties offered by the white men.

Over the next couple of days, the rest of the groups offered their tableaux, with some great thinking and drama. I was delighted to see the level of thinking, the attentiveness of the audience, and the way in which the kids showed ownership of these books. They really knew—and cared about—what they had read.

(To read the complete account of Diane's native-Settler contact in inquiry circles, including more of her reflections on the process, see the website.)

www.heinemann.com/
comprehensionandcollaboration.

INQUIRY: *Writing Circles in Middle and High School*

—JIM VOPAT, MILWAUKEE WRITING PROJECT, MILWAUKEE, WISCONSIN
—NANCY STEINEKE, VICTOR J. ANDREW HIGH SCHOOL, TINLEY PARK, ILLINOIS

After literature circles became popular, teachers began trying to apply this collabora-
tive discussion structure to writing. But nobody ever came up with a model that
worked as well for composing text as it did for discussing it. That is, until our colleague
Jim Vopat sat down with kids and teachers in Milwaukee and created writing circles. In
the following article, adapted from his book Writing Circles *(2009), Jim shares some*
of the key elements of this exciting model, especially how it can help kids grow as non-
fiction writers.

Then Nancy Steineke, from Andrew High School near Chicago, shares how she's
adapted writing circles to her sophomore classes and shows us a sample of one student's
work that progressed from the playful first stage of writing circles to an edited and enter-
taining essay. Read more about this in Assessment Live! *(Steineke 2009).*

*J*im Vopat's Introduction to Writing Circles

Ever wish there was something like literature circles for writing? Writing circles
are here to grant that wish. The structure of writing circles mirrors literature circles,
with kids' writing serving as the text. In writing circles, kids write on an agreed-upon
topic, share their drafts, receive positive responses, choose a new writing idea, and
end with a brief think-back reflection.

What do writing circles look like in the classroom? Circles of four to six
kids—some around tables, some on pillows on the floor, two groups out in the
hall. The Mall Monkeys are furthest down the hall; the Penguins—some sitting,
some standing—are just outside the classroom door. Los Viejitos, Smooth Opera-
tors, and Purple People Eaters sit around tables in classroom corners, listening to
the first writer. Silver Snakes are on pillows near the windows meeting with the
teacher, excited to hear what he's written about unknowingly making camp on a
huge anthill. The Femme Lattes push desks together at the front of the classroom
and one-up each other on the topic "Why we should be able to have cell phones in
school." Los Viejitos' topic is "Favorite animal." "Friends" for the Smooth Opera-
tors, "When I grow up" for Purple People Eaters, "Bugs" for the Silver Snakes, and
"Shipwrecked on an island with your worst enemy" for the Penguins. Each Penguin
has written about enemies in a unique way: a struggle for survival, provisional rec-
onciliation, epitaph, some gore, an unexpected letter to a friend who moved away,
rescue by cruise boat. After hearing each draft, the rest of the Penguins practice
the day's response strategy, called "point out": Tell the writer one thing you liked.
Point out something interesting.

What are all these students in the middle of? The writing circle dynamic includes these activities:

- Groups of kids name their writing circle and choose a common topic.
- Kids write on this topic, using any format or genre.
- Writing circle mini-lessons focus on circle management and writing craft.
- Writing circles meet.
- Kids share their writing.
- Kids respond to each other's writing.
- Each circle chooses its next writing topic.
- The whole class shares new topics and writing from each writing circle.
- Kids write think-back reflections and notes in their writing circle notebooks.
- Periodically, kids review their rough pieces and select the most promising one.
- Writers enter a cycle of collaborative revision, polishing, and publishing.
- Classmates serve as each other's agents, illustrators, reviewers, and editors.
- Finished works are shared and celebrated in public.

The dynamic of writing circles is unique. Kids are given a fun, low-risk opportunity to "just write." They can freely and spontaneously jot about questions or subjects that fascinate them—ranging from issues within a particular content field to matters of personal concern or interest. While the small groups do choose common topics, individuals decide which genre (poem, story, letter, blog) and approach, stance, and specific subject matter suits them best. Then, they share their drafts in a positive, supportive context, with plenty of guidance on how to give friendly feedback. All this helps students to shed their fear of the blank page, build fluency, develop confidence, gain knowledge of content, and sample multiple text structures that they can draw upon as writers.

Writing Circles in Content Areas

In content areas, writing circles provide a structure for every student to explore subject matter in his or her own way; to investigate, learn, and, at the same time, support each other as writers. The groups operate just as they do in language arts classrooms: kids name their writing circles, choose topics through consensus, and write about the topic in whatever way they think will be effective. They may choose to write about a subject they have already studied in, say, social studies or science—or, they may elect to do some research into a new topic before writing. It's a way to get kids thinking and talking, using writing as learning—pure and simple and without penalty.

At Ballard School, the seventh-grade science writing circles were Oh Snap, Benchwarmers, Masterminds, Chick'n Nuggets, the ?'s, and Desperate House Guys.

Their science topics included animal cruelty, cloning, holograms, extinction, diseases, evolution, and space.

The Benchwarmers decided to write about cloning. When they met in their circle, one draft outlined the scientific steps of the cloning process, one described how "awesome" it would be to have a clone "do your homework and chores while you relax and have fun. Then the clone could go to school and you could chill on the couch all day." One student mounted an argument against cloning; another balanced the positive and negative aspects of cloning, and another wrote the first part of a time-travel story entitled "Cloning."

While some pieces remained undeveloped, there was also some good writing right off the bat, like this futuristic flashback (patterned after the lyrics of a country song by Brad Paisley):

CLONING

If I could write a letter to me, I'd send it back in time to myself at 7 years. First I'd prove it's me by saying look under your bed, there's a jewelry box full of jewels you stole from Millie then.

I'd say these are the best times of your life. Your daddy's still cool, but over time from all that stress, he'll lose it just like that. Millie will still be givin' you love, hug her tight 'cause in 17 months, she'll slip away so fast.

Go hug Aunt Jennie, every chance you can. Oh. . . you got so much going for you, going right, but I know at 7 years it's hard to see past Fri. night. You'll grow up and get a cute baby bro name Luke. Haley will move away. You'll get a boyfriend in 6th grade and take it as slow. See you in the mirror, when you're a grown teen.

Meanwhile, the Masterminds were writing about holograms: "They will also be used as trademarks for Disney. Disney will then take over the media to control the brains of little children and bring them to their lair where they will sacrifice them to Mickey Mouse."

Through writing circles, kids interact with content, engage in research, learn from each other, and become stronger writers. When the Chick'n Nuggets share their writing about their chosen topic, disease, it includes a poem from a terminal patient's point of view; a rant about the connection between disease, germs, and handling money; an extended definition of "zooness"; a lively description of the Black Plague; and a gruesome survey of the "Worst Diseases of All Time."

Kids need to write regularly in all content areas if they are to become stronger writers and thinkers. Whether the topic is math, social studies, science, or another content area, writing circles stand ready and able to explore and connect learning through writing. In each circle, concepts are explored from as many points of view as there are kids. Organizing these explorations through kids' writing and response has significant social as well as academic payoffs.

Nancy Steineke Talks About High School Writing Circles

When Jim started telling me about writing circles, I began teaching the structure to my sophomores. What I immediately liked was how the kids connected with the process. They really liked the idea of picking their own topics and prided themselves on writing about them in all different genres and styles. Coming together to read their pieces aloud was almost like a "writing slam": "Hey, look at this!" "Try and top this!" Because they were eager to hear each other's writing, they were very receptive when I taught them different ways of responding constructively. The pieces that resulted had a freshness and sense of craft that I don't typically see. Colin was a good example.

THE SILVER SCREEN

—By Colin Brogan

I see a lot of movies. Over the summer it seemed like I saw one every week. I don't know what it is about movies that I like so much. Maybe I like the way they make me feel, as if I'm in a different world. Whatever it is, I know that the best movies I see are the ones that have moments or lines that you can distinctly remember and reference when you're telling other people about them: *Snakes on a Plane, 300, There Will Be Blood, The Departed,* and most recently, *Batman: The Dark Knight.* Everybody knows "I drink your milkshake!" is the line that crazed Oscar Award Winner Daniel Day-Lewis spews. And then there's "This is SPARTA!" from *300.* And of course, "Why so serious?" the memorable question posed by The Joker, Oscar award winner Heath Ledger, in *Batman.*

My honest favorite, though, will have to be *300.* The best way to sum it up is it's about these 300 Spartans who go out and kill a bunch of Persians, while yelling at the top of their lungs. Deep stuff, I know. The entire movie is done with computer generated animation, and about half of it is in slow motion. Maybe they needed to fill in time to make up for their lack of meaningful dialogue. I also think that there was some historical significance to the whole series of epic battles, but I forgot about it. I think the director and producers forgot too, because they sure didn't seem to care either.

Despite its flaws, the movie was pretty cool once I actually watched it. But the weekend it came out, I went to the movie theatre and it was the only movie I was willing to see. I sat down and the previews started. Eddie Murphy, Eddie Murphy, and more Eddie Murphy. At this point, I start to wonder why I came to see this garbage. But then the movie started, and everyone started dying.

About five minutes into the movie, I questioned why I hated the look of "300" from the previews. The trailer showed the same footage, but I don't think they were allowed to show as much gore, death, and questionable material that they showed during the very R-rated movie. But it's the way that the people who made the movie, the various producers, writers, directors, and actors, put the movie all together. That's why everyone likes movies. Movie magic, if you will. Everything works, all the music, and the acting is perfect, and everyone's happy.

Once the movie was over, I was satisfied. I found myself yelling quotes from the movie for the next few days. "SPARTANS, TONIGHT WE DINE IN HELL!", or "Our arrows will blot out the sun!" Movies like 300 may not win any awards, but they are good time-wasters. And that's really why you go and see movies. To waste time.

I always have kids reflect on their work, and that was especially important with this new activity. Here's what Colin had to say about his writing circle experience.

Dear Ms. Steineke,

I am learning a lot about myself as a writer. I am able to spill my ideas out onto paper and put them into halfway decent form. I usually get stuck when I complete one really good thought and don't know how to follow it up. Another problem I have is not being able to end my pieces on a well-rounded note. When I listen to my group's pieces, I learn that everyone uses different styles and usually everyone just speaks their minds. I can learn from this greatly because it gives me satisfaction knowing I just completed a good piece, and every bit of help can be useful. My writing circle is going great, we all listen carefully and it truly feels like you are on your own Home Court.

Sincerely,

Colin Brogan

See Lesson 12, "Home Court Advantage: Showing Friendliness and Support," p. 127.

I love how kids get into this activity—just their body language, the leaning toward each other, the lively talk and the laughter. They get totally engaged. But a writing circle is much more than a fun variation. This is a whole new kind of writing workshop. The kids get more useful feedback in their writing circles than they do from individual conferences with me. I'm a little uncomfortable saying that I grew up with the original workshop model, where the key structure is one-to-one conferences with the teacher. But with writing circles, I see the kids' writing progressing faster than it does when I am the main source of feedback. When I am doing individual conferences, there's always some distraction and off-task stuff happening with the other twenty-nine kids. But in writing circles, everyone in the room is working and thinking the whole time.

The power comes from the audience, I think. Having three or four other kids as an immediate audience, peers who care about you and attend to your every word and will give you honest feedback—that's the driving motivation, instead of teacher approval or grades. Of course, I had to *teach* them how to do this, with lots of modeling and mini-lessons and great ideas from Jim's writing circle examples. But once they have the language and procedures to work together, they take off.

For many years, we writing teachers struggled to perfect what we used to call "peer editing groups." Now, with writing circles, we have a structure that helps kids support each other's writing at all stages, from topic selection and drafting, through revision, to publication. And that's pretty cool.

Open Inquiries

How many times have we said that school should operate as if kids' questions really matter? Well, in this chapter, kids' own questions take center stage. You'll see many different groups of students investigating their topics in depth, using their developing skills in comprehension, collaboration, and investigation to find information and build understanding.

These open inquiries (sometimes called *negotiated curriculum* projects) are much like the other types we've shown in this book, with one big difference: now, the topics come not from a curriculum unit or a literature circle book, but from kids' own curiosity, wonderings, and concerns. But these open inquiries are in no way a side trip into trivial, divorced-from-school topics. Actually, our own experience has been quite the opposite: when given a *genuine* opportunity to choose their own topics, and when provided with thoughtful guidance by a veteran adult inquirer (like you), kids lean toward topics of significance. They very often choose to investigate subjects that really matter. Kids want to know.

And further, with most of these kid-driven inquiries, teachers find it apple-pie-easy to backmap the students' investigations directly to district or state standards (see pages 261–262 for a detailed example). After all, any inquiry is going to include these basic skills:

- reading a variety of nonfiction text
- identifying main ideas and significant details
- gathering and weighing information
- building understanding
- providing explanations or interpretations
- summarizing or synthesizing information
- sharing or performing newfound knowledge

All of these are uber-standards in every state we know.

The Best for Last?

We have saved these "pure" kid-driven projects for last, not because they are the best (though they can be pretty awesome), but because, for most of us, they represent an especially big stretch of our teaching repertoires. Because such genuinely open-ended, kid-driven investigations are fairly rare in our schools (and perhaps absent from our own personal experience as students or as teachers), they may sound a bit like jumping off a cliff, walking a high wire, tempting fate—pick your own scary metaphor.

It is true that projects like these require us to trust and support kids in ways that we may not have tried before. We are required to step out of the roles of expert, presenter, and authority, and take new stances as partners, consultants, advisors, resource finders, and facilitators. Our job is not to dispense knowledge, but to manage the process of inquiry. We serve as the most experienced researcher in the room, and take the kids under our wing as our apprentices while they conduct their own investigations.

But even if these open inquiries take us out of our teacherly comfort zones in some ways, they are also very highly structured in terms of steps and procedures. This is not turning kids loose to "do their own thing." Instead, these inquiry projects are highly organized, disciplined, and thoughtful.

▲

SMOKEY: Whenever we start talking about these open inquiries, it makes me think of that classic quote we mentioned earlier: "School is a place where young people go to watch old people work."

STEPH: For sure. That's funny, but also sad, don't you think? I mean, we teach and teach and knock our lights out all day long, day after day. When the bells rings, the kids bound out of their seats with limitless leftover energy—and dash off to play sports, ride bikes, hang around the mall or wherever, for hours to come. Meanwhile, we teachers drag our exhausted behinds home and crawl into bed. It should be just the opposite; they should be dragging their exhausted butts out the door on Friday afternoon and we should be skipping off to yoga!

SMOKEY: We are doing too much of the work. These open inquiry projects sure turn that around, where kids are really taking responsibility, doing the work themselves.

STEPH: That's one reason I love this kind of project. You work just as hard, but you are following kids' leads, coaching and supporting them—and not performing, telling, all that stuff that just drains you. It's unpredictable every day, and I love that.

SMOKEY: We always talk about teachers "challenging" the kids, but this kind of teaching challenges us! I'm not going to know the answers to every question

> kids are pursuing or every topic they are digging into. So I am genuinely learning myself, right along with them, and they can watch me doing that.
>
> **STEPH:** Right, people always talk about how teachers should be a guide on the side, not a sage on stage—well, that's exactly what happens here. You are sitting beside the kids, finding out together.
>
> **SMOKEY:** The bonus, for me anyway, is that this is the most fun kind of teaching I ever get to do.
>
> **STEPH:** Amen.

▼

Open inquiry projects have huge potential payoffs for teachers *and* students. Talk about a put-it-all-together activity! Here, kids take full responsibility for their own learning, at a developmentally appropriate level. Instead of plunging in to "instruct," we teachers hold back. We insist that *kids do the work.* We don't feed them topics; we don't preselect their readings; we don't mandate the form of reports. Instead, we teach the way Steph was just describing—and every day brings a string of fresh, spontaneous, here-and-now opportunities to support kids right at the point of need. We think of these as "guaranteed teachable moments," and they simply come with the territory when you hand the reins over to kids.

When we teach the conventional way, preplanning our lessons based upon the district curriculum, state standards, or even our own old lesson plans, we pretty much know in advance what we are going to teach. But when we open up to kid-driven inquiries, where students exercise real choice, we enjoy far less predictability. With different groups pursuing different topics, we can't do very many whole-class content lessons—though we can teach a lot about the inquiry process itself.

We also know, from the research cited in Chapter 1, that this kind of project "works"—we can expect kids to understand and remember content, as well as sharpen inquiry and work habits that will serve them well into the future (see especially Darling-Hammond 2008). In short, with open inquiry projects, we don't tell kids what to think—we help them think for themselves.

On the the next page is our now-familiar inquiry model, adapted for these kid-driven, open topic projects.

Sometimes, these open projects provide kids with life-changing experiences. Shari Storch's fourth graders in Riverview, Florida, read an article that explained that girls were denied equal access to education in high-poverty countries through-out the world. They were stunned, particularly since they believed that the only way to escape a life of poverty was through education. Further research revealed that even in the United States, kids from high-poverty homes had less access to books. The kids' outrage spurred a desire to act. They undertook a project aimed at promoting literacy in high-poverty elementary schools. They decided to hold a dance at their school to raise money for books for one specific high-needs school

Small-Group Inquiry Model Adapted for Open Inquiries

STAGE	TEACHER	KIDS
Immerse *Invite Curiosity, Build Background, Find Topics, and Wonder*	• Invites curiosity, questioning, engagement • Models own inquiry topics and process • Conducts activities that support topic-finding and commitment • Forms kids into inquiry groups by topic affinity • Gathers and organizes relevant materials to support student topics • Confers with small groups and individuals	• Surface curiosity and questions from their own interests and experience • Talk, read, and write with others to develop possible topic choices • Read, listen, and view to build background knowledge and test topic attractiveness • Make tentative commitment to a topic or question • Meet with teams to set schedules, ground rules, and goals
Investigate *Develop Questions, Search for Information, and Discover Answers*	• Floods kids with resources and materials on chosen topics or questions • Models how to read, listen, and view with a question in mind • Models how to take notes by interacting with text, coding text, and writing in margins or on Post-its • Demonstrates how to determine importance • Helps kids sharpen or change their open inquiry focus • Facilitates changes in group membership or topics • Confers with groups and individuals	• Listen, talk, view, and read to gain information • Write, talk, and draw to think about information • Develop questions and read, listen, and view to answer them • Use text and visual features to gain information • Work to better articulate and refine chosen topics or questions • Meet with teams to set and monitor schedules and task completion
Coalesce *Intensify Research, Synthesize Information, and Build Knowledge*	• Shows how to infer answers and draw conclusions • Demonstrates how to read for the gist and synthesize information • Helps students to access increasingly focused or specialized resources • Models how to evaluate sources • Teaches interviewing strategies • Facilitates arrangements for out-of-school resources • Confers with groups and individuals	• Engage in deeper reading and researching; books, articles, websites, videos, library visits • Target key ideas and information • Check sources and determine reliability • Keep asking: So what? What about this really matters? • Practice interviewing • Conduct "people" research—interviews, surveys, questionnaires, focus groups • Synthesize information to build knowledge • Meet with teams to monitor schedules, complete specific tasks, and plan for sharing

continues

Small-Group Inquiry Model Adapted for Open Inquiries, *cont.*		
STAGE	**TEACHER**	**KIDS**
Go Public *Share Learning,* *Demonstrate* *Understanding,* *Take Action*	• Co-constructs expectations and rubrics for final projects • Offers the widest range of possibilities for sharing/performing • Welcomes kids' suggestions for these demonstrations • Helps kids find real audiences and opportunities to share their knowledge and teach others • Helps students reflect on content and process • With students, responds, assesses, and evaluates projects • Supports kids to share the learning by taking action	• Co-construct expectations and rubrics for final projects • Demonstrate learning and understanding in a variety of ways—posters, models, essays, picture books, tableaux, poetry • Become teachers as they share their knowledge with others • Articulate their learning process and how learning changes • Reflect on their knowledge building • Reflect on their cooperative process • Pose and investigate new questions for further research • Consider changes in their own beliefs or behavior • Take action through writing, speaking, community work, advocacy

nearby. They divided into small inquiry groups and all took on specific roles and responsibilities. One group created a marketing strategy. Another sold tickets and managed money. Still another decorated the gym, while a fourth crew selected and played the music. Working together as we do in real life, they organized, planned, promoted, and implemented the first-ever dance at their school, with all of the proceeds going to buy books for the designated school. Their fund-raising effort paid off; they collected $1,500. They read up on books for primary and intermediate students and headed to the bookstore to purchase them for the school. This culminated in a day spent visiting the school, reading to the kids, and leaving the books for the school library. These students still come back and tell Shari it was one of the most meaningful events of their lives.

See Lesson 14, "Making and Using a Work Plan," p. 129.

*T*he Upcoming Stories

In this chapter we share an assortment of open inquiry designs ranging from preschool to high school. First, you'll hear about four-year-old Sadie Montgomery's study of letters, princesses, mermaids, and more in preschool. Next, we visit Brad Buhrow's second-grade classroom in Boulder, Colorado, where a group of kids constructively hijacks the curriculum. Many open inquiries begin with students' spontaneous questions, and when teachers listen carefully, as Brad and Steph do here, or as Shari did with the dance project, they can support kids to investigate with gusto and act with purpose. Next Smokey leads a sixth-grade class through a "pure" open inquiry, where kids carefully sift through possible topics of personal interest, form affinity groups, and pursue a wide-ranging investigation over several weeks. Finally, we move to high school, where a national trend toward performance learning is offering teenagers a chance to become specialists in topics of personal interest. We look to Federal-Hocking High School in Appalachia, where, working with teachers and community mentors, students are creating simple and powerful senior projects.

INQUIRY: *Postal Service, Princesses, and Castles*

—PAMELA BATTIN-SACKS, CHILD STUDY AND DEVELOPMENT CENTER, UNIVERSITY OF NEW HAMPSHIRE, DURHAM, NEW HAMPSHIRE

PRESCHOOL

PRIMARY

Sadie H., age four, attends a New Hampshire preschool where children's questions drive the daily curriculum. Sadie's mother, Kate Montgomery, is one of our best colleagues at Heinemann (and the editor of this book). Here is her mom's-eye view.

At Sadie's school, many of the children's families travel extensively. Whenever a family goes on a trip, the teacher, Pam Battin-Sacks, quite smartly asks the child to send a postcard back to the school. Then, when mail arrives, she reads the card aloud to the class and they talk about the interesting destinations in the world and what their far-flung classmates might be doing.

Early in the year, a postcard with a lovely drawing arrived from England *after* the author, Emily, was back in the class. The kids were in an uproar about that. It was supposed to be a message from an absent person, but there was Emily, sitting right at her desk! "She said she missed us, but we were right there," Sadie reported. It was funny to the children. So Pam leapt on the moment, and they got out maps and traced the way the postcard would have come. But then Randy raised the point that they'd gotten a postcard from Germany before Foche got back, and that was even farther away. So they got out the calendar, did some subtraction, and sure enough, it *had* taken longer. This launched a whole postal system study.

All the kids got a letter to take home asking parents to help them mail a letter from their town to school—envelope, stamp, the whole works. The kids were marking down dates and using calendars, and they had to write a letter, which was great. (After we mailed Sadie's letter, she wanted me to drive fast to the school to make sure we beat it there.) They talked about what would happen to the letters once they were in the mailbox, at the post office, on the truck, and so on. A graphing chart was used to track whose letter came faster; then, looking at their local delivery and pickup times, kids made guesses as to why.

Teachers set up a post office in the dramatic play area—Sadie said it was the best center but it was always too full, because everybody wanted to use all the envelopes and stamps ("which were really stickers because it was only pretend"). The kids mailed the letters to each other's cubbies. They tried addressing the letters too. At home Sadie sent letters to everyone she knew, and delivered the ones in our neighborhood herself.

Now, somewhere along the way, one girl in the class mailed a classmate a drawing of a princess. Another girl in the class told the artist that the picture she'd drawn couldn't be a princess, because she had glasses. Pam, great teacher that she is, jumped on that question. They had a class discussion about it (which included some very strong differences of opinion from the more Disney-fied members of the class). Pam suggested they do some research. The kids started making piles of books about princesses, and they studied them. Pam made sure *Mufaro's Beautiful Daughters* (by John Steptoe) and *The Paper Bag Princess* (by Robert Munsch) were in there. Parents sent in books about Queen Elizabeth (at her grandest and her most plain), and there were some Princess Di clippings.

Apparently, once the children conceived that princesses were actual people, everyone agreed they could have glasses and freckles. They ended up deciding that there were different kinds of princesses—the real kind and "the kind you mostly see," and one group might have freckles and glasses and the kind you mostly see wouldn't. As this study went on, some of the kids quite naturally became interested in studying castles, so another center spun off and gathered inquirers. Kids were looking at David Macaulay's amazing cross-section book *Castles* (1982), building their own castles and so forth. As a culminating project, the kids decided to create a fairy tale about a princess in a castle. So they each wrote one line and illustrated one page of a picture book they called "The Lucky Princess."

This investigation evolved into a study of mythical beasts—not a far jump from the princess, knights, and castles. Kids studied the phoenix (they loved the idea of being born from a fire), unicorns, and dragons and ended up writing and performing (for the other classes and for the parents) their own action play involving the knights and princesses "attacking the bad dragons with safety scissors." This study involved a lot of drawing of the different kinds of legendary creatures. Sadie told me her favorite part was when she taught her friend April to draw a mermaid: "You just draw half a princess and then stop. That's the hard part—April kept forgetting and drawing all of it! And then you put on a tail—but not like a lion tail, fatter."

The same process Sadie is experiencing as a four-year-old works for all learners. With Pam's skillful facilitation, Sadie and her classmates are using the same intellectual processes that proficient, grown-up thinkers use to find stuff out:

- Identify a topic or question or interest

- Seek information from a variety of sources

- View, read, think about, and react to the information

- Evaluate the validity, reliability, and usefulness of the information
- Work with others to leverage your thinking
- Build concepts and knowledge by synthesizing meaning
- Get help from the more experienced researchers around you
- Apply the knowledge to your own life
- Share your new learning with others

Sound familiar? It should. These thinking moves closely overlap the processes we have described all through this book, as small groups of kids conduct quick mini-inquiries, extend their thinking in literature circles, or pursue topics within the curriculum.

Sadie's story also offers a clear picture of the roles that teachers play in these open inquiries. Pam doesn't just stand back and hope that kids stumble onto research-worthy topics or pose rich questions—she is facilitating actively, every step of the way. First of all, she is listening, always on the alert for an emerging hot topic among the kids. When the spark is struck (Can princesses have glasses?) Pam "leaps on the moment" and "jumps on the question." She starts clearing a path for the kids' curiosity to follow. She gathers materials (maps, calendars, chart paper, books, art supplies) and designs activities (graphing, the postal center, coauthoring a book) that allow kids to vigorously pursue their topics. Pam steers the activities and moderates discussions, poses clarifying questions, and helps children move to the next level of thinking. In sum, while the kids enjoy the choice, the ownership, and the energy of pursuing their own interests, there is a very present and steady teacher hand guiding it all—a beautiful example of that rarely glimpsed phenomenon called "leading from behind."

INQUIRY: *Signatures and the Origins of Writing*

PRIMARY

—BRAD BUHROW, COLUMBINE ELEMENTARY, BOULDER, COLORADO

Welcome to Brad Buhrow's second-grade classroom at Columbine Elementary in Boulder, Colorado. The children at Columbine come from many different countries and speak a variety of languages, although most of Brad's kids are native Spanish speakers. Steph has been working on and off in Brad's room for many years. Here they work together with a small group of kids on a surprising inquiry project. For more on ELL inquiry, check out Brad's book, Ladybugs, Tornadoes and Swirling Galaxies: English Language Learners Discover the World Through Inquiry *(2006) written with his teammate Ann Garcia.*

"Where have you been?" Adolfo called to Steph as she entered Brad Buhrow's second-grade classroom one morning.

"Hey, Adolfo, great to see you. Long time no see," Steph answered. Adolfo, an English language learner, scrunched his nose, puzzled.

"What do you think that means, Adolfo, 'long time no see'?" she asked.

"It means you haven't been around here for a while," August chimed in.

"That's right! That is exactly what it means, August. But it sounds weird, doesn't it? It sounds like wrong-way English, which is why you looked so puzzled, Adolfo. You know what good English sounds like when you hear it!" A broad smile spread across Adolfo's face.

Having worked with these kids earlier in the year, Steph now realized how much she missed them as she scanned Brad's delicious room. It was coral reef time, and the entire room had been transformed into a deep-sea habitat—walls covered with ocean-blue poster paper bursting with brightly colored construction-paper clown fish, pop-up sea anemones, and reef creatures of every size and shape, all swimming through a backdrop of staghorn, fan, and brain coral. The coral reef murals were covered with labels, captions, and written summaries of kids' thinking and learning as well as the splendid art. What a magical place!

The kids had oceans of ocean resources to draw upon—Big Books, leveled books, magazines, posters, and visuals of every type as well as markers, construction paper, scissors, Post-its, notebooks, word walls, and graphic organizers for research. Kids were spread throughout the room voraciously reading, writing, and drawing about coral reefs. Brad moved between small groups and individuals, conferring with them and scaffolding their work, supporting them as they did research, read to answer questions, and demonstrated their thinking and learning through writing and drawing. Steph noticed three kids on the floor busily working. Surrounded in visuals and text, Kyky was reading a book about sea creatures, Zeke was working on a chart categorizing types of coral, and Joel was cutting out a clown fish he'd drawn to place on the ocean mural.

"Hey you guys, what are you working on?" Steph asked as she sat down in their midst. They explained that the day before Brad had taught them about symbiosis and how certain ocean creatures, like clown fish and sea anemones, help each other out in order to survive.

"But I have a question," Kyky said as she pointed to a photograph of a coral trout with a cleaner wrasse swimming around its lip. "I know that this little cleaner fish is cleaning out the mouth of this bigger coral trout, because it says so right here in the caption, but I wonder, why doesn't the coral trout eat it?"

"Such a great question. What do you all think?" Steph asked them. As they discussed their thoughts on symbiosis, Steph asked Kyky to write her question on a Post-it note and suggested that Joel and Zeke jot down what they thought might be going on here.

This is a great way to get inquiry circles going—build background for a curricular topic, honor kids' questions, and support them as they research and read to learn answers and build knowledge. All three of the kids shared reasonable inferences about why they thought the coral trout did not eat the cleaner wrasse (see their Post-it notes). After their discussion, Steph wrote the word *inquiry* on a Post-it and asked the kids if they knew what it meant. They were unaware of the term, so she explained that inquiry has to do with asking questions, using background knowledge to better understand, and then searching for more information. She asked them if they would like to be in a symbiosis inquiry circle to learn more about how animals in the ocean support each other in order to survive. They all nodded.

"So cool. I will write *Inquiry Circle* on a large Post-it and you can each put your name on it, sort of like a formal contract that says you are all going to work together in this group to ask questions and find out information about symbiosis." Kyky wrote her name on the Post-it. But before anyone else has a chance to sign, Zeke jumped in:

"Whoa, look at Kyky's name. She wrote it in cursive!"

"Let me see," Joel exclaimed. "I don't know how to write cursive."

"Me neither," Zeke added. "Can you show us, Kyky?"

"I only know how to do it with my own name. My big sister taught me. She's in fourth grade," Kyky answered.

"I really want to know how," Zeke said.

Steph volunteered, "Here Zeke, I'll show you. I'll write your name in cursive and you can trace over it to get a feel for it and then try doing it yourself if you like."

"Me too, please," Joel popped in.

"No problem," Steph answered as she wrote Joel's name in cursive on another Post-it.

All three began practicing writing their names in cursive as Steph paged through another coral reef book to a photo of a sea anemone. "Hey, look you all, another example of symbiosis," Steph said as she read the page. But all three had become so enthralled with writing their name in cursive that they ignored her read-aloud of the paragraph.

"Hey you guys, look at this picture," Steph said as she touched Kyky's shoulder and tapped her pencil in front of Joel, who had now written his name in cursive at least four times. But it was too late. Cursive ruled.

"Why do we write in cursive anyway?" Zeke suddenly asked.

"What a great question, Zeke. I am not completely sure of the answer to that. Actually, my son Alex, who is twenty-eight, never really learned to write in cursive, except for one thing, of course—his signature," Steph commented.

"What is a signature?" Joel asked.

"Another great question. What do you all think a signature is?" Steph asked. They discussed this briefly and didn't seem to have much of a grasp on the concept of signature.

"Well, it is a way of signing your name that is yours and nobody else's. Like fingerprints—no one else has your fingerprints and no one else has your signature. A signature is your name written exactly the way you want to write it. It doesn't have to look just like your own name. For instance, there are many kids called

Alex, but they all have their own signatures. My son Alex's signature looks different from all of the rest of the Alexes' signatures. The letters in a signature don't have to be exactly correct. They can be any size you choose. Some people write a big signature, other people a small signature. Some people use their initials and then their last name as their signature. It is up to you."

"Do you have a signature?" Kyky asked.

"You bet. Here it is." Steph wrote a large *S* for Stephanie with some squiggles in between and then a large *H* for Harvey and a few squiggles before the final *Y*. They all pored over the paper with Steph's signature.

"I can't read it," Zeke said.

"You don't need to be able to read it. It is like a mark, your own personal stamp," Steph explained.

"Can we write our own signature?" Joel asked.

"Of course you can, but you may need some time to figure one out," Steph said as she gave each of them more paper to try out their signatures and contribute to their identity. As they practiced, they burst with questions.

"How did people think of signatures?" Kyky asked.

"How did people figure them out?" Zeke queried.

"When did people first use signatures?" Joel asked.

"How did people learn to write?" Kyky asked.

"What about cursive? How did cursive happen?" Zoe piped in from the sidelines. She had been working alone, drawing a stunning illustration of some fan coral, but suddenly she couldn't ignore the group any more.

"Hey, Zoe. Such a great question. Do you want to find out? Would you like to join our group?" She nodded and sat down with us.

"Now you are four kids! Add your name to the Post-it, Zoe," Steph nudged her.

Inferences followed quickly on the heels of their questions. *I think they started with a stick, then a rock, then they used a pen. I think they used chalk. I think they got a stick and wrote in the sand. I saw a book about mummies with some drawings for writing.* And it was at that moment Steph realized that even though all four of these kids would happily continue working on oceans and fish in science and social studies for quite some time, an authentic spontaneous inquiry into cursive writing and signatures had erupted unannounced right here in the middle of the classroom coral reef. *Sometimes we just have to go with our kids.* We simply can't ignore their energy and excitement. We have to jump on their enthusiasm and support them to learn more about the topic and more about the inquiry process.

"What do you all think about our starting an inquiry circle that finds out about writing and signatures?" Steph suggested.

"YES!" Ezekiel fist-pumped as the others nodded enthusiastically.

"OK, who wants to write down a couple of the questions we have?" Kyky and Zeke agreed to write down two important questions (their work is reproduced

here): How did people learn to write? How did people learn about signatures? "Make sure you sign these questions with your very own signatures," Steph added. "And then on your Post-its, why don't you go ahead and write down what you think might be the answer, what you infer, and we will find out for sure when we start to do our research."

"So how shall we begin?" Steph asked.

"Let's collect signatures of the grown-ups in the school. It's going to be great! It's going to be fun to figure out how each person's signatures are different!" Zeke said. Joel, Zoe, and Kyky agreed.

"What are signatures for anyway?" Joel asked.

"Such a great question, Joel. I am making a point of recording all of your questions, so we don't forget them," Steph said, as she added Joel's question to the list that the others had generated so far.

"To answer your question, Joel, maybe you have seen your parents write a check. They have to write their signature on the check so people know who signed it," Steph said as she pulled her checkbook out of her purse and wrote her signature on a check. This got them talking about how we use signatures. Zoe commented that her mom signs when she uses a credit card. Zeke said he saw his dad write his signature at the end of a letter. Suddenly, it was lunchtime, so Steph suggested that everyone make inquiry circle folders to help keep their questions, information, drawings, and notes organized, and then—of course!—write their signatures on the cover.

So this is how one group of four kids began an investigation into the origins of signatures and the beginning of writing. Their unbridled energy and enthusiasm led Steph to change her plans and go with their interest, to pursue an open inquiry. Steph met with Brad, who happily agreed to facilitate this inquiry circle over the next few weeks. Steph was excited because she knew Brad would fire up these kids. He is a huge advocate for artistic response, and his kids are amazing artists because of it. Steph could envision the incredible images and illustrations that would emerge from this study. Brad is also a teacher who creates lessons with big ideas in mind and fosters thinking about essential questions, which would make this inquiry even better. He would gather as many resources into the origins of writing as he could find and would meet with them daily during reading/writing workshop time. During those times, he might read to them in the small group and facilitate a discussion, help them plan their next steps, or just check in with them to see how things were coming along as they read, wrote, painted, drew, and talked their way through their writing inquiry. To keep a record of the teaching and learning, Brad kept the following journal.

Kid's document their own research process.

See Lesson 3, "Think and Wonder About Images," p. 118, and Lesson 8, "Notetaking: Read with a Question in Mind," p. 123.

From Brad's Teacher Journal: The Journey of the Signature/Writing Inquiry Group
Day 2

After a discussion about the events of the day before, the kids decided they were going to focus first on signatures. They wanted to collect adult signatures in the school to get an idea of how different signatures looked. I wrote them a pass on three different occasions over the next several days so they could visit the office, the library, and the kitchen to collect adult signatures. They asked people to print their name in green and sign it in blue to show the difference between printing and a signature.

When the kids returned to the room, they drew and wrote what they had done. They drew themselves in the office with clipboards showing how they collected signatures from the staff. Later they shared the adult signatures with the rest of the class and explained what a signature was. This was a big hit, and soon all of the kids in the class were practicing their own signatures! We glued all of the signatures onto a large sheet of chart paper and titled it simply "Our Signature Collection."

Day 3

The students' initial signature exploration led to more questions. These went way beyond the issue of signatures:

- When did writing start?
- How did people write without paper?
- How did people invent paper?
- How did people learn to write and read in cursive?
- How did people invent paint and paintbrushes?
- How did people invent ink?
- Is an autograph the same as a signature?

I recorded them on an anchor chart so we could keep track of them. The kids recorded their own questions and learning on their personal Learn/Wonder charts, which they would add to when they found new information as well as new questions. I reminded them to keep their questions in mind as they read and viewed images, particularly those original questions about how writing began and where signatures come from.

Joel asked, "What did they write with on the pyramids?"

Zeke, loaded with background about ancient Egypt, responded to Joel's question: "I think I have an answer to that. Egyptians made symbols on the pyramids to help them understand."

Joel, an English language learner, followed with, "What's a symbol?" That fostered a discussion of the nature of symbols and how a symbol is something people might draw, write, or design to create meaning. We drew a smiley face and talked about what it might symbolize. We talked about how each star on the flag symbolizes one of the fifty states. We talked about equal, plus, and minus signs; question marks and exclamation points; stop signs; green, yellow, red lights—all symbols. So here we found ourselves talking about a big idea, *symbolism*, that emerged from one kid's question. How great is that!

The Egypt discussion spawned a conversation about hieroglyphics. Zoe, having done an earlier investigation of Cleopatra, shared that hieroglyphics represented some of the very first writing. And Kyky mentioned drawings of animals in caves, which she had seen in a book. We all decided that we better head to the library to get more information. I got the principal to cover my class for half an hour so we could go. Once there, we didn't find any resources on cave paintings, but we found quite a few books on ancient Egypt, one titled simply *Hieroglyphics,* which the kids couldn't wait to dive into.

Heiroglyphics collection and one of the kids' "I Learned/ I Wonder" charts

Day 4

We read about hieroglyphics and how the Egyptians used them as symbols. We referred back to one of our questions, Who invented paper and why? And wham—we read that the Egyptians invented papyrus, so

we wrote the answer to our question and coded it with an *A* for *answer*. We also learned that Egyptians used tools to carve symbols, called hieroglyphics, into rock. The kids coded their answers with an *A*, then drew a favorite hieroglyphic. They placed their Post-it questions on their Learn/Wonder charts and matched them to their newly found answers using an arrow.

I asked what they still wondered. Joel said, "I want to know more about papyrus. Let's Google *papyrus!*" All agreed. Zoe suggested that they use *papyrus plants* as keywords rather than simply *papyrus*, which I applauded, since we work to help the kids be more specific in their online searches. Online sources provided great color images of papyrus with captions rife with information. We were all excited, never having seen a papyrus plant, so I got the kids some watercolors and they sketched and painted some papyrus plants. Their paintings added to our growing knowledge base about writing and signatures.

Days 5 and 6

The kids continued their watercolor paintings of papyrus. When they finished, they wrote a caption and labels to go with their paintings. We found a very fun book of hieroglyphic stencils. This was big! Some of the kids worked on creating their own hieroglyphic words while the others finished painting and labeling their papyrus. They couldn't get enough of these hieroglyphic stencils. Zeke set up shop, writing the names of other kids in the class in hieroglyphics. Kids signed up and waited their turn! See how their names turned out in hieroglyphics.

As the kids drew their own hieroglyphics, Zoe mentioned that they were hard to draw, so tiny and perfect. And Egyptians had to carve some of them, which would be really hard, she noted. She decided that they must have really wanted to make sure people knew about their lives. This led to a discussion of yet another big idea, one of the most important—the need for communication. We all agreed that people live to communicate with one another, whether it is with another kid in the class, with their mom and dad, or about history like the Egyptians. Whatever the reason, people need communication. And Zeke made a profound inference that communication was probably why writing began in the first place.

Papyrus watercolor

Names of kids in class in heiroglyphics

Day 7

A week into the inquiry, we needed some time to reflect on where we were. We gathered around some of the work we had done and some of the artifacts we had collected during the study so far. Our signature collection, which held about forty different signatures, was taped to the wall; the books we were using for

See Lesson 17, "Midcourse Corrections: Reflecting and Replanning," p. 132.

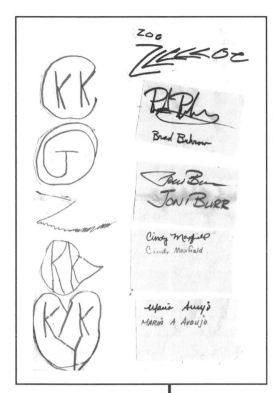

Part of the kids' "Signature Collection."

See Lesson 9, "Drawing Inferences from Images, Features, and Words," p. 124.

sources were leaning against the shelf; the printed images we found of papyrus were taped up and labeled; our signature/writing word wall was posted for all to see; and our signature inquiry group folders were filled with lots of questions, some answers, paintings of information, and drawing and writing of our process.

I took time to have kids reflect on what they had learned so far. I suggested they look at all of the artifacts surrounding them, flip through their folders, and talk to each other about their learning. Kyky spoke of her learning about papyrus and how the Egyptians used it. "And that's why we're holding paper today!" she exclaimed. Joel told us that he now knew what a symbol was and that the stars on the flag were symbols for the states. Zoe added that hieroglyphics were symbols of words. Zeke mentioned that no one could have your signature. "Like fingerprints, your signature belongs to you alone!" he announced.

They also talked about what they had learned about working together—to follow the conversation rather than just shouting out whatever is on your mind, and also to disagree respectfully. Throughout the inquiry, they talked, wrote, and drew about the inquiry process itself. They shared drawings they had made and photos they had taken that recorded their research project.

Day 8

Steph joined us again and read aloud the picture book *First Painter,* a fictionalized account of the earliest cave paintings in France, done in about 15,000 BC. It tells the story of a young girl who is sent by her tribe to draw animals and symbols in a cave in an effort to bring rain to her drought-ridden people. We discussed the fact that this led to the inference about how the first cave paintings came to be. There was no one to record it with a camera. Because no one knows for sure, we had to infer how these paintings originated. We talked about the fact that these cave paintings were drawn even before the Egyptians wrote in hieroglyphics. Joel said, "That answers our question about how writing began. In caves!"

"Great thinking, Joel. Why caves, do you think?" Steph asked. The group began talking and discussing how these paintings could last so many years. Why did these paintings last for so long? Would writing in the sand outside last for thousands of years? Would painting on walls outside last for thousands of years? Our guided discussion led to the realization that the cave paintings lasted so long because the cave was dry and safe from wind and rain and from people, too. This led to a discussion of the notion of permanence and impermanence. We didn't shy away from teaching this vocabulary just because the kids were in second grade. Rather, we

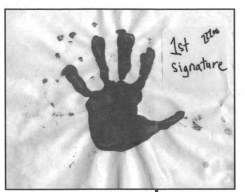

jumped on the opportunity to teach another big idea that emerged from the kids' conversation.

Zeke connected this to hieroglyphics, saying, "Hieroglyphics probably lasted because they were mostly inside tombs, safe from rain and wind."

"And because they were carved in stone, not just painted on," Zoe added. I just sat back and marveled at the amazing thinking kids can do when given a chance.

One of the most amazing discoveries from reading *First Painter* came when Kyky pointed out that the cave paintings in the book also included handprints next to the illustrations. Wow! Could those handprints be the world's first signature? We stopped and considered this momentous possibility. We had talked many times about how signatures and fingerprints belong to you and only you. Now right here in this book, we found handprints next to the paintings that we inferred might well have been the signatures of the painters! And Zeke pointed out that the cave artist in the book seemed to sign her drawings with a handprint! The kids could hardly contain themselves and wanted to test out the first signature idea. We got some paper and nontoxic tempera paint, and the kids went to it. Green, yellow, red, and purple handprints appeared as if by magic. We let our "first signatures" dry and then placed them on the wall for all to see. (Zoe's "signature" is shown here.) Needless to say, it was not long before the first signatures of all of the kids in the class decorated our classroom!

Zeke's inferences about chalk and charcoal writing.

Day 9

In *First Painter*, the young cave artist drew with a "charred stick." We discussed what *charred* meant and how a person might be able to draw with burnt coals. Staying with the idea of permanence, the kids devised some experiments. We talked about what we thought might happen if we wrote with chalk outside. Was chalk permanent? How long would our writing last outside on the sidewalk? Would our chalk writing last through a rainstorm or wind? The kids wrote their signatures with chalk on the sidewalk outside our door. We then checked them daily to see if they were still there, were fading, or had disappeared completely. The kids wrote in their folders what they predicted would happen. And sure enough, the signatures faded quite a bit one afternoon during a thunderstorm. The kids also filled cups with water and put the chalk in the water, wondering if it would dissolve. We learned that it did not, at least not in the three weeks we let the experiment run.

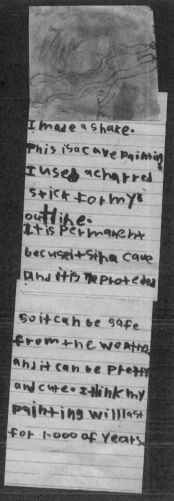

Joel's "cave painting" with commentary.

See Lesson 4, "Use Text and Visual Features to Gain Information," p. 119.

Day 10

Would writing or drawing with a charred stick be permanent? That was our next question. We reread *First Painter*. After talking about it again, we got out the watercolors to create some cave art. I lit a match over the sink, blew it out, and let it cool. Voila—a mini charred stick! I made one for each of the kids and with our charred sticks, we created the outlines of our cave paintings (several of these are shown here). Later we talked and wrote about what we had painted and whether it would be permanent or impermanent. Joel wrote:

> I made a snake. This is a cave painting. I used a charred stick for my outline. It is permanent because it's in a cave and it is protected from the weather and it is pretty and cute. I think my painting will last for 1,000(s) of years.

Day 11

The kids had been interested in some of the tools people throughout history have used to write. Using online sources, we found images of feather pens, porcupine quill pens (ethically procured), and clay tablets that were written with reed pens. Throughout our study, we created a word wall of new vocabulary and grammatical structures. We studied the features of nonfiction: illustrations, lables, arrows, tables of contents, and even glossaries. After I modeled, each of the kids created a personal mini-glossary to hold their own new words so they would develop a better awareness of them and use them more frequently. (Kyky's mini-glossary is shown here.)

Studying these items led us to the Rosetta stone. In the book *Hieroglyphics*, we read and learned more about this important discovery. We learned that the Rosetta stone was discovered in Egypt and that it translated hieroglyphics so they could be understood in other languages. However, we found that the Rosetta stone now rested in a museum in England. "Why is the Rosetta stone in England and not in Egypt?" the kids wondered. This led to critical conversations about the "spoils of war" and the idea of "finders keepers." The Rosetta stone and its translation also

led to a discussion of codes and breaking codes by finding patterns. I showed them how codes work and gave them an example—A=1, B=2, C=3, and so on—and they spent time writing each other code notes and cracking them. Soon they began to create their own codes.

Days 11, 12, 13, 14

The kids, in keeping with our established routine, wanted to present their findings to the class. Some, like Zoe, decided to make a giant research poster. she planned how to organize the artifacts she had created, like the first signature (handprints), and place them on the poster. When she was finished, she had her notes with questions, inferences, answers, and other information she had learned. The painting of the papyrus plant and drawings accompanied a word wall she created for her research. She included a list of her books as well as online and people sources. Finally she presented to the class. She took questions, comments, and connections from the audience after she presented the information.

Although the kids would have happily continued to study the origins of writing for many more weeks, these presentations were the culminating events of our inquiry study. They had learned a lot on the journey. They had answered questions at the onset, about when writing and signatures began. But more importantly, they learned about many more things than they imagined. They learned about the big ideas of communication, permanence, identity, translation, codes, spoils of war, and who has the right to discoveries, among other things. They also learned about the process of inquiry, how to use a variety of sources, and examine their validity and

See Lesson 27, "Response Options: Take Learning Public," p. 142.

Zoe's research poster.

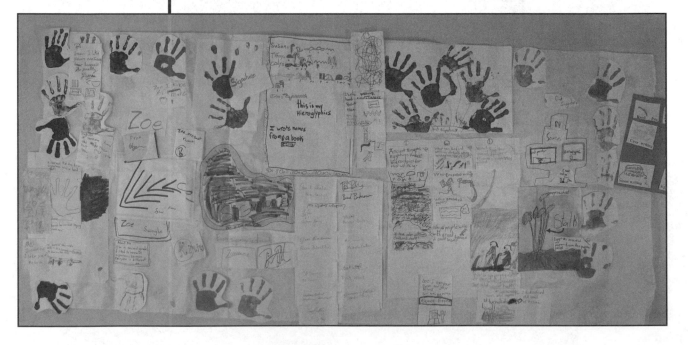

stance. And they got a whole lot better at working together. Amazing to think that this all began when Zeke saw Kyky write her name in cursive! With the kids' inquiring minds and our guidance, they worked their way deeper and deeper into a study of the history of writing and drawing and learned more than we could have dreamed along the way.

INQUIRY: *Kids' Choice Inquiry Projects*

See Lesson 12, "Home Court Advantage," p. 127.

—JOYCE SANCHEZ, SIXTH GRADE, SALAZAR SCHOOL, SANTA FE, NEW MEXICO

Last year, Smokey spent the second semester working with Joyce Sanchez's wonderful sixth graders in Santa Fe, New Mexico. Joyce, an amazing teacher with sixteen years in the classroom, has worked mostly with kids from immigrant neighborhoods. Salazar's student body gets 100 percent free or reduced lunches, and includes quite a few recently arrived English language learners.

Every day in Joyce's classroom begins with the kids scanning, reading, and discussing the local newspaper. The conversation that bubbles up is free-flowing, open-ended, and filled with feeling—laughs, high fives, disagreements, and debates are everyday happenings. Joyce constantly models her own curiosity, questions, concerns, and passions in these conversations. From the first day of the year, Joyce creates an atmosphere of friendship, trust, and mutuality that paves the way for all kinds of collaborative work later on. She creates a "home court advantage."

Today, when Smokey arrives, the kids are already discussing an article and photo about a baby born with two faces. The child is being worshiped in its home village in India, treated as a goddess, and has a potentially graced life. True to sixth-grade form, the kids are speculating madly about the child's future. Shai says, "What if she went to get married and one mouth said 'I do' and the other one said 'no way!'" Looking on the brighter side, Cristina points out, "Think of all the extra kissing you'd get, first one mouth, then the other!"

See Lesson 6, "Ask Questions and Wonder About Information," p. 121.

SELF AND WORLD QUESTIONS

KIDS: *Hey Smokey! Where have you been? We thought you were never coming back!*

SMOKEY: (laughs) Well, you know I always come back to you guys, don't I?

DEVIN: *Where were you this time?*

SMOKEY: Actually, I was in a couple of interesting places. (I roll down the U.S. map and show them the towns in New Hampshire and Maine where I have been consulting with schools.) I hope you all get a chance to see New England someday. It is really different from here in New Mexico—very wet and green with tons of tall trees, not like our desert and mountains and piñon trees at all.

ILSE: *Did you like it?*

SMOKEY: I really did. A lot of my family came from the east and I feel very at home there somehow. Anyway, do you all remember last week, Ms. Sanchez and I were talking with you about doing some inquiry projects where you could choose anything you would really like to know more about?

ASHLEY: *You said we could study anything we wanted.*

SMOKEY: For sure, that's the whole idea—to put all your good reading strategies and collaboration skills to work on something you really care about or wonder about. It is going to be a lot like literature circles, except that instead of picking one book to read, you'll pick one topic or question you want to investigate. Then we'll match up people with overlapping interests and you can read and learn all sorts of stuff about it.

DIEGO: *Can I work on what I want to be when I grow up?*

SMOKEY: Absolutely.

LUIS: *Can I do soccer?*

SMOKEY: You bet.

NADIA: *Animals?*

NAYETZY: *I want to do tigers!*

SMOKEY: Yes, whatever you want.

JORDAN: *But I don't have an idea right now. How do I find a topic?*

SMOKEY: Don't worry. We've only been talking about this for thirty seconds! So, a few people think they already have a topic and others haven't got one yet—no problem there! Let me show you how I go about finding things I want to investigate myself. Sometimes, it works to just brainstorm. You may already be carrying questions around in your head without even knowing it. I think there are two main kinds of big questions that people have—questions about themselves and questions about the world. (I go to the board and make a two-column chart). "Having a question" can mean that we have some problem we want to solve, or some practical job we need help with—or it can just be a subject we are interested in and want to learn about. You know? (The kids nod.) We have talked before about how I haven't been able to be with you as much as I would like because my job has so much travel. My wife says the same thing, actually.

NADIA: *I'll take your job!!*

SMOKEY: If I can be in Ms. Sanchez's class, then I'll take your job, Nadia! It's a deal! So I am going to list this as my first self question. (In the self column, I write How can I get off planes?)

Next, I mention that my wife and I have been thinking about getting a dog, but cannot decide what breed would fit into our somewhat itinerant life. The kids have oodles of suggestions. "Get a Lab," says Luis. "They love to ride in the car!" With each entry, the kids pepper me with questions and advice, and we spend two or

See Lesson 22, "Choosing Topics to Investigate," p. 137.

See Lesson 19, "Model Your Own Inquiry Process," p. 134.

three minutes chatting about each item. I add notes to my chart as they spark my thinking or raise new questions for me.

When I jot my third self question, that I want to study more about a neuro-muscular disease that my grown son has, the kids get quiet.

NADIA: (*in a whisper*) *Is it a killing disease?*

SMOKEY: No, no, it isn't a killing disease—but it can make him get weaker.

JOSE: *I will help you find out about it if you want me to.*

SMOKEY: Thanks for your concern, Jose and everyone, it means a lot to me. (I have brought up this particular topic not just to be honest in my modeling, but also because I want to emphasize that we can pursue truly personal issues in this project.) Nick is a very cool guy; I hope you get to meet him someday. He works in pathology and forensic science and has done hundreds of autopsies. Can you believe that?

Kids holler out comments evenly divided between "Yuck" and "Cool." I plunge ahead to avoid getting sidetracked into a conversation about crime scenes, splatter patterns, and/or murder.

SMOKEY'S SELF AND WORLD QUESTIONS

SELF

How can I get off planes?
Should I get a dog?

Is there any new research on spinal bulbar muscular atrophy?

WORLD

How can I affect the presidential election?

Global warming—what can I do?
Can we stop oil drilling in Santa Fe?

SMOKEY: Now I'm going to move over to the World side, to things I wonder about the larger world, not just my own life and family.

I first make an entry about the upcoming election, which is a big concern to me. Kids blurt out who their parents are voting for, who they like, and want to know who my candidates are. Next, I jot down global warming, which I have been reading a lot about and am eager to learn more. The kids instantly avalanche me with ideas and information. It turns out they have been studying climate change in their down-the-hall science class while I've been away. We plunge into a lively conversation about the worsening drought here in the Southwest, issues about recycling and whether it really works, and more. Finally I add my last topic.

SMOKEY: Remember we saw those articles in the newspaper about how some oil companies are planning to drill right here in Santa Fe? Well, you know what, I went on the website www.santafenotoil.com and they had a map, and it looks like they are going to be drilling very close to my house. And that freaks me out! You guys know that my wife and I just moved here, and we live way out in the desert. We thought we would always have peace and quiet, being so far out. So I am really taking this personally and I need to find out about it. Maybe this is more of a self question, but I know this is happening everywhere.

LUIS: *I read about oil wells. Sometimes they make a big mess, and spill oil all over.*

SMOKEY: Whoa, that's exactly what I am afraid of. But you know, I do realize that I put gas in my car and it has to come from somewhere. I drove here today, right, thirty-two miles round trip. Wherever in the world they drill for oil, there are probably people like me who wish it would happen somewhere else. Have you ever heard the expression NIMBY?

LUKE: *What?*

SMOKEY: (writing on board) N.I.M.B.Y. It stands for Not In My Back Yard. Funny, huh? But it's a good reminder that if everybody yelled "NIMBY" all the time, we'd never be able to drill for oil anywhere, or have a dump anywhere or whatever.

DANIEL: *That's funny, NIMBY.*

SMOKEY: OK, guys, so I have finished my list of questions, three self and three world— and thanks for all the input. You've given me lots of good hints and directions I can use. Now it's your turn. Since we are almost out of time for today, I'm going to give you all a little homework.

KIDS: *Boo, no way! Ms. Sanchez! (The class jokingly shoots appealing looks at Joyce, who just smiles and shrugs.)*

SMOKEY: Too late, you guys. She already gave me permission to oppress you. But look, this is how big your homework is! (I hold up a 3x5 index card.) For tomorrow, I want you to write down some self and world questions of your own, just like I did. Three of each. To help you think, you might talk to your friends on the bus or with your family at home tonight. Just come back tomorrow with at least three questions you have about yourself on one side of the card and three questions about the world on the other. Deal?

KIDS: *Yeah sure. OK.*

As I walk around the room I notice that many kids are already jotting down their own topics, even as they pack up to go to PE.

THE NEXT DAY: FINDING COMMON QUESTIONS

SMOKEY: I see that you guys already have your homework cards out on your desks—it looks like everyone has three self questions and three world questions, right? Some of you have even more than six questions! So now let's see what's on the docket. Get in your regular groups (Joyce's kids normally sit in permanent home groups of four or five) and share with each other all your topics—both sides of the card. Just read them aloud and talk about them briefly. Make sure you hear all of everyone's topics. Go ahead.

Joyce and I move from group to group, listening carefully during this sharing. We know that some kids may mention topics that they won't later raise in the whole group, and we want to be ready to plug those back into the process at some point. We let groups talk for about fifteen minutes, then call the kids back. They are really into it, and we have to forcibly interrupt and drag them out of their conversations.

Teacher Modeling in Open Inquiries

There is a lot to think about when you model this kind of question list for kids. First and above all, you want to be authentic, to represent things you are genuinely curious about. We go for multiple topics because we know that if we share only one or two, the kids are likely to think these are the suggested or "right" topics to choose for themselves. Even when you share many ideas, you always have to double-check if kids pick a topic you have modeled. Are they really interested or does it just seem easier than making their own choice? Or do kids somehow think you are steering them toward a particular topic for some reason? With this group, a few kids did eventually pick up on my global warming topic. But they also showed lots of background knowledge and genuine enthusiasm for the subject. If I had listed arthritis, I doubt they would have come back to it.

Which raises a related point. Within the bounds of authenticity, I avoid listing too many old-person issues that kids really don't care about. I may have burning questions about my retirement investment strategy (actually, I do), but listing them doesn't help kids much. On the other hand, mentioning my wife's and my discussions about getting a dog connects really well. I try hard to list topics that are genuinely mine, but also kid-friendly.

SMOKEY: Wow, this took a little bit of time, didn't it? If I have the math right, if everybody in a group brought six topics, you might have just discussed twenty-four or thirty topics. So you have heard tons of topics, questions, and problems, right? I heard some amazing stuff in the groups where I sat in. Did some of you find that you had the same or similar topics?

KIDS: *Yes. A lot.*

SMOKEY: Great, let's see what are common topics, the big overlaps. Eventually, we'd like to form groups of people who have the same basic interest or question, or closely related questions, so you can work together on your research. But we're not in a hurry. So let's list some of the topics you are raising. We could call them "hot topics" and "burning questions," OK? Let's start with the world questions. Who's got one?

NADIA: *We talked about the war in Iraq.*

DEVIN: *Our group did too.*

SMOKEY: That's a world problem, for sure, isn't it? OK, so we have two groups that overlap already. What other topics or questions did you talk about?

ILSE: *We talked about global warming.*

ALEXANDRA: *So did we.*

LUKE: *Us too.*

SMOKEY: Whoa, lots of people brought up global warming.

The kids continue to pitch in ideas and I jot them on the board (see the photo). Many of these entries spark conversations, and we stop, talk, consider possibilities, and add things to our notes. When we move to the Self side of the chart, there is a sudden wave of energy around the topic of pets. Everyone wants

www.heinemann.com/
comprehensionandcollaboration.

to learn more about their dog, cat, rat, hamster, gerbil, ferret, turtle, goldfish, para-keet, boa constrictor—or the critter they wish they had. All this duly goes up on the board, where we are building a pretty good inventory of topics.

For more of our conversation, go to the website.

SMOKEY: Now, thinking through all those topics—the ones you thought about last night and the ones you have just heard, will you each please write down the two most interesting topics for you right now? This would be the two topics or questions that you are most curious about, most interested in, would really like to know more about. (Kids jot notes.) Now we are going to do something we call a "mingle." Did you ever go to a family party or a barbecue or some event where people mingled? Who knows what I mean by mingling?

JESSICA: *Before my auntie's wedding everybody just kind of walked around outside the church and said hi to everybody for a while, until they had seen everybody else.*

SMOKEY: What a perfect example of mingling. You talk to one person for a while, then you move along and talk to someone else. And then you shift again and talk to some other person. You're just mingling, y'know? Right now, we are going to have "Topic Party" and mingle through the room until we have all talked to everyone else. Bring your two topics and your research notebook so you can write down great topics or questions you hear.

Joyce and I quickly model topic mingling so the kids will understand the process, and then we turn them loose. Kids pair off, read aloud their two hot topics, make quick notes, then break up and form another pair. Joyce and I circulate and keep things moving at first, but the kids quickly get the process. They are pretend-meeting each other, shaking hands, and acting very official and grown-up. Within about eight minutes, all the kids have shared their two topics with every other kid. We are really winnowing down now.

SMOKEY: So let's find out which topics "have legs." By now we have all heard a zillion topics, from every kid in here. Now, let me ask you—and really think about this—what are the most common topics out there, the ones that you just heard over and over as you mingled?

These emerge quickly and easily—a list of seven items.

Possible careers
World of the Future

Global warming
Risky teenage behavior

The French language
Animal extinction

Pet ownership

Kids did *not* want to put down twelve or eighteen topics, even as I kept asking: "Any more, any more hot topics or burning questions? Anyone?" Our winnowing process has led to just eight genuinely big ideas of wide interest. (Jump-starting inquiry groups can be a challenge. To see two other ways we have launched open inquiries, see the website.)

www.heinemann.com/
comprehensionandcollaboration.

Forming Groups

Once again I hand out 3x5 index cards—the go-to tool in this whole negotiating process.

SMOKEY: All right, you guys. Now you're going to pick your topics. At last! Please jot down your top three choices from among our seven finalist topics. We're going to try to give everybody their first choice, but we need your second and third picks just as a backup. And remember that you will be able to investigate your own personal question within the overall group topic if you want. Ready? Cast your votes. Be sure to number them 1-2-3, and don't forget your name! (As the kids complete their ballots, I gather them up.)

Now watch what I am going to do. I have cleared a space on this table so that I can deal out all your cards and you can watch me. I am going to categorize your choices and start to create groups by putting together people with similar interests. I'm going to start by giving everyone their first choice of topics. Then if that doesn't work, we'll look at second choices. But let's see what happens. (I start dealing the cards and I don't mention kids' names, just topics at this stage.)

OK. The first card says "global warming," so I will put it down right here. The next one says "careers," so I am going to put this one over here. The next card says "global warming" again, so I will put this together with the other global warming card. The next one says "the future," which is a third topic, so I'll make a separate place for that one.

I continue going through the deck until I have the following distribution:

6 on global warming
6 on careers

2 on the French language
5 on the world of the future

1 on foreign languages, but not mentioning French
1 on risky teenage behavior

Using just their first choices, I already have nineteen of twenty-one kids in groups with their first-choice topic. Now, I work with the two "outliers." Because Joyce has created such an atmosphere of trust and high morale, I feel comfortable doing this transparently, in front of the class.

> SMOKEY: *You two who are not in a group yet, you have some choices. You can stay with your number one topic and work alone, or you can pick your second or third choice and join an existing group. Maria, you put foreign language in general, but not specifically French.*

> MARIA: *Well, I was really more interested in Italian.*

> SMOKEY: *You French people, what do you think? Can you make room for some Italian in your inquiry?*

> ALEXANDRA: *(She first gets nonverbal assent from the other girls.) Sure.*

> MARIA: *(Thinks for a moment before responding.) I think I'll take global warming instead.*

> SMOKEY: *So you want to move to your second choice, then? Are you sure? I think you could pursue your Italian just fine with this group if you want . . .*

Maria thinks for a moment and then sticks with global warming. I ask, "Are you really sure? Are you truly curious about global warming?" She sounds pretty calm and solid about it, so I put her in that stack of cards.

I go through the same process with Tony, who has just returned to Joyce's class after several months' absence, and seems quite unsure. His own pick, teenage risky behavior, hasn't attracted any other votes. I am a little disappointed about this myself, since the kids are headed to the big scary middle school next year, but obviously, nobody wants to deal with this topic right now. Maybe they have been over-DARE-ed. Anyway, the other students are attentive to Tony; they suggest connections, and several even invite him into their groups. Within two minutes, he's happily matched up with the careers group, ready to investigate his just-remembered dream of becoming an astronaut.

Now everyone has a home. No one has chosen to go it alone, though if they had, Joyce and I would have happily supported them (and looked for natural opportunities for them to work alongside others as appropriate). For more ideas on helping kids who prefer to work alone, see pages 274–277.

Now we need to take a look at group size.

> SMOKEY: *As you guys remember from our work with lit circles, a good size for group projects like these is four, though we can have three or five if that's how the numbers lay out. More than six is really too big for a good group. There are too many ways that members can get lost, sidetracked, or ignored. So you will probably want to split up the career group at some point. Keep that in mind when you get together—see if you find some natural way to divide up, probably based on differences in your questions.*

See Lesson 14, "Making and Using a Work Plan," p. 129.

Now it is time for the kids to meet for the first time in their inquiry groups.

> **SMOKEY:** *What a great start! Such good topics, such a nice, even distribution of people. So now you can get up, take your materials and your journals, and go sit in your new groups. We'll give you some time to just chat about your interests. Then after a while we'll hand out a blank work plan you can use to organize your group and let me and Ms. Sanchez know what help you need. (We hold back on this handout for a while, knowing that kids will immediately fill out any worksheet-like form that's put in front of them, whether they have talked about it or not!)* (See this *Making a Work Plan Form* on the website.)

As kids set to work, we circulate, helping them develop lists of subtopics and questions. There is plenty of fine-tuning going on. The futures group had originally aimed to target the year 3000, but quickly realizes they are more interested in what the world will look like when they will still be alive, so they ratchet down to 2030.

The global warming group quite naturally splits in two. Nadia, Jose, and Nayetzy are really more interested in animal extinction, a topic only partly related to global warming. Each has chosen an animal to investigate (tigers for Nayetzy, elk for Jose, and polar bears for Nadia). Meanwhile, Jordan, Juan, and Luke want to focus their attention on what individuals can do to stop global warming, and they have already posed a solid, researchable question: does recycling really help?

Across the room, the careers kids have also split into two manageable-sized groups. Ashley, Jessica, Diego, and Tony had already developed an affinity while sitting around a computer looking at the average salaries for some jobs on a U.S. Department of Labor website. Daniel and Devin are still unsure about their direction, and they fall in with the very self-sufficient Cristina, who is the sole student looking into a nonscientific career—fashion design. So now, everyone has a posse. Here's how the groups settled out after a first day of working together.

SALAZAR INQUIRY GROUPS

Animal Extinction

Nadia (polar bears)

Jose (elk, hunting)

Nayetzy (tigers)

Global Warming: What Can We Do to Stop It?

Jordan

Juan

Luke

---

www.heinemann.com/
comprehensionandcollaboration.

No "Group Shopping"

Once groups are formed and students see who's in each one, some kids may ask to switch to another team. This, of course, might be a case of social preferences overruling kids' curiosity about a topic. We have to make our best guess about their intentions. To let kids casually switch groups at this stage pretty much undermines the careful process we have just gone through to match people by interests. While there are always exceptions, we usually say no to transfer requests for reasons other than sincere subject matter concerns.

The French Language: Speak, Read, Write, and Eat French!

Maria

Alexandra

Claudia

Careers I

Ashley (pharmacist)

Jessica (doctor)

Diego (video game designer, ophthalmologist, marine biologist, math professor)

Tony (astronaut)

Careers II

Cristina (fashion designer)

Daniel (neuroscientist; later changed to nuclear weapons)

Devin (chemist; later changed to nuclear weapons)

The Future of Humanity: The Year 2030

Shai Rae (generalist)

Louie (future transportation, cars)

Nathan (cloning)

Ilse (houses of the future)

Javier (green building)

It's important to mention that the kids in Joyce's room who are receiving special services are simply integrated into different groups like everyone else. They have arrived there purely through topic selection. Janice Ballard, the special education teacher, has been in on the project from the start, and helps Joyce and me to support these kids. Once groups are formed, she immediately begins seeking appropriate readings and materials on the topics her kids have picked. By the luck of the 3x5 card draw, a couple of the kids who really struggle are now partnered with some of the highest achievers in the class. This proves to be a great advantage as the project unfolds. It is in the very nature of these projects that people contribute according to their interests and talents, so everyone is able to be a full member of the team without having to do the exact same things.

Investigate: The Reading Frenzy

Using the kind of careful topic-finding process we have just described, you can usually help kids find a subject of real interest. But that's just the start. Now it is time for the newly formed groups to explore more deeply, to immerse themselves in the topic. In Joyce's room we called this phase a "Reading Frenzy." Over the

See Lesson 21, "Explore and Use Multiple Sources," p. 136.

Taking Time for Topics

You've probably noticed that this topic finding and group formation took a while. In fact, Smokey and the kids spent *two hours and fifteen minutes* negotiating the curriculum, just to find topics that each student could commit to and sustain over the long haul. Compare this to the tiny amount of time that we typically allocate to helping students pick a topic for traditional research reports! In the old days, we might give kids a list of approved topics and ask them to pick one on the spot, or let them review the list as homework and report back with their choice. Or maybe we'd have a few minutes of class brainstorming and let kids pick their topics from the discussion.

But then what happens? Disturbingly often, the kids don't care enough about their hastily chosen topics to conduct intensive work over days and weeks, and energy peters out quickly. Then, we end up with the Death March to Due Dates, where we have to impose extrinsic rewards and punishments (points, parties, pizzas) rather than rely on young people's curiosity and intrinsic motivation. Instead of a joyous intellectual process, we suffer low morale, rampant plagiarism, parent coauthorship, and lots of whining (not just us, the kids too).

So maybe this seems ironic, but when we want kids to make a truly free and personal choice, we have to provide them *more* support than when we simply give an assignment. With true inquiry, it is the teacher's responsibility to set aside enough time and conduct enough appropriate activities that kids can thoroughly explore, validate, develop, and commit to a topic.

weekend, both of us stripped our own shelves of all books or magazines pertaining to checked out materials at our respective public library branches, the kids' initial topics, and we enlisted the help of the school librarian to deliver a delicious cartful of resources on Monday morning.

SMOKEY: *Hi guys, what's up? I know that some of you have already found some readings about your topics. I came in the room while you were still down the hall for science and I could see all the articles sitting on your desks. Who found stuff over the weekend?*

ALEXANDRA: *I found some things about French food.*

DEVIN: *Ms. Sanchez found lots of articles for us.*

SMOKEY: *Oh, so that's where all those articles came from. Thanks, Ms. S! So we are off to a good start. Over the weekend I also did some Internet searches on your topics, picked books off my own shelves, and rescued magazines from the recycling bin—just in time! And I brought all that stuff in today. I put it all in a plastic bin for each group. You'll see there is plenty of room for more stuff as you collect it. You should make a label for your bin, with all your names on it—you can even decorate it if you like.*

So today we are basically going to have what we call a "Reading Frenzy." We have tons of books, magazines, and Web articles—and we also have a few videos and audio CDs for you Frenchies. This will be your first pass through these materials, and we want you to just read for fun, read fast, and enjoy. Here's a format for a three-column chart that you can use to quickly record your reactions, what you learned, and any new questions that pop up.

REACTIONS: Wow! Cool! No way! Weird!	I LEARNED: Facts, information	I WONDER: Lingering or new questions

SMOKEY: *If something interests you, then slow down and read it more carefully. Use your note-taking strategies, or annotate the text, or mark it with Post-its that hold your questions and reactions. OK? If anything is too hard or seems boring, just put it aside for now and keep looking for the really interesting stuff that looks like it might start to answer your questions. Let's read!*

Kids spend parts of the next three days scanning and studying these resources, following leads to websites, and sorting materials into useful stuff and discards. Throughout the frenzy, Joyce and I constantly circulate, conferring with groups and helping them to hone and deepen their questions.

(To hear more about our Reading Frenzy and the subsequent investigations, see the website.)

Interviewing

Joyce and I wanted the kids to add "live" research to all their information from texts and websites. So we conferred with each group to determine what specialists or experts might be interviewed, either in person, by phone, or via email. Before turning kids loose, we modeled what an effective interview sounds like and helped kids to construct written guidelines for questioning an informant. Groups had little trouble finding experts to help them; at one point, Diego was communicating with two different marine biologists about his career goals. When the animal extinction group set up a conference call with Marc Beckoff, the University of Colorado's world-renowned expert on animal emotions, we weren't about to let those three kids hog the opportunity! Everyone crowded into the school's conference room and listened in rapt attention as Nadia, Jose, and Nayetzy skillfully interviewed Beckoff about his brand-new book. Suddenly, we all had to put our questions aside for a minute when a rare silver fox scampered across the scientist's snowy deck in

www.heinemann.com/
comprehensionandcollaboration.

See Lesson 25, "Demonstrate and Practice Interviewing," p. 140, and Lesson 26, "Co-construct Interview Guidelines," p.141.

Daniel and Devin with their interview subject, Dr. Robert Eisenstein.

www.heinemann.com/
comprehensionandcollaboration.

See Lesson 27, "Response Options: Take Learning Public," p. 142.

Boulder—as Marc described the animal to us on the phone. Indeed, one of the biggest unforeseen outcomes of our inquiry circles was that we all wanted to learn about everybody's topics, not just our own. The same thing happened with Daniel and Devin's atomic bomb inquiry: when Los Alamos nuclear physicist Dr. Robert Eisenstein came to be interviewed, the whole class peppered the patient scientist with questions (the somewhat surprising outcome of this inquiry is recounted on page 268–269).

The sixth graders worked much longer on these inquiries than we had planned. What could we do? Topics kept expanding, new questions kept popping up, something would appear in the newspaper (which we still religiously read each morning) that launched another round of investigations. Or one group would invite an adult expert to come and visit, and then we'd all get interested in each other's projects.

Some days kids worked on the inquiries for the entire morning; other days we spent just an hour or less, and yet other days were taken up entirely by other school events, testing, and previously scheduled field trips. In all, the kids spent about fifty school hours digging into their topics, as well as significant time at home and in the community, reading and extending their inquiries.

To hear more about the kids' deepening inquiries, see the website.

Going Public

Each of the six inquiry groups pushed through to a sharing learning with the world. To read about all the inquiry outcomes, see the website. Meanwhile, here are a few highlights:

- Cristina, who worked quite autonomously within the careers group, studied countless books and websites about fashion design and tried her hand at sewing a variety of looks at home. For her final project, she designed and made beautiful outfits for three of the girls in the class and conducted a highly professional fashion show, after which she answered questions from the crowd about her design vision as well as technicalities of clothing construction. Incidentally, when school restarted the next fall, a new student named Angela reported to Joyce's room, announcing that she wanted to be a fashion designer just like Cristina, who was now at a distant middle school. A few weeks later, Cristina designed a Halloween costume for Angela that won first prize in the school's costume contest. So not only is Cristina getting a reputation around town as a hot young designer—she's getting work!

- The rest of the careers group created a PowerPoint show about finding your just-right career, using four examples keyed to their own interests: physician, pharmacist, marine biologist, and astronaut. Jessica, Ashley, Diego, and Tony took their program on the road to the fourth-grade classes down the hall, supplementing the images with Q&A sessions and handouts.

- Toward the end of the inquiry project, the futures group mingled purposes with the global warming crew. They jointly invited an official from the Sierra Club to come to the classroom and be interviewed. Knocked out by the kids' expertise, the environmentalist turned the tables. A few weeks later, Joyce's class appeared on the front page of the Sierra Club newspaper under the headline: "Sixth Graders Look at Our Future in the Year 2030." The article quoted smart thinking from many of the kids and made quite an impression on parents and school district officials.

- The global warming kids got into a variety of projects, including trying to reduce the staggering amount of waste coming out of the school's kitchen every day after lunch. But at the very end of their inquiry, something really weird came up. The kids discovered a discrepancy in the New Mexico State Standards for sixth-grade science. In the section about climate, the standards listed only volcanoes, glaciers, and asteroid impacts as possible sources of climate change on earth. Nowhere did they mention human impact on the climate. The kids couldn't believe it. In the middle of the global warming crisis and an awful regional drought, the state of New Mexico didn't even acknowledge human beings as a source of greenhouse gases, pollution, and other climate-changing phenomena?

Well, these kids knew better—way better. So they sat down and wrote a letter to the state department of education.

Dear Dr. Lopez,

This spring we have been studying climate change in our school (Salazar School in Santa Fe). Our teachers, Ms. Sanchez and Mr. Daniels always show us the standards for what the state wants us to learn and what will be on the test. We looked at them on your website www.nm.standards.org. We were surprised to see that on page 5 of the 6th grade science standards, it says that only volcanoes, glaciers, and asteroid impacts can change the earth's climate. This is not what we have learned after studying this in our inquiry groups. We have learned that most experts think humans are changing the weather on Earth.

If you would read the article "Beyond the Ivory Tower: The Scientific Consensus on Climate Change," by Naomi Oreskes in Science Magazine from December, 2004, you will see that most scientists from around the world agree that global warming is real and is caused by humans. If you would like some more books and articles to read about this, just let us know.

We are wondering if the state standards for 6th grade could be changed? Can you do that, or is there someone else we should write to? How can we help? Thank you very much for your attention.

Jordan, Juan, and Luke

Salazar School

$\mathcal{B}$ackmapping to the Required Curriculum

As you have already seen, this was an extensive undertaking. We spent parts of twenty-four school days on this project. Maybe you are thinking: "Whoa! That's a big hunk of time!" Indeed, this project consumed about 3 percent of the sixth graders' class time at Salazar last year. And look at all the skills kids strengthen in doing these projects:

They interact appropriately in group settings.

They read a variety of texts (e.g., fiction, nonfiction, newspaper and magazine articles, poetry, drama).

They read independently to increase fluency and build background knowledge.

They choose materials to read independently, identify the main ideas and significant details, and determine the correct sequence of events or information.

They interpret and synthesize information from a variety of sources by:

- reviewing the characteristics of informational works
- restating and summarizing information
- determining the importance of information
- making connections to related topics and information
- monitoring comprehension
- drawing inferences
- generating questions
- using specific strategies to clear up confusing parts of a text (e.g., reread the text, consult another source, ask for help)

They increase fluency, comprehension, and insight through meaningful and comprehensive reading instruction by:

- using effective reading strategies to match type of text
- reading self-selected literature and other materials of individual interest
- reading selections and other materials assigned
- discussing selections in teacher-student discussions and small groups
- taking an active role in class discussions
- investigating examples of distortion and stereotype
- recognizing underlying messages in order to identify recurring themes

They interact with text by:

- making predictions
- formulating questions

- supporting answers from textual information, previous experience, and/or other sources

- drawing on personal, literary, and cultural understandings

- seeking additional information

- expanding and refining vocabulary through wide reading, word study, content area study, writing process elements, writing as a tool, debate, discussions, seminars, and examining the author's craft

They use critical thinking skills and create criteria to evaluate text and multimedia by:

- determining purpose through exploring bias, apparent messages, emotional factors, or persuasive techniques

- identifying and exploring the underlying assumptions of the author

They recognize the point of view of the author by considering alternative points of view or reasons by remaining fair-minded and open to other interpretations.

They develop and apply appropriate criteria to evaluate the quality of communication by:

- drawing conclusions based on evidence, reasons, or relevant information

- considering the implications, consequences, or impact of those conclusions

- using knowledge of language structure and literary or media techniques

They organize information gathered for a research topic into major components based on appropriate criteria.

They use multiple sources of print and nonprint information in developing informational materials such as brochures, newsletters, and advertisements by:

- exploring a variety of sources that provide information (e.g., books, newspapers, the Internet, electronic databases, CD-ROMs)

- distinguishing between primary and secondary sources

They reflect on learning experiences by describing personal learning growth and change in perspective.

If you have been reading this list and thinking, hmm, that doesn't sound like Steph and Smokey talking to me, you are quite right. While this is an accurate (though partial) inventory of the work kids do in inquiry circles, the wording isn't ours. Instead, it comes (with slight reordering) from the New Mexico State Standards—the same document that Smokey and Joyce used to make sure that the time kids spent on their projects addressed the official curriculum and helped prepare them for the statewide test. Take another look—we bet your state's standards look a lot like these.

Note that this list covers only the language arts standards, and within that, only the ones listed for the sixth-grade level. Joyce's kids also hit many language arts standards from seventh, eighth, and even high school levels. And remember, since each inquiry circle studied a content topic, every investigation connected somewhere to the official curriculum. For example, the global warming group also met many state standards in science, social studies, and mathematics as well as dozens of reading and language arts standards.

We hope the point is clear—undertaking these units with kids is *not* a side trip from the official curriculum. These well-structured small-group inquiries allow us to offer students both rigor and engagement, content and process, information and interpretation, ownership and responsibility. This is what becomes possible when we *go deeper into a smaller number of topics*. Kids don't just amass factoids for transient tests; they learn to wonder, read, write, talk, think, collaborate, and *remember*—having been true investigators in the world.

*K*ids should be learning to love to learn and learning to love to think.

Learning to Love to Learn

In her final reflections, Joyce talked about how one particular boy in the class was affected by the open inquiry projects:

> All year I had trouble getting him to work, to turn anything in, and to get motivated or interested in learning. He is a bright boy, he just didn't like school. I literally saw that kid come alive with this project. He became motivated. He was interested in learning. I did not have to constantly get on his back about working or turning in work. I think for the first time in his school career, he actually liked school. His attendance even improved. When you see that happen to a kid, how can you not want to do something like this? The excitement of the kids was too much to contain sometimes. If every teacher in America did these inquiry projects, there would be an explosion of kids actually learning! They would be learning to love to learn, and learning to love to think!

HIGH SCHOOL

Open Inquiry in High School: Capstone and Senior Projects

—Coventry High School, Providence, Rhode Island
—Federal-Hocking High School Faculty, Stewart, Ohio

An increasing number of states are now requiring high school kids to undertake ambitious, self-chosen inquiry projects, much like the ones we have showcased in this book. For example, Rhode Island has recently garnered much admiring press coverage for its statewide "capstone projects," in which seniors "focus in-depth on a core question of his or her own choice" and gradually create a collection of writing, research, documentation, and self-reflection, as well as offering a twenty-minute public exhibition or presentation. Kids are encouraged to make a real "learning stretch," tackling topics that are truly "open-ended and exploratory" (*Education Week* 2008).

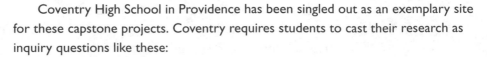

Coventry High School in Providence has been singled out as an exemplary site for these capstone projects. Coventry requires students to cast their research as inquiry questions like these:

- How can I promote cultural diversity at this school?

- How could I prove that the media alters the public's opinion of political candidates?

- How can I alert my classmates to the effects of twentieth-century genocides on school students around the world?

- How can I convince the community to participate in recycling efforts?

- How can I shadow an architect to learn about that profession?

It's not hard to see how pursuing such consequential topics could help "foster student interest and cultivate the active use of knowledge," as the program aims to do (Vernon-Sparks 2008).

If this capstone project idea sounds familiar, perhaps that's because the Coalition of Essential Schools has been advocating and operating a graduation-by-performance model for more than thirty years. In hundreds of coalition-affiliated schools across the country, kids don't complete high school by accumulating "seat time" or piling up course credits. Instead, they have to learn, grow, and show what they know all along the way. Similarly, many of the project-based learning schools we talked about back in Chapter 4 consistently invite kids to demonstrate what they have learned through complex performances. The Forum for Education and Democracy, founded by George Wood, Linda-Darling Hammond, Deborah Meier, and other progressive education luminaries, aims to replace the reign of standardized tests with authentic, teacher-driven, locally developed performance assessments instead (Wood and Darling-Hammond 2008).

The kids and faculty at Federal-Hocking High School in Stewart, Ohio, are getting senior projects right. Students from this spread-out Appalachian district develop portfolios of their work all through school, and also create a special senior project. When kids want to do their projects in groups, the faculty wisely requires them to clearly specify individual goals and outcomes, not just group plans. Smokey has worked with the teachers at Fed-Hock for several years, and has been impressed by their commitment to culminating projects that really mean something to kids. Look at the simplicity and kid-trustingness of their senior project model.

FEDERAL-HOCKING HIGH SCHOOL SENIOR PROJECT PROCESS

Each student at Federal Hocking High School finishes his or her high school career with the opportunity to leave a lasting impact on the school or our community through the Senior Project experience. Your Senior Project gives you the chance to gain new skills, see how you can make a difference in the world around you, and take on something that is of interest to you. While we expect the Senior Project to be a challenge, we believe you can have fun doing it as well.

You may choose from several different types of projects in order to complete this graduation requirement. Most importantly, you should choose a project for which you have a passion. This is your turn to shine, to do your own special piece of work, and to take control of your education.

The first step in the process is submitting a proposal for approval by the advisors for next year's class. Your proposal should be no longer than two pages and should be turned in to your advisor who will present it to all of the advisors for your class. Your proposal should include the following three sections:

SECTION ONE: What type of project will you be doing? You may choose a project that fits in any of the following areas. Remember, the project is worth one full academic credit so make sure it is something that will take about the same amount of time you spend in one class, at least one hundred hours. Be specific in your description and make sure it clearly fits the area you are choosing.

Academic Interest: A project may involve pursuing an area of academic interest in more depth than the student has been able to at school. For example, an extended research project on the Civil War ending in an essay that is submitted to the faculty.

Community Service: A project may involve carrying out a community service which results in something benefiting the local community. For example, fixing up a local park or taking on a church repair project.

Personal Challenge: A project may involve taking on a personal challenge that extends the student's current skills and abilities in a significant way. For example, a student may want to tour the State of Ohio by bicycle, or rebuild a car.

Learn a New Skill: A project may involve a student learning a new skill and presenting that skill. For example, learning to play a Mozart concerto and performing it at a school concert.

School Service: A project may involve a student carrying out a school service project. For example, landscaping a part of the school or creating a piece of public art.

Creating Something New: A project may involve a student creating something new. For example, this may involve the production of a major piece of art or the writing of a musical score for the band.

Research: A project may involve a student working on an original piece of research. For example, a student may take on researching the quality of water in the local watershed or working on a piece of local history research.

Other: For students who can find nothing of passion in the above areas, (s)he may work with her/his advisor to devise yet another approach to the senior project.

SECTION TWO: What will the process be for you to complete the project? Include what steps you think you will be taking, who your outside learning resource person will be (part of the project is to find an outside educational resource—this cannot be a family member or an FH staff member), and what skills you need to learn. You must also include an estimated budget for the project and how you will raise or find the funds for the project. Also, if your project is going to

See Lesson 22, "Choosing Topics to Investigate," p. 137.

See Lesson 14, "Making and Using a Work Plan," p. 129.

involve another agency or part of the school (like the athletics department), you should include a letter indicating that the project is acceptable to that organization. (For example, if you are working with the Humane Society, have a letter attached that indicates that they are willing to have you do the project.)

SECTION THREE: What will the final product be? What will you present as evidence that your project is complete?

You may write up your proposal and turn it in at any time to your advisor. This proposal is a formal piece of work and will only be accepted if it is carefully written and edited. Once they receive it, the advisory teachers for your class will review the proposal and provide you with feedback. Once it is approved, you can start to work on it. There will be a Senior Project Showcase sometime during the academic year for you to show off your work.

Reading this document, you might ask: do we really need more rules than this?

Fed-Hock senior teachers serve as project advisors for the kids, and they are assisted by a "coach" (another faculty member) and a "community resource person," an adult mentor whom students recruit from the community. Typically, these mentors work in the field being investigated by the students. As the guidelines suggest, the kids are free to base their senior projects on a wide range of meaningful activities. Here are some recent FHHS project topics:

Learning about Alzheimer's Disease and Volunteering at a Nursing Home

Collecting a Set of Folk Songs for Use in History Classes

Building and Paddling a Cedar Strip Kayak

Teaching Art Lessons to Kids at the Public Library

Making a Video Yearbook for the School

Training a Seeing-Eye Dog

Rebuilding an Antique Farm Tractor

Making Baby Blankets for the Regional Hospital

Building a New Outhouse for Grandparents

Organizing and Teaching Volleyball Clinics for Younger Kids

Hiking and Photographing the Appalachian Trail for a Week

Raising Funds to Fence and Improve the Softball Field

In one especially noteworthy project from last year, Mason Pesek developed a whole curriculum on United States foreign policy for the school's social studies teachers. His mentor was a history professor at nearby Ohio University and his coach was Principal George Wood. Mason is now continuing his studies as a freshman at Harvard University.

See Lesson 27, "Response Options: Take Learning Public," p. 142.

Though Fed-Hock originally defined the senior projects as solo undertakings, more and more kids are now working together. Two groups of boys have hiked wilderness sections of the Appalachian Trail, which passes not far from the school, documenting their adventures and learnings along the way. Last year four boys made the trek, which involved much more than just a six-day hike. They had to carefully plan the path of the trip using paper and Web maps; study the ecosystem; plot out food and menus; figure out where drinkable water could be found; research the animals they might encounter (including bears) and how to interact with them; and more. Each senior had outlined in his original proposal specific and separate tasks that he would do: one would shoot videos of the trek, another

Brant Day with his rebuilt Allis Chalmers tractor.

would photograph, another would keep a daily journal. When the boys returned, exhausted from their great adventure (hungry and with very stinky feet, their families reported), they went to work on a joint presentation for Senior Project Day.

Early this year, Cristina and Briana noticed that their advisor, math teacher Sue Collins, had adopted a new "healthy lifestyle." One day in the cafeteria, they sidled up and asked how she was doing it. Sue talked about diet and exercise and calories and the girls were hooked. Yes, they wanted to lose some weight for the prom later in the year, but they also sincerely wanted to make permanent changes in their lives. This would make a perfect senior project. The girls set individual goals in writing their proposals but also did numerous activities together: getting their body mass index calculated, grocery shopping for healthy foods, and going to exercise classes together. As this book goes to press, the school year is half over, the girls are working diligently, and the prom is drawing near.

GROWING BETTER
INQUIRY GROUPS

Assessment and Evaluation

We started this book with four stories about kids working in inquiry teams to better understand garbage, prejudice, a crumbling school, and the conflict between settlers and native peoples in America. Now, as we turn to assessing kids' work in inquiry circles, we want to share one more story.

Daniel and Devin were members of the careers inquiry group in Joyce Sanchez's sixth-grade class, recounted back in Chapter 11. Both boys were initially interested in possible scientific careers—chemistry for Devin and neuroscience for Daniel. But then, during their in-class "Reading Frenzy," they came upon that famous picture of Albert Einstein with his tongue hanging out—and a huge nuclear explosion in the background. The guys were hooked—kaboom—and ended up conducting a six-week study of atomic weapons.

The boys' topic choice was not surprising, since their New Mexico school sits just thirty-five miles from Los Alamos National Laboratory, where the bombs dropped on Japan were designed and built. Daniel and Devin began with a mainly prurient interest in the topic; it was all about the blowing up. At the outset of their research, the boys proposed to demonstrate a nuclear blast in the classroom by smashing some ants with a big rock.

At first, Daniel and Devin focused on the mechanics of how atomic bombs work, and amassed a huge amount of technical information on Fat Man and Little Boy. They dug into scientific detail about two different detonation systems the designers used to make sure that at least one bomb would explode as planned. They learned about the series of outcomes from a nuclear blast: heat wave, pressure wave, and radiation. But after watching a History Channel video of the aftermath of Hiroshima, the boys' approach dramatically shifted; they moved away from big bangs and on to the human consequences, and the moral dimension of nuclear weapons.

As a next step they contacted, invited, and skillfully interviewed a veteran nuclear physicist from the lab. Dr. Robert Eisenstein captivated the whole class with his approachable manner and informative drawings. When the boys asked about Hiroshima, the physicist gave a strong endorsement of the atomic bombings

Daniel, Devin, and Albert E. Einstein.

as necessary to end the war and save American lives by avoiding an invasion of the Japanese mainland.

But then Daniel and Devin discovered a document that blew the lid off their inquiry: a visitor-comment journal kept in a corner of the Los Alamos Laboratory's public museum. Several writers in the guest book claimed that Japan had actually offered to surrender to the United States two months before the bombs were dropped. One said that Secretary of War James Stinson had intentionally cajoled President Truman to prolong the battle until his "secret" was ready to be tried out. Another visitor wrote that the bombs were dropped not as a military tactic, but as a warning to Josef Stalin, who was busily marching through Asia, taking over Japan's former colonies. A couple from Japan wrote that the bombs were dropped solely to see whether they worked on humans: "We were just perfect test material at the time," they wrote. Still another entry pointed out that Generals Dwight Eisenhower and Douglas MacArthur both advised President Truman not to drop the bomb; that using it would not shorten the war or save one American soldier.

What? Daniel and Devin had navigated to a place that schools usually avoid: Uncharted Territory. All those people writing in the guest book couldn't be right about the atomic bombings of Japan, could they? Every one of them contradicted what most Americans are taught in school: that the United States used nuclear weapons to avoid a costly, bloody land invasion of Japan.

The boys were now stuck. They'd been sobered by the pictures of the survivors and victims of U.S. nuclear attacks—but had also been told it was the right thing to do, virtually an unavoidable choice for the United States.

Embracing Uncharted Territory

Daniel and Devin's unexpected outcomes in their study of atomic weapons give us food for thought as teacher-planners. One of our own favorite expressions is "teaching with the end in mind," meaning that we always try to know what kids will learn before we launch them on a lesson or inquiry. But at the same time, there is a tension between having valid instructional goals and leaving space for authentic discovery. In our world of standards and benchmarks, it seems like teachers must *always* know what kids will know at the end of a lesson or unit. But consider this: do real researchers, investigators, and authors know exactly where they are going when they begin an inquiry? Hmm, maybe not. After all, what would be the point?

We need to be careful that we are not sponsoring "pretend" or "as-if" inquiry—like having kids "investigate" topics until they have found out the four things we knew they would encounter and filled in the four boxes we prepared in advance. This might be called information gathering, but it sure isn't research or inquiry. If we want curiosity and passion and actual inquiry, there must be times when kids go into uncharted territory, where we don't know exactly what they are going to come back with. We have always admired Bob Probst's challenge to teachers: at least once a year, read a book that you have never read before, right along with your class. Then, they can actually watch you *thinking* about it for the very first time—making predictions, forming hypotheses, reacting and revising, developing inferences, and more—instead of reciting your interpretation of *Catcher in the Rye* for the twenty-eighth year. Wow. In the same way, it is vital (and challenging and rigorous) that kids set off on inquiries where neither we nor they know the ultimate outcome. This is real inquiry, not as-if research.

Daniel and Devin continued digging, trying to assess these different claims. Eisenhower and MacArthur's opposition to the bombings was quickly confirmed. Other results were mixed and perplexing. Some sources seemed reputable and authoritative, while others were linked to websites with crazy, revisionist interpretations of settled historical facts. The Japanese surrender offer was well documented, but it was not clear whether it had reached high enough levels of the U.S. government to be taken seriously. Finally, with the school year running out, the boys needed to pull together what they now understood—and to list the new questions that lingered and loomed.

Daniel and Devin decided that, taking everything into account, the United States should not have dropped the atomic bombs in World War II, and should never use them in the future. They expressed concern about the proliferation of these weapons around the world and wondered, "If America would use atomic bombs, why wouldn't any of these other countries use them, too?" They held a symposium for the class; the boys fielded an array of questions, and the discussion was a thoughtful, sober one. There was no smashing of ants with rocks.

As a final product, Daniel and Devin created a written project and led an engaging classroom discussion. But the boys did not change the world, their community, or their school. Other groups in Ms. Sanchez's room initiated ambitious public-service projects that are continuing today. Other inquiry circles left behind more impressive physical artifacts. But what Daniel and Devin did spectacularly well was *think*. They ended their inquiry with a far more nuanced and thoughtful view of their chosen topic than when they started. They deepened their understanding by undertaking a wide and searching investigation. The main outcome of this particular inquiry circle was *internal;* the boys changed themselves.

Just a few weeks later, Daniel happened to be accepted into a special summer program at a pricey local prep school that was designed to help disadvantaged kids finish high school and get into college. The first topic the summer class took up was—guess what?—nuclear weapons. Daniel dazzled the teachers with his depth of knowledge, quickly became a leader, and reported back to his sixth-grade teacher, Joyce, "I knew exactly what to do."

We'd argue that Daniel and Devin are well on their way to becoming literate, thoughtful, and resourceful citizens of a democracy.

Oh, and by the way, how do we *grade* work like this?

Assessment Versus Evaluation

In this chapter, we are going to be very practical about assessing *and* evaluating kids' work in inquiry circles. We will talk about points and grades, rubrics and accountability, conferences and performances, record keeping and observations. But first, some key distinctions.

There is a huge difference between assessment and grading. Assessment is something we do all day, every day, 180 days a year. Grading is something we do once in a while. In the olden days of teaching, we had it backward. We would grade, grade, grade, and fill that black book with marks, but rarely assess. Now, we work in a constant assess-teach-assess-teach-assess cycle all day long. We use everything we can learn about kids *formatively,* to shape our instruction, moment by moment. And occasionally, we shift into a different activity called evaluation, where we use information about kids *summatively,* not to enhance instruction but to report to someone outside the classroom. Nowadays, we have dropped that old pop quiz–gotcha game, trying to catch kids unawares and unprepared. Instead, we give students plenty of practice and guidance, so that when grading occurs, we catch kids at their best, with the highest likelihood of success. We grade the learning, not the knowing.

Assessment

Assessment fills us in on what our kids are doing. However, it also tells us how effective our instruction has been. When we reflect on evidence of their learning and understanding, we revise and reshape our subsequent instruction. Authentic assessment provides us with three very important pieces of information:

- *Our students' learning and progress.* By looking carefully at our kids' work and listening to their words and thoughts, we derive an authentic understanding of how they are doing and what they have or have not learned.

- *Past instruction.* What kids learn depends on how well we have taught. If kids are not learning, we need to rethink our instruction and change course accordingly. If most of the class doesn't get a lesson, that failure is our responsibility. If 25 percent of the class doesn't get it, it is still our responsibility. And frankly, if one kid doesn't get it, helping that student remains our responsibility. Teaching the same lesson over and over again is not the solution, because that didn't work in the first place. We need to redesign our lessons, keeping in mind what we have learned from our kids and letting that information guide our instruction.

- *Future instruction.* Responsive teaching and assessment go hand in hand. Based on what we see in students' work—the evidence of their understanding—we design subsequent instruction tailored to what they need. We plan our next steps based on what we notice in their work that needs attention and elaboration. Kids all have different needs. Some are quickly ready for independent practice. Others need more time, support, and guided practice. We may convene a small group or we may confer individually, depending on the need (Harvey and Goudvis 2007).

Evaluation

Evaluation, on the other hand, is about putting a value—a grade—on the work. And thoughtful work that demonstrates understanding is much harder to grade than a fill-in-the-blank-worksheet. So how do we grade these inquiry projects?

There is no need to grade students on what they know when they walk in the door. We want to grade them on what they learn from our teaching and their investigating. When we give students grades to evaluate them, we make sure the grades are based on evidence gleaned from ongoing and authentic assessment. This is how assessment informs evaluation. When we assess our kids' progress, we look for a demonstration of understanding.

Work samples, student talk, performances, and artifacts are the evidence we use to assess kids' learning. Grades are all about evaluating what kids have learned through practice. We evaluate and give grades only after students have had time to internalize the strategies and skills we have taught. We base our grades on a substantial body of evidence that stands as proof of kids' learning.

Daily Grading

Regurgitating answers to end-of-chapter questions does not give us enough evidence to accurately evaluate what kids know and what they have learned. Likewise for fill-in-the-blank worksheets and literal comprehension questions. Grading a stack of worksheets or packets doesn't provide us with information about authentic learning. So we look at constructed and more open-ended

responses that require kids to show us their thinking and learning. This day-to-day evidence comes in the form of kids' Post-its, thinksheets, short and longer summary responses, notes from discussions, thoughtful illustrations, journal and notebook entries, and so on.

We constantly check what kids are doing against what we have taught them and the outcomes we hope to achieve. We review and save work that demonstrates understanding as well as work that doesn't, and we design instruction accordingly. After students have had plenty of practice and we have collected a good deal of their work, we grade them, holding them accountable for what they have learned. Much of our grading is done using rubrics that directly correspond with and measure what we have taught. But we also evaluate kids on the content, because if we take time to teach thinking and collaborating, kids *should* learn, understand, and remember the material better than ever before. Our content "quizzes" are not fill-in-the-blank, however; we ask kids to write, talk about, or perform their learning in a way that shows they understand. So in the end, we evaluate students to measure their learning, to "grade" their understanding, and to satisfy the norms of school and society.

*A*ssessing Thinking and Understanding

The only way we can accurately assess our students' understanding is when they share their thinking with us. Learners reveal their comprehension by responding to what they read, hear, or view. Personal responses give us a window into students' minds. When we listen to kids, ask them questions, and watch them closely, we learn not only what they understand but also what they don't. We can then design instruction that is responsive to what they need to learn.

We find out whether kids understand what they are learning in the following ways:

- *We listen to kids.* We can't stress enough how much we learn about kids' reading and thinking by simply listening closely to what they say. If we listen, they will talk. Sometimes kids say, "I'm inferring" or "I wonder." However, using the language isn't enough. We probe to find the substance underlying their statements.

- *We read kids' work.* We read their responses closely, looking for evidence that kids are constructing meaning, then use these responses to design future instruction.

- *We confer with kids.* Individual conferences provide an ideal opportunity to talk one-on-one with students and help them sort out their thinking as well as come to a deeper understanding. Sometimes, all you have to do to discover what kids are thinking is to ask. Those natural talkers are only too happy to fill you in on their thinking, and the more reticent kids may surprise you and open up, too.

- *We listen in on conversations.* Even though we were both taught that eavesdropping is rude, we know that it's invaluable when trying to find out what kids are thinking. Listening in on conversations kids have during an inquiry project is a surefire way to get at their honest thinking.

- *We observe behavior and expressions.* A scrunched-up nose, a raised eyebrow, or a quizzical look lets us know what a student is thinking, so we watch kids' expressions carefully.

- *We chart responses.* We record what kids say in class discussions on charts. This holds their thinking and makes it visible and public. Students can refer to the charts during discussions or use them as guides for future investigations.

- *We use the available technology* to track and document kids' thinking. Electronic portfolios, videos, printouts of class blogs or threaded discussions, and saved PowerPoints give us rich information about what kids are learning, thinking, and creating.

- *We keep anecdotal records of conferences and conversations.* In classrooms where we work, teachers keep track of student thinking by taking notes on interactions they have with kids and reviewing them regularly. Many teachers have three-ring binders with a tab for each student. Behind the tabs, teachers mark the date and record notes about each student's reading, writing, and thinking.

- *We script what kids say,* recording their thoughts and questions. Teachers we work with move about the classroom with clipboards, keeping track of kids' comments by scripting student talk. After school, teachers reflect on their notes to determine whether students are making meaning and building knowledge (Harvey and Goudvis 2007).

*I*ndividual Accountability: The Key to Small-Group Assessment

Recently in Albuquerque, Smokey sat down with twenty-four brand-new high school graduates and asked them to look back on their experience with small-group projects. "I hated it!" Alicia blurted out instantaneously. "Wow," Smokey said, "that was quick. So what was the trouble?" "I always did all the work," she replied. "There were kids in my group who didn't care about their grades. Well, I wanted an *A,* so I had to do the work for everybody. It made me mad." Bobby chimed in with a smile:

Kids show what they know

"Well, I always tried to get into groups with smart kids like you, so I didn't have to do any work," he confessed, earning a low-five from the boy next to him.

What Smokey learned from talking to these kids (and thousands of others in the past) is that *they've never experienced well-structured collaborative learning.* Oh, they've been placed in small groups plenty of times, but without the social skills and tools needed to succeed. Then pile on inappropriate, self-undermining assessment practices, and the door opens to all kinds of mischief and dissatisfaction.

Let's boil it down. The number one small-group problem most American kids have encountered is a *lack of individual accountability.* If you set up a group where everyone gets the same grade regardless of their contribution, it will probably fail, especially with kids who have long been socialized to function in a solitary, competitive mode. In the absence of any contrary training or structures, you can pretty much expect low morale and lower-quality work. But this collaborative learning pitfall can easily be avoided. We simply have to teach and assess kids with individual accountability in mind, all the time.

ENSURING INDIVIDUAL ACCOUNTABILITY IN SMALL GROUPS

1. **Define the concept first.** Explain what individual accountability means right from the start. Even though we may set group goals (e.g., learning about animal extinction), group success means that *each member of the group meets that goal.* It is not enough to have "pooled" some learning among the members; each person must have built knowledge and achieved a full understanding.

2. **Keep the group size small.** It is much easier to establish and maintain genuine individual responsibilities in a group of three or four rather than eight. The more people, the more overlap, the more vagueness, and the harder it is to track who is supposed to be doing what. If lots of kids want to do the same topic, split them up. It is far better to create lots of small groups with high internal social pressure than to have a few big groups with no natural defenses against kids hiding, sleeping, or riding on the coattails of others.

See Lesson 14, "Making and Using a Work Plan," p. 129, and Lesson 17, "Midcourse Corrections: Reflecting and Replanning," p. 132.

3. **Use written work plans and checkpoints.** Groups must specify in advance what each member is responsible for. Have kids clearly list as well as explain verbally what each person will be doing. Then, as the inquiry project unfolds, refer to this document as you observe and talk to groups and individuals. You may also build formal checkpoints into the schedule, official days when you will confer with kids about their progress. Require that individuals bring "visible evidence" of their work; it is *not* enough to just "talk about what you have been doing."

4. **Make grading standards crystal clear.** Once the shape of projects is established, co-create with students an assessment rubric that explicitly lays out how both groups and individuals will be evaluated. If you decide to award points at stages along the way, make sure these tasks involve *thinking* (e.g., being able to contrast the points of view in three different articles) and not merely mechanical compliance (having two hundred index cards by January 12).

5. **Observe group meetings.** When you sit down with a group, you can randomly ask members to explain a key concept or recent finding. Or you can remain quiet and use a simple chart to tally kids' participation and write down memorable quotes during the work session. If participation is asymmetrical (some people slacking, others doing more than their share), this will usually be evident. After your observation, hand your notes over to the students and ask them to discuss ways to equalize effort and airtime. Check back shortly to hear their plans. (You may also make a copy of your observations for use in grading later on.)

6. **Have checkup conferences with individual kids.** During these one-to-one meetings, you may:

    • Ask general questions about how the student is progressing toward his or her original goals, using the written work plan as a basis.

- Have a conversation about the subject matter the student is investigating.

- Ask the student to select an article or source that has proven to be valuable, show you his or her notes or annotations about it, and explain how this resource fits into the broader inquiry.

Don't exhaust yourself trying to schedule too many private conferences; they are inevitably time-consuming, and often you can get equally good information by observing and talking in the groups.

7. **Have "commitment ceremonies."** Save five minutes at the end of every inquiry circle work session. Ask each kid to jot down of exactly what he or she will do to prepare for the next meeting (dig up a contrasting article, prepare a chart, interview someone). Then have kids read this aloud to their small group—or gather the whole class and have some (or all) kids report on their task lists.

8. **What about individual roles?** The literature on collaborative learning recommends assigning kids specific roles or tasks. These might be based on the actual jobs a given group will perform or can draw upon kids' special talents. Thus students might take on roles like Web Wizard, Data Displayer, Number Cruncher, Interviewer, Materials Librarian, Model Maker, or Illustrator. To be honest, we've had mixed results with this strategy. Those attractive-sounding jobs can have pitfalls, as some users of old literature circle role sheets well remember. Roles tend to get stale quickly and may create a mechanical attitude among kids. They often segment the work too narrowly, allowing kids to take an "It's not my job" stance. Some commonly used roles like Encourager and Motivator have no tangible outcomes, and thus are useless for accountability. Finally, roles like Manager and Director explicitly encourage most kids to lay back and wait for the "boss" to get things rolling. Use with care, if at all.

9. **If all of that doesn't work**. Some other strategies may help in certain situations:

- Have an individual student teach what he/she has learned to some other kids not in the same group.

- Give individual tests.

- Assign individual written work along the way (critique an article, take a point of view, explain a chart).

- Have kids bring in individual work, then collect and review it before groups meet.

- Have kids use their individual learning to do a separate task, after a group meeting.

- Let peers evaluate each other's individual contributions to the group's overall success, in writing or via verbal feedback.

- Have kids fill out a short daily form reflecting on their personal learning, progress, and participation.

These last few strategies (especially taking tests and writing reports) are pretty old-school, and may take the edge off the freshness and engagement that inquiry circles provide. Use these more traditional accountability measures sparingly and monitor closely for negative side effects.

Grading Inquiry Circles with Performance Assessment Rubrics

For many years, we have been big fans of performance assessment, and you can see our advocacy for it stranded throughout our previous work. Instead of giving kids low-level, factual recall questions on a timed paper-and-pencil quiz, we access our learners' very best thinking by inviting them to undertake complex, thoughtful performances of valuable learning: engaging in a wide-ranging public debate, creating and displaying a science experiment, writing a letter to the editor, making posters that teach and hanging them in the halls, building a model of a historic building, creating a Web page with multiple texts, writing an extended essay that argues both sides of an issue. And as we lead kids toward these "power tests," we explicitly define the ingredients of a successful performance. We don't leave them to guess what good work looks like; we show them examples and explain exactly what quality means. When we tell kids that *voice* is one key ingredient of excellent written language, and then model it ourselves, define it, and show multiple examples, we are making assessment a part of instruction. Later, we use those same explicit criteria to assess kids' final activities, performances, or products. Take that, SAT!

Today, performance assessment is on a roll. It may well help replace those crude standardized tests that have yielded so much misinformation and distorted school policy for so many years. In the first major education policy speech of his presidency, President Obama called upon the nation's governors and state education chiefs to "develop standards and assessments that don't simply measure whether students can fill in bubble on a test, but whether they possess 21st century skills like problem-solving and critical thinking and enterpreneurship and creativity." So we are very excited to see complex inquiries and their associated performances become part of the official school scene. Indeed, one reason we wrote this book was to provide lessons and structures for teachers leading students through just such projects.

But we also have some cautions. (Again, don't get us wrong, we strongly favor teacher- and student-developed performance assessment rubrics, and we use them in our own teaching every day.) The first problem: in designing state versions of performance assessments, adults sometimes get so worried about meeting countless standards and perseverate so deeply about "student accountability" that the result is counterproductive. They infuse so many hoops, controls, and requirements into these projects that all the energy for kids is driven out.

Some states are now trying to figure out a way to "moderate" locally developed performance assessments, usually by having teachers from some distant school "rescore" your kids' work. This is the mother of all slippery slopes. When we try to convert teacher-made rubrics into public accountability assessments, and insist upon scoring reliability across many schools (AKA: standardization),

*P*erformance assessment may well replace the old bubble and blank tests.

the whole game changes. Performance assessments can become just as tyrannical, arbitrary, and lifeless as any standardized test, if they aren't used properly.

Second, we worry about any educational initiative that focuses too heavily at the accountability end of education—on grading, ranking, and scoring kids. (Arguably, we teachers are already too comfortable with our role as judges of children; it's a tendency that deserves vigilant self-criticism.) In our experience, every reform project that "starts" with evaluation, *ends* with evaluation, and instruction rarely changes. That's really no surprise. How are kids supposed to perform better or differently in some area of knowledge if the grown-ups focus only on the rubrics and matrices that will be used to score them—but never teach them how to think and act differently? To use the tired proverb: you can hang all the thermometers you want on the porch, but it won't change the temperature. Let's not allow this overenthusiasm for measurement repeat itself with the performance assessment movement.

The third problem with official performance assessments is that most of these are tied to individual rather than collaborative efforts. Everyone automatically assumes that any high-stakes or graduation-linked activity must be a solitary one. But why? As much as we honor individual achievement, joint action is vital, too. American schools already do plenty to reinforce the competitive, individualistic, winner-loser value system. We should not miss this natural opportunity for kids to practice the number one skill employers say they want: teamwork!

Finally, we are concerned about reification. *(Reify* is such a cool word, it's a shame hardly anyone ever uses it. It basically means making something real that isn't.) Sometimes we reify our rubrics. Teachers work very hard to create these gorgeously complex scoring guides. (Sometimes they become intricate matrices that look almost like an Escher etching.) Maya Wilson has shown how rubrics can become reductionistic (2006). The more complex you make them, the less likely they are to capture real strengths and the more likely to become a checklist of mechanical subskills. We spoke earlier in the book about states like Rhode Island and Iowa, where schools are pioneering the use of complex performances instead of machine-scored multiple-choice tests. And yet when we look at the scoring guides developed for these mandated performances, they are so infused with layers of requirements, it's hard to imagine how they actually reward a good performance— or allow kids to sustain any enthusiasm for the work.

On the surface, it seems like a good idea to get increasingly complex with scoring guides, creating a matrix with dozens of boxes to score, point totals to add up. The process feels deeper and more sophisticated. But often, the more elaborate these tools get, the more unreliable they become. We've all seen the kind of rubric that claims infinitesimal and essentially meaningless shades of difference (1 point = rarely brings materials; 2 points = somewhat consistently

*W*e should not miss this natural opportunity for kids to practice the number one skill employers say they want: teamwork!

brings materials; 3 points = fairly consistently brings materials; 4 points = consistently brings materials; 5 points = always brings materials). Just because you can develop criteria like these doesn't mean they are significant.

Creating Rubrics

When we use rubrics to grade inquiry circle work, we keep them simple, clear, and focused on kids. As students engage in the inquiry process, we recognize it for what it is, a process. So we evaluate kids' inquiries all along the way, not merely at the end. Too often, the kids who create a great poster or give a compelling live performance are the ones who hit it out of the park in the grade department, even though they might not have been so cooperative when working together or were organizational nightmares when it came to taking notes and synthesizing information. Or we have the kids who worked hard and stayed on task the entire time, but whose final project just doesn't click. These in-depth inquiry projects are really too extensive to receive one grade at the very end.

Fifth-grade teacher Mary Pfau saw this early on as her kids moved through research projects. "Look at all they have to do," Mary shared with Steph. "Come up with researchable questions, read for information and respond to it, organize thinking, synthesize the information, share their learning, maybe take action and work together cooperatively to make it all happen! Grading the final project alone couldn't possibly reflect all of the hard work and thoughtful learning that goes on throughout their inquiries."

And of course, Mary hit on something. Traditionally, the final project grade evaluates only the final phase of the project, without even considering all of the ongoing work and learning that occurs when we teach kids to think, collaborate, and inquire. Grading these extended inquiries needs to be a sustained effort that includes an ongoing evaluation of the interim phases and outcomes as well as the final product. And, as we've stressed throughout, our evaluation system must maintain individual, as well as group, accountability all along the way.

So we stop and evaluate at each phase of the inquiry process: *immersion, investigation, coalescing,* and *going public.* Thus, with every inquiry project we have at least these four grades; we come up with an overall grade by averaging the four grades together. We might lend more weight to one phase over another depending on our preference and, most importantly, our kids' needs. In this way, we really grade what we taught across the entire time period as well as what kids needed and learned throughout the process. And when kids are engaged in a mini-inquiry where they spend only a day or two finding and sharing information, the rubric might have only two categories and thus two grades to average together.

The sample rubrics that follow on page 281 are based on the inquiry model introduced in Chapter 4 and can be adapted to each of the inquiry types we describe in this book. Yours will likely vary depending on your instruction and your students' needs, so as you consider these sample rubrics, keep in mind how you might adapt them. The point totals we have shown are just illustrative—you and your class may make other, finer distinctions. As we have said earlier, we worry when rubrics get so complex and "scientific" that they distort real-life activities.

The best way to use rubrics is to co-create them with your students. In a whole-class session, brainstorm to identify a few (two or three) key skills for each phase of an inquiry. Then build these into a rubric that everyone can understand and support. Let kids define what will count as evidence and what point totals should be attached to each item. Then, when the phase of research is completed, have kids score themselves using the class-created rubric. You can either review these ratings, create your own, or have individual grading conferences where you discuss and reconcile perceptions.

www.heinemann.com/
comprehensionandcollaboration.

For more assessment tools and rubrics from a variety of schools and grade levels, see the website.

Inquiry Circles Rubric: Phase 1 *Immersion: Invite Curiosity, Build Background, Find Topics, and Wonder*

Name:_____ Date: _____ Topic: _____

Traits	Evidence	Score 1–4*
Interacts with a variety of media to explore, learn, and wonder about topics		
Responds to text by jotting or drawing questions, connections, and reactions		
Works productively with teams to set schedules, ground rules, and goals		

*4 = distinguished, 3 = excellent, 2 = good, 1 = still developing

Inquiry Circles Rubric: Phase 2 *Investigate: Develop Questions, Search for Information, and Discover Answers*

Traits	Evidence	Score 1–4*
Listens, talks, views, and reads to gain information		
Develops questions and reads, listens, and views to answer them		
Works productively with teams to monitor schedules and task completion		

*4 = distinguished, 3 = excellent, 2 = good, 1 = still developing

Inquiry Circles Rubric: Phase 3 *Coalesce: Intensify Research, Synthesize Information, and Build Knowledge*

Traits	Evidence	Score 1 4*
Engages in deeper reading and researching: books, articles, websites, videos, library visits		
Checks sources and determines reliability		
Synthesizes information to build knowledge		
Works productively with teams to monitor task completion and plan sharing		

*4 = distinguished, 3 = excellent, 2 = good, 1 = still developing

Inquiry Circles Rubric: Phase 4 *Go Public: Share Learning and Demonstrate Understanding*

Traits	Evidence	Score 1–4*
Demonstrates learning and understanding in a variety of ways: posters, models, persuasive letters, editorials, magazines, picture books, tableaux, and so on		
Reflects upon and articulates the learning process		
Reflects upon and articulates the cooperative process		

*4 = distinguished, 3 = excellent, 2 = good, 1 = still developing

13

Management Q&A

In the water-rich and wooded states of Minnesota and Wisconsin where the two of us grew up, an annual ritual was the traveling carnival that rolled into town for a week or so each summer. After the Ferris wheel, the roller coaster, and the Tilt-a-Whirl, it was a gallery game called Whack-a-Mole that captured both of us.

For those of you who missed Whack-a-Mole in the Coney Islands of your youth, it is a game like no other. The Whack-a-Mole table resembles a large pinball machine minus the glass top. A dozen holes about four inches in diameter and three inches apart cover the table. When play begins, puppetlike creatures remotely resembling prairie dogs pop up helter-skelter out of the holes in the table. A single player with a mallet hits these stuffed animals on the head as fast as possible to keep them below the table surface. Wacky for sure! Sound easy? It's not. Just when you strike one, two more pop up. Isn't classroom management a bit like that? Just when you think you have one mole under control, up pops another! It's enough to drive you crazy.

The Q&A section of this book is primarily focused on how to keep your sanity intact as you lead your kids through inquiry circles. Seriously, there are a few things we can do as teachers to help our inquiry circles roll along smoothly. First and foremost is engagement—the best medicine for management. When kids are engaged, issues of management all but disappear. And inquiry circles by their very nature are highly engaging because it is the kids' thoughts and questions that matter. So you may be surprised to find that when you engage your kids in inquiry circles, management concerns often slide to the back burner. However, some issues will almost certainly arise, as they do whenever kids (or adults) try something a little new and different. We address some common concerns about management, organization, schedules, and time here.

*H*ow Do These Four Types of Inquiry Fit Together?

Our basic inquiry framework derives from a number of long-standing models of inquiry we discussed in Chapter 4. What is a bit different is how we have adapted that framework to four different types of inquiry in schools: mini-inquiry, curricular inquiry, literature circle inquiry, and open inquiry. Since it may not be immediately apparent how these can fit seamlessly into your classroom, here are some suggestions.

Many teachers begin with mini-inquiry. The purposes of these small, quick inquiries are really twofold. Most important, they provide a means for kids to answer their ongoing questions regularly and quickly. But they also give teachers the opportunity to teach some useful comprehension, collaboration, and inquiry strategies, thereby giving kids the necessary research tools for more in-depth inquiry later on. So we often begin teaching about the inquiry process with these mini-inquiry projects. You could call this the Gradual Release of Responsibility for inquiry circles. And of course, mini-research continues all year as kids ask and answer their Quick Find questions.

Often teachers move next to curricular inquiry circles, because most districts require some sort of grade-level curricular project, and adapting the curricular inquiry model to required subject matter is a natural. Teachers whose students already participate in book clubs may find literature circle inquiries to be an appealing alternative to traditional and superficial postbook projects. Lingering questions and potential inquiry topics abound when kids finish reading and talking about their books.

While we probably love the fourth type, open inquiry circles, the most, they seem to occur the least frequently. When we engage our kids in open inquiry circles, there is no denying that their questions matter. These inquiries emerge solely from kids' need to know. Sometimes, teachers save these for the spring of the year, when their curricular inquiries are completed or they have already engaged kids in lit circle inquiries. Some teachers tell us that their kids have learned the process so well by year's end that they really soar with open inquiry circles. Other teachers say that they like to *start* the year with open inquiry circles, because when kids can choose any topic or question under the sun, they almost always pick subjects they know about, wonder about, and care about. Teachers get to know their kids early and discover their interests and quirks from the start. Even though topics may vary wildly, however, we always find that we can easily teach many of the language arts standards through open inquiry. And of course, all of the inquiry adaptations in the book are framed around the original inquiry structure (pages 61–62 in Chapter 4).

Often teachers move next to curricular inquiry circles, because most districts require some sort of grade-level curricular project, and adapting the curricular inquiry model to required subject matter is a natural.

As you can see, there is no right or wrong way to engage kids in inquiry circles. When you take a crack at these, you will begin to see what instructional path works best for you and your kids. But regardless, we are convinced you will agree that any form of inquiry is far superior to the conventional alternatives.

How Do You Schedule Inquiry Circles?

As you might imagine, there is a schedule for every teacher and a teacher for every schedule. After introducing some mini-research strategies, some teachers we know choose to do three inquiry circles a year—one curricular, one lit circle inquiry, and one open inquiry circle. These frequently lay out seasonally, one in the fall, one in the winter, and one in the spring. Others may do an inquiry circle with every curricular unit. The teachers at Burley School, a Chicago public school that has made a whole-hearted commitment to inquiry-based learning, guide kids through six inquiry projects each year at every grade level. What kid wouldn't want to go to that school?!

The inquiry projects in this book vary considerably in length. Mini-inquiry aside, the other three forms of inquiry circles described here took anywhere from a week to two months. In departmentalized middle and high schools, teachers often devoted between five and twenty class periods to a cycle of inquiry circles. In elementary schools, the average inquiry project took about two to four weeks, with the class and teacher focused on them for an hour or so a day. Some teachers, particularly those for whom lit circles were an ongoing practice, used their literacy block to have kids read, write, talk, listen, and investigate in inquiry circles.

Other elementary teachers used their science, social studies, or math time for engaging in curricular inquiry. What better way to spend that time than having kids read, write, research, and talk about the content? Content area teachers typically might conduct a fifteen-minute mini-lesson related to the larger concepts and focus questions in the district curricular standards, then set kids free to work together in their inquiry circles. As the teacher moves around the room and works with different small groups, she makes a point of helping kids see the connections between their inquiry circle discoveries and the overarching curricular concepts. The period often ends with a whole class share.

Elementary teachers often find that kids in self-contained classrooms choose to work on their projects whenever possible during independent work times throughout the day, whether their inquiries stem from science, social studies, math, or language arts. And secondary teachers notice that their kids come in raring to go every day, grabbing a friend and a spot at the computer, or hunkering down with a text that just might answer their question. While middle and high school teachers usually do not offer as much in-class work time as their colleagues in self-contained classrooms, their students use out-of-class and homework time to complete inquiry circle tasks.

Elementary teachers quickly found that kids in self-contained classrooms chose to work on their projects whenever possible during independent work times throughout the day, whether their inquiries stemmed from science, social studies, math, or language arts.

In addition to scheduling these inquiries across the year, we need to figure out daily schedules that support our kids' work in inquiry circles, but also leave room for everything else they need to do each day. Kids can make these plans collaboratively. We can provide them with a time allotment—say an hour a day for three weeks—and then facilitate a discussion about some parameters. We might suggest that they consider how much time to read and research, how and when to contact specialists, how and when to present the findings, and so on. Then we set them loose to work together and come up with a viable schedule that will allow their inquiry circle to complete its work within the time available.

Teachers we know have come up with a variety of ways to help kids manage time in their inquiry circles. We've talked earlier about using written work plans and calendars. Some teachers encourage kids to sign joint inquiry circle contracts to commit to a time horizon for project completion. Others hand out calendars with open squares where kids fill in their plans for the day each morning, set goals to complete one stage of a project over time, and then review their calendars to see if they are close to their predetermined schedule. Other teachers prefer logs where kids write their plan on the top and make daily entries to gauge how they are coming along in relation to their schedule. Many teachers we work with use a flexible three-column form with these headings—*Date/What I Did Today/What I Plan to Do Tomorrow*—and encourage kids to reflect on their progress at the end of each work period.

For some teachers, inquiry-based learning is a way of life that occurs every day, across the curriculum and throughout the year. These teachers weave in all four inquiry models and teach everything from a point of inquiry. They know that in many states you can hit most or all of the required standards by teaching with genuine inquiry. However you choose to implement inquiry circles, building in time to teach the reading, inquiry, and social strategies and then giving kids time to collaborate, read, and research will make all the difference.

See Lesson 14, "Making and Using a Work Plan," p. 129.

What Are the Other Kids Doing?

Any time kids are working in small groups, whether in inquiry circles or another collaborative format, teachers often wonder: when I sit down to work with one of the inquiry circles, how can I be sure good things are happening in the others? Great news here! No more hands waving in the air and shouts of "I'm done!" No more kids staring out the window, bored to death. Students do the bulk of the work in inquiry-based learning environments, so they have a lot to do. Inquiry circles are busy places. Conversations buzz. Information abounds. One question leads to another. In short, kids are working hard. What a concept! There is no need to keep them filled with busywork: worksheets, unrelated activities, and other contrived tasks that have no purpose or meaning. In inquiry-based learning, the important, thoughtful work is never done!

Following is a range of constructive and productive things kids can do collaboratively or independently while you are engaged with another group or conferring with an individual.

WHAT KIDS CAN DO DURING INQUIRY TIME

- **Read to themselves.** Nothing correlates more highly with reading achievement than reading volume. And reading provides the most direct route to finding information and answering questions. So just plain, independent reading is one of the most important things kids can do during inquiry circle time.

- **Read to each other.** Reading together with an inquiry circle partner or the entire inquiry circle can spur conversation and lead kids to discoveries they might not make when reading alone.

- **Conduct research online.** The Internet is often the quickest place to gain information. We encourage kids to keep their Internet evaluation strategies in mind when searching online (see Chapter 6). Also, it is often helpful for inquiry circle partners to work together at the computer.

- **Respond in writing and/or drawing.** Jotting and drawing thinking is especially useful when reading to find information and answer questions. Keeping track of thoughts and questions on Post-its, thinksheets, or in the margins helps kids clarify their understanding and synthesize information. We encourage kids to write and/or draw about their research, whether in books, online, watching a video, or scrutinizing an artifact.

- **Respond by talking.** Talking with one's inquiry circle or an inquiry circle partner goes a long way toward learning and understanding. However, you may need to remind kids about the need for quiet conversation and teach them the skill of using the "inside" or "twelve-inch" voice.

- **Develop interview questions and conduct practice interviews.** Kids can come up with some interview questions and practice interviewing with an inquiry circle partner.

- **Contact specialists and experts.** Kids can work with their inquiry circle partners to come up with a list of people they might want to contact to get more information. Kids can hunt through school for an on-campus specialist, or they can email, call, or write to an "outside" expert in the field.

- **Maintain your research notebook.** We remind kids to sort through their written and drawn responses and write up important findings in their notebooks so they don't lose track of them. Often these discoveries lead to more questions.

- **Plan to actively use knowledge and take action.** Kids can discuss how they plan to actively use the knowledge they have acquired. They might decide to simply share it with the class or they may be moved to take a more public advocacy position. They can talk with each other and then make a collaborative plan.

For further information about how to support kids, especially your younger ones, to work independently, check out *The Daily Five: Fostering Literacy Independence in the Elementary Grades* (Boushey and Moser 2006).

How Do I Help Kids Organize Their Materials and Responses?

One of our first jobs in the organization department is to help kids keep track of their work and the materials they collect. But what's the just-right tool? Our friends Debbie King and Michelle Trimble from Burley School say they have tried everything:

> Over the years we have tried out various tools to help keep our student researchers organized. We have used binders, crates, note cards, file folders, message centers. We exhausted the possibilities. But in the end, we looked to our writer's workshop for inspiration. We realized that the writer's notebook had all the components a researcher needed and more. Researchers need notebooks. It's that simple.

See Lesson 20, "Create Research Notebooks," p. 135.

We agree, and that's why our Lesson 20 (see p. 135) focused on getting kids started with researcher's notebooks. You have seen throughout this book how kids keep notebooks and folders for their inquiries. We have recommended that research notebooks be equipped with pockets on the inside flaps to hold collected materials. But now we can look a little deeper.

We have found that when kids keep all of their written responses in a notebook and all of their collected materials in a folder together with the notebook, they are far more likely to stay on top of their inquiry projects. In elementary grades, kids often refer to these inquiry notebooks as Wonder Books (Harvey 1998); older kids generally call them research or inquiry notebooks. Whatever the name, these books give kids a place to hold their thinking and responding as they engage in inquiry circles.

We model how we keep everything together in our own inquiry notebooks, which generally contain:

- questions and wonderings we want to pursue
- topics that matter to us
- project ideas
- schedules
- work plans
- Post-its that we jot while reading and researching and stick in notebooks after reading

- quotes from books, teachers, and other kids that relate to our inquiry

- notes related to our research

- syntheses of interesting or important information on our topic, including the source citation and page number; great for checking accuracy later

- bibliographic information

- drawings, diagrams, and doodles related to our inquiries

- clippings pasted in from newspapers, magazines, or Internet printouts

- related photographs, pictures, and illustrations

- notes from field research

- lists of specialists we know—people within as well as outside the school community who have expertise in our topic

- notes from interviews

- observation notes

- research findings

- presentation ideas

- action plans

- reflections on our process

*T*here is no greater wealth of resources than the members of the school community.

The accompanying folders hold all of our collected print materials, articles, maps, diagrams, the notebooks themselves—anything that is pertinent to the inquiry study. Our youngest learners have adapted these folders to their inquiry projects. While they don't always keep notebooks, they file everything in their "wonder folder." We use legal-size folders for primary kids rather than the standard size so kids can clip together their larger drawings and thinksheets and slip them in easily. Our elementary kids also love to keep what they call "wonder boxes"—plastic recipe boxes with 3 x 5 index cards where they list their questions alphabetically by topic. They can easily flip through the cards in the box, pull their questions, and search for the answers.

*H*ow Do I Get Community Resources to Support Inquiry-Based Learning?

To marshal community resources, we begin with the school itself. There is no greater wealth of resources than the members of the school community. Early in the year, all the staff members in the school are invited to write down their specialty—something they know a lot about, care a lot about, and would be willing to teach someone. Every child in the school is asked to do the same. We call these

AOS's—areas of specialty, and every school community member has at least one. These vary from dinosaurs to emergency medicine to quilting to cooking. The principal is responsible for collecting the AOS's and creating a chart of all of the members in the school community, their specialties, and their location in the school. This chart is distributed to every teacher, who then posts it in the classroom so kids can easily see who knows about what. When students are engaged in inquiry circles, the AOS chart is the first place they check to see whether anyone on their campus has knowledge about their particular inquiry. This is a terrific resource in elementary, middle, and high school. We are always stunned by the high degree of expertise we find among teachers in our schools and also among the kids.

www.heinemann.com/
comprehensionandcollaboration.

Additionally, we actively enlist people from the outside community to come and share their expertise. We co-create letters and forms with the kids for them to distribute to their families and friends in an effort to get more people with special expertise into the classroom. (See a sample letter on the website.) We also think hard about people we know who have expertise in a certain area and might be willing to share their knowledge with an inquiry circle. You will be surprised how many folks are just waiting for an invitation. Indeed, some organizations have student outreach as part of their official mission; think police and fire departments, museums, and environmental groups. No one has turned us down yet!

Finally, we co-construct a list of community institutions that are top-notch sources of expertise. These might include

- museums
- universities
- state legislatures
- hospitals
- military bases
- city hall
- restaurants

- libraries
- community colleges
- national and state parks
- courthouses
- chambers of commerce
- banks
- grocery and other retail stores

How Can We Introduce Inquiry Circles Throughout Our School? *How long will it take? What will be the benefits?*

We've run across plenty of schools that are on a schoolwide journey toward inquiry-based learning. As you already know, we particularly admire the story of Burley School in Chicago. Burley could be just another skill-and-drill factory, like too many city schools. But for more than a decade, the Burley faculty have gone in a different direction. Principal Barbara Kent and Assistant Principal Mary Beth Cunat share some of the journey:

Understanding at deep and sophisticated levels is the outcome of authentic, student-driven inquiry. These words are not just catchy phrases to us, but reflect beliefs of the professional learning community as we strive to improve our practice. The Burley story is one of incremental and purposeful moves toward building a school culture that values inquiry because it values deep understanding.

These days, on a walk-through at Burley School, you would find evidence of inquiry on the walls, in the halls, in student conversation, and in small groups of students working together. Students are engaged in mathematical investigations, reading independently, participating in literature conversations, writing to learn, and writing about their inquiries. Thinking and learning are framed by meaningful questions that take students deeply into text and content.

If you were visiting in April, you could see the whole school celebrate student inquiry with an event known as Explore More! Working individually and in groups, students pursue topics of choice or explore an area of the content curriculum in depth. Then, the school becomes one big children's museum, filled with performances, installations, multimedia exhibits, and interactive events. This amazing event shows everything we have come to value about student ownership of learning, collaboration, and inquiry. But it was not always this way. When we began our turnaround in 1996, we looked at our test data, and came to the horrifying conclusion that the longer a student stayed at Burley, the worse he/she performed on standardized tests. We were a failing school. Teachers were working hard, but everyone was "doing their own thing." There was a lack of coherence in curriculum and instruction, which, of course, led to major gaps in student learning. Teachers taught what they liked and avoided teaching what they didn't.

We recognized that what we were teaching in science and social studies was redundant, superficial, and cute. It wasn't meaningful. There were several units on seasons, holidays, or dinosaurs, but no depth. In addition, the curriculum didn't increase in complexity or rigor from one grade to the next. The best that could be said was that all students were completing mandatory science and history fair projects. Unfortunately, they were always the same. Everyone was bored with boards!

At that same time, we received an alarming phone call from a parent. This parent, also an educator, was extremely concerned when his third-grade child complained about having to learn about Martin Luther King Jr. "again"! A complaint of boredom about such an important and inspiring person in history was a redefining moment. Certainly, the teachers were increasingly aware of the limitations of the content curriculum, but having it expressed by students and parents created a sense of urgency and a commitment to change.

That summer, in our own collaborative inquiry, a core group of teachers examined content curricula from other districts, combed through content textbooks, and reviewed the Illinois Learning Standards. During our discussions, it became clear that teachers were feeling overwhelmed by the quantity of content coverage and underwhelmed by the quality. To address this, we looked at the entire scope of each content area, and determined a broad developmental and logical sequence for its delivery. Each grade then identified just three major themes for social studies and three for science. (See the website for complete listings.) This process of curricular narrowing, of going deeper in a smaller number of topics, was easier said than done. Veteran teachers had to give up beloved units and resources because their units didn't align with the content maps or adhere to the new expectations of rigor and meaningfulness.

www.heinemann.com/
comprehensionandcollaboration.

Once teachers began to narrow their focus, they were able to increase the depth of study. This structure created the conditions that allowed for authentic learning. Historical perspectives and events since Vietnam could actually take longer than a week! Student work, rather than being based on seasonal activities or holidays, was now based on essential questions structured around the content themes. Furthermore, this learning was supported by fiction and nonfiction literature for each of the themes. Inquiry skills developed through the Burley Language Arts Curriculum could be applied in the content areas, extending and enriching student knowledge and understanding.

Over the past thirteen years, our student achievement has climbed steadily, from less than 25% of kids meeting standards in reading, math, and science to this year's composite score of 93% meeting or exceeding the Illinois standards. We have become one of the top-performing schools for our demographic in our state. Many of our kids are now in the "exceeds standards" category: reading—91.9% (49.3% exceed); math—94.1% (46.6% exceed); science—95.2% (44.6% exceed). We believe inquiry—for both adult learners and students—is a critical component of our continued success.

www.heinemann.com/
comprehensionandcollaboration.

We are so happy that you readers will be able to see Burley kids and teachers in action on our companion inquiry circle DVD.

If you are considering a school or districtwide exploration of inquiry-based learning in general, or of inquiry circles in particular, please consult the Teacher Study Group Guide on our website. We designed this document especially to help groups of teachers think through the opportunities, advantages, procedures, and predictable problems of small-group inquiry across the curriculum and all grades.

As this book went to press, yet another blue-ribbon, "let's fix education" report came across our desks. How many clarion calls for authentic, real-world learning do we need before we actually begin to teach in a way that prepares kids to participate and make a difference in the world they are growing into? *Measuring*

Skills for the 21st Century (Silva 2008) echoes a chorus of voices arguing that too many schools continue to focus on isolated facts rather than the information-seeking skills and problem-solving strategies that matter. As *Education Week* notes: "In an age where facts can be located in seconds on the Internet, schools should teach students such skills as how to critically evaluate what they find, connect it to other subjects, apply it to real world problems, and collaborate well with partners halfway around the globe" (Gewertz 2008).

This approach to teaching and learning describes the essence of inquiry circles. It is our rationale for recommending them, for doing our best to help you implement them, and for giving our kids a real chance to reach for the stars. Yes, we do feel a sense of urgency about this. This is a galvanizing moment. This is our time. We can do this. We have no choice.

Appendices

When we teach with inquiry, offering kids genuine choice and responsibility, they need lots of books, materials, and resources—no matter what their grade level. That's why we are offering you five bibliographies—two right here and three on the website.

All teachers hunger for those extra-great short articles, clips, or images that instantly evoke kids' curiosity or answer their questions about current nonfiction topics. So our first listing focuses on collections of such engaging *short nonfiction,* so you don't have to go searching for them one at a time. Thanks to Liz Stedem for helping us build this unique resource.

Mostly, in inquiry circles we work with nonfiction texts. But when we train middle and high school students in the skills of small group discussion, we love to use a rare literary genre called "short-short stories." On p. 308, Smokey, an aficionado of the form, takes us on an annotated tour of his (and kids') favorites. And don't overlook the bibliographies on our website: series books on a range of topics for all grades, magazines of particular interest to kids, and a collection of cool websites for both students and teachers.

www.heinemann.com/
comprehensionandcollaboration.

Short Text Collections

Ablow, Gail. *A Horse in the House and Other Strange But True Animal Stories.*
Cambridge, MA: Candlewick Press, 2007.
Picture book featuring strange, yet true, stories from newspaper reports around the world. Witty text and fun paintings.
PRIMARY

Armstrong, Jennifer. *The American Story: 100 True Tales from American History.*
New York: Alfred A. Knopf, 2006.
Tales of triumph and tragedy for inventors, athletes, abolitionists, artists, and many more. These one-page narratives could be read aloud.
INTERMEDIATE

Aronson, Marc, and Patty Campbell, eds. *War Is . . . : Soldiers, Survivors, and Storytellers Talk About War.* Cambridge, MA: Candlewick Press, 2008.
Anthology of essays, memoirs, letters, and fiction from twenty contributors, both contemporary and historical. The editors (who represent opposing viewpoints about war) agree strongly that teens need to hear the truthful voices of those who have experienced war firsthand.
HIGH SCHOOL

Ash, Russell. *The Top 10 of Everything*. London: Hamlyn, published yearly.
A collection of facts on the top ten of *lots* of topics. Published annually and released as specific country editions. Includes color photographs and illustrations.
MIDDLE/HIGH SCHOOL

Atkins, S. Beth. *Voices from the Fields*. Boston: Little, Brown, 2000.
Vignettes of migrant children and young adults who tell about their experiences living and moving around as the children of farm workers. The ties and values of Hispanic families come through in poems and interviews, as does the strain of moving constantly to new places and being poor in an affluent culture.
INTERMEDIATE/MIDDLE

Bathroom Readers' Institute. *Uncle John's Bathroom Reader.* Ashland, Oregon: Bathroom Readers' Press.
There are *lots* of these—"The Best," "The Best of the Best," "The Biggest Ever," "The Gigantic," and so on. The titles may not appeal to teachers or librarians, but the information is addicting! Each volume includes a wealth of extremely odd stories. Table of contents is divided by length of pieces as well as subject matter. Subjects include forgotten history, pop science, myths and legends, food for thought, law and order, sports, and more.
HIGH SCHOOL

Bausum, Ann. *Our Country's Presidents*. Washington, DC: National Geographic, 2005.
This slick coffee-table book includes an official portrait of each president, facts, and photos. Articles on the White House, political parties, first ladies, and other pertinent topics are interspersed throughout. Includes a foreword by George W. Bush.
INTERMEDIATE/MIDDLE

Best American Writing series. Various authors. New York: Houghton Mifflin, 2002–present.
These annual volumes are each dedicated to a genre like science, short stories, essays, mysteries, or travel writing, and are guest-edited by an expert in the genre— Lynda Barry on Best Comics of 2008, perfect! All draw from front-line periodicals and books. We love them all, but the Science and Nature title often provides the best classroom materials—and most valuable background for teachers.
MIDDLE/HIGH SCHOOL

Beyer, Rick. *The Greatest Stories Never Told: 100 Tales from History to Astonish, Bewilder, and Stupefy*. New York: HarperCollins, 2003.
This collection of stories that changed the course of history will astonish readers. Based on the Timelab 2000 History Minutes hosted by Sam Waterston on the History Channel. Photographs, drawings, and maps add to the "good stuff."
HIGH SCHOOL

Blumenthal, Karen. *Six Days in October: The Stock Market Crash of 1929.* A *Wall Street Journal* Book for Children. New York: Atheneum, 2002.
The author puts a human face on the crisis with personal stories throughout the text. Chapters follow the six days surrounding the crash. Archival photographs, cartoons, and documents are featured.
MIDDLE/HIGH SCHOOL

————. *Let Me Play: The Story of Title IX: The Law That Changed the Future of Girls in America.* New York: Atheneum, 2005.
This 2006 recommended Orbus Pictus book tells the story of efforts to make sure that girls enjoy the same opportunities in sports and related careers that boys do. Includes many political cartoons, photographs, and personal profiles that add to this history of breaking down cultural barriers.
INTERMEDIATE/MIDDLE/HIGH SCHOOL

Botham, Noel. *Best Book of Useless Information Ever.* New York: Perigee, 2007.
This and other editions by the same author (*Amazing Book of Useless Information, Ultimate Book of Useless Information,* etc.) are presented in a humorous manner and are packed full of trivia.
MIDDLE/HIGH SCHOOL

Bryson, Bill. *A Really Short History of Nearly Everything.* Canada: Doubleday, 2008.
The author's goal for this edition (and *A Short History of Nearly Everything*) is to help people appreciate how we have used science to understand everything from the smallest particles to the vast expanses of space. This is a chapter-by-chapter narrative, not a reference work.
MIDDLE/HIGH SCHOOL

Carle, Eric, Mitsumasa Anno, Quentin Blake, et al. *Artist to Artist: 23 Major Illustrators Talk to Children About Their Art.* New York: Philomel Books, 2007.
Most attractive! Profits from the sales of this book benefit the Eric Carle Museum of Picture Book Art. Older students will enjoy reading about their favorite picture book artists. Teachers will need to read aloud and adapt for younger students. Foldout pages feature photographs of artists' early works, their studios, and their sketches. The self-portraits alone will provoke conversation.
INTERMEDIATE/MIDDLE/HIGH SCHOOL

Chin-Lee, Cynthia. *Akira to Zoltan: Twenty-Six Men Who Changed the World.* Watertown, MA: Charlesbridge, 2006.

————. *Amelia to Zora: Twenty-Six Women Who Changed the World.* Watertown, MA: Charlesbridge, 2005.
These companion volumes have capsule biographies of twenty-six men and women—some famous, some lesser known—representing ethnic diversity and a variety of professions. Mixed-media illustrations.
PRIMARY/INTERMEDIATE/MIDDLE

Claybourne, Anna. *100 Most Dangerous Things on the Planet: What to Do If It Happens to You*. New York: Scholastic, 2008.
Natural disasters, dangerous weather, and dangerous animals are a few of the categories covered in this book. Far-fetched to everyday dangers score a risk rating as well as a survival rating. Pertinent and related facts are part of the short text per topic.
MIDDLE/HIGH SCHOOL

Copeland, Cyrus. *Farewell, Godspeed: The Greatest Eulogies of All Time*. New York: Harmony Books, 2003.
An amazing collection of eulogies of some of the most notable people of all time given by the friends and family members who knew them best. Moving, poignant, funny, and sad, these speeches give us an intimate peek into the lives of these famous scientists, politicians, actors, artists, entrepreneurs, and writers.
HIGH SCHOOL

Cummins, Julie. *Women Daredevils: Thrills, Chills, and Frills*. New York: Dutton Children's Books, 2008.
Presents the stories of fourteen women who performed extraordinary feats and stunts—at a time (1880–1929) when women were not even participating in sports! Meet a cannonballer, a circus bareback rider, an airplane stuntwoman, and a woman who rode down Niagara Falls in a barrel.
PRIMARY/INTERMEDIATE

Davies, Nicola. *Extreme Animals: The Toughest Creatures on Earth.* Cambridge: Candlewick Press, 2006.
Relates how animals have adapted to survive in extreme conditions, from polar wastelands to bubbling volcanoes. This small book contains a wealth of information. Fun, readable text and illustrations will please readers.
PRIMARY/INTERMEDIATE

Denenberg, Dennis, and Lorraine Roscoe. *50 American Heroes Every Kid Should Meet.* Minneapolis, MN: Millbrook Press, 2006.
Foreword by Joy Hakim. Interesting collection of heroes who give of themselves to make the world a better place. Scientists, journalists, teachers, inventors, and athletes are included, some well known, some not. Brief text will encourage further study of these people.
INTERMEDIATE/MIDDLE

Dreifus, Claudia. *Interview*. New York: Seven Stories Press, 2003.
The journalist Claudia Dreifus interviews people she categorizes as saints, philosophers, "media freaks," and poets, including such varied personalities as the Dalai Lama, Kareem Abdul-Jabbar, and Cokie Roberts. Great model for students as they do their own interviews.
HIGH SCHOOL

Earthworks Group. *50 Simple Things Kids Can Do to Save the Earth.* Kansas City: Andrews and McMeel, 1990.
Although this publication is twenty years old, issues such as acid rain, water pollution, the greenhouse effect, too much garbage, and disappearing animals are unfortunately still current. Reader-friendly text reminds children what a difference they can make. Eco-experiments presented in the back. (Note: Updated "new" edition available March 2009.)
PRIMARY/INTERMEDIATE

Eggers, Dave. *Best American Non-Required Reading.* 2008. New York: Houghton-Mifflin. (Annual volume since 2005.)
Always an eclectic collection of fiction, nonfiction, alternative comics, screenplays, blogs, and more, edited by the author of *A Heartbreaking Work of Staggering Genius.* Eggers has made better use of his early fame than any writer in recent memory; he now mostly supports younger writers through his McSweeeny's Press.
HIGH SCHOOL

Feynman, Richard. *The Pleasures of Finding Out.* Cambridge, MA: Helix Books, 1999.
A remarkable treasury of the best of the Nobel laureate's short works—from interviews and speeches to lectures and articles. Always thoughtful and often amusing, a wonderful collection to remember the great physicist.
HIGH SCHOOL

Gallo, Donald. *Owning It: Stories About Teens with Disabilities.* New York: Candlewick Press, 2008.
With wit and courage, ten outstanding young adult authors write about dealing with physical and psychological issues, from ADD to cancer.
HIGH SCHOOL

Guest, John. *True Facts: 1000s of Freaky, Scary, Gross, Extraordinary, and Simply Unbelievable Facts.* Bath, UK: Parragon Books Ltd., 2007.
The title sums it up! The presentation is fun; the text is easy to skim through and includes diagrams, sidebars, and photos. The facts will provoke much discussion and thought.
INTERMEDIATE/MIDDLE

Guinness World Records. London: Guinness, published yearly.
Yes, get the hardback copy with all of the color photographs! Teachers and students will fight over the familiar and addicting volumes published each year. Thousands of exciting new and updated records and superlatives from around the globe. (Also available in mass market paperback, published by Bantam.)
ALL AGES

Hampton, Wilborn. *September 11, 2001: Attack on New York City.* Cambridge, MA: Candlewick Press, 2007.

Facts, personal sagas, and photographs. Some accounts are written so vividly that they are difficult to read.
MIDDLE/HIGH SCHOOL

Hardin, Christopher, Jennifer Vetter, Cheryl Weisman, et al. *Incredible Earth! Eye-opening Photos of Our Powerful Planet.* New York: Play Back Publishing, 2008.
An extraordinary compilation of stunning photographs of earth in all its glory, from volcanoes, baobab trees, and coral reefs to melting glaciers. Each photo is accompanied by interesting short text captions running down the side of the page.
ALL AGES

Homer, Trevor. *The Book of Origins.* New York: Plume, 2007.
For people who want to know how and when things began, where they came from, and why they started. Includes "questionable" origins throughout history and a chapter on sex.
MIDDLE/HIGH SCHOOL

Hoose, Phillip. *We Were There, Too! Young People in U.S. History*. New York: Farrar, Straus, and Giroux, 2001.
Extensive text highlights fascinating stories of young people from diverse cultures through first-person accounts, journals, and interviews.
INTERMEDIATE/MIDDLE/HIGH SCHOOL

Hudson, Wade. *Powerful Words: More Than 200 Years of Extraordinary Writing by African Americans*. New York: Scholastic, 2004.
The black experience in America is chronicled in this book of powerful speeches and writing from figures such as Rosa Parks, Paul Robeson, Thurgood Marshall, and many more. Each piece of writing culminates with a short author biography and a description of the response engendered by the piece. A remarkable book about the power of words!
INTERMEDIATE/MIDDLE/HIGH SCHOOL

Hughes, Susan. *No Girls Allowed: Tales of Daring Women Dressed as Men for Love, Freedom, and Adventure.* Tonowanda, NY: Kids Can Press, 2008.
Stories, in comic book format, highlight women across countries and cultures, from a pharaoh in 1500 BC to a Civil War soldier. Will appeal to boys, too.
MIDDLE/HIGH SCHOOL

Play Bac. *Incredible Animals! Eye-opening Photos of Animals in Action.* New York: Play Bac Publishing, 2008.
Amazing photographs and short text will have students gawking and talking. See a crocodile carrying her newborn between her jaws, camels swimming, or a snake swallowing its prey. Photos were selected to create "energy, emotion, and fun."
PRIMARY/INTERMEDIATE

Jackson, Donna M. *In Your Face: The Facts About Your Features*. New York: Viking, 2004.

This guide to the human face explains how the eyes, ears, mouth, and nose work; discusses the definition of beauty; notes various facial expressions; and includes lots of high-interest facts and authentic stories.

MIDDLE

Jamieson, Wendell. *Father Knows Less: One Dad's Quest to Answer His Son's Most Baffling Questions*. New York: Perigree, 2008.

New York Times editor Wendell Jamieson has a fun premise: What if I got experts to answer my seven-year-old son's questions and those of other young kids? Questions such as, What would hurt more—getting run over by a car or getting stung by a jellyfish? are answered by people in every imaginable profession. The questions are charming and the answers quite fascinating.

INTERMEDIATE/MIDDLE

Janeczko, Paul B. *Top Secret: A Handbook of Codes, Ciphers, and Secret Writing*. Cambridge, MA: Candlewick Press, 2006.

A guide to secret writing. Details the history of code writing, famous codes, and invisible ink recipes, as well as how to crack codes and make your own. Full of sketches, codes, and deciphering exercises. Kids will pore over this for hours.

INTERMEDIATE

Jenkins, Steve, and Robin Page. *How Many Ways Can You Catch a Fly?* Boston: Houghton Mifflin, 2008.

Picture book that can be used as a "short text." Bold, simple illustrations. A few pages of solutions are devoted to such questions as "How many ways can you use a leaf? Hatch an egg? Snare a fish?" Extended information at the end.

PRIMARY/INTERMEDIATE

Jenkins, Steve, and Robin Page. *Sisters and Brothers: Sibling Relationships in the Animal World*. Boston: Houghton Mifflin, 2008.

Each page stands alone and deals with an issue in animal families, like sibling rivalry, competition, playing games, and being an only child. Fun read-aloud.

PRIMARY/INTERMEDIATE

Jones, Charlotte Foltz. *Mistakes That Worked*. New York: Doubleday, 1994.

Many things that are used everyday had haphazard beginnings. A collection of vignettes about some of them.

PRIMARY/INTERMEDIATE/MIDDLE

Keenan, Sheila. *Greetings from the 50 States: How They Got Their Names*. New York: Scholastic, 2008.

Easy to read one-pagers give quick facts (nothing in-depth) on each state.

PRIMARY/INTERMEDIATE

Knight, Margy Burns. *Talking Walls.* Gardiner, ME: Tilbury House, 1995.
Walls around the world—the Lascaux caves in France, the granite walls in
Zimbabwe, Nelson Mandela's prison walls, and Diego Rivera's murals, among
others—introduce children to the art, sculpture, and architecture of different
cultures. Map locates all of the sites. Also see *Talking Walls: The Stories Continue.*
PRIMARY/INTERMEDIATE

Lamb, Brian. *Booknotes: Stories from American History.* New York: Penguin, 2002.
This book is third in the series that comes from interviews conducted by Brian
Lamb, the host of the C-Span program of the same name. This one covers
different facets of U.S. history, from the Boston Tea Party to Dan Rostenkowski's
fall from power, with the greatest emphasis on twentieth-century events. See also
Booknotes: Life Stories: Notable Biographers on the People Who Shaped America and
Booknotes: America's Finest Authors on Reading, Writing, and the Power of Ideas.
HIGH SCHOOL

Lauber, Patricia. *The True-or-False Book of Horses.* New York: HarperCollins, 2000.
Fun True-False format focuses on the history, anatomy, and behavior of horses.
Narrative text (one pagers) and attractive illustrations. True or False? Horses
walk on tiptoe. True or False? A horse's teeth are clues to its age.
PRIMARY/INTERMEDIATE

Lewis, Barbara A. *Kids with Courage: True Stories About People Making a
Difference.* Minneapolis, MN: Free Spirit Publishing, 1992.
Older copyright does not outdate stories of "everyday" kids battling problems
with courage—fighting crime, taking social action, saving the environment, and
being heroes.
MIDDLE/HIGH SCHOOL

Lloyd, John, and John Mitchinson. *The Book of General Ignorance: Everything You
Think You Know Is Wrong.* New York: Harmony Books, 2006.
Fun look at misconceptions, misunderstandings, and flawed facts in history,
literature, science, and other areas. Answers to questions are brief yet
comprehensive and will generate more questions. Readers will appreciate
knowledge to be gleaned in *The Book of Animal Ignorance* (2007 copyright) as
well. Did you know that chameleons do not change color to match the
background? That Antarctica is the driest place on earth? How about that
Cinderella wore fur slippers?
HIGH SCHOOL

Macaulay, David. *The (New) Way Things Work.* Boston: Houghton Mifflin, 1998.
Over-sized reference book about the scientific principles and workings of
hundreds of machines. Includes new material about digital technology.
INTERMEDIATE/MIDDLE

Margulies, Phillip, and Maxine Rosaler. ***The Devil on Trial: Witches, Anarchists, Atheists, Communists, and Terrorists in America's Courtrooms.*** Boston: Houghton Mifflin, 2008.
Fascinating accounts of five different trials. In America, everyone has the right to a fair trial, but what if that person is a threat to our country?
HIGH SCHOOL

Masoff, Joy. ***Oh, Yikes! History's Grossest, Wackiest Moments.*** New York: Workman Publishing, 2006.
"For kids bored with endless dates and unpronounceable battles in history texts." Humorous, conversational writing style. Covers a lot of time! Fun and affordable. Classrooms will need multiple copies.
MIDDLE/HIGH SCHOOL

———. ***Oh, Yuck! The Encyclopedia of Everything Nasty.*** New York: Workman Publishing, 2000.
Touted as "the all-encompassing compendium of gross," these short entries will have readers groaning aloud as they learn the scientific facts about everything from acne to cockroaches to pus and tar pits. Students will love the conversational tone of the writing and will not believe the cover picture. Be sure to buy multiple copies. (The price is right.)
MIDDLE/HIGH SCHOOL

McGrath, Barbara Barbieri. ***The Storm: Students of Biloxi, Mississippi, Remember Hurricane Katrina.*** Watertown, MA: Charlesbridge, 2006.
This collection of writing and artwork created by kids in grades K–12 stems from their personal experience with the devastating hurricane. The book stresses the resilience of children and the healing power of art.
ALL AGES

National Children's Book and Literacy Alliance et al. ***Our White House: Looking In, Looking Out.*** Cambridge, MA: Candlewick Press, 2008.
This coffee-table-size anthology is a collection of essays, short stories, illustrations, presidential letters and speeches, comics, and personal reflections from, about, and by the people who have built and lived in the White House. It includes Nixon's final remarks to the White House staff, Robert Kennedy's response to the assassination of Martin Luther King, Jr., the story of a White House physician, and notes on preparing for the War of 1812. David McCullough wrote the introduction; 108 renowned authors and artists contributed to this publication.
MIDDLE/HIGH SCHOOL

Nelson, Kadir. *We Are the Ship: The Story of Negro League Baseball.* New York: Jump at the Sun/Hyperion, 2008.
Another one for the coffee table. Oil paintings are frameable. "Everyman" narrator tells stories about the unsung heroes who overcame segregation, hatred, terrible conditions. and low pay. Spans 1920–1947 (the year of Jackie Robinson's crossover to the major leagues).
HIGH SCHOOL

New York Times. The New York Times Guide to Essential Knowledge: A Desk Reference for the Curious Mind. 2nd ed. New York: St. Martin's Press, 2007.
This widely expanded edition (vs. the original 2004 edition) defines nearly every facet of contemporary life. Organized alphabetically. Includes essays, tables, and lists.
MIDDLE/HIGH SCHOOL

Nikola-Lisa, W. *How We Are Smart.* New York: Lee & Low Books, 2006.
Explores, in picture book format, the eight basic ways people can be smart. Based on Dr. Howard Gardner's theory of multiple intelligences, this book contains quotes, verse, and prose about a diverse group of people to help readers figure out, "Are you smart like_____?
INTERMEDIATE/MIDDLE/HIGH SCHOOL

Parker, Steve. *Children's Human Body Encyclopedia: Discover How Our Amazing Bodies Work.* Bath, UK: Parragon Books Ltd., 2007.
All systems of the body (including the reproductive system) are explained, diagrammed, and illustrated. Written in a straightforward style. "Amazing" facts are interspersed throughout. Will grab readers' attention and provide lots of answers.
MIDDLE/HIGH SCHOOL

Philip, Neil, ed. *In a Sacred Manner I Live: Native American Wisdom.* New York: Clarion, 2005.
Native Americans write about historical and twentieth-century themes, past and present. Poems, essays, and speeches include Chief Joseph's speech "I Will Fight No More Forever" and Tecumseh's words at a treaty signing: "My heart is a stone, heavy with sadness for my people." Traditions and beliefs about the power of Native American cultures come through in these original writings.
INTERMEDIATE/MIDDLE/HIGH SCHOOL

Rappaport, Doreen. *In the Promised Land: Lives of Jewish Americans.* New York: HarperCollins, 2005.
A picture book with well-researched vignettes of men and women who fought religious barriers and affected American and world history—including Houdini, Salk, and Spielberg.
INTERMEDIATE/MIDDLE

Rappaport, Doreen, and Joan Verniero. ***United No More! Stories of the Civil War.***
New York: HarperCollins, 2006.
Dramatic and thoroughly researched stories about real people whose important
acts made them a part of history. Narrative text is compelling and will work as
short read-alouds.
INTERMEDIATE/MIDDLE

Rappoport, Ken. ***Ladies First: Women Athletes Who Made a Difference.*** Atlanta:
Peachtree Publishers, 2005.
Inspiring profiles of a dozen of the twentieth century's greatest female athletes
who impacted society as well as their sports.
MIDDLE/HIGH SCHOOL

Ripley Entertainment. ***Ripley's Believe It or Not! Prepare to Be Shocked.*** Orlando,
FL: Ripley Publishing, 2008.
This colorful hardback edition will be hard to put down! Topics feature amazing
animals, weird science, startling art, fantastic food. Limited text should provoke
many questions and "out of the box" thinking.
ALL AGES

Rochelle, Belinda. ***Witnesses to Freedom: Young People Who Fought for Civil
Rights.*** New York: Puffin, 1997.
A collection of true stories about brave young people in the 1960s who
integrated schools and fought for civil rights.
INTERMEDIATE/MIDDLE

Rockwell, Lizzy. ***The Busy Body Book: A Kid's Guide to Fitness.*** New York: Random
House, 2004.
Narrative text and interactive cues (what do you do?) make this a good read-
aloud for primary kids. Skeletal, circulatory, muscular, and respiratory systems
are diagrammed and labeled.
PRIMARY/INTERMEDIATE

Roehm, Michelle. ***Girls Who Rocked the World 2: Heroines from Harriet Tubman
to Mia Hamm.*** Hillsboro, OR: Beyond Words, 2000.
This book tells amazing stories about girls who shook things up while they were
teenagers. Oprah was seventeen when she broke into showbiz, and the Bronte sisters
were teenagers when they wrote their novels. You are never too young to go for it!
INTERMEDIATE/MIDDLE

Rusch, Elizabeth. ***Generation Fix: Young Ideas for a Better World.*** Hillsboro, OR:
Beyond Words Publishing, 2002.
Generation Fix tells the inspiring stories of more than fifteen young people who
saw a problem in their community and did something to fix it.
INTERMEDIATE

Salkeld, Audrey. *Climbing Everest: Tales of Triumph and Tragedy on the World's Highest Mountain.* Washington, DC: National Geographic, 2003.
This book explores six of the most famous Everest climbing stories in history—some tragic, some triumphant, all compelling. Great photographs, maps, and time lines.
INTERMEDIATE/MIDDLE/HIGH SCHOOL

Schlosser, Eric, and Charles Wilson. *Chew on This! Everything You Don't Want to Know About Fast Food.* Boston: Houghton Mifflin, 2006.
From the author of *Fast Food Nation,* a behind-the-scenes look at the fast food industry. Well-written and extensively researched (see the footnotes), text encourages teens to think about the "bad habit" of eating fast food. Each chapter stands alone. Action steps, educators' guide, and new afterword included.
MIDDLE/HIGH SCHOOL

Schwartz, David, and Yael Schy. *Where in the Wild? Camouflaged Creatures Concealed . . . and Revealed.* Berkeley, CA: Tricycle Press, 2007.
Beautifully done! Poetry, nonfiction text, and photographs help readers explore how a wide variety of species use camouflage. Fold-out pages promote interaction.
PRIMARY/INTERMEDIATE

Smith, Charles R. Jr. *Winning Words: Sports Stories and Photographs.* New York: Candlewick Press, 2008.
These stories are guaranteed to pump up confidence in young athletes. Stories and quotes inspire striving for your personal best—no matter what the sport.
MIDDLE/HIGH SCHOOL

Solheim, James. *It's Disgusting and We Ate It! True Food Facts from Around the World and Throughout History.* New York: Aladdin, 2001.
An exploration of "edible grub." Divided into three sections including "People Eat the Wildest Things," "From Mammoth Meatballs to Squirrel Stew," and "If You Think That's Sick, Look in Your Fridge." Fun illustrations.
INTERMEDIATE/MIDDLE

Spilsbury, Louise. *Questions and Answers Knowledge: The What, When, Where, How, and Why of Everything You Need to Know.* Bath, UK: Parragon Books, Ltd., 2007.
Oversized reference book. Question-and-answer format will further provoke readers' interest. Why do we need two eyes? What did explorers eat? How do mountain goats get a grip? Topics covered are extensive. Photographs, diagrams, and illustrations support the paragraph-length answers.
INTERMEDIATE/MIDDLE

Stiekel, Bettina, ed. ***The Nobel Book of Answers.*** New York: Atheneum, 2001.
Since 1901, the Nobel Prize has been awarded to the world's most brilliant thinkers in our most important fields. This book shares answers that Nobel Prize winners gave to questions collected from kids throughout the world.
INTERMEDIATE/MIDDLE

Talbott, Hudson. ***United Tweets of America.*** New York: G. P. Putnam's Sons, 2008.
Factual information about state birds and other state trivia. Picture book.
PRIMARY/INTERMEDIATE

Thimmesh, Catherine. ***Madam President: The Extraordinary (True and Evolving) Story of Women in Politics.*** Boston: Houghton Mifflin, 2004.
These picture book vignettes feature contemporary and past women from around the world. See also Thimmesh's *Girls Think of Everything: Stories of Ingenious Inventions by Women.*
MIDDLE/HIGH SCHOOL

Travis, Cathy. ***Constitution Translated for Kids.*** Austin, TX: Ovation Books, 2008.
In a two-column format, the complete text of the U.S. Constitution is translated into kid-friendly (fifth-grade level) language. Further information is included on proposed amendments and the workings of the different branches of government. Also available in Spanish.
INTERMEDIATE/MIDDLE

Tunnell, Michael O., and George W. Chilcoat. ***The Children of Topaz: The Story of a Japanese-American Internment Camp.*** New York: Holiday House, 1996.
Text is based on the diary kept by a third-grade class taught by Anne Yamauchi in 1943 at the Topaz internment camp. The book describes, from a child's point of view, how Miss Yamauchi and her students tried to continue with normal school life despite difficult conditions. Archival photographs provide a detailed look at life in Topaz.
INTERMEDIATE/MIDDLE

Wallechinsky, David, and Amy Wallace. ***The New Book of Lists: The Original Compendium of Curious Information.*** Edinburgh, Scotland: Canongate, 2005.
Weirder than fiction—intriguing facts, unusual statistics, and the incredible stories behind them. Impressive group of contributors.
MIDDLE/HIGH SCHOOL

Walsh, Melanie. ***10 Things I Can Do to Help My World.*** Cambridge, MA: Candlewick Press, 2008.
Simple ways to make a difference—using both sides of writing and drawing paper, planting seeds, turning off the water while brushing teeth are a few. Bold, inviting illustrations.
PRIMARY/INTERMEDIATE

Weisman, Alan. ***The World Without Us.*** New York: Picador, 2008.
> Amazing thought experiment: what would happen to the world, its animals, landforms, ecosystem, if all humans suddenly disappeared from the earth—died of a plague, got raptured up, whatever. Delicious individual scenarios (how a suburban house would rot away, how the greatest human-made edifices would crumble) are curiously engaging. Author defeated Smokey for sophomore class vice president at Northwestern U in 1966, yet we still recommend his book.
> **HIGH SCHOOL**

Whitehead, Sarah. ***How to Speak Dog!*** London: Marshall Editions, 2008.
> Discover why dogs wag their tails, why they sniff other dogs, and how to talk to your dog so your pet responds as you want! Information about owning and caring for dogs as well as photos, facts, and sidebar information throughout the text. Also see *How to Speak Cat!* by the same author.
> **INTERMEDIATE/MIDDLE**

Williams, Maria. ***Hooray for Inventors!*** Cambridge, MA: Candlewick Press, 2005.
> Oversized and in comic book format, this provides the stories behind some of the world's greater and lesser inventions. Pages are busy! Brief information will pique further investigation.
> **PRIMARY/INTERMEDIATE**

Wills, Garry. ***Certain Trumpets: The Nature of Leadership.*** New York: Simon & Schuster, 1995.
> A thoughtful examination from a Pulitzer Prize winner of the characteristics of leadership. Readers will find food for thought in the essays that attempt to compare and contrast styles of leadership by pairing successful leaders with antitypes. For instance, reform leader Eleanor Roosevelt is paired with Nancy Reagan, Napoleon with George McClellan (military), and George Washington with Oliver Cromwell (constitutional).
> **HIGH SCHOOL**

Woodford, Chris. ***Cool Stuff Exploded: Get Inside Modern Technology.*** New York: DK Publishing, 2008.
> Hologram on cover will entice readers to this high-tech publication. A CD-ROM with animations is included in this year's edition. Computer-generated illustrations and vivid photographs and subjects such as "Super-cool science" and "Brilliant inventions" and "Jam-packed with gadgets" will thrill techies.
> **MIDDLE/HIGH SCHOOL**

World Almanac Books. ***The World Almanac and Book of Facts.*** New York: World
  Almanac, published yearly.
  A great resource. Millions of facts. Endless categories including sports,
  personalities/arts/media, population facts, science, and technology.
  Answers abound!
  INTERMEDIATE/MIDDLE/HIGH SCHOOL

Yankee Publishing. ***The Old Farmer's Almanac.*** Dublin, NH: Yankee Publishing,
  published yearly.
  "Besides the large number of Astronomical Calculations and the Farmer's
  Calendar for every month in the year, this book contains a variety of new, useful,
  and entertaining matter." Lots of ads and articles interspersed throughout the
  factual charts.
  INTERMEDIATE/MIDDLE/HIGH SCHOOL

Zehr, Howard. ***Doing Life: Reflections of Men and Women Serving Life Sentences.***
  Intercourse, PA: Good Books, 1996.
  The author hopes that this collection of short vignettes and profiles (and
  haunting black-and-white photos) gives readers "an opportunity to see offenders
  as individuals with their own fears and dreams, rather than stereotypes." People
  featured have been convicted of homicides or as accomplices in homicides and
  have little possibility of ever returning to society.
  HIGH SCHOOL

Short-Short Stories

Biguenet, John. *The Torturer's Apprentice.* New York: HarperCollins. 2001.
    The title says it all: deliciously bizarre stories by a new New Orleans writer. This
    one's for the big kids and grown-ups. Only one really short-short story, "Rose," a
    knockout that deservedly garnered the O. Henry prize in 2000.

Cisneros, Sandra. *The House on Mango Street.* New York: Vintage. 1984 and *Woman
Hollering Creek.* New York: Vintage, 1992.
    The dual mother lodes of fiction/memoir short-shorts. The Queen of the genre.

Eggers, Dave, Sarah Manguso, and Deb Olin. *One Hundred and Forty Five Stories in
a Small Box: Hard to Admit and Harder to Escape, How the Water Feels to the
Fishes, and Minor Robberies.* San Francisco: McSweeney's, 2008.
    The title says it all: three master writers take on the short-short form and deliver a
    trove of delicious, diabolical, and delightful stories—each in less than 500 words.

Kitchen, Judith, and Mary Paumier Jones. *In Short: A Collection of Brief Creative
Nonfiction.* Norton, New York, 1996.
    Mostly short memoirs and essays, not informational text, but cleverly organized,
    with a dozen fine nature/outdoor/science pieces toward the end. Pico Iyer's "In
    Praise of the Humble Comma" is a treat for English teachers.

Kitchen, Judith, and Mary Paumier Jones. *In Brief: Short Takes on the Personal.*
New York: Norton, 1999.
    More of the above; quality stuff. Josephine Jacobsen's "Artifacts of Memory" is
    the best introduction to archaeology you're likely to discover.

Howe, Irving, and Ilana Howe. *Short Shorts: An Anthology of the Shortest Stories.*
New York: Bantam, 1983.
    Not-really-that-short stories, mostly from DWMs like Tolstoy, Chekhov, Borges,
    Kafka, Thurber, etc. If you absolutely must use respectable stuff, this would be
    your source.

Moss, Steve, and John M. Daniel. *The World's Shortest Stories of Love and Death.*
Philadelphia: Running Press, 1999.
    All stories are 55 words or fewer, which you realize while reading them, usually isn't
    enough. Lower ratio of winners than Micro or Flash fiction, but some goodies.

PEN-Faulkner Foundation. *Three Minutes or Less: Life Lessons from America's
Greatest Writers.* New York: Bloomsbury Press, 2000.
    Short speeches by PEN awardees. Have a defibrillator at hand for Pat Conroy's; it
    may stop your heart.

Shapard, Robert, and James Thomas. ***Sudden Fiction: American Short-Short Stories***. New York: Norton, 1986.
Mostly 3–4 pagers from mainstream 20th century writers like Hemingway, Malamud, Bradbury, Hughes. In an afterword, 40 writers comment on the short-short form.

Shapard, Robert, and James Thomas. ***Sudden Fiction Continued: 60 New Short-Short Stories***. New York: Norton, 1996.
More of the above. Margaret Atwood's lead-off story "My Life as a Bat" is worth the price. Alice Walker's "Flowers" is a chiller.

Shapard, Robert, and James Thomas. ***Sudden Fiction International: 60 Short-Short Stories.*** New York: Norton, 1996.
Every other country gets one writer, the U.S. gets about 12. So much for international. Included: Jamaica Kincaid, Nadine Gordimer, Isak Dinesen, Margaret Atwood.

Stern, Jerome. ***Microfiction: An Anthology of Really Short Stories.*** New York: Norton, 1996.
Winners from a contest requiring fully formed stories in one-typed page. A gold mine for middle and high school readers. One kid favorite: "This Is How I Remember It" by Betsy Kemper.

Stern, Jerome. ***Radios: Short Takes on Life and Culture***. New York: Norton, 1997.
From his NPR commentaries. Some pungent, funny ones like "Library;" many about his illness.

Thomas, James, Denise Thomas, and Tom Hazuka. ***Flash Fiction: 72 Very Short Stories***. New York: Norton, 1992.
Highlights: Julia Alvarez's "Snow," Tim O'Brien's "Stockings."

References

Chapter 1

Beane, James. 2005. *A Reason to Teach: Creating Classrooms of Dignity and Hope.* Portsmouth, NH: Heinemann.

Daniels, Harvey, and Marilyn Bizar. 2004. *Teaching the Best Practice Way.* Portland, ME: Stenhouse.

Daniels, Harvey, Marilyn Bizar, and Steven Zemelman. 2001. *Rethinking High School: Best Practice in Teaching, Learning, and Leadership.* Portsmouth, NH: Heinemann.

Darling-Hammond, Linda, Brigid Barron, P. David Pearson, Alan H. Schoenfeld, Elizabeth K. Stage, Timothy D. Zimmerman, Gina N. Cervetti, and Jennifer L. Tilson. 2008. *Powerful Learning: What We Know About Teaching for Understanding.* San Francisco: Jossey-Bass.

Heathfield, Susan. 2008. "How to Build a Teamwork Culture: Do the Hard Stuff for Teams," available online at http://humanresources.about.com/od/involvementteams/a/team_culture.htm.

Newmann, Fred. 1996. *Authentic Achievement: Restructuring Schools for Intellectual Quality.* San Francisco, CA: Jossey-Bass.

Newmann Fred et al. 1996. "Authentic Intellectual Work and Standardized Tests: Conflict or Coexistence?" Chicago, IL: Consortium Chicago School Research.

Pianta, Robert C., Jay Belsky, Renate Houts, Fred Morrison, and The National Institute of Child Health and Human Development (NICHD) Early Child Care Research Network. 2007. "Teaching: Opportunities to Learn in America's Classrooms." *Science* 315: 1795–96.

Smith, Julia et al. 2001. "Instruction and Achievement in Chicago Elementary Schools." Chicago, IL: Consortium on Chicago Schools.

Schultz, Brian. 2008. *Spectacular Things Happen Along the Way: Lessons from an Urban Classroom.* New York: Teachers College Press.

University of Illinois at Urbana-Champaign. 2008. "10 Years On, High-school Social Skills Predict Better Earnings than Test Scores." *ScienceDaily* (October 16), available online at http://www.sciencedaily.com /releases/2008/10/081015120749.htm.

Zemelman, Steven, Harvey Daniels, and Arthur Hyde. 2005. *Best Practice: Today's Standards for Teaching and Learning in America's Schools* (Third Edition). Portsmouth, NH: Heinemann.

Chapter 2

Allington, Richard. 2003. "The Three Principles of Reading." February. Keynote Address at CCIRA.

Block, Cathy Collins and Michael Pressley, eds. 2002. *Comprehension Instruction Research-Based Best Practices.* New York: Guilford.

Block, Cathy Collins, Linda B. Gambrell, and Michael Pressley, eds. 2002. *Improving Comprehension Instruction: Rethinking Research, Theory, and Classroom Practice.* San Francisco: Jossey-Bass.

Brown, Ann L., and Jeanne D. Day. 1983. "Macrorules for Summarizing Texts: The Development of Expertise." *Journal of Verbal Learning and Verbal Behavior* 22: 1–4.

Costa, Arthur L. 2008. "The Thought-Filled Curriculum." *Educational Leadership* 65: 20–24.

Cunningham, Anne E., and Keith E. Stanovich. 1998. "What Reading Does for the Mind." *The American Educator* (Spring/Summer): 8–15. American Federation of Teachers.

Daniels, Harvey and Steven Zemelman. 2004. *Subjects Matter: Every Teacher's Guide to Content-Area Reading.* Portsmouth, NH: Heinemann.

Gavelek, James R., and Taffy E. Raphael. 1985. "Metacognition, Instruction, and the Role of Questioning Activities." *Metacognition, Cognition, and Human Performance, I: Theoretical Perspectives; II: Instructional Practices,* 103–136. Orlando, FL: Harcourt Brace Jovanovich.

Guthrie, John T. 2003. "Concept Oriented Reading Instruction." In *Rethinking Reading Comprehension (Solving Problems in the Teaching of Literacy).* Eds. Catherine E. Snow and Anne P. Sweet. New York: Guilford.

Hansen, Jane. 1981. "The Effects of Inference Training and Practice on Young Children's Reading Comprehension." *Reading Research Quarterly* 16: 391–417.

Harvey, Stephanie, and Anne Goudvis. 2005. *The Comprehension Toolkit: Language and Lessons for Active Literacy.* Portsmouth, NH: Heinemann.

———. 2007. *Strategies That Work: Teaching Comprehension for Understanding and Engagement* (Second Edition). Portland, ME: Stenhouse.

———. 2008. *Primary Comprehension Toolkit: Language and Lessons for K–2.* Portsmouth, NH: Heinemann.

Keene, Ellin O. 2008. *To Understand: New Horizons in Reading Comprehension.* Portsmouth, NH: Heinemann.

Langenberg, Donald N. 2000. Report of the National Reading Panel, "Teaching Children to Read." Bethesda, MD: National Institute of Child Health and Development.

Miller, Debbie. 2002. *Reading with Meaning.* Portland, ME: Stenhouse.

———. 2008. *Teaching with Intention.* Portland, ME: Stenhouse.

Palinscar, Annemarie S., and Ann L. Brown. 1984. "Reciprocal Teaching of Comprehension-Fostering and Comprehension-Monitoring Activities." *Cognition and Instruction* 1: 117–175.

Pearson, P. David, and M. C. Gallagher. 1983. "The Instruction of Reading Comprehension." *Contemporary Educational Psychology* 8: 317–344.

Pearson, P. David, and Nell Duke. 2001. "Comprehension Instruction in the Primary Grades." In *Comprehension Instruction Research Based Practices*. Eds. Cathy Collins-Block and Michael Pressley. New York: Guilford.

Pearson, P. David, L. R. Roehler, J. A. Dole, and G. G. Duffy. 1992. "Developing Expertise in Reading Comprehension: What Should be Taught and Who Should Teach It." In *What Research Has to Say About Reading Instruction* (Second Edition). Eds. Jay Samuels and Alan Farstrup. Newark, DE: International Reading Association.

Perkins, David. 1995. *Smart Schools: Better Thinking and Learning for Every Child*. New York: Free Press.

Pressley, Michael. 1976. "Mental Imagery Helps Eight-Year-Olds Remember What They Read." *Journal of Educational Psychology*. 68: 355–359.

———. 2002. *Reading Instruction That Works: The Case for Balanced Teaching* (Second Edition). New York: Guilford.

Reutzel, D. Ray, John A. Smith, and Parker C. Fawson. 2005. "An Evaluation of Two Approaches for Teaching Reading Comprehension Strategies in the Primary Years Using Science Information Texts." *Early Childhood Research Quarterly* 20: 276–305.

Rosenblatt, Louise M. 1938. *Literature as Exploration* (Fifth Edition). New York: MLA, 1995.

Ruddell, Robert B., and Norman J. Unrau, eds. 2004. *Theoretical Models and Processes of Reading* (Fifth Edition). Newark, DE: International Reading Association.

Shefelbine, John. 1998. *Reading Voluminously and Voluntarily*. Scholastic Reading Council Research.

Tovani, Cris. 2000. *I Read It, but I Don't Get It: Comprehension Strategies for Adolescent Readers*. Portland, ME: Stenhouse.

Trobasso, Tom, and Edward Bouchard. 2002. "Teaching Readers How to Comprehend Text Strategically." In *Comprehension Instruction: Research-Based Practices*. Eds. Cathy Collins-Block and Michael Pressley. New York: Guilford.

Chapter 3

American Association for the Advancement of Science. 1989. *Science for All Americans: A Project 2061 Report on Literacy Goals in Science, Mathematics, and Technology*. Washington: AAAS.

Daniels, Harvey, and Nancy Steineke. 2004. *Mini-lessons for Literature Circles*. Portsmouth, NH: Heinemann.

Darling-Hammond, Linda, et al. 2008. *Powerful Learning: What We Know About Teaching for Understanding*. San Francisco: Jossey-Bass.

Harvey, Stephanie. 1998. *Nonfiction Matters: Reading, Writing, and Research in Grades 3–8*. Portland, ME: Stenhouse.

National Institutes of Health. 2008. "New Program Teaches Preschoolers Reading Skills, Getting Along with Others." *ScienceDaily*. (November 14), available online at http://www.sciencedaily.com/releases/2008/11/081114080933.htm.

Schmuck, Richard A., and Patricia Schmuck. 2001. *Group Processes in the Classroom* (Eighth Edition). New York: McGraw-Hill.

Sharan, Shlomo. 1999. *Handbook of Cooperative Learning.* Westport, CT: Greenwood.

———. 1992. *Expanding Cooperative Learning Through Group Investigations.* New York: Teachers College Press.

Slavin, Robert. 1994. *Cooperative Learning: Theory, Research and Practice.* Boston: Allyn & Bacon.

Stanley, Diane. 1990. *The Conversation Club.* New York: Aladdin.

Steineke, Nancy. 2002. *Reading and Writing Together: Collaborative Literacy in Action.* Portsmouth, NH: Heinemann.

Wheelock, Anne. 1993. *Crossing the Tracks: How "Untracking" Can Save America's Schools.* New York: New Press.

Zemelman, Steven, Harvey Daniels, and Arthur Hyde. 2005. *Best Practice: Today's Standards for Teaching and Learning in America's Schools* (Third Edition). Portsmouth, NH: Heinemann.

Chapter 4

Allensworth, Elaine, Macarena Correa, and Steve Ponisciak. 2008. *From High School to the Future: ACT Preparation—Too Much, Too Late.* Chicago: Consortium on Chicago School Research at the University of Chicago.

Beane, James. 1997. *Curriculum Integration: Designing the Core of Democratic Education.* New York: Teachers College Press.

Darling-Hammond, Linda, et al. 2008. *Powerful Learning: What We Know About Teaching for Understanding.* San Francisco: Jossey-Bass.

Harvey, Stephanie.1998. *Nonfiction Matters: Reading, Writing, and Research in Grades 3–8.* Portland, ME: Stenhouse.

McTighe, Jay, Elliott Seif, and Grant Wiggins. 2004. "You Can Teach for Meaning." *Educational Leadership* (September) 62: 26–30.

Short, Kathy, Jerry Harste, and Carolyn Burke. 1995. *Creating Classrooms for Authors and Inquirers.* Portsmouth, NH: Heinemann.

Weglinsky, Harold. 2004. "The Link Between Instructional Practice and the Racial Gap in Middle Schools." *Research in Middle Level Education* 28: 1–13.

Wilhelm, Jeffrey. 2007. *Engaging Readers and Writers with Inquiry.* New York: Scholastic.

Wolk, Steven. 2008. "School as Inquiry." *Phi Delta Kappan* (October) 90: 115–122.

Worthy, Jo, Karen Broaddus, and Melinda Ivey. 2001. *Pathways to Independence: Reading, Writing, and Learning in Grades 3–8.* New York: Guilford, Press.

Chapter 5

Feynman, Richard. 1999. *The Pleasure of Finding Things Out: The Best Short Works of Richard Feynman.* Cambridge, MA: Perseus Books.

Harvey, Stephanie, and Anne Goudvis. 2007. *Toolkit Texts: Grades 2–3; Grades 4–5; Grades 6–7.* Portsmouth, NH: Heinemann.

Hidi, S., and Renninger A. 2006. "A Four Phase Model of Interest Development." *Educational Psychologist* 41: 111–127.

Johnston, Peter. 2004. *Choice Words: How Our Teaching Language Affects Children's Learning*. Portland, ME: Stenhouse.

McGregor, Tanny. 2007. *Comprehension Connections: Bridges to Strategic Reading*. Portsmouth, NH: Heinemann.

Nichols, Maria. 2006. *Comprehension Through Conversation: The Power of Purposeful Talk in the Reading Workshop*. Portsmouth, NH: Heinemann.

Perkins, David. 1995. *Smart Schools: Better Thinking and Learning for Every Child*. New York: Free Press.

President and Fellows of Harvard College. 2006. "Interrogating Texts: 6 Reading Habits to Develop in Your First Year at Harvard," available online at http://hcl.harvard.edu/research/guides/lamont_handouts/interrogatingtexts.html.

Probst, Robert. 2004. *Response and Analysis* (Second Edition). Portsmouth, NH: Heinemann.

Rosenblatt, Louise. 1996. *Literature as Exploration* (Fifth Edition). New York: Modern Language Association of America.

Schwarz, Patrick. and Paula Kluth. 2007. *You're Welcome: 30 Innovative Ideas for the Inclusive Classroom*. Portsmouth, NH: Heinemann.

Tishman, Shari. 2008. "The Object of Their Attention." *Educational Leadership* (February) 65: 44–46.

Chapter 6

Gilmore, Barry. 2009. *Plagiarism: A How-Not-To Guide for Students*. Portsmouth, NH: Heinemann.

McCain, John, and Mark Salter. 1999. *Faith of My Fathers*. New York: Random House.

National School Boards Association. 2007. "Creating and Connecting: Research and Guidelines on Social and Educational Networking."

Obama, Barack. 2006. *The Audacity of Hope: Thoughts on Reclaiming the American Dream*. New York: Crown Publishing.

Richardson, Will. 2008. "Footprints in the Digital Age." *Educational Leadership* (November) 66: 16–19.

Chapter 7

Fielding, Linda G., and P. David Pearson. 1994. "Reading Comprehension: What Works." *Educational Leadership* (February) 51: 62–68.

Harvey, Stephanie, and Anne Goudvis. 2005. *The Comprehension Toolkit: Language and Lessons for Active Literacy*. Portsmouth, NH: Heinemann.

Pearson, P. David, and Margaret C. Gallagher. 1983. "The Instruction of Reading Comprehension." *Contemporary Educational Psychology* (July) 8: 317–344.

Perkins, David. 2003. "Making Thinking Visible." *New Horizons for Learning Online Journal* (December), available online at http://www.newhorizons.org/strategies/thinking/perkins.htm.

Chapter 8

2007. "Recycling Without Sorting: Engineers Create Recycling Plant that Removes the Need to Sort." *Science Daily.* (October), available online at http://www.sciencedaily.com/videos/2007/1002-recycling_without_sorting.htm.

Bond, G.R. 2003. "Home Syrup of Ipecac Use Does Not Reduce Emergency Department Use or Improve Outcome." *Pediatrics* (November) 112: 1061–1064. American Academy of Pediatrics.

Harvey, Stephanie and Anne Goudvis. 2007. *Toolkit Texts: Grades 2–3; Grades 4–5; Grades 6–7.* Portsmouth, NH: Heinemann.

Harvey, Stephanie. 1998. *Nonfiction Matters.* York, ME: Stenhouse Publishers.

Kemper, Betsy. 1996. "This is How I Remember It," in Jerome Stern, ed. *Micro Fiction.* New York: Norton.

Pearson, P. David. 2005. National Geographic Literacy Conference speech. National Geographic School Publishing and LARC (Literacy Achievement Resource Center). July. Washington, DC.

Time for Kids. March 28, 2008. Available online at http://www.timeforkids.com/TFK/kids/wr/0,28393,080328,00.html.

International Labor Organization. 2004. "Study on Economic Costs and Benefits of Eliminating Child Labor." ILO February. www.ilo.org.

Chapter 9

Author Unknown. 1998. "Forced Labour on Sugar Cane Plantations in the Dominican Republic." Available online at http://www.antislavery.org/archive/submission/submission1998–05Dominican.htm.Erickson, Paul. 2001. *Daily Life on a Southern Plantation.* New York: Sagebrush.

Harvey, Stephanie, and Anne Goudvis. 2005. *The Comprehension Toolkit: Language and Lessons for Active Literacy.* Portsmouth, NH: Heinemann.

Wiggins, Grant, and Jay McTighe. 2005. *Understanding by Design* (Expanded Second Edition). Englewood Cliffs, NJ: Prentice-Hall.

Woolley, Marilyn. 2006. *In Antarctica.* Curtain Communications New Zealand distributed in U.S. by Okapi.

Unicef, Caroline Castle, and John Birmingham. 2001. *Every Child: The Rights of the Child of the World.* New York: Dial.

Chapter 10

Daniels, Harvey. 2002. *Literature Circles: Voice and Choice in Book Clubs and Reading Groups* (Second Edition). Portland, ME: Stenhouse.

Daniels, Harvey, and Nancy Steineke. 2004. *Mini-lessons for Literature Circles.* Portsmouth, NH: Heinemann.

Harste, Jerome C., Kathy G. Short, and Carolyn Burke. 1988. *Creating Classrooms for Authors: The Reading Writing Connection.* Portsmouth, NH: Heinemann.

AND/OR: Harste, Jerome C., Kathy G. Short, and Carolyn Burke. 1995. *Creating Classrooms for Authors and Inquirers* (Second Edition). Portsmouth, NH: Heinemann.

National Council of Teachers of English and the International Reading Association. 1996.

Peterson, Ralph, and Maryann Eeds. 1990. *Grand Conversations.* New York: Scholastic.

Steineke, Nancy. 2009. *Assessment Live!* Portsmouth, NH: Heinemann.

Vopat, Jim. 2009. *Writing Circles: Kids Revolutionize Workshop.* Portsmouth, NH: Heinemann.

Chapter 11

Buhrow, Brad, and Anne Garcia. 2006. *Ladybugs, Tornadoes, and Swirling Galaxies: English Language Learners Discover Their World Through Inquiry.* Portland, ME: Stenhouse.

Darling-Hammond, Linda, et al. 2008. *Powerful Learning: What We Know About Teaching for Understanding.* San Francisco: Jossey-Bass.

Education Week. 2008. "Showing What They Know: In Rhode Island, Performance-based Assessments Are Now Required for High School Graduation." Vol 27, #42, June 18, 2008.

Federal Hocking High School: Rules for Senior Projects. Available online at http://www.federalhocking.k12.oh.us/extra/hs/fhhs_htmls/academics/seniorproject.html.

Vernon-Sparks, Lisa. 2008. "Policy Makers Study Coventry High." *Providence Journal.* March 14, 2008.

Wood, George H., and Linda Darling-Hammond. 2008. "Refocusing Accountability: Using Local Performance Assessments to Enhance Teaching and Learning for Higher Order Skills." *The Forum for Education and Democracy.* Available online at http://forumforeducation.org/node/368.

Chapter 12

Harvey, Stephanie, and Anne Goudvis. 2007. *Strategies That Work: Teaching Comprehension for Understanding and Engagement* (Second Edition). Portland, ME: Stenhouse.

Wilson, Maya. 2006. *Rethinking Rubrics in Writing Assessment.* Portsmouth, NH: Heinemann.

Chapter 13

Boushey, Gail, and Joan Moser. The Daily Five: Fostering Literacy Independence in the Elementary Grades. 2006. York, ME: Stenhouse.

Gewertz, Catherine. 2008. "Assessing 21st-Century Skills Won't Be Easy." *Education Week.* November 12, p. 8. Accessed at http://www.edweek.org/login.html?source=http://www.edweek.org/ew/articles/2008/11/12/12skills.h28.html&destination=http://www.edweek.org/ew/articles/2008/11/12/12skills.h28.html&levelId=2100)

Silva, Elena. 2008. "*Measuring Skills for the 21st Century.*" *Education Sector Reports* (November). Accessed at http://www.educationsector.org/usr_doc/MeasuringSkills.pdf.

Index